The Practice of Global History

Also Available from Bloomsbury

Forthcoming:

Doing Global History, Roland Wenzlhuemer
Writing Transnational History, Fiona Paisley and Pamela Scully

Published:

Scarcity in the Modern World (2019),
Edited by John Brewer, Neil Fromer, Fredrik Albritton Jonsson
and Frank Trentmann
Global History, Globally (2018),
Edited by Sven Beckert and Dominic Sachsenmaier
Global Economic History (2018),
Edited by Tirthankar Roy and Giorgio Riello
Empire in Asia: A New Global History (2018),
Edited by Brian P. Farrell
Economic Development and Environmental History in the Anthropocene (2017),
Edited by Gareth Austin
Global Conceptual History: A Reader (2016),
Edited by Margrit Pernau and Dominic Sachsenmaier

The Practice of Global History

European Perspectives

Edited by Matthias Middell

BLOOMSBURY ACADEMIC
LONDON • NEW YORK • OXFORD • NEW DELHI • SYDNEY

BLOOMSBURY ACADEMIC
Bloomsbury Publishing Plc
50 Bedford Square, London, WC1B 3DP, UK
1385 Broadway, New York, NY 10018, USA

BLOOMSBURY, BLOOMSBURY ACADEMIC and the Diana logo are trademarks of
Bloomsbury Publishing Plc

First published in Great Britain 2019

Copyright © Matthias Middell and contributors, 2019

Matthias Middell has asserted his right under the Copyright, Designs and Patents
Act, 1988, to be identified as Editor of this work.

Cover image: Demonstration Against Decolonization in Brussels, 1960
(© Keystone-France/Gamma-Keystone via Getty Images)

All rights reserved. No part of this publication may be reproduced or transmitted
in any form or by any means, electronic or mechanical, including photocopying,
recording, or any information storage or retrieval system, without prior
permission in writing from the publishers.

Bloomsbury Publishing Plc does not have any control over, or responsibility for,
any third-party websites referred to or in this book. All internet addresses given
in this book were correct at the time of going to press. The author and publisher
regret any inconvenience caused if addresses have changed or sites have
ceased to exist, but can accept no responsibility for any such changes.

A catalogue record for this book is available from the British Library.

A catalog record for this book is available from the Library of Congress.

ISBN: HB: 978-1-4742-9215-3
       ePDF: 978-1-4742-9217-7
       eBook: 978-1-4742-9216-0

Typeset by Integra Software Services Pvt. Ltd.
Printed and bound in Great Britain

To find out more about our authors and books visit www.bloomsbury.com and sign up for
our newsletters.

Contents

List of Tables	vi
List of Contributors	vii
Introduction: European Perspectives in Global History? Recent Development in Practicing Global History across the European Continent *Matthias Middell*	1
1 Plural Globality and Shift in Perspective *Michel Espagne*	29
2 Paris: National, International, Transnational, Cultural Capital City? (19th–20th Century) *Christophe Charle*	45
3 The Socialist World in Global History: From Absentee to Victim to Co-producer *James Mark and Tobias Rupprecht*	81
4 Russian Economic History in Global Perspective *Alessandro Stanziani*	115
5 Labour History Goes Global *Marcel van der Linden*	137
6 Towards a Transnational and Global History of Demographic and Migratory Processes and Discourses *Attila Melegh*	149
7 The Idea of Africa in History: From Eurocentrism to World History *Catherine Coquery-Vidrovitch*	169
8 Global and Regional Comparisons: The Great Divergence Debate and Europe *Eric Vanhaute*	183
Index	206

List of Tables

1	Paris Salon Admissions	48
2	Number of Theatres in Five European Capitals	48
3	Conferences in Paris and London and in Their Respective Countries in Exposition Years	54
4	Percentage of Foreign Students by Faculty in 1897/98 in Berlin and Paris	56
5	Country of Origin of Foreign Students in Paris in 1898	57
6	Proportion of Foreign Artists in Various Art Salons in Paris and Berlin (Percentage)	61

List of Contributors

Christophe Charle (1951) is professor of modern history (19th–20th c.) at Paris 1-Panthéon Sorbonne University since 1993. Historian of European cultures and societies he published or edited more than 40 volumes. Among the most recent: *Théâtres en capitales, naissance de la société du spectacle à Paris, Berlin, Londres et Vienne 1860–1914* (2008), *Le temps des capitales culturelles XVIIIe–XXe siècles* (2009), *Discordance des temps, une brève histoire de la modernité* (2011), *Histoire des universités XIIe–XXIe siècles* (with J. Verger, 2012), *La dérégulation culturelle. Essai d'histoire des cultures en Europe au XIXe siècle* (2015). He coedited, with Laurent Jeanpierre, *La vie intellectuelle en France depuis la Révolution* (2 vols, Paris: Seuil, 2016), and with Daniel Roche and others *L'Europe, encyclopédie historique* (Arles: Actes Sud, 2018). Currently, he prepares a book on Paris during the 19th century.

Catherine Coquery-Vidrovitch is a former student of the École Normale Supérieure de Sèvres and agrégée d'histoire (1959). Her doctoral thesis dealt with 'Brazza and the taking of possession of the Congo. The mission of West Africa, 1883–1885' (1966) and her second thesis entitled 'The Congo at the time of the big concessionary companies: 1898–1930' was defended in 1970. She became in 1975 a professor at the University Paris VII Denis Diderot from where she retired in 2001. In the *late* 1970s, she founded and directed the Third World Knowledge / Africa laboratory, which became SEDET (Societies in Development: Transdisciplinary Studies) and, later on, a component of the Center for Social Science Studies on African, American and Asian worlds. From 2000 to 2005 she served as a member of the board of the Comité international des sciences historiques. Among her many publications are *Afrique noire: permanences et ruptures* (Paris: Éditions Payot, 1985); *Histoire des villes d'Afrique noire: Des origines à la colonisation* (Paris: Albin Michel, 1993); *Les Africaines. Histoire des femmes d'Afrique du XIXe au XXe siècle* (Paris: Desjonquères, 1994); *L'Afrique et les Africains au XIXe siècle* (Paris: Armand Colin, 1999); *Enjeux politiques de l'histoire coloniale* (Marseille, Agone, 2009); *Petite histoire de l'Afrique: l'Afrique au sud du Sahara de la préhistoire à nos jours* (Paris: La Découverte, 2010); *Les Routes de l'esclavage. Histoire des traites africaines VIe–XXe siècles* (Paris: Albin Michel, 2018).

Michel Espagne is a historian of culture and served since 1989 as directeur de recherche at the Centre Nationale de la Recherche scientifique in Paris. From 2011 to 2018 he was head of the Laboratoire d'excellence TransferS and from 2011 till 2014 he served as president of the European Network of Universal and Global History. His main research interest focuses on cultural transfers between different societies, both European and non-European. Among his recent publications are *Les transferts culturels franco-allemands* (PUF, 1999); Le creuset allemand. Histoire interculturelle de la Saxe au XVIIIe et XIXe siècles (PUF, 2000); *L'histoire de l'art comme transfert culturel. L'itinéraire d'Anton Springer* (Paris: Belin, 2009); *L'ambre et le fossile. Transferts germano-russes dans les sciences humaines XIXe–XXe siècle* (Paris: Armand Colin, 2014); (with Jin Guangyao) *Conférences chinoises de la rue d'Ulm* (Paris: Demopolis, 2017); (with Pavel Alexeiev and Ekaterina Dmitrieva) *Transferts culturels en Sibérie. De l'Altaï à la Iakoutie* (Paris: Demopolis, 2018); (with Li Hongtu) *Chine France – Europe Asie. Itinéraire de concepts* (Paris: Editions rue d'Ulm, 2018).

Marcel van der Linden is Senior Fellow at the International Institute of Social History, where he served as Research Director between 2001 and 2014. He was also, since 1997, professor of Social Movement History at the University of Amsterdam (UvA). He is President of the International Social History Association (2005–10, 2010–15, 2015–20). Research interests: labour history and the history of radical thought. His books and articles have been published in seventeen languages. Forthcoming: *The Social Question in the 21st Century* (co-edited; University of California Press, 2019), and *The Worldwide Web of Work* (Amsterdam University Press, 2020).

James Mark is Professor of History at the University of Exeter His research interests include politics of memory, and the social and cultural history of state socialism in central-eastern Europe. His recent work aims to connect the region to broader global histories. He is the author of *The Unfinished Revolution: Making Sense of the Communist Past in Central-Eastern Europe* (2010), and co-author of *Europe's 1968: Voices of Revolt* (2013) and *1989: A Global History of Eastern Europe* (2019).

Attila Melegh is a sociologist, economist and historian. He has taught widely in the United States, Russia, Georgia and Hungary. He is associate professor at Corvinus University, Budapest, and a senior researcher at the Demographic Research Institute. His research focuses on the global social change in the

20th century, and international migration. Among other books and publications he authored *On the East/West Slope. Globalization, Nationalism, Racism and Discourses on Eastern Europe* (New York-Budapest: CEU Press, 2006), He is the founding director of Karl Polányi Research Center at Corvinus University of Budapest.

Matthias Middell, professor of cultural history at Leipzig University, is director of the Global and European Studies Institute at that University. Since 2015 he is a member of the Board of the Comité International des Sciences Historiques. Since 1991 he serves as editor of *Comparativ. Journal of Global History*. His main research interests include global and transregional histories with emphasis on spatial configurations; the history of revolutions and the history of intercultural transfers as well as the history of historiography in the 19th and 20th century. Most recently he published the *Handbuch der transnationalen Geschichte Ostmitteleuropas 1750–1918* (with Frank Hadler; Göttingen: Vandenhoeck & Ruprecht, 2017) and the *Routledge Handbook of Transregional Studies* (London: Routledge, 2018).

Tobias Rupprecht is a Lecturer in Latin American and Caribbean History at the University of Exeter. He has held research and teaching positions at Free University of Berlin, the University of Aarhus/Denmark, the Catholic University in Santiago de Chile, Fudan University in Shanghai, and the German Historical Institute in Moscow. His research mostly addresses contacts between the Second and Third Worlds during the Cold War and its aftermath, the role of culture and religion in international relations, and the position of both Latin America and Russia in the global history of the late 20th century. His monograph *Soviet Internationalism after Stalin. Interaction and Exchange between the USSR and Latin America during the Cold War* (Cambridge: Cambridge University Press, 2015) explored Latin American encounters with the Soviet Union and the ways in which arts and culture shaped how people made sense of the Global Cold War. With James Mark, Bogdan Iacob and Ljubica Spaskovska, he is co-author of *1989: A Global History of Eastern Europe* (Cambridge: Cambridge University Press, 2019). He is currently studying the role of liberal economists in late state socialism and the transition.

Alessandro Stanziani is Directeur d'études at the Ecole des Hautes Etudes en Sciences Sociales and Directeur de recherche at the Centre National de la Recherche Scientifique in Paris. He is a specialist of the history of labour in transregional perspective and has a focus on Russian history. His most recent books include *Les entrelacements du monde, Histoire globale, pensée globale* (Paris: CNRS éditions 2018) and *Labor in the Fringes of Empire* (London: Palgrave, 2018)

Eric Vanhaute is Professor of Economic History and World History at the History Department of Ghent University. His publications include books and articles on agrarian and rural history and global history such as *World History. An Introduction* (London: Routledge, 2013), and *Peasants in World History* (London: Routledge, forthcoming).

Introduction: European Perspectives in Global History? Recent Development in Practicing Global History across the European Continent

Matthias Middell

A recent global turn in historiography

Although world and universal histories have been written since the first historiographies were embarked upon,[1] the term global history describes a relatively new field that has received considerable attention since the second half of the 1990s. Subsequently it has grown exponentially, including the number of scholars devoting their work to this field and the many new aspects covered by their research. Almost everything that was considered a relevant topic for history writing has seen its global turn – for instance, from consumption to finance, from politics to migration and from social order to cultural patterns. People specializing in the history of various geographical areas have joined forces to cover planetwide narratives with their expertise,[2] and a few authors have even risked writing global histories as single-authored overviews of periods such as the eighteenth or the nineteenth centuries.[3] Such collective and individual efforts are a response to the increasing demand for global history works.

However, the new enthusiasm for global history has not only – and perhaps not even primarily – led to ambitious all-encompassing narratives, but has also first and foremost led to the intensification of research that has a conscious global or transregional focus. There is a general agreement among scholars today that global history is a specific perspective on history rather than the history of everything under the sun.[4] Global history therefore is not necessarily only the history of longue durée processes: proponents look more often at parallel and simultaneous processes in different arenas and the probability of their synchronization. While parallelism is more often observed in the times before the Seven Years War (as historians of increasing global competition between imperial powers argue),[5] or 1820 (as economic historians insist upon by hinting at the emergence of a world market and price convergence),[6] the situation changed dramatically during the nineteenth century towards something that has been referred to by Charles Bright and Michael Geyer as the global condition.[7] With this global condition, the mutual dependency and co-constitution of local, regional, national and imperial developments have become the most prominent subjects of global history writing and research. As a consequence, comparison has lost its former prominence as the royal road to scientific knowledge in the humanities and social sciences.[8] For this reason, new theories and methodologies have had to be found to fill the gap left by the decline of comparative strategies that isolate cases – and therefore construct them as fixed and naturalized entities – and select variables to be measured for the purpose of comparison. This does not mean that comparing phenomena is no longer of importance in global history. On the contrary, comparison has received more attention over recent decades, but more as a practice exercised by the historical actors when constructing the global than as a methodological tool applied by the scholar imagined as a neutral observer.[9] This comparative nature can be seen in connected[10] and entangled histories[11] as well as research on intercultural transfers[12] or on histoires croisées.[13]

Within such approaches, the idea that the world consists of fixed entities (usually as states or societies) and that the construction of variables helps to understand their position within the system has been criticized for being driven by methodological nationalism,[14] remaining ahistorical and ignorant towards the achievements of historiography, being stuck in the generalization of the Western experience of statehood or nationalization of society, as well as being so far immune to the challenge of post-colonial arguments. The very recent emergence of a global historical sociology can be interpreted as a reaction to the gap between global history, on the one hand, and globalization research in the social sciences, on the other.[15]

Arguments have also been made from various points of departure as to why and how the world entered the global condition. Technological innovation and a revolution in the tools for long-distance communication undoubtedly played an important role. However, there is also concern about a resulting techno-determinism and a 'teleology of globalization rhetoric'[16] when overlooking, on the one hand, the contingencies of such processes[17] and the violence and major crises of many societies as well as the international system, on the other, with which this transformation came together in and following the nineteenth century.[18]

Within less than two decades, global history has gained considerable historical interest, and there is a debate as to whether the former dominance of national history writing has been broken and replaced by a paradigm of 'we are all global historians', as Harvard historian David Armitage put it in an interview in 2012.[19] Others remain more sceptical, and there are parts of the world where one can find much less enthusiasm about the global turn for the simple reason that it is seen as another tool for renewed Western dominance over processes of history writing and memory-building.[20] In this view, world or global history are nothing other than instruments of certain projects of globalization – instruments targeting sovereignty over one's own past, or better, a society's past. These sovereignty arguments often translate into defending national history narratives and can be found in many universities around the world. Interestingly, such opposition to global history in the name of national sovereignty and as part of anti-hegemonic discourses uses explanatory patterns with a global appeal as well, from dependency theory and world-system theories to post-colonial argumentations. One can suggest that these arguments are paradoxically, and even against their own intentions, a very important and particularly inspiring part of the global history movement and at the same time proof that global history is anything but monolithic. This is also reflected in an ongoing dispute about terminology. The term universal history came under attack in the early 1990s when North American scholars drew a strong line between their own new concepts and a European tradition that seemed to be stuck in a Hegelian speculative philosophy of history. The problem with this argument was not so much a farewell to naive Hegelianism but rather the need to have it addressed by the US reception of nineteenth-century European world history writing instead of targeting the debate in both Eastern and Western European historiographies since the 1970s, where a more differentiated picture had already been drawn.[21] While a negative connotation was attached to universal history during these debates, world history remained the more neutral term in contrast to global history, which in the early 1990s became loaded with the meaning of either a more advanced version of world history (even culminating in Bruce Mazlish's proposal to speak of new global history)[22] or sympathies for the ideology of globalism, openly rejected above all by French scholars. Over the years, however, this struggle with words seemed ever more fruitless and a sort of relaxation took place. The result was that these terms became no longer relevant for the identification of different schools of thought within the broader stream of historians dealing with topics larger than their continent.

A European perspective: The institutions

At the start of the twenty-first century, reaching into the first decade, global history was particularly strong in the US, originating from the world history movement that had already appeared in various places throughout the country in the early 1980s. The movement – within which academics and high school teachers were critical towards traditional 'Western Civ' courses[23] (amusingly labelled 'From Plato to NATO') – combined forces to challenge a teaching concept that seemed to be stable and without any alternative. For various reasons, introductory courses at American colleges as well as the cooperation between history departments and area studies centres provided fruitful grounds for the emergence of the new subfield. History departments at North American research universities profited in one way or another from the institutional crisis of area studies,[24] in turn becoming the new home for specialists in non-Western developments. This position allowed them to offer courses on worldwide entanglements and transregional encounters.[25] Dominic Sachsenmaier describes the German development of global history in his comparative analysis, published in 2010 and based upon data from the previous ten years, as remaining very much behind not only North American but also Chinese efforts.[26] To some extent, this echoes the main argument made by Patrick Manning, who presented in the early 2000s the renewal of global history as being rooted in a long European tradition, on the one hand, but also as being completely transformed by American scholarship after 1945, on the other.[27]

German global historian Jürgen Osterhammel confirmed this narrative by pointing out that the new interest in global history was much less anchored in any sort of German tradition and was more inspired by the North American debate. He stated in 2009:

> Some of the best work by German historians is now published in English, and it is extremely difficult, and ultimately futile, to look for traces of its 'Germanness'. A growing number of these historians, especially among the younger generation, have migrated to universities in the United States, Great Britain, Japan or to such extraterritorial and cosmopolitan academic locations as the European University Institute at Florence. They carry with them their German training without self-consciously transplanting any characteristically German tradition.

Regarding his own work, he denies that it has ever 'been self-consciously German'.[28] The most prominent German global historian to date describes himself as 'not [being] representative of world/global history in "Germany"' and sees himself not writing 'from within the "field" ... but rather from the point of view of a semi-detached observer'.[29] He continues with a description of six pathways towards global history that is typical of German historians: starting either (1) from European expansion and colonialism, or (2) from historiography and theory, or (3) with migration; coming (4) from international relations and global economic history; focusing (5) on cross-cultural comparisons; or finally taking (6) area histories with an emerging interest in transregional ties as the point of departure. He insists on the sixth as the most fruitful in terms of numbers of scholars now comprising the field of global history in Germany. This departs from the assumption that there has not been proper training at the university level in world or global history before 2000. This might be true for West Germany, with its rather individualized system of study where students had a broad choice from more or less specialized courses but not necessarily a course introducing them to world history (or the history of the West or similar broad topics). Osterhammel rightly insists on a substantial change to the organization of study, which affects students' training and the necessity to train faculty in order to be able to offer this kind of general course.

Things had been quite different in East Germany, where since the late 1950s the idea of a well-regulated curriculum allowed, at least in some places, introductory courses in world history. The idea not only fitted well with the holistic aim of Marxism but also continued local traditions that went far beyond the Communist Party's takeover in 1945. Leipzig University's history department had to deal with the legacy of Karl Lamprecht's Institute for Universal History, founded in 1909 and integrated into the department again through a painful process between 1947 and 1951. The details[30] are not of particular interest here since the local story is part of a wider process. In a large number of countries today, history is taught by distinguishing national and world history, while in other countries the two are presented together (often at the expense of the world history part).

Counting the number of professorships devoted to non-Western history in a national academic system therefore only provides a rough indicator for the global orientation of a whole academic system. It is true that such quantification allows competencies to be measured within a history department relating to topics that need linguistic skills and familiarity with archives abroad. These competencies, without a doubt, display the weaknesses of many higher education systems in Europe. However, focusing on history departments only modifies the indicator in a problematic way, considering the outcome of the area studies crisis that occurred in the 1990s in the US, which is considered a benchmark for global development. Up until this time, area studies were rather weakly institutionalized in North American academia. Generally, they were organized in temporarily funded centres and profited from double appointments between departments. They remained in most cases a product of contemporary political interest during the two world wars, and then suffered from discontinued funding from private foundations and the state.[31] During the crisis – when funding declined or stopped abruptly and when the entire concept of area studies was criticized for its lack of foresight with regard to the collapse of the Soviet Union or 9/11 – ties with the department proved stronger, with people searching for protection under the umbrella of history or sociology departments, for example, or establishing new ones, as in international or global studies departments. In contrast, area studies in many European countries, with a strong emphasis on philology and cultural studies, had already been established in the late nineteenth and early twentieth centuries with institutes independent from history departments. Profiting from continued state funding when setting their own multi-disciplinary agenda, some of them have worked on historical topics while others have not paid very much attention to developments in professional historiography.[32]

Evidently, this system of having institutes separate from history departments has had a series of disadvantages when it comes to supporting the development of global history approaches. Firstly, its (often lamented slow) reactivity to new developments has depended almost exclusively on the willingness of the tenured faculty, and since the institutes have usually been very small, there has been little room to manoeuvre when hiring new staff. Although this gap has been partly filled with external funding, the resulting problem is that highly qualified young researchers remain for a very long time in a precarious situation and depend on continuous streams of money from outside the universities. Secondly, this system has treated regions as isolated containers instead of looking at their transregional and global connections. Thirdly, institutionally separated area studies have above all had a tendency to strengthen their ties with academic institutions in the region under investigation instead of integrating into joint analyses of global processes. True, all these disadvantages have not necessarily played out in every situation; however, in contrast to the very rapid development of global history in the US, it is evident in many European countries that the field has emerged rather slowly despite the fact that the area expertise was available.

The situation in Europe is not only diverse because of the different positions world history had in the school curriculum but also due to the fact that in some countries strong institutions existed with an explicit programme for comparing historical and contemporary processes across regional boundaries. The School of Oriental and African Studies (SOAS) in London and the École des Hautes Études en Sciences Sociales are the most famous examples that encouraged the establishment of similar institutions outside universities in Germany; for instance, the Hamburg-based Global and Area Studies Institute is primarily a think tank with a strong political focus similar to a series of institutions in Scandinavia and the Anglo-Saxon world, while the Centre of Modern Oriental Studies in Berlin took inspiration from the more historical SOAS approach. There is not adequate space here to list all the state- and privately-funded institutions dealing with global issues across the European continent and also hosting, to a certain extent, historical research. That being said, they are numerous and some are devoted to clearly demarcated topics: for example, the Stockholm International Peace Research Institute, with its research on the arms trade; the Institut du Monde Arabe in Paris, with its concentration on the North African region; and the famous Archivo General de Indias in Seville, cataloguing the archival legacy of Spanish colonialism. Additionally, European states have founded and are still founding institutes on other continents for the purpose of cultural and academic diplomacy, which became research hubs in global connections.[33]

This leads us to consider another factor of diversity: the relationship between higher education and extra-university institutions. This relationship, and collaboration, is typically seen as a product of communist intervention in the academic landscape because the academies of sciences developed after the Second World War in the former East from a point of academic exchange into powerful research centres. We should, however, not forget that the Centre National de la Recherche Scientifique (CNRS) in France dates back to the late 1930s and has so far resisted all attempts at its dissolution. Whereas in former East Germany the research institutes of the Academy of Science were dissolved after unification, in most other parts of the former Soviet bloc institutes with a regional focus or institutes for world history survived and joined up with the international movement towards research on globalization in one way or another.[34]

Even this short and very cursory overview of the institutional landscape shows that the European situation is very diverse and far from homogenous. With Osterhammel's six pathways towards global history in mind, we see that in only a few places in the late 1990s and early 2000s had the preconditions for the emergence of this new field been present.

A European perspective: The scholars

Institutions are one thing, and they are important for attracting funding as well as for the training of the next generation of scholars. Nevertheless, individuals are decisive when it comes to the formulation of a new research agenda. Gareth Austin recently gave a remarkable overview of scholars and global history debates, paying special attention to northwestern Europe. Austin's overview refers to the same difficulties we are confronted with concerning the Europeaness of such debates. He voluntarily focuses on contributions in English and French, and as an economic historian, he gives more weight to the 'great divergence' debate in organizing the field than other scholars would probably do.[35] But there is no doubt that Patrick O'Brien – who took a very important initiative in establishing a proper global history debate in the UK by starting, in 1996, a regular seminar at the Institute of Historical Research in London – was among the first to connect colleagues across the continent (and beyond) through his Global Economic History Network.[36] Global history, in this context, fought against a Eurocentric tradition in the interpretation of the so-called 'great divergence', which maintains that the division of the world into those who are rich and those who remain poor[37] has deep historical and structural roots that cannot be overcome by following the Western model of development. In contrast to this opinion, there are differing debates inspired by Andre Gunder Frank's call to ReOrient established views[38] and especially by Kenneth Pomeranz's powerful attempt to turn the comparative scheme between Europe and China upside down by insisting on reciprocal comparison and on a more reflexive definition of the appropriate scale of research objects, for example 'China' and the Yangtze Delta or 'Europe' and the British Midlands.[39]

It is evident that the multiple variants of Eurocentrism and the polemics around it are a unique challenge for European global historians.[40] The variety of reactions to this challenge range from new imperial history, advocating the mutual constituency of metropolis and colonies, to the emphasis given more recently to alternatives to Western globalization, with studies on 'red globalization'[41] or 'socialism goes global'.[42] Although part of the background to the debate on the 'great divergence' lies in modernization theory, a similar discussion occurred in the East around the holistic ambition of Marxism.[43] Such parallel developments mirror the division of the European continent during the Cold War. However, the fact that today socialist globalization is investigated more intensively in the United Kingdom than in East Central Europe,[44] with the Russian journal *Ab Imperio* becoming an important platform for the comparison of imperial histories,[45] hints at the increasing entanglement of historiographic landscapes that were formerly separated from each other. The same holds true for the international network addressing questions of global labour history, with its European centres, for example the Amsterdam-based International Institute of Social History and the re:work Centre in Berlin.[46]

Even though diversity is the first characteristic of the European landscape in global history due to national intellectual traditions and organizational trajectories, transnational cooperation and mutual inspiration have increasingly come to the fore. A variety of academic journals have emerged, and when looking at their authorship it becomes clear that they are not, on the whole, platforms for national discourse communities as the leading journals of the nineteenth and twentieth centuries were.[47] Although they are edited from a certain national background, they are intended to facilitate transnational communication while working simultaneously as mediums to different audiences and linguistic communities. *Itinerario*, edited in the Netherlands since 1977, continues the Dutch tradition of interest in early modern colonialism and transregional encounter, and since the early 2000s has opened up widely to global interactions from the fifteenth century to the present.[48] *Comparativ*, founded in Leipzig in 1991, publishes four to six thematic issues a year, providing collections of articles that look at different world regions, mobilizing the expertise of area studies for collaboratively produced global or transregional histories.[49] While the multilingual journal bridges gaps between germanophone, anglophone and francophone readerships, another German periodical, *Zeitschrift für Weltgeschichte*, was founded in 2000 in Hannover by a specialist in Russian history, Hans-Heinrich Nolte, which collects articles mainly in German and English.[50] It was followed in 2006 by the *Journal of Global History*,[51] initiated by the influential group in global economic history at the London School of Economics including Patrick O'Brien and Gareth Austin,[52] which was also an expression of the ongoing institutionalization of global history in the UK as the examples of the Global History and Culture Centre at the University of Warwick[53] and the Centre for Global History at the University of Oxford[54] demonstrate. The more recent conjuncture of global history in France is reflected in the establishment in 2012 of the journal *Monde(s)* by a new generation of French historians who connect national, imperial and global history in an innovative way.[55]

But these are only the most obvious developments in the field of academic journals. Many of the traditional journals started to welcome contributions from a global or transnational perspective, and some also became platforms for an extended methodological debate about how to integrate these new trends into the established historiographical landscape.[56] During this time, global history became a field in its own right and a perspective taken by many more historians in cases where it was suitable for the topics covered. After a relatively short period of transformation, starting in the early 2000s, there is today a broad spectrum of global historians all over the European continent, which is also well connected not only with its counterparts in the Americas, Australia and New Zealand, as well as in Asia, but also with renascent African scholarship.

The European network in universal and global history

The increasing number of global historians can also be seen in the European Congresses in World and Global History, which bring together every three years between 500 and 800 participants. The initiative for these congresses was taken at a meeting in Leipzig in 2002, with Patrick O'Brien from London, Peer Vries, at the time from Leiden, and Margarete Grandner from Vienna being among the founders. Everyone present at this seminar at the then rather embryonic stage of global history debates in Europe found it both unsatisfying to simply follow the US-based World History Association (WHA) – with its strong focus on the improvement of the teaching situation at US colleges (while still recognizing how fruitful many of the WHA initiatives have also been for European scholarship) – as well as the organization of national platforms or organizations. At the time, it was not only the relatively small number of active global historians that led to doubts as to whether national organizations might become successful, given the strong dominance of national historians almost everywhere in Europe. All participants were also convinced that a separation of global historians from other streams in historiography would conflict with the notion that the global is not simply a separate (and separable) scale of the historical object but is, out of necessity, a perspective to be taken on almost every object. To globalize national histories was seen as a task just as much as the (re)discovery of global connections long forgotten.

It also became clear at the same meeting that global perspectives may mean different things to historians from other contexts. Some historians felt encouraged to risk comparison on larger scales than before, while others focused on the study of connections. Some started from the analysis of economic performance, while others were interested in cultural practices and imaginations. At the same time, practicing global history does not mean to be completely free from any influence of national priorities in looking at history –

as is clear with regard to the role of empire and colonialism or Cold War engagement on both sides of the Iron Curtain. Historians from what have been referred to as small nations[57] may see global processes differently from those who were trained at the universities of former large empires, not to mention those who experienced the hegemonic position of their own country in world affairs. Critical distance from the formative effects of one's own socialization is a prerequisite of any good historian; however, confrontation with other world views in the same field of interest obviously helps to realize some biases that remain overlooked.

It took no more than an evening at a Mexican restaurant to formulate the rules of a European Network in Universal and Global History (ENIUGH) that should become responsible for the organization of a regular European congress and facilitate initiatives for joint graduate programmes. These small beginnings resulted three years later in the first gathering of just over 200 people presenting papers in Leipzig. The idea of bringing the global history torch to East Central Europe in 2008 failed at the very last moment, and the congress had to be transferred to Dresden, which saw an increase in participation to about 250 presenters. The numbers for the following two congresses indicate that global history in Europe was on the rise and that the UK and France were successively mobilizing scholars in large numbers from within their own borders as well as far beyond. London in 2011 had 483 participants and Paris three years later had 701.[58] The congress in 2017 in Budapest (with 663 people offering papers to more than 150 panels) demonstrates that global history has in the meantime grown into a stable field of study, which now brings together a second generation of scholars. Participants come not only from all over Europe but also from, to name a few: Gabon, Hong Kong, Israel, Japan, Kazakhstan, Pakistan, Senegal, Singapore, South Africa, Thailand, Togo, Trinidad and Tobago, as well as from the US. Taken together, all congresses organized since 2005 by ENIUGH have brought together scholars from seventy-six countries.

But what is more impressive is the European character of the congresses, with relatively stable participation (more than ten participants for all the congresses) from Austria, Belgium, Denmark, France, Germany, Italy, the Netherlands, Russia, Spain, Sweden, Switzerland, Turkey and the UK. The location of the congress has an effect on the participation of the French (peaking in Paris with 129 but shrinking to 28 again three years later, which is a little less than the 32 in London 2011) but not of the British historians, who were as strongly represented in London as at the two subsequent congresses with more than 70 participants. German global historians (with more than 100 per congress and as many as 164 in Paris) have established the congresses as their main forum, and this may relate to the fact that the headquarters of the European Network is located in Leipzig as well as to the slow reaction of the biannual German National Congress of Historians towards global history. These large congresses of historians, with more than 3,000 participants and open to high school teachers who have to teach a mainly national and partly European history curriculum, have a few sections on global issues. However, in general, there is not enough space to present ongoing research on topics not relevant for the nexus between teachers training at universities and high school practices.

The participation numbers at the European congresses show that a truly transnational platform has been built, which, interestingly enough, is also highly attractive for scholars from Africa, Asia and North America. This was possible because the European Network was involved in a second initiative to establish a world and global history organization within the Comité International des Sciences Historiques (CISH). The first attempt, which was related to a major theme section at the congress of the CISH in 2000 in Oslo, failed as a result of mistrust between North American and European scholars. However, the foundation of the Network of Organizations in World and Global History (NOGWHISTO) in 2008 in Dresden led to the acceptance of NOGWHISTO as an affiliate of the CISH in 2010. Since the CISH congress in Jinan in 2015, NOGWHISTO has not only regularly held panels but has also maintained close contact with its sister organizations in Asia and North America as well as with initiatives in Latin America and Africa. Such activities at a regional level invite further reflection upon the European character of certain forms of global history, which came to light with a first bibliography covering the years 2010 to 2015.[59]

Accordingly, historians with a background in the history of world regions other than Europe looked for opportunities to discuss their subject fields. At the same time, the exponential growth of funding in the field of global history (among others) has no equivalent in tenured positions at German universities. The first chairs in global history are only just now being established. Therefore, one can observe the emergence of a 'reserve army' (to use the old Marxian term) that looks for opportunities for international career development and that feels the particular need to network across boundaries. All this together played out in favour of an organization of global historians in Europe at the continental instead of the national level.

An intertwined approach to European global history and historiography

Our collection of essays written by European scholars from France, Germany, Hungary, the Netherlands, Switzerland and the UK reflects the state of global history in the second decade of the twenty-first century. Claire Lipscomb, Emily Rose and Beatriz López subsequently welcomed the idea of collecting a series of examples that demonstrate the different ways to understand and write global or transnational history across the European continent. This is quite different from any sort of congress proceedings, even if some of the chapters in this volume originate from papers given at the congress. The steering committee of the European Network commissioned the editor to select from the many topics and historiographical cultures, while insisting on two criteria. First, the volume is intended to reflect the focus of the respective congress, in our case the one in Paris, which was the first big conference and mobilization of global historians on French soil. Second, the volume is meant as a cross section of different trends, topics and interpretations across various European historiographies. What is not intended is any attempt to mirror the diversity of approaches characteristic of these congresses given the enormous mobilization of scholarly energies by the very concept of global history. In contrast, our intention is to provide as far as possible a coherent picture of the innovations presented at the congress. Such innovation can be measured against two backgrounds: the previous situation or the situation somewhere else. To make the European perspectives (evidently plural) visible is the main purpose of such a volume, and this is facilitated by the fact that historians from all over the continent know each other and refer to each other just as well as they do with scholars from other world regions. The congress in Paris in 2014 was a landmark in the development of such European perspectives as there was an explicit debate about the specific contribution made by European global historians to the field.

All the authors are eminent specialists in their subfield and have an excellent overview of what happens internationally in their domain. We invited them not only to present their personal research but also to introduce the historiographical environment to which they belong. The chapters therefore provide an overview of what are very inspiring developments within the European historiographies and what happens in other academic landscapes with regard to the same topic. The chapters reflect the high degree of entanglement in international global history writing nowadays much more than only specialized expertise. Global history as practiced in Europe is a connected history in itself.

This is well known in the case of the British Empire, for which specialized chairs at the most famous universities in the UK provide a background since the late nineteenth century. The mobility between the academic systems of the UK, Australia, New Zealand, the USA and Canada has created a sort of global historiographical complex that facilitated a leading role in the transnational use of archives, the combination of intellectual inspirations across the oceans for the development of new methodologies and theories, as well as careers between more research- and more teaching-oriented institutions of higher education. This structure profits from the harsh competition within a large English-speaking space, which has, furthermore, grown to include a series of Asian, Caribbean and South African universities as another consequence of the long history of British colonialism and the post-colonial constellations that emerged step by step since 1776 in different parts of the world.[60] All of this is to some extent unique, and the interesting effects of such a large market for academic innovation were observed during the London ENIUGH congress in 2011. Consequently, we asked for similarities and differences with the French system when organizing the Paris congress three years later.

There is also a francophone space of transregional reach, and probably its political organization is even stronger than in the British case.[61] But the relationship between universities in France and those in sub-Saharan Africa or Southeast Asia was characterized rather by unidirectional mobility towards places in the former colonial metropolises instead of a comparable circular mobility as in the case of anglophone universities. The interest in French colonial histories also has long roots, but a post-colonial approach to it emerged rather late.[62] It was under the presidency of Nicolas Sarkozy that the public debate in France on the relationship with its colonial past received a decisive boost. Sarkozy, with his intervention into the politics of history, not only provoked strong reactions in the field of colonial history but also helped a new generation of French scholars to definitively overcome scepticism towards global history.[63] Building on the traditions of the Annales school and on Lucien Febvre's *Cahiers d'histoire mondiale* – with which he pushed the United Nations Educational, Scientific and Cultural Organization's project in the 1950s on a history of mankind[64] – as well as on the discussions around the concept of intercultural transfers,[65] a series of translations as well as original pieces of new research within a relatively short period of time flooded the French book market with global histories of all kinds.[66] The mobilization of French intellectuals in favour of a global history of France during the election campaign in 2017, when Marine Le Pen's Front National was on the doorstep of the Elysée Palace, is just a continuation of this earlier movement.⁶⁷ It was against this background that the Paris congress of ENIUGH was held at the ENS. Special emphasis was given to the history of French-African connections, to the history of warfare (the opening at the Collège de France occurred on the centenary of the First World War), and to the method of intercultural transfer histories as a way to investigate encounters and appropriations across the borders of countries as well as continents.

The intention of our book is to present for the first time an overview of the most debated topics and to highlight the most recent developments in global history practiced by Europeans. Such an overview is unique both for the timeliness of the data and for the diversity of European ways of writing global and transnational history. One of this volume's aims is to overcome a certain parochialism of students in global history, who only know research trends from their own country or linguistic community but do not sufficiently reach out to the wealth of already completed research in other historiographies.

Even though in this volume considerable attention is given to the French way of doing world and global history as well as to the particular place intercultural transfers, colonial history and area studies have in this tradition, we do this with the clear intention of complementing this focus in subsequent volumes with other national or regional foci. Compared to British imperial history and its various legacies, the French turn towards the global has not yet received the necessary attention it deserves. Still, it nevertheless allows for a very interesting comparative setting. Both the role of France in global connections and the (re)positioning of French-speaking Africa are topics that enrich the analysis of European interventions in the competition around global projects targeting very different world regions spanning all continents.

The general layout

Michel Espagne, who in the 1980s had already begun (together with Michael Werner⁶⁸) the study of French–German cultural transfers, has consequently globalized this originally transnational and very European setting of research.⁶⁹ As he demonstrates in his chapter, the question of intercultural appropriation is not limited to the encounter of two nationalized cultural landscapes. On the contrary, the methodology developed by French cultural historians applies equally well to non-European contexts, and such transfers are constitutive of units that understand their culture as specific and separate. A global history that focuses on entanglements and connections as well as on brokers who facilitate the mobility of cultural patterns will find in this approach an appropriate methodology for further precise analysis. Espagne also applies his approach to historiographies of the global, underlining the fact that the seeming universalism of such historiographies is rather an illusion and that an investigation into how and why different historiographies borrow (selectively) from each other (or renounce them for one reason or another) can be very illuminating.

Christophe Charle's discussion of the role of Paris as an international cultural capital and a hub of transnationalism is much more than an impressive list of all the cultural innovations for which Paris has been known. The author suggests a distinction between the international dimension of the French capital's function of being home to many creative artists and giving space to an unbelievable number of congresses, expositions and meetings, on the one hand, and its transnational function, on the other, which is less related to the idea of everything being subordinated under French superiority and more to the practice of cultural transfers. The latter produces something beyond a clear division between French and foreign, addressing the productivity of the encounter, which results in something mixed and fertile. Charle clearly explains the methodological innovation of the intercultural transfer approach and its potential for a truly transnational history of modern times.

James Mark and Tobias Rupprecht analyse three different readings of the role socialist countries played in the overall story of globalization and react critically both to the ignorance of scholars towards the Eastern bloc's impact and to its downplaying as a victim of global forces, border opening and international connectivity by free mobility and markets. Instead, the authors appeal for a thorough analysis of the role of the socialist camp as a co-producer of globality over the past 70, or even 100, years in order to avoid a one-sided picture of globalization as the expansion of neo-liberalism. They hint at the fact that globalization as a paradigm started dominating the social sciences exactly when the Soviet Union and the bloc it had formed since the Second World War collapsed. But this should not prevent us from seeing the impact of socialist internationalism, the mobilities supported by communist organizations across borders, and the ideas of collectivism all over the planet. Analysis of the Eastern bloc's activities during the so-called global Cold War[70] and its attempts to mobilize support for its revolutionary aspirations[71] provides us with a much more complex picture of international relations during the twentieth century and is thought-provoking with regard to the recalibration of a periodization that reflects only a part of the world rather than its whole, for example with 1956, 1968, 1979 or 1989.[72]

Alessandro Stanziani, a specialist in Russian history teaching in Paris, places not only the history of Eastern Europe into a long-term perspective but also opens it up for comparative studies of socio-economic performance. He argues against the reigning normativity centred around England's transformation towards a modern industrial society and emphasizes that Russia had itself great potential to move from proto-industrialization to modern heavy industry. Characteristics of this pathway were relative little resistance from the 'subalterns' and the lack of both democratic institutions and a developed welfare state. This allowed for a labour-intensive pathway towards industrialization that profited from comparably low wages paid to workers but suffered simultaneously from problems with the quality of products and the effects of such an extreme degree of exploitation. But Russia was not alone; on the contrary, it is interesting to see that this pathway was taken by other European societies as well until the very last quarter of the nineteenth century when another crossroads emerged that allowed new decisions to be made and opened up opportunities to leave this pathway (whereas Russian society was neither able nor were its elites willing to do so).

Marcel van der Linden sheds light on the renewal of global labour history after the almost complete decline of the sub-discipline with the breakdown of the orthodox Marxist version of it as practiced in Eastern Europe until 1989. With the outsourcing of old industries to countries of the Global South, the interest in factors influencing working conditions, the role of wage levels for the type of capitalism possible, and the various forms of resistance (local, regional, national, as well as transregional) by the subalterns grew considerably in Brazil, India, South Africa and elsewhere in the former 'Third World'. This brought the message back to Europe that so-called classical free labour and the formation of a well-organized and relatively homogenous proletariat is rather the exception than the rule. Capitalism is also possible on the basis of slavery or coerced labour of all kinds, and this is also true for parts of the West. This influences the ability of a labour movement to politicize a common interest for all those who can be called workers when their living conditions range from complete misery to privileged participation in welfare states, with the details of their contracts differing tremendously. Global labour history is one of the most impressive examples of how European experiences can be provincialized to the profit of new narratives to be researched and written for the twenty-first century. It becomes clear that Europeans are not exempt from increasingly transregional value chains and that it is worthwhile to investigate the changes that happen to their position within such new constellations.

Attila Melegh, a historian of population development from Hungary, describes a similar development in the field of demography. Scholars here were for a long time convinced that growth and decline of population can be influenced at a national level only, if at all. Global perspectives have therefore provided an addition to national figures and trends; furthermore, with the availability of new databases and with the concern over Europe's relatively declining proportion of the world's population, the discussion of global tendencies has gained steam. While these debates focus on fertility, mortality and nuptiality, they are also related to questions of transregional mobility and global migration systems.[73] It has become evident over the past five years or so that Europeans are very much concerned with the growth of immigration; nevertheless, neither global demography nor the reasons for any change in the direction or size of global migration systems play very much of a role in these heated discussions. Melegh suggests that taking a global view and not limiting the perspective to (Western) Europe will lead in the near future to a turning point in demographic interpretations; however, he also assumes that resistance from the general public will remain strong against such a process, therefore deepening dichotomies between expert and public discourse.

Catherine Coquery-Vidrovitch, the doyen of French studies on Africa and one of the most active (and few) promoters of the integration of African voices into the French historiographical discourse since the 1970s,[74] takes the argument of provincializing Europe from the other end. She attacks African exceptionalism and proposes to provincialize the history of the continent as simply another part of global history (with its labour force, raw material, imaginations, etc.), which in her eyes has been ignored for too long. Liberating Africa from the ascribed role of a victim in global history fits with a couple of recent developments in international historiography, which depends above all, as Coquery-Vidrovitch demonstrates with many examples, on the full integration of African historians into the international community of scholars, a process she has contributed to a great deal.[75] The recognition of African historiography, she claims, is the precondition for Western historiography to not confuse its own particular contribution to global history with the field itself.

Finally, Eric Vanhaute from Ghent University, where he coordinates a Centre for Global Studies, comes back to the debate on the 'great divergence', which is arguably the most widespread discussion among global historians of the last twenty years,[76] although it is still not yet covering the whole world but mostly remains limited to a European–Asian comparison.[77] Vanhaute points out that the debate has brought enormous progress in terms of data, theories and methodologies that go far beyond the question of socio-economic performance of East Asia and northwestern Europe during the transformation from proto- to modern industrialization. This encourages a recalibration of comparative strategies and the study of connections. The selection of the units of analysis has an enormous impact on such studies; therefore, one should not take Europe for granted as a unit nor other continents. Vanhaute shows that, first, Europe has to be dismantled in the sense of a much more nuanced variety of pathways taken by different European regions and, second, that Europe also forms a part of larger socio-economic systems as is the case for the big Afro-Eurasian ecumene, maritime regions or a series of border areas. Global historians should be aware that the relevant spatialities change over time and do not work as simple containers within which history happens. To understand globalization as a historical long-term and uneven process means to analyse the dialectics of de- and respatialization that are repeatedly at work. These dialectics, as Vanhaute shows with a series of examples from recent research initiatives, produce an increasing number of new frontiers of globalization where the people on the ground interact with the systemic forces of macro-structural processes.

It would be a complete misunderstanding to take the selection of themes and approaches presented here to the reader as the whole of global history as practiced in Europe. A long list of topics would unfold if we were to aim for any kind of completeness. Environmental history or military history have been subjects of panels during the congress days of Paris as well as gender and culture, and so many others come to mind. But our intention is neither an encyclopaedia nor a handbook. In contrast, this collection of essays is meant as a stimulus for further debates about the European character of certain approaches in global history and it will hopefully be followed by subsequent volumes presenting other dimensions of this perspective.

Global history in Europe, as the chapters in this volume show, critically engages the challenge of the Eurocentric traditions of history writing in the West. It joins forces and develops a widely diversified set of strategies to overcome a legacy that has its roots in an intellectual haughtiness already developed before 1800 but seemingly confirmed by all the elements of supremacy of some European societies over parts of the planet during the (later) nineteenth century. Global history is not simply a reconstruction of the global processes of the past but it is – in Europe as elsewhere – confronted by the need to put this history into perspective.

Leipzig, August 2019

Notes

1. Hervé Inglebert, *Le monde, l'histoire: Essai sur les histoires universelles* (Paris: Presses Universitaires de France, 2014).
2. It is interesting to observe the fast emergence of a new book format that seems to respond best to this kind of collective effort. Many leading publishers now offer their own handbook series, which both allows a kind of shared authorship when it comes to global processes as well as satisfying the demand for short articles electronically available for use in university seminars. Handbooks, therefore, have in recent years become the main instrument for the global expansion of higher education since they provide an overview on current scholarship and facilitate the very flexible recomposition of such knowledge according to local needs.
3. On some of the most recent works on world or global history such as the ones published by Cambridge University Press, Harvard University Press and C.H. Beck in Munich, see Matthias Middell and Katja Naumann (eds), *New Global Historical Synthesis* (*Comparativ. Journal of Global History* 28, no. 2) (Leipzig: Leipzig University Press, 2018).
4. Sebastian Conrad, *What Is Global History?* (Princeton, NJ: Princeton University Press, 2016).
5. Among many others, we hint here at Patrick K. O'Brien, *Mercantilist Institutions for the Pursuit of Power with Profit: The Management of Britain's National Debt, 1756–1815* (Working Paper LSE Department of Economic History 95) (London: LSE, 2006), and Lynn Hunt, 'The Global Financial Origins of 1789', in *The French Revolution in Global Perspective*, eds Suzanne Desan, Lynn Hunt and William Max Nelson (Ithaca, NY: Cornell University Press, 2013), since they connect the argument of imperial competition with the one on growing economic entanglement.
6. Kevin H. O'Rourke and Jeffrey G. Williamson, 'When Did Globalisation Begin?', *European Review of Economic History* 6 (2002): 23–50.
7. Charles Bright and Michael Geyer, 'Benchmarks of Globalization: The Global Condition 1850–2010', in *A Companion to World History*, ed. Douglas Northrop (Hoboken, NJ: Wiley-Blackwell, 2012), 285–302.
8. Michel Espagne, 'Sur les limites du comparatisme en histoire culturelle', *Genèses* 17 (1994): 112–121.
9. Angelika Epple and Walter Erhart (eds), *Die Welt beobachten: Praktiken des Vergleichens* (Frankfurt: Campus, 2015).
10. Sanjay Subrahmanyam, 'Connected Histories: Notes towards a Reconfiguration of Early Modern Eurasia', *Modern Asian Studies* 31, no. 3 (1997): 735–762.
11. Shalini Randeria, 'Entangled Histories of Uneven Modernities: Civil Society, Caste Solidarities, and the Post-colonial State in India', in *Unraveling Ties: From Social*

Cohesion to New Practices of Connectedness, eds Yehuda Elkana, Ivan Krastev, Elisio Macamo and Shalini Randeria (Frankfurt: Campus, 2001), 284–311.

12 Michel Espagne, *Les transferts culturels franco-allemands* (Paris: Presses Universitaires de France, 1999); Matthias Middell, 'The Intercultural Transfer Paradigm in its Transnational and Transregional Setting', *The Yearbook of Transnational History* 1 (2018): 46–60. See the article by Espagne in this volume.

13 Michael Werner and Bénédicte Zimmermann, 'Beyond Comparison: Histoire Croisée and the Challenge of Reflexivity', *History and Theory* 45 (2006): 30–50.

14 Andreas Wimmer and Nina Glick-Schiller, 'Methodological Nationalism and Beyond: Nation-state Building, Migration and the Social Sciences', *Global Networks* 2, no. 4 (2002): 301–334.

15 See the heavy critique from inside the social sciences by Julian Go and George Lawson, 'Introduction: For a Global Historical Sociology', in *Global Historical Sociology*, eds Julian Go and George Lawson (Cambridge: Cambridge University Press, 2017), 1–34.

16 Conrad, *Global History*, 212.

17 Roland Wenzlhuemer, *Globalgeschichte schreiben: Eine Einführung in 6 Episoden* (Konstanz, Munich: UVK Lucius, 2017); Roland Wenzlhuemer, 'The Ship, the Media, and the World: Conceptualizing Connections in Global History', *Journal of Global History* 11, no. 2 (2016): 163–186.

18 Michael Geyer and Charles Bright, 'Global Violence and Nationalizing: Wars in Eurasia and America: The Geopolitics of War in the Mid-nineteenth Century', in *The Modes of Comparison*, ed. A. Yengoyan (Ann Arbor, MI: University of Michigan Press, 2006), 226–271.

19 Martine van Ittersum and Jaap Jacobs, 'Are We All Global Historians Now? An Interview with David Armitage', *Itinerario* 36, no. 2 (2012): 7–28.

20 Dipesh Chakrabarty is probably the best known author who has expressed this dissatisfaction with the difficulties of disconnecting the very concept of history from the now largely criticized concept of Eurocentrism; that being said, one is also confronted with the argument that global history is a renewed form of intellectual imperialism in many places.

21 See, for example, the reader edited by Ernst Schulin under the title *Universalgeschichte* (Cologne: Kiepenheuer & Witsch, 1974) and the insistence on the many uses of the terms universal and world history in Marx's work by Manfred Kossok, *Karl Marx und der Begriff der Weltgeschichte* (Sitzungsberichte der AdW der DDR, Gesellschaftswissenschaften 4 G/1984) (Berlin: Akademieverlag, 1984).

22 Bruce Mazlish, *The New Global History* (New York: Routledge, 2006).

23 In contrast to this narrative Katja Naumann recently insisted on the long and complex history of world history conceptualizations in the USA since the end of the First World War: Katja Naumann, *Laboratorien der Weltgeschichtsschreibung:*

Lehre und Forschung an den Universitäten Chicago, Columbia und Harvard von 1918 bis 1968 (Göttingen: Vandenhoeck & Ruprecht, 2018).

24. David L. Szanton (ed.), *Politics of Knowledge: Area Studies and the Disciplines* (Berkeley: University of California Press, 2004); David C. Engerman, *Know Your Enemy: The Rise and Fall of America's Soviet Experts* (Oxford: Oxford University Press, 2011).

25. The most influential perhaps within an impressive series of textbooks introducing students to the history of the world: Jerry H. Bentley and Herbert F. Ziegler, *Traditions & Encounters: A Global Perspective on the Past* (Boston, MA: McGraw-Hill, 2000).

26. Dominic Sachsenmaier, *Global Perspectives on Global History: Theories and Approaches in a Connected World* (Cambridge: Cambridge University Press, 2011).

27. Patrick Manning, *Navigating World History: Historians Create a Global Past* (New York: Palgrave Macmillan, 2003).

28. Jürgen Osterhammel, 'Global History in a National Context: The Case of Germany', *Österreichische Zeitschrift für Geschichtswissenschaften* 20, no. 2 (2009): 41.

29. Ibid., 42.

30. See the history of this institute described in its foundational period by Roger Chickering and Karl Lamprecht, *A German Academic Life (1856–1915)* (Princeton, NJ: Princeton University Press, 1993), and the later continuation of the world history tradition until the early 1990s: Matthias Middell, *Weltgeschichtsschreibung im Zeitalter der Verfachlichung und Professionalisierung: Das Leipziger Institut für Kultur- und Universalgeschichte 1890–1990*, vol. 3 (Leipzig: Akademische Verlagsanstalt, 2005).

31. Torsten Loschke, *Area Studies Revisited: Die Geschichte der Lateinamerikastudien in den USA, 1940 bis 1970* (Göttingen: Vandenhoeck & Ruprecht, 2017).

32. Katja Naumann, Torsten Loschke, Steffi Marung and Matthias Middell (eds), *In Search of Other Worlds: Towards a Cross-regional History of Area Studies* (Leipzig: Leipzig University Press, 2018).

33. See, for example, Pierre Singaravélou, *L'École française d'Extrême-Orient ou L'institution des marges (1898–1956): Essai d'histoire sociale et politique de la science coloniale* (Paris: L'Harmattan, 1999); Germany disposing already of a very active network of historical institutes in Rome, Paris, London, Washington, Tokyo, Moscow and Warsaw decided recently to create similar centres in Delhi, Accra and a series of Latin American cities, among them Guadalajara and Buenos Aires.

34. To refer here to only two, among many other initiatives, to the *Journal of World History* published by the Hungarian Academy of Science or the recent multi-volume world history published by the Institute of World History at the Russian Academy of Sciences, continuing a tradition that goes back at least to the famous ten volumes of world history edited by Evgenij M. Zhukov in the 1950s.

35 Gareth Austin, 'Global History in (Northwestern) Europe: Explortions and Debates', in *Global History, Globally: Research and Practice around the World*, ed. Sven Beckert and Dominic Sachsenmaier (London: Bloomsbury, 2018), 21–44.

36 As a sort of summary of his approach towards the traditions of world and global history writing, see Patrick K. O'Brien, 'Historiographical Traditions and Modern Imperatives for the Restoration of Global History', *Journal of Global History* 1 (2006): 3–39.

37 David Landes, *The Wealth and Poverty of Nations: Why Some Are So Rich and Some So Poor* (New York: Norton & Co, 1998).

38 Andre Gunder Frank, *ReOrient: Global Economy in the Asian Age* (Berkeley: University of California Press, 1998).

39 Kenneth Pomeranz, *The Great Divergence: China, Europe, and the Making of the Modern World* (Princeton, NJ: Princeton University Press, 2001). On reciprocal comparison with regard to other regions, see also Gareth Austin, 'Reciprocal Comparison and African History: Tackling Conceptual Eurocentrism in the Study of Africa's Economic Past', *African Studies Review* 50, no. 3 (2007): 1–28.

40 For a recent critical summary of the debate about the category of the West, see Rolf Petri, *A Short History of Western Ideology: A Critical Account* (London: Bloomsbury, 2018).

41 Oscar Sanchez-Sibony, *Red Globalization: The Political Economy of the Soviet Cold War from Stalin to Khrushchev* (New York: Cambridge University Press, 2014).

42 James Mark and Péter Apor, 'Socialism Goes Global: Decolonization and the Making of a New Culture of Internationalism in Socialist Hungary, 1956–1989', *The Journal of Modern History* 87, no. 4 (2015): 852–891.

43 The work of Manfred Kossok became part of the renewal of global history when he presented at a workshop in Bellagio in 1991, later published as Ralph Buultjens and Bruce Mazlish (eds), *Conceptualizing Global History* (Boulder, CO: Avalon Publishing, 1993); see also with regard to Kossok's interpretation of Latin American colonial history as part of global history: Matthias Middell, 'De la historia colonial de Latinoamérica a la historia global a trés de la historia comparada de la revolución: La obra de Manfred Kossok', in *De revoluciones, Guerra Fría y muros historiográficos: Acerca de la obra de Manfred Kossok*, ed. Manuel Chust Calero (Zaragoza: Zaragoza University Press, 2017), 15–44. Recently, the journal *Review*, published by the Braudel Centre in Binghamton, devoted an entire thematic issue to Kossok's contribution to the debate on global inequality and comparative history of revolutions.

44 See the chapter by James Mark and Tobias Rupprecht in this volume on how 'red globalization' has been researched in recent years.

45 *Ab Imperio*. Available online: https://abimperio.net (accessed 11 July 2018).

46 Among many other contributions to this fast-expanding field: Marcel van der Linden, *Workers of the World: Essays Toward a Global Labor History* (Leiden: Brill, 2008); Jürgen Kocka and Marcel van der Linden (eds), *Capitalism: The Reemergence of a Historical Concept* (London: Bloomsbury, 2016); Andreas Eckert (ed.), *Global Histories of Work* (Berlin and Boston: De Gruyter, 2016).

47 See for detailed investigation of the mainly national contributors to the national journals that were founded in the second half of the nineteenth century and to those established at the height of social history in the period from the 1950s to 1970s: Margaret F. Stieg, *Origin and Development of Scholarly Historical Periodicals* (Alabama: University of Alabama Press, 1986); Alain Corbin, 'La Revue historique: Analyse du contenu d'une publication rivale des Annales', in *Au berceau des Annales*, eds Ch.-O. Carbonell and G. Livet (Toulouse: IEP, 1983), 205–137; Nicolas Roussellier, 'Les revues d'histoire', in *L'histoire et le métier d'historien en France 1945–1995*, ed. F. Bédarida (Paris: Éditions de la Maison des sciences de l'homme, 1995), 127–147; Matthias Middell (ed.), *Historische Zeitschriften im internationalen Vergleich* (Leipzig: Leipzig University Press, 1999).

48 *Itinerario*. Available online: https://www.cambridge.org/core/journals/itinerario (accessed 11 July 2018).

49 *Comparativ*. Available online: http://research.uni-leipzig.de/comparativ/ (accessed 11 July 2018). For the general context of the foundation, see Matthias Middell and Katja Naumann, 'World History and Global Studies at the University of Leipzig', in *Global Practice in World History: Advances Worldwide*, ed. Patrick Manning (Princeton, NJ: Markus Wiener, 2011), 81–98.

50 *Zeitschrift für Weltgeschichte*. Available online: https://www.peterlang.com/view/journals/zwg/zwg-overview.xml (accessed 11 July 2018); Hans-Heinrich Nolte, *Zur Institutionalisierung von welt- und globalhistorischer Forschung und Lehre im deutschsprachigen Raum* (*VGWS Discussion Papers* 7, 2014). Available online: http://www.vgws.org/files/vgws_dp_007.pdf (accessed 1 April 2018).

51 *Journal of Global History*. Available online: https://www.cambridge.org/core/journals/journal-of-global-history (accessed 11 July 2018).

52 Gareth Austin, 'Global History and Economic History: A View of the L.S.E. Experience in Research and Graduate Training', in *Global Practice in World History: Advances Worldwide*, ed. Patrick Manning (Princeton, NJ: Markus Wiener, 2011), 99–111.

53 Maxine Berg (ed.), *Writing the History of the Global: Challenges for the 21st Century* (Oxford: Oxford University Press, 2013).

54 James Belich, John Darwin, Margret Frenz and Chris Wickham (eds), *The Prospect of Global History* (Oxford: Oxford University Press, 2016).

55 *Monde(s)*. Available online: http://www.monde-s.com/ (accessed 11 July 2018).

56 One can think of the discussion about transnational history between 2002 and 2006 in Germany's leading journal of social history, *Geschichte und Gesellschaft*, or

of the reopening of the French *Annales* since the early 2000s to consider questions of global reach after a period of strong nationalization of its content and authorship after Braudel had retired from editorial duties. The *Revue d'histoire moderne et contemporaine* had, in 2007, a special issue on the relationship between global history and connected histories. The new wave of recently founded journals in the field of European history contains many examples where individual authors or the editors of thematic issues recognize the mutual inspiration global and European histories have to offer each other. Sometimes it may remain pure lip service, but as journals like the *European History Quarterly* or the *Journal of Modern European History* demonstrate, there are the various aspects of imperial history increasingly present on their pages. The same holds true for journals specializing in the histories of technology or communication as well as in cultural history or human geography, but it would greatly inflate the size of this chapter to mention them all in detail.

57 Miroslav Hroch, *Das Europa der Nationen: Die moderne Nationsbildung im europäischen Vergleich* (Göttingen: Vandenhoeck & Ruprecht, 2005).

58 I would very much like to thank Julia Yakovleva, who helped with assembling and calculating the figures from the database of the four congresses of Dresden, London, Paris and Budapest.

59 Matthias Middell and Katja Naumann (eds), *Bibliography of Global History 2010–2015*, with a foreword by Jie-Hyun Lim (Leipzig: Leipzig University Press, 2017), soon available online both at the website of the European Network as well as of the International Committee for Historical Sciences.

60 It is, of course, impossible to list here all contributions to the history of the British Empire; we limit it to John Darwin, *After Tamerlane: The Global History of Empire* (London: Bloomsbury, 2008); John Darwin, *The Empire Project: The Rise and Fall of the British World-system, 1830–1970* (Cambridge: Cambridge University Press, 2011) and A. G. Hopkins, *American Empire: A Global History* (Princeton, NJ: Princeton University Press, 2018).

61 Jürgen Erfurt, *Frankophonie: Sprache, Diskurs, Politik* (Tübingen: Francke, 2005).

62 Nicolas Bancel, Pascal Blanchard and Françoise Vergès (eds), *La république coloniale: Essai sur une utopie* (Paris: Albin Michel, 2003); Elisabeth Mudimbe-Boyi (ed.), *Empire Lost: France and its Other Worlds* (Lanham, MD: Rowman & Littlefield, 2008); Catherine Coquery-Vidrovitch, *Enjeux politiques de l'histoire coloniale* (Marseille: Agone, 2009); Nicolas Bancel (ed.), *Ruptures postcoloniales: Les nouveaux visages de la société française* (Paris: La Découverte, 2010).

63 As an example of the polemics raised by the simple notion of global history and possible implications for national sovereignty, see the negative statement by Chloé Maurel, 'La World/Global History: questions et débats', *Vingtième Siècle. Revue d'histoire* 104, no. 4 (2009): 153–166, and the response by Pierre Grosser, 'L'histoire

mondiale/globale, une jeunesse exubérante mais difficile', *Vingtième Siècle. Revue d'histoire* 110 (2011): 3–18.

64 Étienne Anhim, Romain Bertrand, Antoine Lilti, and Stephen Sawyer, *The Annales and the Tradition of World History* (Paris: EHESS, 2012) (a collection of texts from the Annales, 1946 to 2007, that were meant to 'stimulate a growing awareness of the variety of approaches to World History, even within the Annales itself and further international dialogue in this field' (from the introduction)); Krzysztof Pomian, 'World History: Histoire mondiale, histoire universelle', *Le Débat* 154 (2009): 14–40.

65 See the contribution by Michel Espagne, the local organizer of the Paris congress, to this volume as well as his book on the theory of intercultural transfers: Espagne, *Les transferts culturels franco-allemands*.

66 Among them, for example, Philippe Beaujard, Laurent Berger and Philippe Norel (eds), *Histoire globale, mondialisations et capitalisme* (Paris: La Découverte, 2009); Romain Bertrand, *L'histoire à parts égales. Récits d'une rencontre, Orient-Occident (XVIe-XVIIe siècle)* (Paris: Seuil, 2011); Hélène Blais, Florence Deprest and Pierre Singaravélou (eds), *Territoires impériaux: Une histoire spatiale du fait colonial* (Paris: Publications de la Sorbonne, 2011); Philippe Beaujard, *Les Mondes de l'Océan Indien. T. 1: De la formation de l'Etat au premier system-monde afro-eurasien (4e millénaire av. J.-C. – 6e siècle ap. J.-C.); T. 2: L'océan Indien, aux cœur des globalisations de l'Ancien Monde (7e-15e siècle)* (Paris: Armand Colin, 2012); Patrick Boucheron (ed.), *Pour une histoire-monde* (Paris: Presses Universitaires de France, 2013).

67 See the broad project for a global history of France: Patrick Boucheron (ed.), *Histoire mondiale de la France* (Paris: Seuil, 2016).

68 Michel Espagne and Michael Werner, 'La construction d'une référence culturelle allemande en France: Génèse et Histoire (1750–1914)', *Annales ESC* 4 (1987): 969–992.

69 Among the many books he has devoted to this: Michel Espagne (ed.), *Russie-France-Allemagne-Italie: Transferts quadrangulaires du néoclassicisme aux avant-gardes* (Tusson: Du Lérot, 2005); Hoai-Huong Aubert-Nguyen and Michel Espagne (eds), *Le Vietnam, une histoire de transferts culturels* (Paris: Demopolis, 2015); Michel Espagne, Svetlana Gorshenina, Frantz Grenet, Shahin Mustfayev and Claude Rapin (eds), *Asie centrale: Transferts culturels le long de la route de la soie* (Paris: Vendemiaire, 2016).

70 Odd Arne Westad, *The Global Cold War: Third World Interventions and the Making of Our Times* (Cambridge: Cambridge University Press, 2008).

71 Odd Arne Westad, 'Rethinking Revolutions: The Cold War in the Third World', *Journal of Peace Research* 29, no. 4 (1992): 455–464.

72 Carole Fink, Frank Hadler and Tomasz Schramm, *1956: European and Global Perspectives* (Leipzig: Leipzig University Press, 2006); Carole Fink, Phillip Gassert,

and Detlef Junker (eds), *1968: The World Transformed* (Cambridge: Cambridge University Press, 1998); Niall Ferguson, Charles S. Maier, Erez Manela and Daniel J. Sargent (eds), *The Shock of the Global: The 1970s in Perspective* (Cambridge: Belknap Press, 2010); Ulf Engel, Frank Hadler and Matthias Middell (eds), *1989 in a Global Perspective* (Leipzig: Leipzig University Press, 2015).

73 Adam McKeown, 'Global Migration 1846–1940', *Journal of World History* 15, no. 2 (2004): 155–189.

74 Catherine Coquery-Vidrovitch, 'Le tropisme de l'Université française face aux postcolonial studies', in *Ruptures postcoloniales: Les nouveaux visages de la société française*, ed. Nicolas Bancel (Paris: La Découverte, 2010), 317–327.

75 For more details see also Catherine Coquery-Vidrovitch, 'L'historiographie africaine en Afrique', *Revue Tiers-Monde* 216, no. 4 (2013): 111–127.

76 Kent Deng, 'The Great Divergence and Global Studies', in *The Many Facets of Global Studies*, eds Konstanze Loeke and Matthias Middell (Leipzig: Leipzig University Press, 2018).

77 Peer Vries, 'What we do and do not Know about the Great Divergence at the Beginning of 2016', *Historische Mitteilungen der Ranke Gesellschaft* 28 (2016): 249–297; Matthias Middell and Philipp Robinson Rössner, 'The Great Divergence Debate', *Comparativ. Zeitschrift für Globalgeschichte und vergleichende Gesellschaftsforschung* 26, no. 3 (2016): 7–24.

1

Plural Globality and Shift in Perspective

Michel Espagne

The first European Congress on World and Global History took place in Leipzig in 2005. This was a natural point of departure because Leipzig was the place where the idea of universal history – *Universal- und Kulturgeschichte* – was developed and promoted by Karl Lamprecht. Karl Lamprecht used the tools developed in scientific psychology to inspire a new form of historiography. This universal history had to incorporate the field of representations, aesthetic tendencies, as well as religious issues and mentality. As a project of Karl Lamprecht, the first steps towards this universal history is the legacy of Wilhelm Wundt's psychology, which through the journal *Revue de synthèse* profoundly shaped the French history of human mentalities. While the second congress in Dresden was devoted to world orders and the third congress in London focused on connections and comparisons, the Paris congress had the general title 'Encounters, Circulations and Conflicts'. These all-encompassing titles are certainly not perfect indicators of the specific themes that each of these congresses addressed. They do, however, have at least the one quality of underlining from the very start that global history is nonetheless plural, and it is around this question of plurality that I would like to focus my contribution.

Depending on where one situates oneself in relation to the perspective adopted, the language employed and the historiographic traditions that this language conveys, globality can take different forms. This certainly does not mean that it is necessary to renounce the idea of a historiography transcending the various frontiers between nations, languages and empires. Rather, it should be acknowledged that this transcendence is made more difficult by a characteristic inherent in all historiographic approaches, which is that transnational history is tensely caught between globality and specificity. Global history is no more than a gratuitous assessment if it only summarizes a global network framing a historical period and applies the main tendencies as interpretation patterns without diving into operational details of every transnational connection. While the term seems paradoxical, there are forms of micro-globality: in other words, approaches to universal history from a particular viewpoint. The global approach to the world prevailing at the time of Vasco da Gama, described in *The Lusiads* by Luís de Camões, represents a global perception of history well beyond the frontiers of Portugal. In 1377, when Ibn Khaldun wrote *The Muqqadima, a Discourse on Universal History* he did so by using ideas borrowed from Koranic traditions and the Arab language, which he advocated to be preserved while wishing to defend its purity. His argument has obviously little in common with the *Discours sur l'histoire universelle* by Jacques-Bénigne Bossuet, which contrasts sharply with Voltaire's *Essai sur les mœurs*. While all of these are global histories or prolegomena to global histories, the geographical breakdowns of the world that they propose depend largely on the cultural context from which they emerged. The concept of globality cannot be defined without being extremely ambiguous because its diversity of meanings fits into the special context of every historical tradition. Without a doubt, there are convergences between the arguments of Ibn Khaldun, Bossuet and Voltaire, such as the question of customs and culture in the search for a historical globality. Notwithstanding, this aspiration to universality is offset by religious aspirations and divergent traditions.

In the francophone tradition, which provided an important context for the congress in Paris, it is tempting to recall some landmark moments. There is, firstly, the famous 1928 article in which Marc Bloch reminds us of the need to place national history in a context that can provide a point of comparison. In fact, this comparison immediately places the emphasis on common substrata, contaminations and works such as Fernand Braudel's *Méditerranée*, which is less oriented towards the comparison of cities and peoples in the Mediterranean region than on the procedures of exchange and circulation that structure it. It seems that in the French context, the effort has been more focused on modes of exchange than on word-for-word comparison when it comes to moving beyond the limits of national historiographies. Cultural transfers are traditionally focused on circulation, on forms of resemantization, which always accompany the import of a cultural asset, and on entanglements that are characteristic of historiography itself. Even more recently, the watchwords 'equal shares of history', the common thread of Romain Bertrand's books on Javanese history, underline the contribution of non-European and non-dominant sources to the understanding of the encounters that have marked global history. It is aligned here with the approaches to universal histories characteristic of eighteenth-century Germany, which included the histories of faraway peoples in a universal history only from the time when their sources became readily available, thereby allowing a retrospective insight to be gained into their respective history or traditions.

Cultural transfers

Every historical contribution to a global history is rooted in a cultural context and is confronted with events described in a special language. We may neglect the special cultural relatedness of every historical matter and be satisfied with an overview; however, such a method cannot be considered as a contribution to transnational or global history. A lot of linguistic and cultural knowledge should be required to cover even a restricted field of enquiry at the crossroads of two or three national narratives. That is to say, global human sciences have to be satisfied by inchoative states of global history.

Unquestionably, it is appropriate to distinguish between national traditions, where in the long term the representation of a national ethnic homogeneity dominated, and traditions in which a unifying idea represented the cement necessary for forming the nation. If the most natural way to link homogenous entities is through comparison, the groupings that from the outset are presented as multi-ethnic and of mixed descent are more likely to question their constituent elements and to adopt a global perspective. The historiography of Brazil is naturally more likely to concentrate on the Portuguese, Amerindian, French and African elements that it is made up of – that is to say, on the multiple links that connect it to universal history – than countries whose history is the deployment of a postulated homogeneity. The history of migrations and the transformations that they bring to contexts of reception in the host country obviously depend on the relative importance of migrations in the countries concerned.

While no country has escaped the 'melting pot' phenomena, be it accepted or repressed, it is, numerically speaking, more noticeable in the history of Australia than that of China. No country can be presented as a homogenous whole; even China is the result of encounters with Sogdian, Tibetan, Manchu and Uighur ethnic groups. The mixed backgrounds of countries have often been forgotten; accordingly, transnational history aims precisely at exploring those legacies that have been downplayed. This variety of circumstances naturally determines the historical science of the different countries concerned and, more specifically, their perception of transnational history and global history. Historiography, in brief, is not independent of national traditions, even in its approach to globality.

In truth, this assertion should be supplemented, or nuanced, by observing the spread of models. Anglo-Saxon, German and French models are spread beyond the academic arenas that gave birth to them. Between relative globality and the domination of largely Anglo-Saxon models, transnational history is likely to be located.

The problem with universality and globality, however, is not that they are absent from historiographic arguments; on the contrary, it could be argued that few historical works are exempt. The problem is that globality is seen from one or several centres and is frequently based on the opposition between one or several centres and their peripheries. There cannot be a true globality, or at least authentically transcultural history, without taking into account the problem posed by the opposition between centre and periphery while becoming conscious of the plurality of possible centres. The Anglo-Saxon centre, from which global historiography has been developed, even if some of its representatives are, for example, acculturated Indians, is only one of a number of others.

First of all, the issue at hand directly concerns cartography. For Anaximander, as for Hecate, the map of the world featured the Mediterranean area at the centre, in particular the eastern regions and the coast of the Aegean Sea, which Herodotus also considered to be the centre of the world. We know that the emperors of China commissioned the Jesuits to create maps of China on the condition that the country occupied a central place in the world space. The current maps that show the Pacific with China and the United States facing each other are simply a modified version of the maps that prevailed at the time of Matteo Ricci. We also know that the pan-Turanism, which developed during the time of Kemal Atatürk and which substituted the universality of the Ottoman Empire with a turkophone universality, placed Anatolia at the centre of its maps in a space that extended east as far as Central Asia. Heirs of the Chinese emperors as well as imitators of their claims of centrality, the Vietnamese emperors asserted in their recorded history the same centrality, which was exerted on other peoples of Southeast Asia, such as Cambodia. In the link that exists between geography and the centre of the transnational or global historical narrative, anamorphosis is the rule.

Multiple interactions prove to be possible between the centre and the periphery: interactions that characterize both the value and the limits of this feature of historiographic discourse. Let us take, for example, the case of Greece. It constitutes, a priori, a territory that has been entirely peripheral to European history from the moment that it was freed from the Ottoman Empire. At the same time, Greece (as we shall call it, to simplify the philhellenism) was one of the breeding grounds for cultural unity in Europe, at least for Germany and France in the nineteenth century, and could be called a prototype of the common European project. For the European powers, it was a matter of imposing upon Greece a physiognomy that conformed to identity constructs, which was imprinted in the very architecture of Athens. To this extent, Greece is both a demonstration of the periphery and a facilitator of the formation of a European centre.

Next to a Greek Germany there is also a German Greece. After hesitating among the different families of the smaller principalities that posed no threat to the major European nations, we know that Greece became German, more specifically Bavarian, and was entrusted to the Wittelsbach family. A Bavarian administration was set up at Nafplio, later moved to Athens, which lasted until 1862. Even though not all of the German servants of the new Greek state were Bavarian, all of them, such as Leopold von Klenze, the architect of Walhalla, had gone by way of Bavaria and had become servants of the fiery philhellene that was Ludwig I. Germany's first intervention in Greek history was of a geographical nature. It was not so much a question of drawing the borders of a country that had just liberated itself as it was one of drawing the imaginary borders of a myth. This myth required the drawing of a circle, whose ideal centre was out of necessity the Acropolis from the age of Pericles and whose radius corresponded approximately to the straight line out to Cape Matapan. This geographical decision, which seems naturally self-evident, was in fact particularly brutal since it excluded or marginalized places that had been fundamental to Greece's long-lasting cultural history: Constantinople, Alexandria or Smyrna. The Megali Idea, dear to the Cretan Eleftherios Venizelos, is in fact more of a theme of Greek nationalism than of the European great power protectors of Greece. Right from the very beginning of the history of the new Greek state, the prescriptive dimension of the protective powers and especially of the German states was manifest in the affair of Jakob Philipp Fallmerayer. In his book on the Isthmus of Morea, written in 1830, he asserts that the Europeans are completely mistaken in believing that the Christian inhabitants of the Greek region are the descendants of the ancient Greeks, stating rather that they are likely a Slavic population. He further declares that this Slavic incursion, incidentally, is dangerous for the rest of Europe. Transforming these degenerate Greeks into authentic Greeks – that is to say, Greeks who conform to German philology – would prove itself to be a titanic undertaking. We know that Constantine Paparrigopoulos, the author of a history of the Hellenes and professor at the University of Athens beginning in the mid-nineteenth century, had to engage in a polemic against Fallmerayer in order to impose his idea of a continuity from antiquity to the modern era and above all from Byzantium to the modern era, which supported the nationalism of the Megali Idea. As the Greek nation was being drawn up by Germany, Greek nationalism itself had to defend itself through historiography against the German prescriptions.

Another interesting case is that of Scandinavia. It is also peripheral to European history even if some moments, for example, the role Sweden played in the Great Northern War until the Battle of Poltava, gave it much more weight. That said, the phenomenon of sanctioning this centre-peripheral perspective was often at work for Nordic writers and artists in the French or German capitals. It was in Paris that one became a great Danish or Norwegian writer, and in Berlin that one became a great Finnish musician. The Nordic cultural identity was constructed at the centre. But this centre itself took advantage of an assumed periphery and there are many artists or philosophers who served as links between France and Germany. From the traveller Jens Baggesen, who was responsible for making Johann Gottlieb Fichte known in France, to the philosopher Harald Høffding, who around 1900 formed a link between France and Germany via the comparativist Georg Brandes, it was as if the periphery – whose originality and specificities were formed at the centre – had another function in the formation of this same centre, or at least in the interconnection of its composite features.

A very distinct periphery in European history is that of Russia. This theme is constantly being encountered in the history of a country that, with Peter the Great giving in to the seductions of Western Europe and Holland, sought to bring classicism to the banks of the Neva. Russia developed the idea of a Third Rome, a translation of Ancient Rome to the very limits of Europe. The role of a German princess such as Catherine II at the head of the empire can also be interpreted as a displacement of Russia towards the periphery. While in the nineteenth century the occidentalists thematized the question of the margins, wishing to attach themselves to the centre, the Slavophiles themselves drew arguments from Germany, which was thought necessary to combat the occidentalists. This time, Eurasianism also placed Russia at the margins of the Asian continent. Yet, from the Cossacks on the Champs-Elysées at the end of the Napoleonic era to the Russian soldiers on the roof of the Reichstag at the end of the Second World War, there is no doubt that Russia has played a determining role throughout European life for at least two centuries, and that it has been just as central as other national entities. Russian ballet defined the Parisian artistic landscape in 1900, and it would be difficult to conceive of structuralism without the introduction of Russian formalism. Russia is a paradoxical periphery as it occupies an essential part of the Eurasian continent, but it is also a periphery reinforced by the location of the capital Saint Petersburg at the limits of the territory, which are the limits of Europe as well. This then is a transnational historiography related to transversality because sometimes it is the limits of Europe that prevail and at other times it is the limits of Asia. As these examples have shown, the Russian periphery can be analysed as being the result of cultural transfers.

After an overview of the examples within German-Russian history, one may wonder what are the new perspectives as well as contributions related to the methodology of cultural transfers. The first point relates to the detection of the very heterogeneous structure of memory, which does not reflect any archival order and is very much oriented towards highlighting nationalism. One assumes more or less that any country develops itself on the basis of internal dynamics. Saxony, as the core of a future German identity,[1] appropriates such foreign cultural objects, whose link with a foreign country is gradually repressed in German history. Who will remember that Polish and Ukrainian Jewish merchants in the eighteenth century had made a fortune from the leading fair in Germany? In the dynamics of owning something foreign, isolated social groups can play a prominent role disproportionate to their demographic weight. For comparativism, which confronts these historical phenomena, these groups, who fully deserve a historical analysis, play no role. Research on cultural transfers is further able to analyse the transformations that the receiving context owes to foreign exportation. For example, the Leipzig fair has no actual independent existence from the Polish Jews' and Greek traders' seasonal immigration. The reception of Russian music in France in the late nineteenth century profoundly modified the Parisian musical context by offering an alternative to the dominance of German music. Although they were mainly interested in their own business, the German merchants who ran the export of Bordeaux wines in the eighteenth and nineteenth centuries changed the face of this city as well as of the French province. The difference between the original context and the host, which does not have much sense in a historical comparativist context, is crucial for addressing cultural transfers, showing the imbrication of two cultural systems. From this point of view, Saxony is a piece of Poland or France and the import of any foreign cultural property corresponds to a transformation of the characteristics of the receiving culture.

The second contribution of the research on cultural transfers seems to rest on the fact that the distribution of European space is transformed through cultural transfers. The link between regions formulates new ideas and detaches regions from their various national frameworks, so much to the point that it is possible to make a historiography that is no longer ethnocentric. A new form of transnational historiography could be based on the failure to consider the specific territories not as comparable units but as interweaving parts of a puzzle. Besides the artificially constructed national or territorial identities, there would be in fact a seminal foreignness to be introduced into a historical consciousness. Specifically in the case of the historical perception of regions with small populations, this approach avoids relegation in peripheral positions. Generally speaking, the opposition between a centre and a periphery is irrelevant in the research on cultural transfers. In this perspective, this is because many Scandinavians asserted that their country is an important mediator between France and Germany and that their story deserves as much attention as the European centre. Russia is just as central in Europe as France or Germany because one would not conceive the French intellectual history of the last 100 years, for example, without a structural link with Russia, from Russian novels to the history of science passing through the aesthetics of the early twentieth century. What is very characteristic here is the history of the relationship with Greece: that is to say, of philhellenism in European countries from the nineteenth to the twentieth century. In fact, we deal with a common denominator where the political position of the countries crystallizes. Despite the diversity of viewpoints, there is a common aspiration towards asserting cosmopolitanism.

Even though the Greek reference in the construction of Berlin as a German capital during the nineteenth century was central – think, for example, of the Museumsinsel in the heart of the city – the case of Munich is still among the most striking manifestations in the nineteenth century of German Hellenism. Munich, often referred to as the Athens of the Isar, combines a prominent role in the political philhellenism of the times, asserting more than other regions not only the German presence in Greece but also showing the ambiguity of the Greek reference. We have to remember that it is King Ludwig I, initially a liberal ruler who became increasingly despotic, who triggers the Bavarian philhellenic movement, and it is in Munich that the Greek decor reached a stage of inauthenticity, which contributed to the emergence of the kitsch concept. Accordingly, the Greek periphery sits at the centre of Germany.

It is clear that any applied research of these phenomena of imbrication – together with the reinterpretation linked to imbrication – is likely to exceed the national history of humanities while opening up a wide field of investigation that could be the coming form of the cultural history of Europe. Even if there is no need to stress here that Russia is part of Europe, especially of German or French cultural history, and conversely Europe is part of Russia, the systematic history of these imbrications still largely needs to be written. Russia is only one case among others; it is the *ensemble* of cultural areas forming the European space that could now be examined in this way.

The language of global history

One of the principal challenges confronted by global history is that of language. This challenge is related to more than just the fact that each language divides up the social world in a particular way and that written narratives in the language take account of this redivision and even reproduce it. A truly transnational or global historiography should take account of those works by historians in the various languages in which the history is written. One only has to study the extremely revealing phenomenon of bibliographies or footnotes to observe that not only are we far away from achieving this but on many points we are digressing from it. French and German works, for example, are increasingly unlikely to discuss what is written in the neighbouring country unless it has been translated into English, which represents a minority of publications. An article in Russian or Chinese has significantly less chance of appearing in the notes of a work aiming at presenting an aspect of global history. This deficiency in the documentation naturally results in the construction of a transnational history with an incomplete and also biased foundation. It could be argued that the problem could be resolved if a single language, English, was chosen for debate in historical sciences, as is the case for the natural sciences. The first problem with this would be that it puts historical discourse through a filter, which could result in uniformity. But even if we accept this type of communication to be possible for the most contemporary of history, it seems difficult to achieve when history addresses past epochs and there is a need to consult older works. In this case, documentation and sources are out of necessity written in a plurality of languages because an overly monolingual historiography would be naturally neglectful. An anglophone global history is ultimately only possible for recent history. In other words, it would reduce history to political science, if not to scientific popularization and journalism.

The historical narrative is based on the use of universals, terms that serve to describe and analyse historical processes. The worker, the citizen, the constitution, the philosophers of the Age of Enlightenment, the nation, the state, the Renaissance, the French Revolution, etc. are, among numerous others, terms to which we refer in any historical narrative or analysis. But these terms, or rather the semantic field that they indicate, must be placed in a temporal context. They are themselves historical objects. In this regard, the work of Reinhart Koselleck represents a fundamental rupture in the historical sciences. Koselleck demonstrated that the vocabulary of history corresponded to stratifications, that concepts had their own histories, and that the moment of reflexivity on the meaning of words was part of the historian's work. Obviously, the notion of globality should be investigated as one of these universals, but the intersection of the idea of *Begriffsgeschichte* (history of concepts), with the idea of transnational history, invites further investigation. As an example, let us take the Age of Enlightenment, which in China corresponded to a part of the Qing era. It is immediately clear that the Enlightenment has as little meaning for this period of Chinese history as the characteristics of the Qing dynasty have for Europe in the eighteenth century. If the term 'nation' has a different meaning in France and in Germany, why should we assume it has the same value in Italy and Japan? Here, once again, unless a standardized lexicon is adopted, to the detriment of the others, the focus of any transnational historiography should be on the displacements of meaning linked to the import or export of universals in history. In fact, Koselleck opened up an avenue that merits further exploration. He argued that the stratifications of meaning linked to the use of fundamental concepts in a linguistic space – in this case, Germany – should be supplemented by an exploration of fundamental concepts in their synchronic chain, from one linguistic space to another. In this view, we would thus not be dealing with a fixed globality but one that is always virtual.

A map of the world showing the density of historiographic publications shows that there are more historic works produced in England than in Central African or Southeast Asian countries. Furthermore, these works are likely to address Central Africa or Southeast Asia from the perspective of Europe or the United States. It would be equally absurd to be surprised by the differences that result from the marked inequality between the places where science is produced: for example, universities and libraries. However, this inequality, which in itself limits the scope of all discourse about global or transnational history, can be reduced if we endeavour to restore to the less fortunate regions of the world not just the status of historical actors, which nobody will deny, but also the status of producers of historical analysis. To this end, it is appropriate to seek, use and highlight the value of texts produced by peoples of social groups from the countries that are most often the subjects of historiography.

Here again, the linguistic question also remains important as there are historiographic traditions that are at least embryonic in languages spoken only by a few. Following the work of Romain Bertrand, it is this trend towards a broader recognition of a status as producers of historical narratives that begins to develop under the name of 'equal shares of history'. African accounts of Africa must be sought out, which for earlier historical periods could be an Arab historiographic tradition. Nevertheless, let us note that it is not necessary to take an interest in the early history of colonial territories in order to recognize the relevance of an approach that aims to vary the perspectives taken in historical analyses. It should be remembered that it is possible to *not* address Baltic countries primarily through German or Russian sources but to take into account local memories and local sources.

Africa in global history

The region of the world most often addressed by historiographies from outside its territory is certainly Africa, and it is Africa that the congress held in Paris in 2014 wished to particularly focus on. Because of the interest in the library of Timbuktu, it is well known that Africa, too, has a written history. Recent works, such as *Le rhinocéros d'or* (François-Xavier Fauvelle-Aymar 2013), show in an ever more convincing way that this history stretches far back in time and above all that it was already global: in other words, that Africa was involved in networks, notably commercial networks, which extended beyond the limits of the continent. From the inscriptions at Aksum to the correspondence of the Jews of Cairo discussing trade between East Africa and India, this ancient history of Africa is documented in written form. The Arab historian from Andalusia, Al-Bakri, described the history of Ghana as early as the eleventh century. In the fourteenth century, Ethiopia had chronicles written in the Ge'ez language. With respect to Africa, there are two basic opposing positions. The first states that Africa is outside of history. Here we are obviously thinking about some stereotypical politician who argues that Africa has never entered into history; the German Hegelianism at the turn of the eighteenth and nineteenth centuries is basically not very far from this position. The other argument considers Africa as the origin of history since the Egyptian civilization, itself considered as one of the sources of Greek civilization and thereby European, is the direct heir of Africa and thus Africa should be assigned a founding role. This construction, notably promoted by Cheikh Anta Diop, is based both on reliable findings and on questionable extrapolations. Following Cheikh Anta Diop, Martin Bernal, as much in the linguistic domain as the archaeological one, echoed this by illustrating in great detail the representation of a black Athena in a Greece marked by Africa. Well beyond the proto-historic questions that it addresses, this construction lays the foundations for a very modern Afrocentrism, clearly reacting to colonial dominations, that places Africa at the centre while giving rise to new reflections on the history of the continent.

The limits of Afrocentrism reside perhaps in an undervaluation of the intricacies that situate the history of Africa in complex groupings. Beyond national histories of particular African countries, which certainly merit exploration by African historians themselves and which are of particular concern to them, there is a clear and overriding necessity to consider African history from a global perspective. It is about addressing the interactions between Africa and the rest of the world. These interactions range from a history of global phenomena – such as the deportation of slaves to America or the Arab world and its role in the subsequent development of countries that practiced slavery – to a history of modes of consumption (coffee, chocolate, fruit, exotic wood, etc.) linked to African imports. We also must not neglect aesthetic forms such as Cubism, which owe their inspiration to African models. The role of African countries as providers of raw materials such as uranium and gas, which notably supply nuclear power stations, are part of this globality. It is hardly necessary to mention that the company Areva is both a provider of a significant proportion of energy in France as well as a controversial element in contemporary African history.

Global history is also at work in the migratory flows towards European countries, and in the make-up of an African migrant population living in precariousness and a workforce with few qualifications in these countries. Global history is active in the complex relationships of at least partially reciprocal dependence between the governments of European capitals and the home countries of the migrants. It is at work in the military aid operations that take place in previously colonized countries. More optimistically, the presence of African students in European or American universities and their contribution is also part of these global movements. The multiplicity of these relations of reciprocal dependence makes Africa part of European history, which is still very relevant for the future of Africa.

The entry of Africa into a global or transnational history implies studying post-colonial history because it is often as a former colony that African countries participate in the circulation of goods or persons, as well as in international political games. Curiously, post-colonialism, including historiographic forms known as subaltern studies, has received limited attention in France. It is not that the anti-colonial movements from Aimé Césaire to Frantz Fanon have been absent in France; it is quite the contrary. Nevertheless, they have not taken this form of post-colonialism per se and are even less developed in Africa than in Anglo-Saxon countries, notably the United States, which has never been a colonial power. Rather than Africans, it is the anglophone Indians who have been long established in the United States that have defined this line of thought. Often looked upon very favourably by African historians, post-colonialism is itself, through its main representatives together with their intellectual identities, the symptom of a globalization. It nevertheless has the disadvantage of linking the history of Africa with colonization, even if this only really covers two centuries in the history of the continent. Then it adopts North American historiography as the centre of reference, which once again demonstrates the difficulty for a global history to take into account the multiplicity of possible centres.

The centenary of the First World War

With the centenary of the outbreak of the First World War, it is imperative to recall that world wars are also global historic phenomena because they mobilized almost all European countries from Britain to Russia, notably France, Germany, Italy, Bulgaria and Turkey. Additionally, the populations of distant colonies were, for the first time, mobilized to fight in Europe, while battles could, for example, take place in the east of the Congo between the colonial troops of the various warring sides. Chinese or Vietnamese people were used in France, if not always to fight at least to support the war effort. Lastly, we know that commercial exchanges were, indirectly, able to continue during the war itself. The war of 1914–18 also generated pacifist actions and institutions that gave rise to the first international organizations. It would be difficult to discuss the League of Nations without referring to the impact of the First World War on the frame of mind of European countries. The transnational dimension of international organizations that were inspired by the war is clearly shown in the fact that the League of Nations was an initiative of American President Woodrow Wilson, that Iraq and Egypt were counted among its members and that Esperanto, the universal language, was able to be envisaged for a moment as the common language of communications.

The issue of war must not be limited to the First World War, however. The Napoleonic wars already had a global dimension as they encompassed territories from Spain to Russia, involving relations with Persia or the Ottoman Empire. Virtually the entire world was involved. Troop movements also corresponded to demographic intermingling between nations: for example, the Napoleonic troops included a number of German soldiers who participated in the Russian campaign. The innumerable proclamations in several languages and the distribution of institutions such as civil codes and laws are indicators of the global dimension of these conflicts. To an even greater extent, virtually no part of the world remained untouched by the Second World War, even if small islands of neutrality survived. For the Second World War as for the First World War, the idea of a world government brought about a transnational organization aimed at conflict resolution: the United Nations.

The wars were moments of global history also on account of the population contacts they enabled. There is the phenomenon of the prisoners for whom the First World War had unexpected consequences when German Africanists improved the analysis of African languages by questioning French prisoners of African origin. But the intermingling of populations was no doubt even greater during the Second World War when all types of European populations passed through the doors of German prisoner-of-war camps. The Second World War resulted in numerous population transfers, which were part of these global demographic movements. One might think here of the Polish populations moving from Lviv towards Warsaw, or the transition of the Jewish peoples of Central Europe towards Palestine.

The question of foreign occupations also feeds the progress towards a global history. One obvious example is the German occupation of the European mainland, and also the occupation of Germany itself and the Soviet presence in the countries of Central Europe that lasted for forty years. These occupations must not be considered only as military operations but also as encounters between cultural spaces where relationships have always been highly tenuous. This is what happened with the American occupation of Japan, the successor to the Japanese occupation of China and Korea. The First World War resulted in a dislocation of what remained of the Ottoman Empire as well as in the reconfiguration of Middle Eastern territories controlled by European powers. Long-isolated countries accordingly became part of a global history.

The relations that were established during the conflicts had an effect on the internal organization of countries active in the conflict. The Napoleonic wars exported legal models or modes of organization of religious minorities throughout Europe. A French model became widespread in a series of societal dimensions following these wars. The great momentum given to the educational sciences in the final third of the nineteenth century in France was directly linked to the conflict between France and Germany in 1870. This time it was the German model of the university and science that became the structural element in France. This transformation of the enemy into a model in a transnational exchange of social models is doubtlessly less apparent following the First World War, although popular culture in Berlin in the 1920s took advantage of the American impetus. After the Second World War, the exchanges between former enemies seem to have been much more intense. From existentialism in the immediate post-war period to legal representations, post-war Germany was profoundly marked by the United States or France. It is true that for its part, Eastern Europe was also marked by Russia. Other examples include the changes to Japanese civil society after Japan's surrender, in a direction determined by the American model.

Above all, the war weakened the colonial powers and pushed the populations who had participated in the conflict to claim independence. These emancipation movements were supported by models borrowed from European powers that were claimed and adapted to colonial wars. The protagonists of the Vietnam war of liberation were trained in freedom fighting in a French cultural context, which they shared with the leaders of the freedom fighters in Algeria. The construction of the intellectual references of anti-colonial wars were to a large part borrowed from their enemies, illustrating once again the necessity to address wars, and notably those of the twentieth century, from a transnational and global point of view.

The encounters, circulations and conflicts that have been analysed during the days of the Paris congress highlighted the innumerable facets of a transnational historiography. It is precisely this multiplicity of scenarios that should provide the opportunity to reflect upon the question of opposition between centre and periphery as well as different perspectives on the very meaning of globality. Correspondingly, the question of centres and peripheries should be a major focus for transnational history because the meaning of world history depends exactly on the position of the historian.

Note

1   Michel Espagne, *Le creuset allemand: Histoire interculturelle de la Saxe (XVIIIe – XIXe siècles)*, 1st edn (Paris: Presses Universitaires de France, 2000).

2

Paris: National, International, Transnational, Cultural Capital City? (19th–20th Century)

Christophe Charle

A cultural capital city, if I may quote my own understanding, is:

> An urban space where sufficient converging indicators allow it to be established, which is, during the period under consideration, a place of attraction and structuring power of individual fields of symbolic production (or even, for the most important, like Paris, London and sometimes Rome, the majority of fields).[1]

This concept therefore does not necessarily imply that the city also has a political role, even if most political capitals have aspired to additionally playing a cultural role, which comes from the tradition of royal or noble patronage; or today, when the keyword for world capitals is attractiveness, through cultural or symbolic activities. In the case of Paris, the two functions have gone hand in hand, but, as will be shown, they have sometimes led to conflict. The main difficulty in approaching the subject, however, lies elsewhere: how to encompass this in a very limited framework.

Since the Middle Ages and especially since what we today call 'la belle époque', Paris has undeniably generated an enormous body of literature, which exalts its function as a capital, notably as a cultural capital. This article does not aim to remind the reader of these unverified and unhistoricized clichés according to the definition outlined above, but rather to try to measure its effects and its origins at three different imbricated scales. The distinction of three levels is necessary in order to demonstrate possible inner contradictions. The conventional literature on these themes is content with qualitative accounts, positive or negative, from heterogeneous informants who only communicate their personal experiences, concerning which it cannot be determined if they are representative of all, thereby producing a mirror effect. To escape from this vicious cycle, I will attempt to implement new approaches through comparison by using objective criteria, although it is particularly difficult in the various fields of culture; by studying cultural transfers and measuring their medium- and long-term impacts; and by inventorying connections with other national and international spaces and their effects on French and foreign cultural dynamics.

To this end, it is also necessary to break away from shared meanings. The cultural domination of Paris throughout the last two centuries is not only the fruit of what was inherited from the monarchy and the French Revolution. The domination has become more pronounced over time, and it has done so despite the constant accusations levelled against it regarding adverse effects as well as the attempts to reduce Paris's influence since the middle of the twentieth century (the policy known as 'cultural decentralization'). We need to understand why this has been so.

This domination has been at the heart of an intellectual and ideological battle within the national and international space, a battle that is still relevant today, being a time of growing power for 'global cities', which are increasingly located outside Europe and which are not necessarily capitals in the political sense but also new networks of cultural transmission. These global cities no longer represent, as they did up until the 1980s, a concentration of cultural resources in one single central place, able to advance cultural domination, as has been the case with the United States, where the centres of cultural creation and dissemination have been much more dispersed and rely on multinational companies. Because of my historical field of specialization, I will address in particular the nineteenth century and the early twentieth century, precisely before the mass culture industries based on the US model asserted their long-lasting hegemony over the Western world, and partly over the non-Western world.

Parisian cultural domination on the national level

The increasing role of Paris as a cultural capital is linked to the revolutionary and imperial era, when the centralizing ideal prevailed over the attempt at decentralization during the initial period of the National Constituent Assembly. What could have been just an administrative and military response to the threats of counter-revolutionary subversion and external war was expanded to the entire culture, to the extent that the political revolution was accompanied by a general cultural revolution. The new regimes that came from the revolutionary decade wished to leave a mark on the Parisian space that reflected the magnitude of the political rupture with, notably, the foundation of the Museum Central at the Louvre, a palace that became national property; with revolutionary celebrations held at symbolically charged locations; and with the cult of the 'Great Men' at the Panthéon, all precedents that would be continued, with occasional interruptions, throughout other eras or by other regimes. Institutions of teaching and sanctioned learning, which were inherited from the monarchy (*Écoles*, academies) or from the Middle Ages (universities, colleges), had to be reorganized. Even if the Consulate, the Empire, the Restoration or the July Monarchy partly effaced some painful memories of this bloody decade, marked by frequent conflicts, the deletion of traces or the new interest in heritage, in reaction to the vandalism of some radical episodes, allowed for the erection of new cultural or heritage symbols. These symbols were always located in the capital, thereby modifying the symbolic image but always with the same reasoning based on the cultural centrality of the capital.

This permanence of a symbolic and cultural policy centred on Paris is all the more paradoxical because the regimes recruited their elites from groups of notables with strong roots in the provinces, and even rural areas. Some – for example, the counter-revolutionary nobility of the Restoration – even fostered an undisguised animosity towards the capital and its popular classes, who were in constant upheaval throughout the nineteenth century. It must be recognized, however, that before the 1860s no political force seriously contested this hyper-centralization of all the most important cultural activities and Paris even became, from this time onwards, in the eyes of foreign intellectuals a virtually identical phenomenon for French identity. Johann Wolfgang Goethe, in his *Conversations with Eckermann* in 1827–28, reflects upon this in remarks that are both admirable and dubious. For the positive aspect, based on a comparison with the contrary German situation, he declares to his confidant:

> Imagine a city like Paris, where the best minds of a great empire are gathered together in the same place, where everything remarkable that all the realms of nature and the art of all parts of the earth can offer is open to study every day; imagine such a world city where every step on a bridge or square recalls a glorious past, and where at every street corner a fragment of history has taken place. And above all do not imagine Paris at a time without light and spirit, but the Paris of the nineteenth century, in which for three generations men like Molière, Voltaire, Diderot and the like have kept up a current of intellectual life which cannot be found anywhere else on the whole earth.[2]

In 1832, Heinrich Heine went even further with this image of a city absorbing all the intellectual forces of the nation:

Paris is, actually, all of France, and France is but the great suburb of Paris. Except for its beautiful countryside and the amiable qualities of its inhabitants, in general, all of France is deserted, at least intellectually speaking.[3]

Pending the reawakening of forces of contestation in 1865 with the Nancy programme, then with the renaissance of regional cultural movements like the Félibrige and arguments in favour of decentralization, all available cultural indicators demonstrate a unique concentration of all the powers of a national cultural commission. This included publishing, theatre or plastic arts, with the central role of the Salon du Louvre (Table 1), then in other places specifically for exhibitions, as well as creations for theatre, music or opera, the general or cultural press and lastly, the university setting.

Until the end of the nineteenth century, Paris had the greatest concentration of venues for theatre, opera and various shows and performances in Europe (Table 2). These venues hosted the majority of new creations and cultivated the

Table 1 Paris Salon Admissions

- 1810: 100,000 visitors
- 1827: 120,000–200,000?
- 1830s: 200,000–300,000 visitors
- 1846: > 1 million?
- 1855: 935,601 visitors
- 1870s: 496,000–520,000 tickets sold; • 20,000 persons on free admission days

Sources: E. Bouillo, 'La fréquentation du Salon de 1817 à 1827', in *'Ce Salon à quoi tout se ramène'. Le Salon de peinture et de sculpture, 1791–1890*, eds J. Kearns and P. Vaisse (Berne: Peter Lang, 2010), 37, and E. Bouillo, *Le Salon de 1827, classique ou romantique?* (Rennes: PUR, 2009), 165–166; C. Allemand-Cosneau, 'Le Salon à Paris de 1815 à 1850', in *Les années romantiques: La peinture française de 1815 à 1850* (Paris: RMN, 1996), 106–129.

Table 2 Number of Theatres in Five European Capitals

	1850	1890	1900	1910
Paris	21	33	36	47
London	22	30	38+23	42+9
Berlin	7	20	22	30
Vienna	6	10	10	16
Madrid	8	15	22	36

Sources: C. Charle, *Théâtres en capitales. Naissance de la société du spectacle à Paris, Berlin, Londres et Vienne, 1860–1914* (Paris: Albin Michel, 2008), and J. Moisand, *Scènes capitales. Madrid, Barcelone et le monde théâtral fin de siècle* (Madrid: Casa de Velàzquez, 2013).

established repertoire. Apart from Madrid, Paris possessed the greatest number of seats available per inhabitant even though it was not the capital with the highest population in Europe, which at that time was London.

While in the twentieth century other great cities overtook Paris in terms of performance venues and facilities, its national and international strength as a city for shows and performance maintained the capacity to export its greatest successes, which is a point we shall return to in the second part of this chapter.

Notwithstanding Paris's centrality, this does not mean, as Goethe appears to indicate, that the provinces or large towns did not play any cultural role. They contented themselves with hosting new shows from Paris (such was the case for theatrical productions and publishing) or following Parisian fashions through the reading of novels or specialized newspapers. They even invented analogous institutions that served as stepping stones towards the centre, such as local painters' exhibitions, scientific societies and local musical societies, which were always seeking patronage or links to their peers in the centre via the stranglehold of the academic system over the arts, literature and sciences.

Many novelists, social scientists, statisticians and commentators highlighted the negative effects of the excessive attraction of Paris on young people aspiring to cultural glory, and the corrupting power of the concentration of all the powers of cultural gatekeeping in the hands of a small group of men – but to no avail – whether it was academies distributing prizes and favours, or colleges, lycées and schools for the elite enabling access to state or university summits, or newspaper critics assuring the success of the latest hit show. Centralized domination facilitated the corruption of close-knit networks, as Honoré de Balzac highlights in *Illusions perdues* in the part titled 'A Great Man of the Provinces in Paris' and his *Monographie de la presse parisienne*,[4] or for the Second Empire in Jules Vallès' *Le Bachelier*, and for the Third Republic several Parisian novels, including Guy de Maupassant's *Bel-Ami* (1885). We know that this discourse, critical of 'Parisian cliques', can be found almost unchanged to the present day, where it especially flourishes on the occasion of literary award ceremonies each autumn.

Although successive regimes were very active in cultural life – for example, through the control and censoring of theatres, public commissions for new works of art, purchases for museums and strict control of the press until the 1880s – we cannot say that they used these weapons to weaken the national domination of Paris. Almost half of French students lived in the Latin Quarter, a contributing factor to the agitation and troubles in the periods of contestation that regularly occurred in the nineteenth century. This contestation was rekindled by some demonstrations encouraged by the extreme right during the interwar period, or by the extreme left with the struggles in the 1960s against the war in Algeria, then Vietnam, and finally the events of May 1968. The university reforms of the Third Republic may have tried hard to strengthen the universities of other cities, but the gap between their faculties and establishments and those of the capital was not greatly reduced.

In comparison with other capitals, the academic institutions of Paris, in absolute numbers as well as for relative percentages, had a much greater concentration of students than any other city in Europe, and doubtless in the world: in 1900, 42.4 per cent of French students were in Paris, compared to the 13.2 per cent of German students in Berlin, for example, and in 1928, 41.4 per cent and 15.3 per cent respectively. This educational role was also accompanied by the concentration of resources and research capabilities during each period as well as domination of the rarest of academic specializations. Although at the end of the nineteenth century London and Berlin also gathered a considerable proportion of national university resources, there were important counterbalances that slowed this trend. In England, these were Oxford and Cambridge, always extremely well funded thanks to their own wealth, or Scottish universities that were autonomous in relation to the centre. In imperial Germany, the federal states supported their universities against Prussian domination, as Saxony did with regard to Leipzig University, or Bavaria with Munich.

Paris – contested national capital

How to explain, beyond a lingering historic effect, the persistence of these long-term phenomena, existing in a context where regionalist movements were developing under the Third Republic and the political class was dominated by elected representatives from the provinces, proud of their origins and often with a vision that was very local and hostile to the capital? Why was the movement for decentralization, especially in cultural matters, regularly failing in France? Was it solely an effect of long-lasting structures reinforced by mechanisms for the concentration of economic resources for cultural activities coming from the commercial sector (publishing, press, theatre, the art market) – through the presence of great aristocratic and bourgeois fortunes that began to practise cultural sponsorship (the founding of private museums, donations to museums and universities) – while also being located in the capital, which follows a classic 'Matthew effect'?

The hysteresis of the movement towards cultural decentralization is not only due to these global factors – which we also find, for example, in London and

Madrid – as they do not prevent the emergence of other cultural centres, for example the large industrial cities in the north of England or Scotland in the former and Barcelona in the latter. In order to understand the strengthening of Parisian cultural domination even in a period of liberalization and democratization or the rise of regionalist arguments, one must take into account the previous dual catastrophe that no other European capital had yet experienced: the terrible siege of 1870–71 and the deadly civil war that pitted the Paris Commune and the Versailles government against each other from March to May 1871. This dual trauma had no equivalent in any other capital, with the last comparable events dating back to 1812 in Russia (the Great Fire of Moscow that broke out as Napoleon invaded), or in 1848 in Central Europe (the revolutions in Berlin, Vienna and Budapest).

That partly explains the still very specific atmosphere of Paris thirty years later. As a city risen from its ashes, it endeavoured throughout the four decades that followed to recapture its European and world ranking. This obsession was clearly mirrored in the series of world expositions, culminating in the 1900 World Fair. Without these tragic memories, it would also not be possible to understand the thirst for liberty and innovation, the frenzy for amusement and derision, the uneasy political passions and the obsession for surpassing achievements felt by not only elites, writers, artists and intellectuals but also the majority of the Paris-born inhabitants, migrants and visitors passing through the city – a city of considerable contrasts and challenges. The fires of the Paris Commune, the mortar shelling during the siege, the partial migration of political functions away from the capital until 1878, and the extension of the military regime well beyond the war have shown that even the capital of revolutions – even the city that thought itself the centre of the civilized world during the World Exhibition of 1867, which almost all the monarchs visited in person – could in the span of a few months lose its ranking, lose a part of its population, become despised by its elites and a large part of the general public, and be subjected to severe internal and external violence.

The greater part of the Third Republic, despite its flaunted provincialism, represented a new sequence of restoration and reinforcement of Paris as a national capital and, above all, a symbolic and international capital. In this country, humiliated and disgraced after 1871, a country uncertain of its future with the rise in power of a unified Germany and imperial England (and soon the USA), a large part of the political elite, intellectuals, writers and artists – at least those who did not adhere to the minority's regionalism – wished to wipe clean this terrible past. They desired to restore to Paris – the secular, symbolic capital – its full function in the increasingly competitive battle in which France was, on the whole, constantly losing ground compared to the beginning of the nineteenth century, particularly in regard to economic and social issues.

International cultural capital city

To conclude this first group of analyses, Paris was characterized, from the last part of the nineteenth century onwards, by its overpowering cultural domination within its own national space as well as by its key international function compared to other European capitals, whose powers of attraction remained generally inferior even for cities that rivalled it or surpassed it demographically.

The proof through expositions and congresses

This framework for interpreting the obsession with preserving Paris's national and international role can appear abstract and in part unable to be proven as it concerns the history of disjointed representations and initiatives, some of which were non-concerted. However, it is clearly illustrated in the major symbolic and cultural events that dominated the period until 1937: for example, the policy of holding great exhibitions, which mobilized, following a very French tradition, private and public actors as well as local and national elites. These expositions were the opportunity for promoting major national and international cultural events. In the first place, there are some features that must be highlighted. In the nineteenth century, and up until 1940, Paris was the city that hosted the most world expositions, with a total of seven, as opposed to only two or three in London, and none in Berlin: 1855, 1867, 1878, 1889, 1900, 1925 (Decorative Arts) and 1937 (Arts and Technology). Moreover, the world expositions in Paris were the most visited and brought in the most money overall: the number of visitors rose from just over 5 million in 1855 to 11 million in 1867, 16 million in 1878, 25 million (paying visitors) in 1889, 50 million in 1900, 15 million in 1925 and 31 million in 1937.[5] The record for the absolute number, the year 1900, was surpassed only at the end of the twentieth century when ease of transportation was greatly improved compared to the era of trains and steamboats.

The 1900 World Fair

The great success of this exposition was due firstly to Paris's international and long-standing prestige, demonstrated by the fact that in 1900, when Berlin, capital of imperial Germany, wished to finally host an exposition, Paris was chosen again. Two reasons were cited: the success of its previous expositions and the desire of the state to maintain a regular frequency of every eleven years, regarded as a way to maintain the project of national recovery, instituted in 1878 to wipe clean the trauma of 1871. With this decision in mind, it must be asked what were the more substantial advantages that gave Paris the edge compared to its rivals in the race for the title 'capital of all capitals'?

The available statistics make it possible to determine the geographic breadth of Paris's international profile as a capital of culture in the last year of the nineteenth century: over 211 days 50,860,801 admissions were recorded, of which 41,027,177 were paid. The average daily admissions were 241,046, with peaks on Sunday of 409,376, with 438,577 on the free-entrance day in November.[6] If this latter indicator underlines the strong presence of a Parisian public, the traffic in train stations and ports then also indicates a notable influx of visitors from the provinces and abroad. The traffic at Parisian train stations also experienced a peak with 102 million passengers, 25 million more than in 1899, and 56 million more passengers than in 1889, another exposition year. The *Album Statistique* from the year 1900 makes it possible to go further in the analysis of geographical origin: 439,976 passengers came on foreign railways and 150,763 by sea. Not surprisingly, the countries that sent the most visitors were both the nearest and the richest. By order of importance, they were the United Kingdom, Belgium, Holland, Switzerland, Germany, Austria and Italy. It is difficult to determine the importance of the American contingent as many travelled via English transatlantic lines and then recrossed the Channel after having stopped over in Liverpool or London. The statistics consulted also show the extent of the exposition's influence, as extremely far-off places of origin can be noted: more than 10,000 passengers came from South America, over 3,600 from China and Japan, over 8,000 from the East Indies and Australia, more than 14,000 Russians came by boat (to which must be added those who travelled by the Paris/Berlin/Moscow railway lines, absorbed into the 'German' contingent), and over 28,000 came from the eastern Mediterranean basin. Algeria accounted for 59,753 passengers, Tunisia for 14,556 and Indochina for 2,974. During this exposition, Paris thus appeared as one of the capitals of what is called the first era of globalization.

The surface area of the exposition was enormous, with 216 hectares over two sites (Champ de Mars/Champs-Elysées, the hill of Chaillot and the Bois de Vincennes). However, the way the pavilions were crowded together, judging from aerial photographs, gives the impression of a crowded space, where the organizers wished to feature every part of the world. All architectural, artistic or musical styles rubbed shoulders. The exhibition space was organized incongruously between the ancient and the modern, the nearby and the exotic.

Alongside the recreational dimension of Parisian culture, the exposition of 1900 also highlighted another trait of the international centrality of Paris, with a proliferation of scientific and professional congresses that took place at the same time. Organizing a conference in Paris guaranteed its standing and attracted participants who also wished to take advantage of the cultural, social, political and entertainment resources offered by the only capital to concentrate them into one single space. This exposition, like those in the past, hosted a great many congresses, which increasingly structured the field of international knowledge in all domains throughout the nineteenth century and beyond: 3 took place in 1855, 14 in 1867, 48 in 1878, 101 in 1889, and twice that number in 1900 with 203 conferences, with a total of 68,000 participants.[7] Due to its ability to gather together all these experts and thinkers, Paris played the role of the intellectual capital of the world for several months. It was at this time that Paris won its title as the city having hosted the greatest number of congresses. On a national scale, organizers preferred to concentrate congresses along the banks of the Seine, in contrast to London, where even in an exposition year barely half (or less) of British conferences were held in the capital (Table 3).

Table 3 Conferences in Paris and London and in Their Respective Countries in Exposition Years

City	Conferences during the exposition	Conferences held that year nationally	Percentage
Paris 1855	3	3	100%
Paris 1867	14	24	58%
Paris 1878	48	65	73%
Paris 1889	101	111	90%
Paris 1900	203	232	87%
London 1851	2	4	50%
London 1862	4	9	44%
London 1886	3	24	12%

Source: Claude Tapia, 'Paris, ville des congrès de 1850 à nos jours', in *Le Paris des étrangers depuis un siècle*, ed. André Kaspi and Antoine Marès (Paris: Imprimerie nationale, 1989), 39.

This centrality was obviously a double-edged sword. It also reflected the imbalance in the French urban network compared to other countries; the other large French cities did not have the advantageous features necessary for gaining a place on the international scene in this way. A city such as Brussels, hardly bigger than Lyon or Marseilles on the international scale, had a perfectly eminent ranking on the list, which did not prevent Belgian cities like Ghent and Antwerp from also launching themselves into the organization of grand expositions.

This unifying function, which Paris possessed, drew its power from scientific considerations – its proximity to the largest concentration of students and high-level researchers – as well as non-scientific factors: beyond the conferences, the participants were guaranteed to find intellectual, artistic or entertainment activities without equal elsewhere. Finally, for a country like republican France that had felt disgraced since 1871, the congresses were themselves symbolic gestures. The authorities supported congresses by demonstrating hospitality or prestige in a policy of image-making not practiced by traditional monarchies; while these were entrenched in the rigid rituals of the royal court or aristocratic ethos, the culture of the congresses was more in line with the democratic and egalitarian ideal. This point is also related to the second important centrality of Paris, linked to its historical scholarly function.

The international scholarly function of Paris can be described more precisely by examining the influence of Parisian academic institutions. A new factor, originating internationally, counteracted the desire for partial decentralization of the Republic, born after the defeat of 1871. This factor was the growth in the flow of foreign students into the city, a prestigious element in the competition between nations. In all advanced European countries, as Victor Karady has demonstrated, students and increasingly students from other places (if we exclude Switzerland, whose universities welcomed large numbers of Russian students) tended to be concentrated in the capitals, although the cost of living there was much higher than elsewhere. In the capital cities students could, however, construct support networks or find additional activities to survive financially. This is especially true in Paris, as the comparison with Berlin or provincial universities shows.

In Paris, the power of attraction that its university possessed, far from diminishing, increased under the Third Republic. However, the attraction of foreign students to other great European universities, such as Berlin, tended on the contrary to regress in the 1920s despite the general growth in enrolment at Friedrich-Wilhelms University (now Humboldt University of Berlin) during the Weimar era. Paris went from having a little less than 10 per cent of foreign students (1890) enrolled to 17.7 per cent in 1910 and 24 per cent in 1928 (as opposed to 13 per cent in Berlin).

The difference in the presence of foreign students according to faculty (Table 4) clearly highlights the varying studies in Paris depending on discipline and country of origin (Table 5). Paradoxically, the professional faculties (law and medicine), dominant in terms of enrolment and Parisian centrality, were the most cosmopolitan. This reflects the practical concerns of the students, who came markedly from the poor areas of Eastern and Southern Europe in order to obtain a professional qualification that, thanks to its Parisian origin, was prestigious in their home countries. Inversely, the other faculties recruited their foreign students from the old nations, particularly when it came to the faculty of general culture par excellence, the Faculté des Lettres. While in other faculties they were not numerous, students from Germany, North America or the Nordic countries wished to immerse themselves in French civilization by attending courses at the Sorbonne. Be that as it may, the idea never occurred to them to learn the basics of science and medicine in Paris because they had institutions at their disposal in their own countries that were equivalent or even superior in terms of premises and facilities.

Russian students were noticeably numerous in sciences and medicine because they came from a less-developed country and found in France a superior climate of liberty and tolerance, even more accentuated in a metropolis like Paris. A good number of these Russians belonged in fact to ethnic or religious groups dominated or persecuted in tsarist Russia, such as Polish and Jewish people. Learning French from an early age further facilitated their integration into this part of Europe. At the turn of the twentieth century, the international cultural space over which Paris specifically exerted its grasp was essentially towards the Southeast European countries (Romanian, the Balkans, Greece), French enclaves (Belgium, Switzerland, Russian and Slavic elites in general), the Middle East where there was a long-standing presence of French-teaching institutions

Table 4 Percentage of Foreign Students by Faculty in 1897/98 in Berlin and Paris

	Law	Medicine	Humanities	Sciences
Paris	9.4%	13.7%	6.4%	8.3%
Berlin	4.26%	15.6%	21.3%	17.02%

Source: Christophe Charle, *Paris fin de siècle, culture et politique* (Paris: Le Seuil, 1998), 35–36.

Table 5 Country of Origin of Foreign Students in Paris in 1898

Country	Faculty of Humanities	Faculty of Sciences	Faculty of Medicine	Faculty of Law	Total	Percentage (of Total Students)
United Kingdom	3	2	8	9	22	1.8%
USA/Canada	18	6	7	3	34	2.9%
Russia	8	30	182	17	237	20.2%
Benelux countries	6	6	13	9	34	2.9%
Austria-Hungary	7	3	6	3	19	1.6%
Germany	31	2	19	5	57	4.8%
Switzerland	7	5	21	10	43	3.6%
Spain/Portugal	–	1	10	1	12	1.0%
Italy	–	–	5	2	7	0.6%
Nordic countries	5	2	2	–	9	0.7%
Bulgaria	4	1	–	–	5	0.4%
Serbia	6	1	5	23	35	2.99%
Romania	8	26	74	117	225	19.2%
Ottoman Empire	4	13	88	47	152	12.9%
Greece	2	3	24	31	60	5.1%
Japan	1	–	–	2	3	0.2%
Latin America	–	4	58	26	88	7.5%
Subtotal	*110*	*106*	*546*	*344*	*1106*	*94.5%*
Egypt	–	1	6	32	39	3.3%
Persia	–	–	3	1	4	0.3%
Africa	–	–	15	6	21	1.8%
General Total	*110*	*107*	*570*	*383*	*1170*	*100%*

Sources: *Annuaire statistique de la ville de Paris*; Charle, *Paris fin de siècle*, 35–36.

(Egypt, Lebanon, Turkey) as well as especially a link to Catholicism and a rather classic and conservative culture.[8] While this differing geography would be confirmed during the interwar years, it would be completely transformed in the 1950s and 1960s with the massive influx of students from the colonies, then, later, from the former French Empire.

This growth in power of Paris's international academic function was for a long time left without a distinct direction, and was produced by the individual choices of those concerned, whether it be researchers or scholars, or the students themselves. Gradually, however, still with the aim of competing internationally with other major countries, official initiatives or patronage dealt with several problems: inviting foreign academics to Parisian faculties (in particular, the establishment of regular exchanges with Columbia and Harvard),[9] creating a department of academic cooperation with Latin America, and, above all, founding and developing the Cité universitaire internationale (International University Campus in Paris) after the First World War, on the occasion of the liberation of land in the south of the Latin Quarter after the destruction of fortifications.

The student residential colleges of the established university were in large part financed by foreign, even private, donors as the chronological list and names show: Fondation Deutsch de la Meurthe (a large petroleum group), Fondation Rosa de Abreu-Grancher (Cuba), Fondation Nuber Pacha (Armenia) and Fondation Biermans-Lapôtre (Belgium). The construction of the student residential colleges in the centre of park grounds was inspired by the American campus model or English colleges (it was referred to as a 'French Oxford'); but the donors or states who consented to such a formation did so because the cosmopolitan residences were only a few kilometres from the Paris centre, which had been mythicized at the end of the nineteenth century. The ideal that presided over the arrival of students was of a mix of nationalities – despite the clear national affiliation of each house – which was also in line with the pacifist message that followed the great massacre of a whole young generation during the First World War. The order in which the houses were established was an accurate reflection of the alliance system of French diplomacy and the imagined cultural proximity between France and other nations, which explains why the Canadian and Belgian student residential colleges were at the top of the list, followed by Latin nations and those affiliated with France's ally, Britain. The old enemies were permanently excluded.

Paris – international capital of books

To explain the influence and attractiveness of Paris, the literary dimension of the image of this international city must be introduced to the discussion. Before even coming to Paris, inhabitants of the provinces or foreigners, intellectuals or not, whether coming as tourists or to settle there permanently for studies or business, had already formed a certain image of the place. This image was transmitted, certainly, by the new media platforms specific to the end of the century: the illustrated press, postcards, railway posters and paintings exported overseas. We are obviously thinking here of the Parisian scenes painted by some Impressionists, and at the same time by other painters, less modern, who specialized in scenes of Parisian life. But perhaps what most affected people of that time in terms of forming a representation of Paris – from a distance – were the images and characters, being more or less accurate and more or less stereotypical, found in the abundant number of novels or in the plays of boulevard theatres. The latter were translated and exported to other European countries throughout the nineteenth century before being taken up by interwar cinematographic production, where the social and cultural landscape of Paris was strongly present in a realist or imagined form (see, in particular, the romantic Paris of *Les Enfants du Paradis* by Marcel Carné). This output was massive; attempts have been made to undertake a detailed study, but its sheer size is discouraging, as is the extremely repetitive character of the ensemble of 'Parisian novels', the 'boulevard comedies' or various films. What is important is less the content, for the majority of these works were often conventional and destined for a mass audience, but more the fact that their export to other countries was direct, with the original French for the upper classes who were able to read the language, or with the translation of the novels that were most successful. The nineteenth century and the beginning of the twentieth century was marked by the domination of English and French novels being exported to Europe, but the difference between them was that the English novels were mostly exported to anglophone areas as well as being constrained by a moral censure much more rigid than that in France. They were much less centred on London, or presented an image of the city that was rather negative, if we think of Charles Dickens or Arthur Conan Doyle. The French novels were able to be translated into many languages and were, above all, works by authors living in Paris, given the concentration of the literary scene in the capital. They frequently set their plots or characters in Paris, often in order to present a more or less realist and informed portrait of the city, with a very clear distortion of the city that was leaning towards the top of the social ladder. Conversely, some internationally successful naturalistic novels, like those by Émile Zola, chose as their subjects groups long placed at the margins of literature, such as workers, employees, prostitutes, artists and journalists (see *L'Assommoir, Au Bonheur des dames, Nana* and *L'Oeuvre* by Zola, and *Bel-Ami* by Maupassant). This does not mean that thought-provoking Parisian literature crossed frontiers unhindered, as certain licences could not be taken in other countries subject to more severe censorship. At least these works, even when they provoked scandal or were quite freely adapted, maintained a complex and fascinating image of Paris for readers in other countries. Neither London, nor, a priori, any other European capital, had enjoyed this continuous literary support that existed from the eighteenth century onwards, with internationally known works, characters, urban locations and authors. This intimate relationship between Paris as a literary capital (the centre of the French literary field), a capital of books (as a centre of national publishing and press) and a capital *within* books, which was a central theme for numerous works of fiction or theatre, explains three phenomena:

1. Some French international bestsellers were centred around the capital, from the publication of Les mystères de Paris and Les Misérables, up to Paris by Zola, to mention the works still known today.
2. The *roman parisien* (Parisian novel) as a specific genre was imitated in other emerging European capitals like St Petersburg with Dostoevsky's Crime and Punishment, Vienna with Arthur Schnitzler and Robert Musil, Rome with Gabriele D'Annunzio, and Berlin with Theodor Fontane and Alfred Döblin, to speak only of authors still known today.
3. The images conveyed both take into account urban changes and, at the same time, delay addressing them. On the one hand, the authors willingly set their plots in a time slightly in the past, or, on the other, the delay in translation and adaptation for other countries comes into play. Eugène Sue, for example, was still being read in Russia at the end of the century, as was Balzac. Zola was not read without some delay in the most conservative countries.

This literary internationalism was amplified by the international artistic role Paris played in the same period.

Paris – international capital of art

The attraction of Paris internationally developed throughout the nineteenth century, in time eclipsing the function acquired by Rome as a place of post-Renaissance learning (except for sculpture). This is attested by the foundation of the Académie de France in Rome and the establishment of the Prix de Rome, which in some domains was still playing a central role in the nineteenth century, and even twentieth century, in the designation of a future artistic elite, at least as defined in academic terms.[10] Contrary to this, there was an increase in the proportion of foreign students at the École des Beaux-Arts in Paris or in private studios, which were appearing in great numbers, together with artists holding exhibits in the major Parisian salons (Table 6).

Table 6 Proportion of Foreign Artists in Various Art Salons in Paris and Berlin (Percentage)

	Société Nationale des Beaux-Arts (1899)	Société des artistes français (1899)	Société Nationale des Beaux-Arts (1909)	Société des artistes français (1909)	Salon d'automne (1909)
Paris	34.7%	21.3%	34.1%	30.3%	35.2%
Berlin 1897	9.1%				

Source: *Annuaire statistique de la ville de Paris* and Charle, *Paris fin de siècle*.

In 1899, there were 34.7 per cent foreign artists exhibiting at the Société Nationale des Beaux-Arts and 21.3 per cent at the Société des artistes français, and in 1909, 35.1 per cent at the Salon d'Automne, the most internationally diverse. This data acts as a new indicator of both the attractiveness and the influence of the Parisian art world. Even if the official institutions remained rather conservative, there were, at least, spaces of freedom that the avant-gardes seized and made use of.

Similar to the upsurge in the number of international conferences or the enrolment of foreign students at Parisian university faculties, the movement first appeared under the Second Empire and was cultivated under the Third Republic when three phenomena converged. Firstly, there was the flourishing of the avant-gardes and the artistic polemics against academic painting. Secondly, there was the rise in power of the contemporary art market in Paris – be it innovative or traditional – together with the development of a merchant-critic system, encouraged by the power of the mainstream or specialized Parisian press outlets. Thirdly, there was the arrival of new foreign collectors on the Parisian market, notably American, who succumbed in turn to the myth of Paris, being regarded as the capital of good taste, civilization and luxury since the eighteenth century; for the less conformist among them, there was an interest in innovative trends relating to the symbolic victory of the theme of 'modernity' in art.

The old idea, and one unique to Paris due to its specific revolutionary history, that in art, as in literature and in all cultural domains, the future belongs to those that break with tradition, is based on proof through the success of past movements that were appropriated for exhibition purposes,[11] even at the price of a certain distortion of historical reality. Such movements included Romanticism in its literary, pictorial and musical dimension (see the painting *Hommage à Delacroix* by Fantin-Latour (1864), which features all the representatives of the young generation of painters in the 1860s); Realism, although with more difficulty, with the success of Courbet in Germany and the specific mise en scène of his own glory and that of his friends in *L'Atelier du peintre*, which was presented to and refused by the international exhibition of 1855; and especially Impressionism, whose international success coincided with the centennial exposition that took place during the World Exposition of 1889. This glorious history of artistic innovation masks the mass of failures of individual careers in a world that was more and more competitive owing to centralization processes. The golden legend of 'Modernism' implied, in the eyes of the foreigner, that those who produced 'new' paintings and who would soon be called the avant-garde, as if history had already been written, had every chance of soon being artistic victors according to that historicized representation, orientated towards the future, already underway in the 1860s and in time theorized by Charles Baudelaire, Zola and others.

This image of Paris as a place of the most brilliant artistic success did not concern only innovative painters but also more traditional painters who achieved worldly success, like the American John Singer Sargent, educated at the École des Beaux-Arts, or the Italian Giovanni Boldini, as well as foreigners close to avant-garde artists like James McNeill Whistler and Mary Cassatt, being travelling companions to the Impressionists. This influence and this attractiveness are found with the avant-gardes in '-isms', characteristic of the end of the nineteenth century and the first decade of the twentieth century: in the field of painting with the Divisionism of Georges Seurat and Paul Signac (1886); the Nabi movement (1899); the founding of the Salon d'Automne (1903), where Fauvism took off in 1905 and Cubism in 1908; or painters at the École de Paris after 1910. These innovators in different genres were often linked together by friendship or a concern for solidarity, or were neighbours. Many foreign painters, being either permanent or temporary residents, represented this period (1890–1930). Some attached themselves to these artistic movements, while others followed traditional routes. Alfons Mucha and František Kupka, both from Bohemia, had their debuts in Parisian satirical newspapers in 1896 before joining the avant-garde. Kees van Dongen, from Holland, settled in Paris in 1896. The Norwegian Edvard Munch was present in the capital in 1896 and regularly sent paintings to the art salons of Paris, as did Wassily Kandinsky, who spent a year there in 1906. Pablo Picasso, trained in Barcelona, after a first visit to the exposition of 1900, moved to Paris permanently in 1904. Sonia Terk, future wife of Robert Delaunay, came from Russia via Germany, and settled in the French capital in 1905 as did Modiglani, from Livorno.[12] Marc Chagall arrived in 1910; both he and Amedeo Modiglani stayed in La Ruche, the artists' residence, in the Passage de Dantzig (in the 15th arrondissement of Paris) in a metal pavilion acquired from the 1900 exposition and opened in 1902.[13] The same phenomenon exists in Montmartre with 'le bateau lavoir', birthplace of the Cubist movement.

Coming from all over the world, these artists were at times obliged to make their names known by exhibiting outside official venues, in cafés, or overseas. Not having full mastery of French, they depended even more than indigenous artists on the articles written by young writers or journalists published in small review magazines like *Mercure de France* and *La Revue blanche*. They could rarely avail themselves of authoritative works such as that by Paul Signac, *D'Eugène Delacroix au néo-impressionnisme* (1899), or manifestos – placed with difficulty in mainstream press outlets – like that of the Italian Futurists, who appeared on the front page of the *Figaro* in February 1909 in order to make themselves known.[14]

Paris played the role of international cultural capital not only because of its multinational concentration of artists of all nationalities and types, but also because of the great number of art merchants, sales, numerous exhibition venues; the presence of colonies of rich foreign amateurs or collectors; and the multitude of foreign tourists that regularly came to purchase luxury goods, including *objets d'art* produced or exhibited in the capital. There is no doubt that Brussels, Vienna, Munich or Berlin, and even St Petersburg or Moscow, climbed the hierarchy of artistic prestige, and increasingly acquired the same facilities (new museums, exhibition venues, etc.), as Béatrice Joyeux-Prunel shows in her book *Nul n'est prophète en son pays*.[15] However, the growth curve in numbers of modern art exhibitions in the major European cities demonstrates that up until 1914, despite some cities catching up after 1905, the dominant position was still occupied by the French capital.

The interwar period, with the proliferation of economic difficulties in France in the 1930s and the worldwide emergence of the avant-garde phenomenon, as shown by the likes of Futurism and the Russian and German avant-gardes independent from Parisian influences, marks a beginning of the decline of Paris as a world capital of art. Nevertheless, the political tensions of the 1930s restored to Paris the function of being a place of safety for the avant-garde movements persecuted by dictators; however, it was also the moment when the art market collapsed due to the 1929 economic crisis and the drying up of American purchases. The decline was accentuated by the Second World War and occupation, with the rise of new artistic centres, particularly in the south of France and especially in the United States with New York, as avant-gardism became impossible in the French capital, which had become one of the bastions of Nazism and its collaborators. The same alternating highs and lows occurred in the 1950s and 1960s, as Julie Verlaine and Raymonde Moulin have shown, before the polycentrism of the art market triumphed to the benefit of New York and today to numerous other cities, and their biennials or international fairs, like those being held in Basel.[16]

Paris – international capital of opera and music

As regards opera and music, Parisian cosmopolitanism is even more ancient than in the case of the plastic arts. Since the time of Louis XIV, musical relations with Italy, for example in opera, have been active and stable, with Paris welcoming numerous foreign composers and performers into positions within its cultural institutions, starting with Gaspare Spontini, Gioachino Rossini, Gaetano Donizetti, Anton Reicha at the Conservatoire or the Opera and Théâtre italien, then Frédéric Chopin and Franz Liszt as partly exiled performers or creators, to name but the most famous. In the second half of the nineteenth century, this opening up to other musical traditions or musicians continued and spread to more diverse and far-off new lands, such as Russia, Spain and Germany. It was Parisian operatic and musical creations, in particular, which were exported overseas on a new scale, facilitated by growing means of communication and mediatization. It was a moment when the French school of music, and specifically the production of operas or of comic operas, enjoyed real and long-lasting success abroad with the operas of Daniel Auber and Giacomo Meyerbeer (based on the librettos of Eugène Scribe, the most performed French author in Europe), Charles Gounod's *Faust* and Georges Bizet's *Carmen*, not to mention the operettas of Jacques Offenbach, Hervé and Charles Lecoq, which were performed throughout Europe. The excessive focus on the battle between the partisans and adversaries of Richard Wagner, which reduces this era to a new form of Franco-German confrontation, gives a distorted image that the works of William Weber, Jann Pasler and Myriam Chimènes have significantly corrected.[17] Without a doubt, Wagner's access to official institutions was delayed after the 1861 *Tannhäuser* scandal and the rejection of the composer due to his hateful stance towards France during the 1870 conflict. Excluded from the Paris Opera until 1891 (the premiere of *Lohengrin*), Wagner was nevertheless very present, with extracts from his works included in the concerts organized by the major Parisian *sociétés* from the 1880s onward.

But this aspect of the life of the opera – disrupted by national tensions – must not conceal the most important phenomenon characterizing this period: the strong internationalism of the works created in Paris, and, in the opposite sense, the many foreign authors arriving on Parisian stages or of new music unknown in the first part of the nineteenth century. This dual movement was linked to unique features already discussed; however, a comparative perspective must be mentioned: Paris was the theatrical capital of Europe, whether in terms of spoken theatre or musical theatre. Paris possessed several specialized theatres as well as an ensemble of general or specific periodicals that were read beyond its borders, which contributed to greater awareness of the failures and successes performed on Parisian stages. The directors of venues in other countries imported these shows when they got wind of a success that had been able to please audiences in Paris, audiences reputed to be very demanding due to their high level of cultural education and the plethora of new shows. It was hoped that success with such audiences could be reproduced beyond the boundaries of Paris.[18] These exports were often supported by the oversea tours of some stars (singers and actors), conductors or composers.

Finally, French operatic theatre benefited from a new generation of innovative musicians, who took over from the generation that had dominated the era since the 1830s. I have, incidentally, analysed in detail the names of those musicians whose works were most often exported overseas: apart from the deceased Offenbach and Bizet, there was a new productive generation comprised of Gounod, Jules Massenet, Camille Saint-Saëns, Claude Debussy and Gustave Charpentier. Some old successes like Bizet's *Carmen*, first performed at the Opéra-Comique in 1875, continued to be performed throughout Europe as well as in the United States or other cities both near and far, such as Oslo, Johannesburg, Sofia or Shanghai.[19]

This international outlook towards music in Paris is also found in the abundance of concerts given in the French capital, which included programmes that willingly mixed music of French, German, Italian or Spanish origins. Recent research undertaken by the various American scholars previously mentioned shows that despite the nationalist climate, the world expositions – like those in 1900 and, before it, those in 1889 or 1878 – were occasions for the import of new music from foreign artists that were not at the centre of European musical creation: the folk music of Northern Europe or Central Europe and the exotic music of Asia and the Far East. In 1889, a music critic, Julien Tiersot, was already able to write about the globalization of music that occurred thanks to the exposition:

Rome is no longer in Rome; Cairo is no longer in Egypt, nor is the Isle of Java in the East Indies. All of that has come to the Champ de Mars, on the esplanade des Invalides and the Trocadéro. So that without leaving Paris, it would be possible to study for six months, at least in their outward expression, the traditions and customs of the most far-off peoples. And music being, between all of these displays, one of the most striking, none of the exotic visitors to the Exposition have dared forget it. Not to mention the grand orchestral concerts, vocal music, the organ, et cetera, a series of which having just opened at the Trocadéro, we find in the diverse sections of the World Exposition numerous occasions to study the musical forms belonging to the races in which art is understood in a very different way to our own.[20]

The field of music and opera, less bound to the national language, obviously guarantees the best transition towards the possible third qualification of Paris as a cultural capital in the nineteenth and twentieth centuries. Incontestably a national and international capital, is Paris also a transnational capital? This is what remains for us to ask in the very last part of this chapter.

Paris, a transnational capital city?

Some preliminary definitions

The distinction between the international function of a cultural capital like Paris and its transnational function can appear a little specious as these two phenomena are closely interwoven, as the examples we have given so far have shown. The distinction will be made here according to the following criteria: *international* is the temporary presence of the cultures of several nations in the same place (the case of expositions and congresses, as well as students, writers or artists staying temporarily) or long lasting (the presence of intellectuals, writers or immigrant artists who find a permanent host environment in Paris or those of foreign origin during their stay). For all the actors involved in culture, the issue was the ability to take advantage of encounters with others or of the influence of a city central to the European or worldwide cultural dynamic, but without renouncing their own identity. Sometimes these encounters were sought out in order to discover, through contrast, the different shocks produced by exchanges with the local culture or with the cultures of those other simultaneously present nationalities.

The *transnational* dimension, in my view, is achieved only when this confrontation produces supplementary effects that make the initial national culture's dynamic – in the co-presence (that of host country and that of exporting country) of an artwork, an identity or a specific ideological affirmation – become a new synthesis that is original or aspires to originality, where the elements of the initial cultures are transformed. Paris, because of its long national and international domination, may appear to have been a privileged location for the emergence of this new dimension. But this is far from being the case since the transnational dimension has often been in contradiction to the two other very significant dimensions of the role this city plays: the national dimension has often been asserted through the rejection of foreign elements by those who claim to be the guardians and natural spokespeople for a national identity – members of the Académie française and academics of all types – notably when they evoke 'the French spirit', 'the French tradition' or, worse still, 'the Parisian spirit'.[21]

The international dimension is always unbalanced, tipping in favour of the dominant culture or cultures according to the fields discussed, which marginalize or 'exoticize' the representatives of the dominated cultures, in this way going against balanced or constant cultural transfers. This explains why some more modest cultural capitals are sometimes the best places for transfers or the emergence of truly transnational cultural productions. One might think here of Brussels, Geneva, Weimar or, by way of mass culture, Hollywood during the great period when European filmmakers and artists, driven from their countries by dictators, contributed to the Europeanization of early American cinema and to the rise of its intellectual ambition.

Foreign artists or intellectuals – attracted to Paris through a steadily constructed myth of a welcoming city that was open to all and was breaking away from rules inherited from the past, including the French Revolution and the other symbolic revolutions with international dimensions that had taken place there – rapidly discovered the magnitude of the factors of exclusion and opposition to their integration. The local intellectuals or creators of art frequently displayed a certain arrogance or a dominating and assimilating cultural imperialism, be it political, social or linguistic. They accepted foreign creators only in as far as they made themselves more French or accepted their peripheral and dominated positions, as Heine had already noted with irony. These negative factors worsened as France generally declined in other domains and continued on through national crises. The former was expressed through anti-Semitic, xenophobic, racist ideologies or certain types of 'calls to order', like the classical or Latin myth, launched at the turn of the nineteenth and twentieth century by the extreme right[22] while the latter included the Boulangist crisis, the Dreyfus affair, the First World War, the Great Depression, the Vichy era and the period of decolonization. These crises tended to reinforce the 'national' capital function of Paris, notably with the anti-cosmopolitan and anti-internationalist forces, who had their own appointed intellectuals and artists as well as presenting foreign works or artists' colonies or writers from elsewhere as threats to the cultural identity of the country. The avant-gardes themselves, groups providing a more welcoming space to foreigners, as demonstrated by movements such as Impressionism (with Whistler, Cassatt or Alfred Sisley), Symbolism where writers of Belgian, Greek (Jean Moréas), American (Stuart Merril or Francis Viellé-Griffin) origin could be found, Cubism (with Picasso, Juan Gris or Guillaume Apollinaire) and Surrealism (Salvador Dalí, Man Ray, Joan Miró, Francis Picabia or Max Ernst). Because of the extreme competition and centralization, they were not spared from this intolerance and fear of mixing, which is, however, the strength and very essence of a transnational capital.

It must also be noted that this recent notion of 'transnational' obviously did not exist during most of the period analysed. This cultural orientation, produced by multiple cultural transfers, was designated by vague fuzzy epithets like 'cosmopolitan' or by frankly negative adjectives such as 'displaced' or 'transplanted', or even hostile ones like 'métèques' (metic) or 'barbarian' by the guardians of national identity, who were the dominant critics and ideologues of the right and extreme right, and also sometimes of the left. The transnational function of Paris is thus more complicated to map out than the two previous functions, which are more substantial and easier to identify through objective criteria. This transnational aspect most often appears only through in-depth monographic analyses of cultural minorities or specific conjunctures closely linked to precise political contexts. Recourse to the objectivist approach, such as that attempted in the two previous parts of this contribution, proves difficult here in the absence of possible connections or exhaustive inventories and the discontinuous character of the process, as the research on cultural transfers led by Michel Espagne has shown. At the risk of falling victim to the trap of sources, only a few examples will be mentioned here (as previously pointed out in the introduction). Three themes will be focused on: the internationalist and pacifist theme, the theme of voluntary or involuntary exile, and the theme of modernity, with all its ambiguities.

Pacifist and internationalist utopia

During the nineteenth and twentieth centuries – when nationalism and patriotism were the central values in most European countries, noticeably in France, which was deeply marked by a series of major conflicts from the time of the Revolution and the Empire up to the wars of decolonization – the cultural and political affirmation of a pacifist ideal as a regulative idea of history is far from self-evident. Yet, Paris was, together with Geneva, one of the rare cultural capitals where militant intellectuals, sometimes writers and artists, attempted to connect the ideal to the city, thereby making a reality that would encourage progress towards peace. The first such occasion was the organization of the International Peace Congress in 1849, at which the most famous French writer at the time, Victor Hugo, gave the inaugural and closing speeches.[23] The choice of Paris as the host for the event, and of Victor Hugo for its rhetorical orchestration, was obviously no accident. It had been about a year since the revolutions of 1848, which began in Paris in February. At the congress, the idea was advanced of a transnational solidarity of the liberal and democratic revolutions against the Holy Alliance of monarchies and aristocracies. As we know, this solidarity was relative. Owing to the German national ideal quickly coming into conflict primarily with the Slavic national ideal, the counter-revolutionary camp was able to exploit the social, political and national divisions that existed among the actors of 1848, thereby restoring the political situation back to normal and even bringing about some regression. At the time, Paris – despite the June 1848 upheaval as well as the victory of the conservatives in the legislative elections in 1849 and their support of the papacy with the French expedition to Rome – was one of the last cities where the pacifist spirit of 1848 still existed to some extent and where national or exiled foreign intellectuals attempted to maintain the internationalist spirit of the previous year. Hugo summed it up:

> You have wished to adopt Paris as the centre of this meeting, whose sympathies, full of gravity and conviction, do not merely apply to one nation, but to the whole world. *(Applause)* You come to add another principle of a still superior – of a more august kind – to those that now direct statesmen, rulers and legislators. You turn over, as it were, the last page of the Gospel – that page which imposes peace on the children of the same God; and in this capital, which has as yet only decreed fraternity amongst citizens, you are about to proclaim the brotherhood of mankind.[24]

In the quoted extract, the combination of a political vocabulary ('sympathies ... to one nation'), the reference to democratic revolutions and to transnational humanism, inherited from the Enlightenment ('whose sympathies ... apply ... to the whole world'), while mixing a universalist religious openness of a

Christian type ('of a more august kind ... the last page of the Gospel'), due to the strong presence of anglophone Protestant pacifists, is an effective feature of Victor Hugo's pre-exile concern, having not yet asserted the full measure of his republican radicalism to reconcile the various European intellectual currents. At this level of generality, their compatibility was more postulated than demonstrated, all the more so as the previous year another internationalism, proletarian this time, had been announced in the manifesto of the Communist Party of Karl Marx and Friedrich Engels, of which Victor Hugo was obviously unaware. However, Engels would assert the same conviction forty years later at the same location, with the founding of the Second International on the occasion of the 100-year anniversary of 1789 and of the World Exposition by the International Socialist Workers' Congress in Paris held 14–21 July 1889.

This second moment of transnational affirmation by the French capital can also be made apparent with two reminders from the past and the present. What could be more logical than to re-establish – after the failure of the First International owing to the splits between Marxists and anarchists, the Franco-German War and, above all, the crushing of the Paris Commune, or the related revolutionary movements in Spain – the new internationalist organ in the sole republican capital on the continent, having been the first victim of the negative effects of national hatred with the siege, defeat and civil war? This slightly simple reading of the issue, however, ignores that Paris too had only just emerged from a serious national crisis with the Boulangist movement, where the nationalism and bellicosity of the Parisian population (including the working-class districts) were clearly expressed during the street demonstrations and a partial election in favour of General Georges Boulanger, who was called 'le général Revanche'. Additionally, it forgets that of all the socialist or related parties that were being formed in Europe and who attempted to unite, the French socialists were the most divided and the weakest, and were far from totally adhering to the internationalism that inspired the new organization, to the extent that a rival congress, organized by the Possibilists and the mostly English delegates, was held at the same time, refusing to join forces with the congress organized by the Marxists.[25] The same problem occurred when the new congress of the Second International took place in September 1900.

Symbolic places, even loaded with revolutionary history, were not sufficient to efface the scars of memories linked to the more or less recent national history. Where Paris was most successful in asserting its transnational role was in those critical moments where it became the theatre for large intellectual or political demonstrations, as in October 1909 with the protests against the execution of

Francisco Ferrer, a Spanish anarchist and educator, victim of the militarist and clerical repression that triggered two socialist demonstrations on the boulevards of Paris and a number throughout Europe.[26] This was the case again with the emergence of an international anti-fascist movement twenty-five years later, the International Congress of Writers for the Defence of Culture organized by the Association des écrivains et artistes révolutionnaires (Association of Revolutionary Writers and Artists), where writers and intellectuals – both French and also exiled foreigners from countries that had fallen under fascist domination – attempted to mobilize international opinion in June 1935. These critical moments allowed the secondary political tensions, inequalities between cultures and excessive national expressions to be partially forgotten.

Translation and exile

The research undertaken on cultural transfers or the transnational dimension of cultural developments places great emphasis on the role of certain personalities marked by the experience of exile, with much recent work allowing research to emerge from the purely empathetic or biographic approach that has largely dominated. Michel Espagne's book *Les juifs allemands à Paris à l'époque de Heine*[27] can be cited here as well as other works, stemming from a thesis by Delphine Diaz on exiles in France in the first half of the nineteenth century;[28] to the two books edited by André Kaspi and Antoine Marès, *Le Paris des étrangers*, which discussed the Paris of foreigners, pre- and post-1945;[29] to the studies (partly divergent) by Pascale Casanova, *La République mondiale des lettres*, and Anna Boschetti with *L'espace culturel transnational* and her very recent work *Ismes*;[30] and also to the research on translations by Blaise Wilfert and Gisèle Sapiro in which Paris is accorded a great, if not central, importance. It is obviously impossible to summarize this ensemble of research, which maintains conclusions that are not always convergent because of the marked historic variations depending on the period addressed. Some emphasize the transnational function of Paris in literature, as Pascale Casanova[31] and Gisèle Sapiro do, while others, like Blaise Wilfert or Delphine Diaz, rather underline the resistance to foreign imports or the compulsory integration of exiled intellectuals into Parisian cultural life. Anna Boschetti also paints a more nuanced picture than that offered by the usual golden legend about Paris, addressing the truly transnational character of some literary or artistic avant-gardes among Realism, Futurism and Surrealism.

Pascale Casanova speaks of a 'Greenwich Meridian' of innovative literature located in Paris in order to construct an alternative central hub for the circulation of works, which demanded autonomy in the face of a mainstream literature or of an industrial and commercial publishing hub that is increasingly dominated by the anglophone conglomerates. Likewise, in terms of literary translation (especially since the 1970s and 1980s) Gisèle Sapiro sees in Paris a central place of exchanges between literature of smaller nations and literature of dominant countries. Previously, because of francophone imperialism, Parisian publishers exported a great deal to other countries but translated little (as Blaise Wilfert has shown in detail in the case of the nineteenth century and the beginning of the twentieth century) compared to German, Italian, Spanish or Russian publishers.[32] From the moment in the 1980s when French as a language of international translation became more and more clearly surpassed by English, the French publishing industry opened up, not only increasingly to English (a long-standing phenomenon since the eighteenth century) but also to new languages, thereby contributing to the transnational renaissance of literatures written in languages that have been less well situated within the hierarchy of internationality and whose productions have not necessarily addressed the dominant model of the globalized literature of the anglophone novel. The international success of the Latin American novel, of some German speaking authors (Heinrich Böll, Günter Grass and Ellfriede Jellinek), Italian novelists (Pier Paolo Pasolini, Dino Buzzati, Umberto Eco, Leonardo Sciascia, etc.), Spanish authors, Czech writers (Milan Kundera) or even more exotic literature (from Japan, China, the Caribbean and Africa) is constructed, according to Gisèle Sapiro and Pascale Casanova, largely in Paris's literary field due to its transnational function as a sort of stock exchange, together with the construction of an image of Paris as a transnational critic, for authors from peripheral countries or languages.

The opening up to other literary traditions and some French authors' return to sources more diverse than the Greco-Latin tradition, so predominant in France due to the ancient construction of Classicism, the basic education of most of the dominant writers and intellectuals since the nineteenth century, clearly depends on the accessibility of these new worlds of foreign literature that characterize the references of the new authors from the dawn of the twentieth century. These alternative literatures are read a priori by a scholarly public and, at the forefront of that public, by authors themselves looking for a certain innovation. Very few French authors in the past possessed a linguistic culture beyond French and Latin (rarely English or German) that would allow them to immerse themselves in literature from elsewhere without depending on translations. Yet, as the research cited has shown, those translations were for a long time rather remote from the current canons of original authenticity (especially the rarer the language was). The Russian novels, the Scandinavian plays and the Italian novels that readers, especially Parisians, were able to read in French from the end of the nineteenth century onwards were more likely adaptations than translations due to the imperialism of French taste, a notion as vast as it is imprecise, imposed by critical and editorial authorities, as Blaise Wilfert shows in detail regarding, for example, D'Annunzio or other research on the Russian novel.[33]

This Parisian literary factory that was producing new foreign works thus represented a process of transnational construction insofar as these French 'infidels' often served as a foundation for translations in Italian, Spanish or English. All of this occurs due to the specific rules of functioning of the Parisian literary field, owing to its centralized and conflict-charged history (foreign authors are appropriated in internal struggles by Parisian writers) as well as the collaboration of French authors or critics with translators. These translators, whose presence was often rather ghostly or was even reduced to anonymity, were drawn from the exiled communities in the capital, given that French-origin experts in foreign languages were for a long time quite few in number, especially in rare languages.[34] It must be emphasized that similar phenomena occurred in the humanities, where leading foreign scholars were gradually introduced into or adapted to internal intellectual debates via intellectuals from those countries, with Structuralism and Russian Formalism in linguistics coming to mind.[35]

Conclusion: Paris – paradoxical capital city of 'modernity'

At the end of this analysis, necessarily incomplete because the diversity of themes and the scope of the period addressed would demand manifold supplementary elements and nuances – as well as, paradoxically, new research, if only to have continuous comparable data beyond the same recurring examples or key cities – two conclusions can be made that are also working hypotheses for other research. The first was expected, namely the multi-dimensionality of Paris's role as a cultural capital and, something that is too often forgotten, the marked variations in reality of its diverse functions depending on contrasting historical phases. Unlike the usual image of Paris's dominant role being permanent, the maximum intensity and the ability to take on the three possible dimensions of the role of a cultural capital are in Paris inversely proportional to the ability of France to claim the role of imperial society. It was after the failure of the First Empire to fulfil its dream of European domination that Paris became once again an attractive cultural, influential capital and opened up, due to Romanticism, to new elements from elsewhere and began to split from the Neoclassicism imposed in all domains by Napoleon. After the failure of Charles X's dream of a partial return to the Ancien Régime in 1830, Paris was the destination of choice for those exiled and persecuted in Europe by the Holy Alliance. It was after the 1871 defeat, the failure of another Empire and being faced with the obsession with decadence that preoccupied the political and intellectual elites that the universities were renovated and thus played, in Paris, an international role that was much more extensive than before. At the same time, following the 1880s, republican France and Paris once again became a home for all the intellectuals and artists who found themselves facing obstacles and hardships in the Europe of monarchies and non-liberal empires. As we have seen, this also does not exclude the possibility of reactions of internal rejection (as shown by the Dreyfus affair). Nevertheless, every eleven years, Paris provisionally became the capital of modernity and the Western world during world expositions and the congresses taking place there. The artistic, poetic or novelistic avant-gardes exerted a strong influence on their foreign counterparts. It was once more after the dark years of 1940–44, when Paris lost its function as a capital for four years, that the Parisian intellectual field temporarily regained its central position in international and transnational modernity, with Jean-Paul Sartre and Albert Camus, influential in Italy, Germany, Japan and even in the United States; with the new abstract avant-garde painters whose works were selling, especially overseas; with the Theatre of the Absurd, the majority of whose authors were transnational authors (such as Samuel Beckett, Eugène Ionesco, Arthur Adamov and Armand Gatti); with experimental music; with the New Wave in cinema; and with the renewed internationalism of the academic sphere. All the same, these culturally rich years corresponded politically to the collapse of the colonial empire and to a lingering crisis in the parliamentary Republic.

Fernand Braudel, in a passage from *Civilisation matérielle, économie et capitalisme*, which has been little commented upon, had noted, at least for the years that concerned him in his three-volume study of the sixteenth to eighteenth centuries, the gap between the dominant city of the world economy of each period and the most influential cultural centre at the same time, as if economic modernity did not have the same requirements as cultural modernity.[36] This conclusion was relatively paradoxical for the period of the cultural Ancien Régime, when princely or ecclesiastic patronage was one of the first conditions for the emergence of new cultural forms, and whose first audience was composed of the circles of the royal court.

For the new cultural regime that progressively established itself over the nineteenth century, which featured growing differentiation and diversity of audiences, competition between forms dominated by market mechanisms and forms that tried to escape from all constraints inherited from the past or linked to concerns for profitability, the divergence is much more logical.[37] Freed early from the court society (and even the origin of its destruction in the most concrete sense, through the radicalization of the Enlightenment thinkers, being then the days of revolution that wiped Versailles and the monarchy off the power map), a proportion of the Parisian artists and creators of all types fought constantly on several fronts. These fronts included fighting against the still burdensome tutelage of the state, which had not renounced its role inherited from the past of regulator and patron with the Bourbon Restoration, against the rising cultural commodification, partly inspired by the London model, and against the other parts of each cultural field ready to comply with these tutelages stirred up by the centralization, which was constant and unmatched in the other cultural capitals. These contradictory dynamics would occur *mutatis mutandis* as similar factors made their appearance a little later in Brussels, Berlin, Vienna, Rome, St Petersburg, Madrid and Moscow. In contrast, factors are much more difficult to identify in London or New York before an even more recent date (in the 1900s), although London and then New York were at the time centres of financial and imperialist capitalism, which is in accord with Braudel's remarks, as previously cited.

The Parisian model partly spread to and was in return influenced by these new cultural capitals, via the intensification of international and transnational exchanges. If it endured beyond that which could have been expected, despite the growing power of the United States or new cultural powers from the dawn of the twentieth century, it is because its paradoxical modernity – in the sense of its pretension to embody the future before the others – arose from the persistent and entirely paradoxical archaism of France in general during these two centuries. By concentrating a disproportionate amount of cultural resources and capacity for innovation in its capital, France, for a longer time than elsewhere, maintained provincial societies in a state of external cultural domination and nurtured a cycle of cultural centralization, on the one hand productive thanks to the intensity of the competition and the exchanges in an enclosed space, but on the other hand also numbing for the rest of the country, as Goethe had already made luminously clear in his *Conversations with Eckermann*.[38] Thanks to the hysteresis of the representations transmitted by the works produced there and the reverberation of its myth by the groups of foreigners that it attracted relatively constantly, Paris succeeded in maintaining its symbolic grip up to the 1960s, even as the conditions that made this hegemony possible were gradually crumbling away.

From the 1960s, at the time when Gaullist France was launching itself into another modernity, inspired by the American example in terms of economy and technology, we entered another cultural world largely dominated by the American hub. It was in the world of contemporary art that this disengagement occurred earliest, as Julie Verlaine and Raymonde Moulin[39] have shown, then increasingly spread out to other domains, where for a long time the national language remained a major obstacle to the transnational and the international.

Today, the idea of a central cultural capital is now doubtlessly meaningless in the age of fairs, festivals, temporary congresses, invisible colleges and electronic networks. This organization, however, does not prevent persistence, as various recent episodes have revealed, of forms of mainly American cultural imperialism, which is just as limiting, in favour of invisible or unattainable centres because they are organized in networks or multi-polarities. They concern quite different cultural forms that are directed much more towards mass audiences than to the literate and cultivated elites that I have particularly described here and who are typical of the culture originating in Paris.[40]

Notes

1. Christophe Charle, 'Introduction', in *Le temps des capitales culturelles (XVIII-XXe siècles)*, ed. Christophe Charle (Seyssel: Champ Vallon, 2009), 15.
2. Johann Wolfgang von Goethe, '3 May 1827', in *Conversations*, trans. J. Chuzeville (Paris: Gallimard, 1988), 517.
3. Heinrich Heine, *De la France*, trans. G. Höhn (1832–33; Paris: Gallimard, 1994), 69.
4. 'How strange! The most serious books, the *oeuvres d'art* honed to perfection, that have been worked on night and day, for whole months receive no attention whatsoever from newspapers and are met with complete silence,' translated from Honoré de Balzac, *Monographie de la presse parisienne* (1843; Paris: J.-J. Pauvert, 1965), 140.
5. Brigitte Schroeder-Gudehus and Anne Rasmussen, *Les fastes du progrès, guide des expositions universelles 1851–1992* (Paris: Flammarion, 1992).
6. Préfecture de la Seine, *Annuaire statistique de la ville de Paris 1900* (Paris: Masson, 1902), 516.
7. Figures given by Claude Tapia, 'Paris, ville des congrès de 1850 à nos jours', in *Le Paris des étrangers depuis un siècle*, ed. André Kaspi and Antoine Marès (Paris:

Imprimerie nationale, 1989), 35–43. Figures from other sources, such as the report of the 1900 exhibition, are slightly different but nevertheless similar to the national set.

8 Victor Karady, 'La migration internationale d'étudiants en Europe', *Actes de la recherche en sciences sociales*, no. 145 (2002): 47–60; Pierre Moulinier, *Les étudiants étrangers à Paris au XIXe siècle* (Rennes: PUR, 2011).

9 Christophe Charle, *La République des universitaires (1870–1940)* (Paris: Le Seuil, 1994), and Guillaume Tronchet, 'Savoirs en diplomatie: Une histoire sociale et transnationale de la politique universitaire internationale de la France (années 1870-années 1930)' (PhD diss., University of Paris 1, 2014).

10 Maria Pia Donato, Giovanna Capitelli and Matteo Lafranconi, 'Rome capitale des arts au XIXe siècle', in *Le temps des capitales culturelles (XVIII-XXe siècles)*, ed. Christophe Charle (Seyssel: Champ Vallon, 2009), 65–99, in particular p. 72 and sq.

11 Théodore Duret, *Critique d'avant-garde* (1885; Paris: ENSB, 1998), 42.

12 Gérard Audinet, Juliette Laffon, Suzanne Pagé and Jacqueline Munck, *Le fauvisme ou 'l'épreuve du feu', eruption de la modernité en Europe: Catalogue de l'exposition, Musée d'art moderne* (Paris: Paris Museums, 1999), 451, 462, 464, 477, 481.

13 Catalogue, *La Ruche cité des artistes: 1902–2008, Exhibition at the Palais Lumière* (Evian: Éditions alternatives, 2009).

14 Françoise Cachin, 'Introduction' and 'Notes' in *Manifeste du futurisme* (1909; Paris: Hermann, 1978), 68 (first published in *Le Figaro* on 20 February 1909). Reproduced and commented in Fanette Roche-Pezard, *L'aventure futuriste 1909–1916* (Rome: École française de Rome, 1983).

15 Béatrice Joyeux-Prunel, *Nul n'est prophète en son pays: L'internationalisation de la peinture des avant-gardes parisiennes 1855–1914* (Paris: Nicolas Chaudun/Musée d'Orsay, 2009), 88 and 231.

16 Julie Verlaine, *Les galeries d'art contemporain à Paris 1944–1970* (Paris: Publications de la Sorbonne, 2012), chapters 8 and 9; Raymonde Moulin, *Le marché de la peinture en France* (1967; Paris: Éditions de Minuit, 1989).

17 Jann Pasler, *Composing the Citizen: Music as Public Utility in Third Republic France* (Berkeley: University of California Press, 2009); Myriam Chimènes, *Mécènes et musiciens: Du Salon au concert sous la IIIe République* (Paris: Fayard, 2004); W. Weber, 'Richard Wagner, Concert Life, and Musical Canon in Paris, 1860–1914', unpublished article provided with grateful acknowledgement by the author. To appear in the *Revue de musicologie*.

18 Christophe Charle, *Théâtres en capitales: Naissance de la société du spectacle à Paris, Berlin, Londres et Vienne, 1860–1914* (Paris: Albin Michel, 2008), chapter 8; Christophe Charle, 'Circulations théâtrales entre Paris, Vienne, Berlin, Munich et Stuttgart (1815–1860), Essai de mesure et d'interprétation d'un échange inégal', in *'Die Bienen fremder Literaturen': Der literarische Transfer zwischen Großbritannien, Frankreich und dem deutschsprachigen Raum im Zeitalter der Weltliteratur (1770–*

1850), ed. Norbert Bachleitner and Murray G. Hall (Wiesbaden: Harrassowitz, 2012), 229–260.

19. Christophe Charle, 'Opera in France 1870–1914, between Nationalism and Foreign Imports', in *Opera and Society in Italy and France from Monteverdi to Bourdieu*, ed. Victoria Johnson, Jane F. Fulcher and Thomas Ertman (Cambridge: Cambridge University Press, 2007), 243–266.

20. Julien Tiersot, 'Promenades musicales à l'Exposition', in *Le Ménestrel* (Paris: Librairie Fischbacher, 1889), 165–166. See also: Annegret Fauser, *Musical Encounters at the 1889 Paris World's Fair* (Rochester, NY: University of Rochester Press, 2005), chapters 4 and 5.

21. See too the Parisian mythology around the figure or myth of 'la Parisienne' as a quintessence of elegance, preciousness and even erotic charm: Emmanuelle Retaillaud, 'La figure de la Parisienne des années 1760 aux années 1960: Histoire sociale et culturelle d'un type féminin urbain' (PhD diss., University of Paris 1-Panthéon-Sorbonne, Paris, 2016).

22. Amotz Giladi, 'Écrivains étrangers à Paris et constructions d'identité supranationale: Le cas de la panlatinité, 1900–1939' (PhD diss., École des hautes études en sciences sociales, Paris, 2010). For earlier periods see: Blaise Wilfert, 'Paris, la France et le reste … Importations littéraires et nationalisme culturel en France, 1885–1930' (PhD diss., University of Paris 1, Paris, 2003). For later periods see Gisèle Sapiro, *La guerre des écrivains 1940–1953* (Paris: Fayard, 1999), American translation: *The French Writers' War, 1940–1953* (Durham, NC: Duke University Press, 2014).

23. Évelyne Lejeune-Resnick, 'L'idée d'États-Unis d'Europe au Congrès de la paix de 1849', *Revue d'histoire du XIXe siècle* [online], 7 (1991).

24. Victor Hugo, 'Discours d'ouverture au Congrès de la paix 21 août 1849', in *Oeuvres complètes: Politique* (Paris: Robert Laffont, 1989), 299.

25. Georges Haupt, *La Deuxième Internationale 1889–1914* (Paris, La Haye: Mouton, 1964), 106–113.

26. Gilles Candar and Vincent Duclert, *Jean Jaurès* (Paris: Fayard, 2014), 377–378; Vincent Robert, 'La "protestation universelle" lors de l'exécution de Ferrer: Les manifestations d'octobre 1909', *Revue d'histoire moderne et contemporaine*, no. 36 (1989): 245–265.

27. Michel Espagne, *Les juifs allemands à Paris à l'époque de Heine, la translation ashkénaze* (Paris: Presses Universitaires de France, 1996).

28. Delphine Diaz, *Un asile pour tous les peuples? Proscrits, exilés, réfugiés étrangers en France 1813–1852* (Paris: A. Colin, 2014).

29. Kaspi and Marès, *Le Paris des étrangers depuis un siècle*; Antoine Marès and Pierre Milza (eds), *Le Paris des étrangers depuis 1945* (Paris: Publications de la Sorbonne, 1994).

30 Anna Boschetti (ed.), L'espace culturel transnational (Paris: Nouveau Monde éditions, 2010); Anna Boschetti, 'Ismes', du réalisme au post-modernisme: Genèse et usages, pratiques et savants (Paris: CNRS éditions, 2014).

31 Pascale Casanova, La République mondiale des lettres (Paris: Le Seuil, 1999), American translation: The World Republic of Letters (Cambridge, MA: Harvard University Press, 2004).

32 Gisèle Sapiro (ed.), Translatio, le marché de la traduction en France à l'heure de la mondialisation (Paris: CNRS éditions, 2008).

33 Blaise Wilfert, 'Littérature, capitale culturelle et nation à la fin du XIXe siècle, Paul Bourget et Gabriele d'Annunzio entre Paris et Rome 1880–1905', in Charle (ed.), Le temps des capitales culturelles.

34 Blaise Wilfert, 'Cosmopolis et l'Homme invisible: Les importateurs de littérature étrangère en France, 1885–1914', Actes de la recherche en sciences sociales, no. 144 (2002); Blaise Wilfert, 'Traduction littéraire: Approche bibliométrique', in Histoire des traductions en langue française. XIXe siècle 1815–1914, ed. Yves Chevrel, Lieven d'Hulst and Christine Lombez (Lagrasse: Verdier, 2012), 255–344.

35 Boschetti, 'Ismes', du réalisme au post-modernisme, chapter 4; Frédérique Matonti, 'L'anneau de Moebius; La réception en France des formalistes russes', Actes de la recherche en sciences sociales, no. 176–177 (2009): 52–67.

36 Fernand Braudel, Civilisation matérielle, économie et capitalisme, XVe-XVIIIe siècle, vol. 3, Le temps du monde (Paris: A. Colin, 1979), 52–54, American translation: The Perspective of the World (Berkeley: University of California Press, 1992).

37 See Christophe Charle, La dérégulation culturelle: Essai d'histoire des cultures en Europe au XIXe siècle (Paris: Presses Universitaires de France, 2015).

38 Goethe, Conversations with Eckermann (23 October 1828), 574.

39 Verlaine, Les galeries d'art contemporain; Moulin, Le marché de la peinture en France.

40 Patrice Higonnet, Paris capitale mondiale des Lumières au surréalisme (Paris: Tallandier, 2004), American translation: Paris Capital of the World (Cambridge: Belknap Press, 2005).

3

The Socialist World in Global History: From Absentee to Victim to Co-Producer

James Mark and Tobias Rupprecht

'Globalization' in contemporary common parlance has been equated with the globalization of neo-liberalism.[1] In everyday conversation, people will think of deregulation, finance capitalism and cheap labour in Asian countries. Read or hear of 'globalization' in the news and you may be sure that journalists refer to the post-Bretton Woods world economy from the early 1970s. In other words, they will be referring to monetarism, the dwindling efficacy of the nation state, the erosion of welfare and social security, and by the same token to the growth of multinational corporations and a vertically integrated 'global factory' with China as the world's workbench and India as its office. Depending on political sympathies, this process is presented as favouring an ever less restricted exploitation of nature and of the world's poor by a transnational managerial elite and as threatening national and traditional ways of life – or as a chance for non-Western regions to catch up with the economic performance and living standards of Europe, North America and Japan.

Economic and global historians, by contrast, tend to define 'globalization' in a much broader and less normative way, as a not always linear process of increasing interconnectedness of different parts of the globe in not only economic but also political and cultural spheres. This interconnectedness begins, in some accounts, as early as the first urban high civilizations, and gathers pace with the European overseas discoveries from the fifteenth century. Modern globalization, too, long predates Chicago neo-liberal economists, and it came in two waves. The first one in the late nineteenth century, based on enormous technological

---

The authors would like to thank Matthias Middell, Felix Wemheuer, Alena Alamgir and Christina Schwenkel, who commented and provided useful insights that have been incorporated into this chapter.

developments in transport and communication and dominated by the British free trade empire, was brought to a halt with the First World War and the rise of economic nationalism in the wake of the 1929 Great Depression. Some global historians agree that the second wave of modern globalization began in the 1950s against the backdrop of the Cold War. In a world politically divided between capitalist and socialist camps, they contend, a *geteilte Globalisierung* (divided globalization) occurred.[2]

Yet in their assessments of renewed worldwide integrative processes, they neglect the socialist side of the story.[3] For the most part, those historians who do look at the longue durée of globalization have assumed the inevitability of its capitalist neo-liberal form.[4] Accounts of the contestation of neo-liberal globalization have been left to studies of anti-globalization movements from the 1990s onwards, mainly by sociologists and political scientists.[5] There is a grave lacuna in the historiography, particularly considering that the 'socialist world', at the height of its expansion around 1980, encompassed roughly one-third of the world's population.[6] Socialist states were party to all major global conflicts and developments in the second half of the twentieth century; many of them were founding members of important international organizations. The Soviet Union alone was, in the early 1970s, a member of over 200 political (such as the United Nations and its substructures) and non-governmental (such as the Red Cross or the Olympic Committee) organizations. Restrictions on movement of their populations notwithstanding, socialist states were increasingly connected among themselves and with the rest of the world at multiple levels. A global history of the second half of the twentieth century is not possible without them. In this chapter, we address the now growing literature that has begun to take into account the contribution of the socialist world to 'post-war reglobalization' – focusing on the debates, contestations and clashes that marked its evolution. We argue that the second wave of modern globalization was a political, cultural and scientific, as much as an economic, phenomenon, and that it happened within and across both avowedly capitalist and socialist states and regions.

The writing of the socialist story into the literature on globally integrative processes also challenges a model of globalization that focuses for the most part on centre-periphery models, usually juxtaposing the West with the rest, and encourages us to consider the role of periphery-periphery interaction. The idea of Western capitalism as the sole engine of globalization has left us with a distorted view of socialist and Third World states as inward-looking, isolated and cut off from global trends until the long transition to capitalism in the 1980s and 1990s.[7] A too narrow definition of globalization in public discourse is a historical template shaped by the claims of the self-proclaimed winners at these conjunctures. It presents all integrative processes as precursors to a world dominated by neo-liberal forms of globalization and avoids any consideration of more contingent and less linear developments occurring at an earlier date.[8] Even those historians who call for a decentred, less Western-centric and multi-polar approach to modern global history often fail to practise what they preach.[9]

How do we define a 'socialist world' in the post-war period? As a shorthand, we include those states which adapted a variety of forms of socialism that embodied, at different moments and to different degrees, resistance to what they considered capitalist or imperialist forms of political, cultural and economic global integration. Here we include the Soviet Union, socialist Eastern Europe, China, Mongolia, Cuba and Vietnam, together with other states in Asia, Latin America, Africa and the Middle East with a self-declared 'socialist orientation'. We also note that these states were often located in the more marginal zones of the world economy; indeed, as some have argued, socialist revolutions in the twentieth century usually occurred in what world-systems theorists called 'semi-peripheral' or 'peripheral' locations, representing as they did a way of resisting exclusion from the core of the capitalist world system. From this perspective, socialist systems provided strong state-led developmental pathways that promised either a catching up with, or even an eventual challenge to, the dominant capitalist core.[10]

We also wish to draw attention to the difficulties that arise in defining the nature of, and boundaries to, a 'socialist world'. Certainly, similar concepts – the socialist camp, an anti-imperialist world or the 'socialist world system' – were evoked both by contemporaries to assist in the construction of political communities that might challenge the dominance of capitalism, and by scholars who privileged political ideology in their studies of the Cold War.[11] Yet these concepts have also been hotly contested, and often by contemporaries. Mao, for instance, portrayed the Soviet Union, alongside the USA, as part of a 'First World' of imperialism that exploited both a 'Second World' of Europe and Japan and a 'Third World' of less developed states in the Global South that should look to China for leadership. From the 1970s onwards, scholars – particularly those influenced by world-systems theory – challenged the very concept of distinct socialist and capitalist worlds.[12]

It has been suggested that the idea of a 'socialist world' needs itself to be understood as a matter of Cold War discourse, a consequence of the political legitimacy that ideological boundary-making provided for states on both sides of the Cold War.[13] Within socialist states, political and cultural elites intent upon bolstering their regimes needed constantly to reaffirm those ideological divides that gave them legitimacy in a world of growing interconnections, which threatened to undermine the perceived reality of such boundaries.[14] For the purposes of this survey, we do not wish to offer a concrete definition but rather to demonstrate how differing understandings of what constituted the 'socialist world' – or indeed the questioning of whether such an entity ever really existed – have been central to scholars' conceptions of the role of socialist states in globalization.

We discern four chief reasons why the socialist states have for a long time not been accorded a significant role in accounts of globalization. First of all, the study of globalization was born in a moment of high capitalist triumphalism in the 1990s, a moment of confidence for the neo-liberal capitalist system that appeared to rest on the defeat of communism in most regions of the world. In the eyes of the West, the communist world was represented by walls and barbed wire that had prevented the penetration of 'the global', barriers that had only fallen away with the collapse of communist regimes and the spread of liberal capitalism. Forms of socialist global integration and interconnectedness were seen as blind alleys, as oddities outstripped by history. Second, in some cases, the perception of the socialist countries as isolated and self-contained units is a legacy of certain aspects of the communist regimes' own self-understanding and self-representation. Even as many socialist states started to collaborate with international organizations, to contribute to broader debates about the future of society and humanity and to augment their foreign trade, they continued to legitimize themselves through the rhetoric of confrontation: they claimed to be the bulwark against international capitalism, and the great protectors of national cultures. Associating cosmopolitanism with capitalism, communists wrote themselves out of the story of globalization.

Third, those writing histories of countries that had once been state socialist displayed scant desire to write their experience of these systems back into histories of globalization. East European post-Cold War historiography, for instance, was very often rather the search for a new national story after the experience of communist internationalism.[15] Fourth, the division between post-communist and post-colonial scholars has meant that there has been, until recently, little interest in bringing together stories of a wider socialist world, which included Central and Eastern Europe, broad swathes of Central Asia, alongside dozens of states from four continents, from Cuba, Nicaragua and Chile to Vietnam, Laos and Cambodia, from North Korea to Afghanistan, from China to Ethiopia, and from Sri Lanka to Angola and Mozambique.[16]

Here, we will explore the ways in which the absence of the socialist world from the history of modern globalization is currently being challenged, and we will suggest a number of approaches that might be developed in the future. The current reawakening of interest in 'entanglements' within the socialist world also derives, or so we would argue, from a specific political context. The Western triumphalist vision of the 1990s has given way to an acknowledgement that large parts of the former socialist world are not content to blindly follow the path of Western modernization. China resisted the 'liberal' in liberal capitalism and has become a very successful global player in Asia and Africa; Russia has turned away from the West and pursues its ideas of a polycentric world in explicitly anti-Western alliances, which are often built on connections derived from Cold War Soviet internationalism. In Viktor Orbán's Hungary, scholars and political figures have rediscovered links with Moscow and a shared contempt for Western liberalism. Cuba, Venezuela and Nicaragua, the latter again ruled by the former socialist Daniel Ortega, are – at least rhetorically – supporting Russia's neo-imperialism in the South Caucasus and Ukraine.

The secular dictators of Syria and Egypt are enjoying military support from the Kremlin, just as they were fifty years ago. Vietnam, following the Chinese path of communist rule-cum-economic liberalism, is still Russia's strategic partner in the area of military-technical cooperation. Both Egypt and Vietnam have recently signed free trade agreements with the Eurasian Customs Union, Russia's great 'alternative' geopolitical project under Putin. At the same time, there is a growing desire on the left and right of the political spectrum in today's Western world to find alternatives to capitalist globalization. The much-debated connections linking Greece and Cyprus to Russia reveal not only an all but forgotten Orthodox internationalism, but also the fact that some Southern European socialists and nationalists seek to move away from a West-rest model in order to address the variety of globalizing circulations. In these contexts, the histories of alternative globalizations appear relevant to contemporary shifts in geopolitics.

An established way of writing the socialist world into the story of globalization – as a victim

Regional specialists working on Chinese, Soviet and East European history have long considered connections between the socialist world and globalization. Yet, by and large they have not been interested in the question of alternative globalizations or the contribution of socialist states to the emergence of the second wave of modern globalization. In most of these accounts, rather, the socialist world is depicted as being solely the victim of *economic* globalization from the 1970s, following the narrow definition that is most commonly used. Taking the collapse of state socialism in the Soviet Union and Eastern Europe as their cue, these scholars chart the failures of socialist states to integrate effectively into the global economy, and examine how the pressures of neo-liberal globalization sounded the death knell of socialist regimes.[17] Some economists and economic historians argue that the struggle against the Soviet bloc was essentially won by the mid-1970s as, with the penetration of Western investment into this 'socialist periphery' and increasing reliance on Western export markets, the region was already being slowly reintegrated into a capitalist world economy on Western terms.[18]

Socialist states were indeed unable to keep up with Western industrial development and be competitive on the world market after import substitution strategies had lost their lustre in the 1970s. Technology transfer from the West, many scholars rightly claim, had depressing effects on innovation within the bloc, and import of Western consumer goods, virus-like, instilled Western values from within.[19] In what some of them called the 'globalization project' – the deterritorialization of production and capitalism, the increasing dominance of finance and supranational political and economic institutions – planned economies could not keep up.[20] The servicing of debt to Western institutions from the mid-1970s insinuated the processes and values of a Western capitalist system 'from within'; their growing dependency on Western credits left them exposed.[21] In such accounts of deficit and defeat, the socialist world failed to escape from an inward-looking regional integration at a moment when the rest of the world was embracing deterritorialized markets, and when the other 'world peripheries' that had opted for this model of globalization (such as the East Asian Tiger economies) were catching up economically with the West.

Some take the story even further back: according to Oscar Sanchez-Sibony's account *Red Globalization*, the power of the Cold War story of superpower rivalry has long obscured the fact that the Soviet Union was never a powerful economy. Rather, it was no larger than that of France or of the UK, and was therefore never really capable of mounting a challenge to a US-dominated global economy, whatever its propaganda claimed.[22] Indeed, the idea of the Soviet Union as an 'Upper Volta with rockets'[23] dates back at least to the 1980s and reminds us that the later Cold War was not really based on the fear of a viable economic alternative to Western capitalism; rather, it was a geopolitical struggle and one over different approaches to the political and cultural organization of modern non-Western societies. As early as 1968, Samuel Huntington observed in his *Political Order in Changing Societies* that the strength of Soviet communism was not in its economics, but in the political theory and practice of Leninism.[24] Sanchez-Sibony's thesis reflects a contemporary tendency to dismiss Russia as no more than a regional power, and has less to say about the attraction of the Soviet model for Third World leaders and intellectuals well into the 1980s. The Union of Soviet Socialist Republics (USSR) was certainly more than only a 'second-best partner of the Global South' in such socialist states as Vietnam, Ethiopia, Angola and Cuba. Countless visitors and admirers abroad believed in the political and moral superiority of the Soviet system, and so did many Soviet citizens.

All these deficit stories, powerful as some of them are in their analysis of the economic underdevelopment of socialist economies, tend to project today's neo-liberal definition of globalization back to the 1950s and 1960s. In so doing, they present state socialism as a project that was doomed to fail from the beginning, destined not to keep up with economic developments in the West, and to miss the digital and ecological course of post-industrial modernity. Those scholars who adopt this perspective fail to acknowledge that in the post-war world many in the West did fear that such an alternative was indeed viable.

Within this literature, accordingly, '1989' becomes the year when the forces of globalization and 'deterritorialization' finally caught up with the Eastern bloc.[25] Gale Stokes describes 1989 as 'removing a temporary roadblock to globalization, ending traditional colonialism, and permitting Eastern Europe to enter post-history – 1989 becomes less a revolutionary moment and more an enabling moment that cleared the deck for underlying processes to proceed towards whatever lies ahead'.[26] Bill Clinton echoed this train of thought as he announced the establishment of the North American Free Trade Agreement in 1993: 'If we learn anything from the collapse of the Berlin Wall and the fall of the governments in Eastern Europe, even a totally controlled society cannot resist the winds of change that economics and technology and information flow have imposed in this world of ours.'[27] Jürgen Habermas wrote of the 'rectifying revolutions' of 1989, which represented the idea that, as Talcott Parsons put it, 'the great civilisations of the world would converge towards the institutional and cultural configurations of Western society'.[28]

True enough, in the long run, globalizing forces contributed to the erosion of the legitimacy of socialist regimes, also in – even for East European standards quite extraordinary – economically nationalist countries like Romania, which had never experimented with market socialism. Ironically, Ceaușescu's neo-

Stalinist regime fell from power because he, unlike his East European colleagues, insisted on repaying foreign debts in order to maintain Romania's autarky, and underestimated the popular backlash to sinking living standards.[29] And quite understandably, the enthusiasm about the 'Wende' and the liberation of Eastern Europe from authoritarian communism superseded other ways of viewing recent history. Yet, while the pressures of neo-liberal globalization are clearly an important part of the story of the decline of the socialist world, we close off many other illuminating ways of considering the role of the socialist world in the emergence of modern global interconnectedness by defining our questions primarily in terms of the victory of neo-liberal capitalist globalization. We will therefore now consider how it is that scholars are beginning to write other actors from the socialist or non-capitalist world into the story of globalization.

The socialist world as co-producer of modern globalization

We should not consider the socialist world to be solely the victim of increasing interconnectedness; if we go back to the 1950s, we discover that many socialist states drove new forms of it. Questioning accounts of globalization that start in the early 1970s with the rise of a finance capitalism, some scholars seek rather to view new globalizing impulses as a response to the acceleration of decolonization in the 1950s and the apparent opportunities this opened up for recasting international trade. As global trading routes shaped by empire began to disintegrate, they contend, the form of what would later become known as globalization was 'up for grabs'. The swing back to an internationalization of trade in the late 1950s followed a period of isolationist economics that had lasted since the 1930s – a shift in which the socialist world played an important role.

Soviet and East European planning in particular can be considered one of the main globalizing forces of the mid- to late twentieth century that proved attractive to decolonizing states in the Global South looking to build their own economic sovereignty in the late 1950s and 1960s.[30] A good number of post-colonial states from Indonesia to Tanzania drew inspiration for their nation-building from the authoritarian socialism of the Eastern bloc.[31] New models of market socialism developed in Eastern Europe became of interest in East Asia and Africa from the 1970s onwards.[32] Networks of experts circulated throughout the socialist world. Architects, for instance, oversaw projects in post-colonial Africa, from Zanzibar to Accra; in East Asia, from Hanoi to Pyongyang; and in Latin America, from Havana to Santiago de Chile. The 'travelling architecture' of the socialist world served quite literally to cement a shared imagery on a global scale. Its constructions are a visible and tangible legacy of such contacts all over the former socialist world, and in some places its popularity lasted: witness the ongoing construction of North Korean statues in the style of socialist realism all over Africa, from Senegal to Botswana, and from Zimbabwe to Angola.[33]

China's industrialization began with one variant of socialist globalization, when the USSR invested heavily after the 1949 revolution. One-third of all projects in China's first five-year plan were financed and executed by the USSR and East European states. Tens of thousands of advisers and technicians from the socialist world flocked to all parts of the country. An even higher number of Chinese students and skilled workers were trained in other socialist countries.[34] China in the 1950s was influenced by the Soviet model of society in spheres from education to agriculture, from the army to the state party, and from cultural institutions to labour camps. Odd Arne Westad thus calls this transfer 'history's biggest foreign assistance program', which has profoundly shaped modern China.[35] As late as 2002, one-third of the members of the Chinese Communist Party's Politburo had studied in the Soviet Union and/or Eastern Europe; to this day, the educational, legal and political systems in China still bear signs of that Soviet influence. Ironically, the Chinese Communist Party's nemesis, the Guomindang, had also taken its cue for the build-up of their one-party dictatorship, mass mobilization and propaganda from Leninism, when Chiang Kai-shek was still enjoying Stalin's support in the 1920s. His Soviet-educated son Chiang Ching-kuo, known as Nikolay Elizarov during his twelve years in Moscow and the Urals, reformed the Chinese military along Soviet lines in the 1930s, and later oversaw Taiwan's economic miracle in the 1970s and eventually its transition to democracy in the 1980s.[36]

A crucial element of globalization was the technical development of the infrastructure of transport, communication and energy. Assessments of the construction of railways, of cars and highways, of an international air traffic system, and of international telephone networks and mass media in the West have found only few equivalents in histories of the socialist world.[37] It would certainly be of interest to know if and how trips on cheap Aeroflot and LOT tickets, or the expansion of telephone networks between East European states, or the construction of roads in Southeast Asia contributed to a 'shrinking' of time and space and an altered self-perception of the interconnectedness between socialist states. They certainly contributed to increased labour migration between socialist states: ever higher numbers of Cuban, Angolan, Mozambican and Vietnamese guest workers came to Eastern Europe.[38] Labourers, experts and companies from across the socialist camp worked together on large-scale infrastructure projects, on the construction of the Druzhba (Friendship) oil pipeline between 1958 and 1964, for example, or on the Soyuz (Brotherhood) gas pipeline (1978–83).[39] Even in states with very tight border controls, such as the German Democratic Republic (GDR) and the USSR, improved and affordable transport systems meant that many citizens could travel in their holidays to other states of the socialist world – and often brought home lasting impressions of the economic and political situation abroad.[40] Some scholars have traced the post-Cold War legacies of such travel and exchanges. Susan Bayly coined the term 'socialist ecumene' to describe the endurance of socialist-era values in forms of trade and assistance to other parts of the world in a similar peripheral position to the neo-liberal globalized order.[41] Socialist-era trading networks and labour migration from Eastern Europe to the Far East still survive, while patterns of migration established across the Comecon states now shape patterns of transnational religious evangelism.[42]

One of the most direct links between the local and the global within the socialist world was the presence of thousands of students from Third World countries in Eastern Europe. Experiences were clearly mixed: some experienced racism, or were dismayed by the degree of poverty or the lack of freedom of expression.[43] Nevertheless, many others were left with positive impressions of their stays and returned not as communists but nonetheless with a sense of gratitude and respect towards their host countries.[44] For citizens of the socialist world, the presence of foreign students confirmed a somewhat paternalistic sense of the economic and cultural superiority of their own societies: it was the rest of the world, after all, that came to learn from them. Alumni from Eastern bloc universities were spread across many countries of the Global South, and some rose to prominent positions. Beyond the aforementioned Chinese political elite, they include Chile's president Michelle Bachelet, who holds a medical degree from the GDR, and also Angola's president José Eduardo dos Santos, the Palestinian president Mahmud Abbas, and Iran's Supreme Leader Ali Khamenei, who all studied in the Soviet Union. Former political leaders from the Global South with degrees from the socialist world include South Africa's Thabo Mbeki, Mali's Amadou Touré, Honduras's Porfirio Lobo Sosa and Guyana's Bharrat Jagdeo. Hafiz al-Assad, Hosni Mubarak and many more Syrians and Egyptians spent considerable periods of time in the Soviet Union for military training.

Many Vietnamese cabinet members obtained university degrees in socialist Eastern Europe. Norodom Sihamoni, the Cambodian king, spent most of his childhood at schools in Czechoslovakia.[45] An estimated 100,000 students from

Soviet universities, and many more from other socialist states, returned to their home countries. Today, post-socialist countries profit from the links that the invitation of students had created. Many members of Vietnamese political and economic elites today, for instance, are still fluent in Russian, German and, to a lesser extent, Hungarian and Polish. Among the students from developing countries, there were even theologians, who came to study Orthodox Christianity in Leningrad and Bucharest, and Islam in Tashkent, from the 1960s onwards. Their numbers were not as impressive, but these contacts evoke a sense of belonging along the lines of religion (Serbian, Romanian, Greek, Egyptian, Ethiopian, Armenian and Palestinian Orthodox Christians as well as Arab and Central Asian Muslims), which often reflected geopolitical alliances that remain influential to this day.[46]

'Socialist globalization' should not only be seen as a transfer from the 'Second World' to the 'Third'; the Soviets sometimes gained insights about development from their interactions with 'Third World' partners.[47] It was a multi-directional story – beneficiaries were also benefactors.[48] Chinese advisers would thus finance projects, and send experts, around the socialist world.[49] Africa and the Middle East were of particular interest to them following the 1950s. In the wake of the Sino-Soviet split, China competed for leadership of the developing world with both the West and the Eastern bloc: by 1964, China had developed a policy of economic and technical aid that was offered without conditions.[50] The best known project was the Chinese financed Tanzania-Zambia railway inaugurated in 1975, which was used to demonstrate the possibilities of two countries united in a common socialist vision.[51] The ideology of Maoism also appealed to the critics of the conservative turn in Eastern bloc socialism, and to radical anti-imperialists in the Third World and the West.[52] So-called 'South-South connections' between socialist countries and movements also became important: from the mid-1970s onwards, the Cubans, often financed by the Soviets, organized their own military, educational, medical, administrative and civilian assistance programmes in Angola, as well as military support for the Derg government in Ethiopia.[53]

The very idea of a common anti-imperialist world located on the world's peripheries, a trailblazer, it was hoped, for an advanced socialist world, provided a coherent world view for many political decision-makers, cultural figures and citizens – and created global links and transnational communities. Some of these came together in international organizations. Indeed, according to Johanna Bockman, who has sought to recover the history of the 'Second'-'Third World' relationship as a nexus of alternative non- and even anti-Western globalization:

if we examine economic globalization more closely and from the perspective of Second and Third World institutions, we can see that the Non-Aligned Movement, the Second World, and the Third World more broadly worked hard to create a global economy in the face of active resistance by the United States and other current and former colonial powers, which sought to maintain the economic status quo of the colonial system.

She then argues: 'only later, in the 1980s and 1990s, after the defeat of Second and Third World internationalism, could the United States and other core capitalist countries co-opt and exploit the emergent global economy for their own benefit, and appear as agents, rather than enemies of globalization'.[54]

Whether these forces had the capacity to influence a still powerful post-war international capitalism is an open question. The Soviet *economic* threat was limited. But what is crucial here is the fact that new progressive forces in the so-called 'Second' and 'Third' Worlds perceived they had the power to do so, and that Western powers at least in part believed them. Many in the 1960s, Che Guevara among them, believed that what was later called globalization had some socialist and anti-imperialist content; they advocated free trade that might break earlier patterns of imperial protectionism. The United Nations Commission for Trade and Development (UNCTAD) played a crucial role: its leaders fought for the creation of trading blocs that would keep the supply of raw materials and industrial production within regions and deprive Western metropoles of their capacity to capture previous levels of profit from global trade. Eastern bloc countries were often reluctant to fully commit themselves to a region-to-region project which, they saw, was led by the Global South: they were often more enthusiastic about the United Nations Industrial Development Organization (UNIDO), through which they could finance bilateral development projects in the Global South.

In the 1970s, these earlier initiatives developed into the 'New International Economic Order' – a political imaginary that stood for a real economic alliance, taken seriously throughout the world, that gave real form to the idea, for a short time and in the wake of the 'oil shock', that the global hegemony of the industrial North might be coming to an end.[55] Such initiatives and contexts thus offered opportunities for new forms of global interconnection. Regardless of the true import of this challenge, such attempts are worthy of note as a reminder that globalization has historically been a contested process with multiple forms.

Even if we remain sceptical about the role of the socialist world in the globalization story, we might nevertheless be prepared to acknowledge that the perception of difference and threat was a crucial dynamic in the creation of globalized forms of trade and culture following the 1950s. The spectre of socialist globalization created new forms of capitalist globalization, such as those we see today: US elites, for instance, enabled the consolidation of the power of their oil multinationals in the 1960s – against campaigns to break them up as excessive monopolies – in order to counter the Soviet challenge.[56] The US was also prepared to let Japanese and Korean economies grow without the interference of their corporations while guaranteeing access to their large home markets, rather than let them become peripheries open to other ideological influences.[57] Indeed, the rise of neo-liberalism and the Washington Consensus can be understood as a reaction to the power of the challenge from a new alterative world order in the 1970s.[58]

Many global integrative after the Second World War in fact served to stabilize regimes in the socialist world. Within Europe, the transnational integration necessary to produce the so-called 'Eastern bloc' created a remarkably stable economic and political structure for over four decades.[59] Seeking to get beyond the idea of the 'bloc' as simply an artificial construct imposed by force, scholars now trace the elite and expert connections that laid the foundations for common identities and transnational circulations, which in addition helped to create an international community transcending its constituent nations.[60] In recent years, various studies have focused on the advantages that different countries could accrue through political and economic cooperation, whereas others have emphasized the overbearing and deleterious role of the Soviets in maintaining these relationships.[61] Questioning the narrative of the socialist world as a victim of globalization, there is reason to argue that, following the early 1970s, increasing global interconnectedness appeared to be stabilizing the socialist world in Europe. Trade with the West brought modern technology and foreign exchange. This 'transition from endogenous to exogenous modernization'[62] was most pronounced in Poland and Hungary, where it improved – at least in the short term – living standards and thus stifled popular resistance to communist rule.[63] Nevertheless, East European states remained suspicious of excessive integration into Comecon, and in the case of poorer states, such as Romania, they were resistant to any attempts to enforce a division of labour between Comecon states, which would, they feared, consign them to a periphery within the Eastern bloc. This partly explains why the encounter between the 'Second' and 'Third' Worlds could for the most part not be organized regionally but emerged as a series of bilateral relationships between East European countries and their partners in Africa, Asia and the rest of the South. Indeed, bloc countries often found themselves engaged in competitive 'proxy wars in expertise exports to the "Third World"'.[64]

The Helsinki Accords – mostly considered today for their long-term destabilizing consequences – also initially provided political legitimacy to communist parties in the East, as their rule and their states' borders were recognized internationally.[65] The decision of the Organization of the Petroleum Exporting Countries (OPEC), a cartel of oil exporting countries from the Global South, to raise the price of crude petroleum, was a portent of the decreasing influence of the West in global politics – and flushed money into Soviet coffers.[66] A paternalistic stance towards an ever more visible Third World and the admiration voiced by the many visitors to the motherlands of socialism reassured many citizens of the superiority of their own system, if not to the West then at least to the rest of the world. In this view, the disintegration of the socialist camp appears as much a consequence of internal factors as it was an undermining from outside.[67] There is reason to believe, indeed, that it was an active repositioning of the political leaders themselves in Eastern Europe and in the Soviet Union that brought about the changes of the 1980s that eventually led to the unforeseen and unplanned end of state socialism. This repositioning drew on new models of economic and cultural development across the world, and on semi-peripheral modernization projects – a process that had become possible only thanks to a revived, post-war socialist internationalism that flourished during the second wave of modern globalization.

In order to gauge the impact of globalizing processes, it helps to remind ourselves that these were actually two parallel developments for peoples east of the Iron Curtain.[68] On the one hand, socialist states integrated among themselves, at both the state level and between the communist parties, and with non-aligned states from the Global South, under the putative tutelage of both the Soviet Union and Maoist China – and positioned themselves against an allegedly hostile, imperialist, capitalist West. On the other hand, European socialist states in particular were part of, and, as we argue here, co-producers of, many modern social, political and cultural developments that happened all over the Northern hemisphere, irrespective of Cold War divisions.[69] Research has been produced recently on both integrative processes, although they often remain separated in the scholarly literature.

Much of the scholarship on integrative processes *within* the socialist world and the Third World focuses on those elements that substantiate the idea of the Cold War divide – ironically, this is a perspective that conservative, triumphalist Cold War scholars share with contemporary radical leftist historians. Yet, it is important to question whether it makes sense to describe a socialist world apart from a capitalist world order. Should we not rather focus on parallel developments and entangledness across a politically divided world?[70] Some scholars, playing down the importance of the East-West conflict, suggest that a shared industrial modernity originated across the 'North' and was exported to the 'South', a process in which the socialist world played a major role, as a co-producer and globalizer of industrial modernity. Both capitalist and socialist states encouraged urbanization, the belief in progress, secularization, Fordist production, technological development (and environmental damage), as well as an appreciation of science and higher education, the merits of hygiene and medicine, mass mobilization, international integration, the spread of bureaucracy and efforts to control and manage populations.[71] In this view, a socialist conception of modern civilization was not so very different from the way it was imagined in the West.[72] The socialist and capitalist worlds may have claimed to be different: for instance, socialist states often claimed that their developmental policies were superior because they respected national cultures and tradition, which led to more equal outcomes. Nevertheless, there were frequently many more similarities than differences.[73]

The growth of networks of expertise that transcended the 'Iron Curtain' illustrates this point. Disciplines aimed at a world opening up in the late 1950s – such as international economics or revived area studies – arose at similar points in the West and in the Eastern bloc.[74] Experts based in such centres were certainly not shut off from the capitalist world: many travelled, worked for UN organizations and alongside Western colleagues, and engaged in broader debates around, for example, underdevelopment, inequality, culture and heritage.[75] Countries of socialist orientation in Africa and Southeast Asia sought expertise from both camps: 24 per cent of the more than 3,000 experts working in Vietnam in 1979 were from non-socialist countries, and the Vietnamese sent their students for training to places such as Sweden.[76] Scholars in the European parts of the socialist world, if not always in the others, had their own concepts of world and global history. What was called global studies in the West assumed the form of Soviet *globalistika*, surfacing in institutes for world economy and journals of world history such as the Hungarian *Világtörténelem*.

Thus one can argue that globalizing impulses emerging from socialist states in fact fostered enhanced integration between capitalist and socialist worlds rather than serving to reinforce an alternative. The attempts at building a specifically socialist globalization in the 1960s laid the foundations for a 'transideological' integrative globalization of the 1970s. Some socialist states gave up on exporting a specific socialist industrial modernity to the Global South, now viewing less developed countries as a source of raw materials, just as their Western counterparts did.[77] By the mid-1970s, under the conditions of détente, so-called 'tripartite' industrial projects brought together West and East European firms in development projects in Africa and elsewhere.[78] Links between West and East European economies proliferated: joint enterprises were established in Hungary from 1973; Central European countries began to privilege export to West European markets; Comecon and the European Community strengthened their ties in the 1970s and 1980s.[79] 'Export processing zones', within which Western companies could create enterprises, were established in socialist states in Eastern Europe and Southeast Asia – such innovations brought capitalist practices into the socialist world.[80]

Agency, globalization and the transformations of state socialism

A shift in emphasis from 'globalization dismantling socialism' to 'socialist globalization' encourages us to ask new questions about the transition of 1989/91. Accepting the agency of the socialist world in the context of globalization has led some scholars to investigate the complex relationships across ideological frontiers in the late twentieth century. Such an approach has had particular resonance in the case of Southeast Asia, where socialist elites enjoyed far more success in negotiating a globalizing path while retaining power. The role of the political elite behind China's 'globalizing turn' from 1978 has now received much attention.[81] This was a propitious moment for the Chinese state to engineer such a shift: Western economies were weak, international capital was looking for new areas to invest in, and Singapore and South Korea provided a model of global transformation that retained strong state control.[82] They displayed some interest in East European experiments with the 'socialist market' – which they eventually rejected.[83] China, instead, drew important lessons from the models provided by both Japan and the East Asian Tigers.[84]

Some writers have wondered how and why it was that Asian socialist states were able to negotiate new global pressures far more effectively than the European socialist states, and why the one-party state there did not collapse.[85] Unlike dictatorships in Eastern Europe and Latin America, they were not fettered by foreign debt that gave outsiders too much leverage, and they had at their disposal larger overseas ethnic communities that were willing to invest in their economies.[86] Internal factors also made a difference: China, unlike Eastern

Europe, was not beset with urgent demands for material well-being encouraged by the party itself.[87]

The agency that is afforded to elites in East Asian socialist countries is usually absent in accounts that focus on the Eastern bloc; the dominant narrative for a long time has been one of defeat by powerful economic forces that originated outside the region itself. Insofar as the East European transition is connected to global history, this is mainly in terms of its corrosive effects across the rest of the socialist world. The collapse of state socialism in the Eastern bloc helped to delegitimize leftist movements in Africa and Latin America, and removed a fear of communism among the right across the entire world, which in turn, in places like South Africa, enabled a range of political forces to embrace democracy.[88]

Nevertheless, one should consider alternative stories. There is much to be said for the view that the integration of the socialist world into a globalized economy cannot be viewed simply as a story of defeat, but one of common contributions to the creation of modern globalized economic forms from the 1970s. Leftist scholars such as Leslie Sklair explored the rise of 'socialist multinationals' in the late 1970s, which were 'more active in the rest of the world than TNCs [transnational corporations] from capitalist countries were in Comecon countries'.[89] The Soviet Union's desire to protect their dollar reserves was instrumental in the late 1950s in the creation of the so-called 'Eurodollar market', which was to become by far the largest source of global finance in the late twentieth century.[90]

These socialist elites and experts, as co-producers of globalization, contributed to the transformations of the socialist world in the 1980s and 1990s towards free markets and global integration, and, in some cases (as in Eastern Europe), towards liberal democracy. We would do well to remember that these changes, to varying degrees from state to state, were dominated by elites. We still do not know enough about the way in which late socialist elites reimagined the world around them, and the extent to which they adopted new political and economic languages from across the world. We still lack stories of how economic terms and concepts associated with globalization – such as the international division of labour, multi-polarity and interdependence – entered the lexicon that expert groups and political decision-makers used to communicate. To what extent was the confidence of elites in a specifically socialist future undermined by, for example, the abandonment of Marxism-Leninism by China[91] or the embracing of liberal democracy by those struggling against right-wing authoritarianism in Southern Europe and then in Latin America? How did the everyday interaction with a new globalizing economy, through trade and thus 'transideological' collaborations between enterprises, influence 'global thinking'? To what extent were socialist economists and leaders of industries that engaged with the world market important drivers of change? Important, too, were the relationships of socialist experts to political elites: when were they successful in convincing leaders to face new forms of global economics, and when did they fail?[92]

Johanna Bockman claimed that East European socialist economists were co-contributors to the neo-liberal economic consensus of the late twentieth century. Her work explored the resilience of neoclassical economics within the Eastern bloc and the belief of socialist economists that markets were compatible with multiple types of social and political systems, including the socialist state. Furthermore, she examined the way in which experts, particularly from Hungary and Yugoslavia, were able to promote the idea of markets 'across the Iron Curtain' from the mid-1970s onwards.[93] In countries such as Poland, Hungary and Russia, prior to the formal political collapse of their socialist systems, there was already a substantial domestic consensus behind neo-liberal reforms. This consensus ensured that such reforms were maintained despite their deleterious social consequences in the early 1990s.[94] Thus the story of 1989 as a simple West-East transfer, in which the influence of Western advisers as bearers of a new ideology is paramount, may well be overstated.[95]

Adjusting to new global flows did not necessarily mean an adaptation to Western concepts of social, economic or political organization. The rise of new authoritarian capitalisms has the potential to prompt a rethinking of our history of this period. The 1980s were not only about a Westernization of the East and the rise of a new democratic market culture; they also witnessed the circulation of a range of different solutions for a socialist world in crisis. Yet the now long-standing emphasis on 1989/91 as a moment of defeat diminished interest in these alternative models of globalization for a region outside the core of the world economy – which existed right up until the collapse of state socialism in Europe. More work could be done on the appeal of authoritarian transitions in the 'world market' in the 1980s; for instance, in Eastern Europe there were political elites who attempted to open up to new global forces while seeking to maintain the one-party state. The seemingly successful authoritarian models of integration into the global economy developed in Singapore, Malaysia, South Korea and Chile (under Pinochet) were influential in this regard.[96] The fact that important authoritarian transition models continued to circulate and influence actors in the socialist and formerly socialist world, such as Putin's Russia, Orbán's Hungary and Duda's Poland, lent these earlier experiences a new relevance. Attempts at an alternative globalization in the form of Russia's Eurasian project and economic and political links with former Soviet partners have emerged in response to the pressures of neo-liberal globalization.[97]

Conclusion: rethinking globalization and the legacies of state socialism

The second wave of modern globalization in the economic, cultural and political spheres following the 1950s included the socialist world as well. The Somali-Italian writer Igiaba Scego reminded her readers how, in the 1970s, she could easily travel between Mogadishu, Rome and Prague (where her brother studied) and how this compared favourably with the restriction of movement she and her Somali family face today. From her perspective, the world of the Cold War, which Europeans associate with barbed wire, was in some ways more interconnected.[98] The European, Asian, African and Latin American parts of the socialist world increasingly integrated among themselves as much as with the rest of the world. If it were not for socialist globalization, there would have been no Mozambican and Angolan contract workers in Saxony, no Chinese development aid workers in Tirana, no Soviet-Cuban encounters in Addis Ababa, no Cuban female factory workers in Hungary and no Polish engineers in Ghana. North Koreans would not have shared their preferred architectural styles with colleagues in Bucharest, their expertise in stadium choreography with Ethiopians and their military strategies with Mexican and Namibian guerrillas. South Yemenites would not have studied together with Sri Lankans at universities in Ukraine, and Vietnamese and Cuban doctors would not have worked in Congo and Angola.

These encounters have left political, cultural and economic legacies all over the world. The hundreds of thousands of alumni from 'socialist' universities work in almost all the states of the Global South. Vietnamese restaurants are legion in Berlin, and so are North Korean statues all over Africa. There is a large presence of Russian tourists, artists and freelance online workers in Southeast Asia. Even the North Atlantic Treaty Organization and the US have drawn on some of the connections of the socialist world: in 2003, former Yugoslav engineers were enlisted in the search for Saddam Hussein as it was they who had built many of the dictator's underground bunkers. In the Afghanistan War, Czech army pilots, who had been trained with Soviet technology during the Cold War, instructed both Afghans and Americans to fly Russian helicopters better suited to local conditions than US-made machines.[99] There is no socialist content left in these connections, and neither is there in the fact that Russian businessmen buy up entire islands off Cambodia, that Russian warships cruise off the Venezuelan coast and that Chinese companies dominate the mining and construction business in most African states. But the roots of all these contacts go back to entanglements within the socialist world during the Cold War.

The revolutions of 1989/91, as we have argued in this chapter, did not bring about a sudden exposure to globalization in the socialist world. Rather, socialist and now ex-socialist countries adapted their relationship to these globalizing forms. Some states came to adopt, and keep to, Western rules. Others, such as Putin's Russia, look for new alternative forms that echo the relationships of the socialist era. The socialist project in these regions might be envisaged as one episode in a longer story of searching for political and economic alternatives, particularly in what have been called the global 'peripheries' or 'semi-peripheries'. The notion of the victory of neo-liberal capitalism in this conflict has been used to gloss over the more complex range of legacies of socialist-era trade and geopolitical imaginaries and alliances. In this sense, we might think of 1989 not as the victory of Western liberal capitalism but as the victory of its historical narrative, which has exerted a powerful influence over the academic world. It has enforced the orthodoxy that the antithesis of socialism was the market, democracy and globalization.

Writing about the transformation of Southeast Asia, Christina Schwenkel notes the change from a centrally planned economy to a competitive, mixed market regime ('market socialism') is often framed in dichotomous terms that suggest a trajectory of progress and rupture from the past: from isolation to integration; closure to opening; stasis to development. These oppositions contrast an era of presumed socialist immobility, inwardness and constraint to one of capitalist mobility, externality, newness, and release. There are obvious problems with this teleology that ignores continuities between past and present economic and sociocultural practices.[100]

As a consequence of this bias, there are many stories waiting to be uncovered that are likely to complicate and add nuance to this narrative. In the context of shifting geopolitical alignments that echo some of the relationships of the Cold War, and new leftist critiques of 'neo-liberal globalization', scholars began to reconsider socialism's attempts in the mid-twentieth century to globalize on different terms. There is a growing sense that, if we are ever to do justice to a history that proclaims itself to be 'global', it is necessary to study the interconnectedness of all parts of the planet.

Enhanced interconnectedness or globalization is not synonymous with Westernization. Scholars have too often fallen into the trap of a retroactive teleology, in which all worldwide entanglements were predestined to finally merge into free markets and liberal democracies. Recent studies have considered various attempts from new Western socialist 'peripheries' to challenge imperial trading networks or the construction of a new antiimperialist global imaginary, or have addressed the circulation of ideas about modernization, tradition or rights 'from the periphery'. Other scholars have begun writing socialism into the history of globalization, not by highlighting its distinctiveness but rather by showing its similarity with its capitalist counterpart as it sought to bring industrial modernity and social progress to the globe. Indeed, some have noted that through studying the actors in globalization – such as experts working together in international organizations or through industrial cooperation between the Eastern bloc and the West in the Global South – that the socialist and capitalist worlds of the North were brought together. Such a perspective encourages us to consider how socialist elites themselves helped develop some of the globalizing forces that their regimes had to contend with.

Studies are now indicating the variety of ways in which socialist states attempted to cope with globalization. In all states of the socialist world, to varying degrees, a number of reformers believed that one-party state socialism might be able to guide their countries on a journey towards an authoritarian globalized capitalism. While the story of Chinese success in this regard is well known, attempts in other states of the socialist world, especially the dominating East European ones, are drowned out by the celebratory narratives of 1989 produced in the expectation of a long-lived unipolarity. As those studying the legacies of socialism are showing us, the idea of a socialist world, the geopolitical ambitions it nurtured, the attitudes towards international relations it inspired, the transnational communities based around collectivism, social rights and tradition it created and the trade routes it built have by no means disappeared. The study of socialist globalization is not a matter of nostalgia. It helps us to understand not only the forms of the second wave of modern globalization following the 1950s, but also the behaviour of entire world regions and the many shifts occurring in contemporary geopolitics.

Notes

1. For a discussion of the concept, see: Philipp Ther, *Die neue Ordnung auf dem alten Kontinent: Geschichte des neoliberalen Europa* (Berlin: Suhrkamp, 2014), 22–26.
2. On 'divided globalization', see: Jürgen Osterhammel and Niels Petersson, *Geschichte der Globalisierung: Dimensionen, Prozesse, Epochen* (Munich: Beck, 2003); Akira Iriye (ed.), *Global Interdependence: The World after 1945* (Cambridge, MA: Harvard University Press, 2014).
3. On the need to theorize 'alternative globalizations', see: Leslie Sklair, 'A Transnational Framework for Theory and Research in the Study of Globalization', in *Frontiers of Globalization Research: Theoretical and Methodological Approaches*, ed. Ino Rossi (Berlin: Springer, 2007), 93–108; Leslie Sklair, 'Challenges of Globalization Theory to World-systems Analysis', in *Routledge Handbook of World-systems Analysis*, ed. Salvatore Babones and Christopher Chase-Dunn (Abingdon /New York: Routledge, 2012), 189–192; Robert J. Holton, *Making Globalization* (Basingstoke: Palgrave, 2005). On the socialist world's relationship to globalization, see also: Zsuzsa Gille, 'Is There a Global Post-socialist Condition?', *Global Society* 1 (2010): 9–30, esp. 9–11.
4. For globalization as a form of Western imperialism: Andreas Eckert and Shalini Randeira, *Vom Imperialismus zum Empire: Nicht-westliche Perspektiven auf Globalisierung* (Frankfurt: Suhrkamp, 2009).
5. Nick Bisley, *Rethinking Globalization* (New York: Palgrave Macmillan, 2007); Elisabeth Mudimbe Boyi, *Beyond Dichotomies: Histories, Identities, Cultures, and the Challenge of Globalization* (New York: State University Press, 2002).
6. Contemporary political science took the claim of an expanding Soviet-dominated world very seriously indeed: see, e.g., Raymond L. Garthoff, *Détente and Confrontation: American-Soviet Relations from Nixon to Reagan* (Washington, DC: Brooklings Institute, 1985).
7. For an account along these lines: André Steiner, 'The Globalisation Process and the Eastern Bloc Countries in the 1970s and 1980s', *European Review of History* 2 (2014): 165–181.
8. We also note Lefebvre's distinction between 'mondialisation' (the process of coming to conceptualize the globe in its totality) and the more recent phenomenon of 'globalisation', which describes only one (mainly economic and technological) form of this, and is generally associated with its neo-liberal variant. Our challenge is to suggest that a socialist variant also existed and is worth investigating: hence, we are more interested in broadening out the term 'globalisation' than critiquing it for its limitations. For a useful discussion, see: Stuart Elden, 'Mondialisation before Globalization: Lefebvre and Axelos', in *Space, Difference, Everyday Life: Reading*

Henri Lefebvre, ed. Kanishka Goonewardena, Stefan Kipfer, Richard Milgrom and Christian Schmid (Abingdon: Routledge, 2008), 80–93.

9   Even Iriye does not treat the socialist world as an active player in the creation of 'global interdependence'.

10 As Manfred Kossok put it, the twentieth century was the 'era of peripheral revolutions': Manfred Kossok, 'Das 20. Jahrhundert – eine Epoche der peripheren Revolution?', in *Manfred Kossok, Ausgewählte Schriften, Bd. 3: Zwischen Reform und Revolution. Übergänge von der Universal- zur Globalgeschichte*, ed. Katharina Middell and Matthias Middell (Leipzig: UniVerlag, 2000), 289–296. World-systems theorists have been particularly interested in the catching up role played by socialist states within the broader global economy: see, e.g., Immanuel Wallerstein, *The Capitalist World-economy* (Cambridge: Cambridge University Press, 1979), 284. See also: Manuela Boatcă, 'Semiperipheries in the World-system: Reflecting Eastern European and Latin American Experiences', *Journal of World-systems Research* 2 (2006): 334–336, here 322; József Böröcz, 'Dual Dependency and Property Vacuum: Social Change on the State Socialist Semiperiphery', *Theory and Society* 1 (1992): 77–104.

11 On the concept of the socialist world system, see Jonas Flury, 'The Political Idea of a Socialist World System', paper presented at the conference "Alternative Encounters: The 'Second World' and the 'Global South', 1945–1991. Jena. 03. -04.11. 2014.

12 Cf. Wallerstein, *Capitalist World-economy*, 35.

13 The illusion of bipolarity is central to the thesis of Oscar Sanchez-Sibony, *Red Globalization: The Political Economy of the Soviet Cold War from Stalin to Khrushchev* (Cambridge: Cambridge University Press, 2014). See the literature on the production of the idea of a strictly ideologically divided world in domestic cultures during the Cold War, for instance: James Mark and Péter Apor, 'Socialism Goes Global: Decolonization and the Making of a New Culture of Internationalism in Socialist Hungary, 1956–1989', *Journal of Modern History* 87 (2015): 1–40.

14 On this tension, see: György Péteri, 'Introduction: The Oblique Coordinate Systems of Modern Identity', in *Imagining the West in Eastern Europe and the Soviet Union*, ed. György Péteri (Pittsburgh, PA: University of Pittsburgh Press, 2010), 1–12, 8. On using divides to discipline domestic populations in the Cold War, see: Mary Kaldor, *The Imaginary War: Understanding the East-West Conflict* (Hoboken, NJ: Blackwell, 1991).

15 Histories of globalization in Eastern Europe usually start in 1989. See for example: Katalin Fábián (ed.), *Globalization: Perspectives from Central and Eastern Europe* (Bingley: Emerald, 2007).

16 On this divide, see: Sharad Chari and Katherine Verdery, 'Thinking between the Posts: Postcolonialism, Postsocialism, and Ethnography after the Cold War', *Comparative Studies in Society and History* 1 (2009): 6–34, at 16.

17 See for example: Matthias Middell, '1989 and the Collapse of Communism', in *OUP Handbook of History of Communism*, ed. Stephen Smith (Oxford: Oxford University Press, 2014), 171–184, at 173; for a nuanced account of the pressures of the 'world market', see Gareth Dale, *Between State Capitalism and Globalisation: The Collapse of the East German Economy* (Oxford et al.: Peter Lang, 2004), esp. 341–342.

18 André Gunder Frank, 'Long Live Transideological Enterprise! The Socialist Economies in the Capitalist International Division of Labor', *Review (Fernand Braudel Center)* 1, no. 1 (1977): 91–140; Immanuel Wallerstein, *The Politics of the World Economy* (New York: Cambridge University Press, 1984), 93. On the idea that the Second World increasingly competed with the Third for foreign investment from the 1970s, see Herbert Giersch, 'Perspektiven der Entwicklung der Weltwirtschaft', *Rheinisch-Westfälische Akademie der Wissenschaften Vorträge* 266 (1977): 7–22. For a different argument that incorporation starts only in 1986, see: David Lane, 'From State Socialism to Capitalism: The Role of Class and the World System', *Communist and Post-communist Studies* 39 (2006): 135–152; David Lane, 'Global Capitalism and the Transformation of State Socialism', *St Comp Int Dev* 44 (2009): esp. 98–102; David Lane, 'Post-socialist States and the World Economy: The Impact of Global Economic Crisis', *Historische Sozialforschung* 35, no. 2 (2010): 220.

19 David Lockwood, *The Destruction of the Soviet Union: A Study in Globalization* (Basingstoke: Palgrave, 2000), esp. 106–108; Lewis Siegelbaum, *Cars for Comrades: The Life of the Soviet Automobile* (Ithaca, NY: Cornell University Press, 2008); Yale Richmond, *Cultural Exchange and the Cold War: Raising the Iron Curtain* (University Park: Pennsylvania State University Press, 2000).

20 Philip McMichael, 'Globalization: Myths and Realities', *Rural Sociology* 1 (1996): 25–55.

21 Stephen Kotkin, 'The Kiss of Debt: The East Bloc Goes Borrowing', in *Shock of the Global: The 1970s in Perspective*, ed. Niall Ferguson et al. (Cambridge, MA: Harvard University Press, 2010), 80–96.

22 Sanchez-Sibony, *Red Globalization*: it is a great study of Soviet political economy and its limits. Some remark on the limitations to his claims, noting his focus on the economy and on a small group of actors, mostly in the Soviet Ministry of Foreign Trade, as well as his narrow neoliberal definition of globalization.

23 The phrase has been attributed to a variety of political leaders, including Margaret Thatcher, Ronald Reagan, Bill Clinton and Helmut Schmidt, but was probably coined by the *Daily Telegraph*'s Moscow correspondent Xan Smiley, an expert on both Russia and Africa.

24 Samuel Huntington, *Political Order in Changing Societies* (New Haven, CT: Yale University Press, 1968).

25 Middell, *1989 and the Collapse of Communism*; Christoph Boyer, 'Big "1989", Small "1989": A Comparative View on Eastern Central Europe and China on Their Way into Globalization', in *1989 in Global Perspective*, ed. Ulf Engel, Frank Hadler and Matthias Middell (Leipzig: Leipzig University Press, 2015), 78-79.
26 Gale Stokes, 'Purposes of the Past', in *The End and the Beginning: The Revolutions of 1989 and the Resurgence of History*, ed. Vladimir Tismăneanu and Bogdan Iacob (Budapest: CEU Press, 2012), 35-54, at 52.
27 President William J. Clinton, 'Remarks at the Signing Ceremony for the Supplemental Agreements to the North American Free Trade Agreement', 14 September 1993.
28 Talcott Parsons, quoted in Gareth Dale, *Between State Capitalism and Globalisation: The Collapse of the East German Economy* (Bern: Peter Lang, 2004), 9-10; Jürgen Habermas, 'What Does Socialism Mean Today? The Rectifying Revolution and the Need for New Thinking on The Left', *New Left Review* 183 (1990): 3-21.
29 Cornel Ban, 'Sovereign Debt, Austerity, and Regime Change: The Case of Nicolae Ceausescu's Rumania', *East European Politics and Societies* 26 (2012): 743-776.
30 For an overview of the field: David Engerman, 'The Second World's Third World', *Kritika* 1 (2011): 183-211; Tobias Rupprecht, 'Die Sowjetunion und die Welt im Kalten Krieg: Neue Forschungsperspektiven auf eine vermeintlich hermetisch abgeschlossene Gesellschaft', *Jahrbücher für Geschichte Osteuropas* 3 (2010): 381-399; Philip Muehlenbeck, *Czechoslovakia in Africa, 1945-1968* (Basingstoke: Palgrave Macmillan, 2015); William S. Logan, *Hanoi: Biography of a City* (Seattle: University of Washington Press, 2000); Sánchez Sibony, *Red Globalization*, chapter 5.
31 Francis Fukuyama, *Political Order and Political Decay: From the Industrialization to the Globalization of Democracy* (London: Profile Books, 2014), 328-334.
32 Péter Vámos, 'A Hungarian Model for China? Economic Reforms in China and Sino-Hungarian Relations, 1979-1989' (paper presented at the conference 'Beyond the Kremlin's Reach? Eastern Europe and China during the Cold War Era – Transfers and Entanglements' Leipzig, Geisteswissenschaftliches Zentrum Geschichte und Kultur Ostmitteleuropas (GWZO) an der Universität Leipzig, 30 June-2 July 2015).
33 Massimiliano Trentin, 'Modernization as State Building: The Two Germanies in Syria, 1963-1972', *Diplomatic History* 33, no. 3 (2009): 487-505. Alessandro Iandolo, 'The Rise and Fall of the "Soviet Model of Development" in West Africa, 1957-64', *Cold War History* 12, no. 4 (2012): 683-704. See the useful discussion in Engerman, *Second World's*, 198-202. Lukasz Stanek, 'Socialist Networks and the Internationalization of Building Culture after 1945', *ABE Journal* 6 (2004), last access 16 June 2015, http://abe.revues.org/1266; David Basulto, 'Chile's "Monolith Controversies" – Winner of the Silver Lion at the Venice Biennale',

Archdaily. Available online: http://www.archdaily.com/516268/chile-s-monolith-controversies-winner-of-the-silver-lion-at-the-venice-biennale (accessed 16 June 2015); Elizabeth Shim, 'North Korea's Artful Diplomacy: Building Big Bronze Statues in Africa', *UPI*. Available online: http://www.upi.com/Top_News/World-News/2015/05/01/North-Koreas-artful-diplomacy-Building-big-bronze-statues-in-Africa/4011430338164/ph2 (accessed 11 February 2016); Christina Schwenkel, 'Socialist Palimpsests in Urban Vietnam', *ABE Journal* 6 (2014). Available online: http://journals.openedition.org/abe/909 (accessed 11 April 2019).

34 Austin Jersild, *The Sino-Soviet Alliance: An International History* (Chapel Hill: University of North Carolina Press, 2014), esp. Introduction and chapter 2. Thomas Bernstein and Hua-Yu Li (ed.), *China Learns from the Soviet Union, 1949–Present* (Cambridge, MA: Harvard University Press, 2011); Lorenz Lüthi, *The Sino-Soviet Split: Cold War in the Communist World* (Princeton, NJ: Princeton University Press, 2008), 19–87; Odd Arne Westad (ed.), *Brothers in Arms: The Rise and Fall of the Sino-Soviet Alliance* (Stanford, CA: Stanford University Press, 1998).

35 Odd Arne Westad, *Restless Empire: China and the World since 1750* (London: Vintage/Random House, 2013), 304.

36 Ibid., 239; Harry Harding, *China's Second Revolution: Reform after Mao* (Washington, DC: Brookings Institution Press, 1987), 22; Alexander Eckstein, *China's Economic Revolution* (Cambridge: Cambridge University Press, 1977), 141.

37 See, e.g.: Peter Svik, '"Fighting for the Third World: The Eastern Bloc Airlines" Penetration of Non-aligned Countries and the US Response' (paper presented at the Transatlantic Studies Association Annual Conference, Gent, Belgium, 7–10 July 2014).

38 In the early years of the Czechoslovak use of Vietnamese labour, transport by train took two weeks; by the 1980s chartered flights sustained a much larger programme of labour exchange. See, e.g.: Alena K. Alamgir, 'Race Is Elsewhere: State-socialist Ideology and the Racialisation of Vietnamese Workers in Czechoslovakia', *Race Class* 4 (2013): 67–85; Christina Schwenkel, 'Socialist Migration and Post-socialist Repatriation of Vietnamese Contract Workers in East Germany', *Critical Asian Studies* 46, no. 2 (2014): 235–258.

39 Jan Lomíček, 'Troubles of Socialist Economic Integration: Czechoslovakia and Joint Projects within the CMEA in 1970s and 1980s', *Prager wirtschafts- und sozialhistorische Mitteilungen* 1 (2014): 61–74; László Csaba, *Eastern Europe in the World Economy* (Cambridge: Cambridge University Press, 1990).

40 Anne Gorsuch and Diane Koenker (eds), *The Socialist Sixties: Crossing Borders in the Second World* (Bloomington: Indiana University Press, 2013); Anne Gorsuch, *All This Is Your World: Soviet Tourism at Home and Abroad after Stalin* (New York: Oxford University Press, 2011); Anne Gorsuch and Diane Koenker (eds), *Turizm:*

The Russian and East European Tourist under Capitalism and Socialism (Ithaca, NY: Cornell University Press, 2006); by the late socialist period, party and trade union elites in the USSR, after decades of service, were allowed a vacation in such 'exotic' locations as Cuba.

41 Susan Bayly, 'Vietnamese Narratives of Tradition, Exchange and Friendship in the Worlds of the Global Socialist Ecumene', in *Enduring Socialism: Explorations of Revolution and Transformation, Restoration and Continuation*, ed. Harry West and Parvathi Raman (Oxford: Berghahn, 2008), 125–147.

42 Christina Schwenkel, 'Affective Solidarities and East German Reconstruction of Postwar Vietnam', in *Comrades of Colour: East Germany in the Cold War World*, ed. Quinn Slobodian (Oxford: Berghahn, 2015); Gertrud Hüwelmeier, 'Postsocialist Bazaars: Diversity, Solidarity, and Conflict in the Marketplace', *Laboratorium. Russian Review of Social Research* 1 (2013): 52–72; Gertrud Hüwelmeier, 'Socialist Cosmopolitanism Meets Global Pentecostalism: Charismatic Christianity among Vietnamese Migrants after the Fall of the Berlin Wall', *Ethnic and Racial Studies* 3 (2011): 436–453; Pal Nyiri, *Chinese in Russia and Eastern Europe: A Middleman Minority in a Transnational Era* (London: Routledge, 2007).

43 Abigail Judge Kret, '"We Unite with Knowledge": The Peoples' Friendship University and Soviet Education for the Third World', *Comparative Studies of South Asia, Africa and the Middle East* 33, no. 2 (2013): 248.

44 Tobias Rupprecht, *Soviet Internationalism after Stalin: Interaction and Exchange between the USSR and Latin America during the Cold War* (Cambridge: Cambridge University Press, 2015), 191–228. Tanja Müller, *Legacies of Socialist Solidarity: East Germany in Mozambique* (Lanham, MD: Lexington Books, 2014).

45 Daniela Lazarova, 'King Sihamoni of Cambodia receives warm welcome in Prague', *Radio Praha*. Available online: http://www.radio.cz/en/section/curraffrs/king-sihamoni-of-cambodia-receives-warm-welcome-in-prague (accessed 8 November 2015). Thanks to Alena Alamgir for this information.

46 Tobias Rupprecht, 'Orthodox Internationalism. State and Church in Modern Russia and Ethiopia', *Comparative Studies in Society and History* 60, no. 1 (2018): 212–235.

47 David C. Engerman, 'Learning from the East: Soviet Experts and India in the Era of Competitive Coexistence', *Comparative Studies of South Asia, Africa and the Middle East* 33, no. 2 (2013): 227–238.

48 On multi-directionality, see: Schwenkel, 'Socialist Palimpsests'.

49 Deborah Brautigam, *The Dragon's Gift: The Real Story of China in Africa* (Oxford: Oxford University Press, 2010); Jeremy Friedman, *Shadow Cold War: The Sino-Soviet Competition for the Third World* (Chapel Hill: University of North Carolina Press, 2015).

50 Robert I. Rotberg (ed.), *China into Africa: Trade, Aid and Influence* (Washington, DC: Brookings Institution Press, 2008), ix.

51 Jamie Monson, *Africa's Freedom Railway: How a Chinese Development Project Changed Lives and Livelihoods in Tanzania* (Bloomington: Indiana University Press, 2009).

52 Alexander Cook (ed.), *Mao's Little Red Book: A Global History* (Cambridge: Cambridge University Press, 2014).

53 Christine Hatzky, *Cubans in Angola; South-South Cooperation and Transfer of Knowledge, 1976–1991* (Wisconsin: University of Wisconsin Press, 2015). Piero Gleijeses, 'Moscow's Proxy? Cuba and Africa 1975–1988', *Journal of Cold War Studies* 8, no. 2 (2006): 3–51; Piero Gleijeses, *Conflicting Missions: Havana, Washington, and Africa, 1959–1976* (Chapel Hill: University of North Carolina Press, 2002).

54 Johanna Bockman, 'Socialist Globalization and Capitalist Neocolonialism: The Economic Ideas behind the New International Economic Order', *Humanity* 6, no. 1 (2015): 109–128.

55 Nils Gilman, 'The New International Economic Order: A Reintroduction', *Humanity* 6, no. 1 (2015): 1–2. See the whole special issue to the NIEO which this article introduces. On its 'defeat', see: Mark Mazower, *Governing the World: The History of an Idea* (New York: Penguin Press, 2012). Giuliano Garavini, *After Empires: European Integration, Decolonization, and the Challenge from the Global South, 1957–1986* (Oxford: Oxford University Press, 2012), esp. chapter 1.

56 Douglas Rogers, 'Petrobarter: Oil, Inequality, and the Political Imagination in and after the Cold War', *Current Anthropology* 55 (2014): 137–138.

57 Christopher Chase-Dunn, 'Globalization: A World-systems Perspective', *Journal of World-systems Research* 2 (1999): 187–216.

58 Mazower, *Governing the World*, chapter 12; Gilman, 'The New International Economic Order', 6–8. Quinn Slobodian, *Globalists: The End of Empire and the Birth of Neoliberalism* (Harvard, MA: Harvard University Press, 2018), 24–25.

59 Simon Godard, 'Shaping the "Bloc" through Economics: Reconfiguration of Socialist Territories and Identities in the Council for Mutual Economic Assistance (COMECON). 1949–1989' (PhD diss., University of Geneva, 2014). Also: Simon Godard, 'Construire le bloc de l'Est par l'économie?', *Vingtième Siècle. Revue d'histoire* 109, no. 1 (2011): 45–58.

60 See in particular the special issue of *Vingtième Siècle* titled 'The Eastern Bloc in Question' 109, no. 1 (2011).

61 Cf. Austin Jersild, 'The Soviet State as Imperial Scavenger: "Catch Up and Surpass" in the Transnational Socialist Bloc, 1950–1960', *The American Historical Review* 116, no. 1 (2011): 109–132.

62 Ther, *Die neue Ordnung*, 169.

63 Paulina Bren and Mary Neuburger (eds), *Communism Unwrapped: Consumption in Cold War Eastern Europe* (Oxford: Oxford University Press, 2012); Eszter Bartha,

Alienating Labour. Workers on the Road from Socialism to Capitalism in East Germany and Hungary (New York: Berghahn, 2013).

64 On the different approaches in the field of architecture that resulted from this bilateralism, see Stanek, 'Socialist Networks'.

65 Sarah B. Snyder, *Human Rights Activism and the End of the Cold War: A Transnational History of the Helsinki Network* (Cambridge: Cambridge University Press, 2011), 16; Jacques Rupnik, 'Afterword', in *Samizdat, Tamizdat, and Beyond: Transnational Media during and after Socialism*, ed. Friederike Kind-Kovacs and Jessie Labov (New York and Oxford: Berghahn, 2013), 320.

66 Kotkin argues that the oil crisis spurred on neo-liberalism in the West. But the Soviets, rich from oil money, did not feel the need to reform as intensely as Western countries that were suffering from the 'oil shock': Stephen Kotkin, *Armageddon Averted: The Soviet Collapse 1970–2000* (New York: Oxford University Press, 2008), 15–18.

67 See, for example, Kotkin, who blames the collapse on Gorbachev, while Timothy Garton-Ash and Zsuzsa Gille focus on internal dissent.

68 For a discussion of the perception of these different internationalisms, see: Rupprecht, *Soviet Internationalism after Stalin*, esp. 1–10.

69 Immanuel Wallerstein describes this tension in some of his work from the 1970s and notes that the anti-imperialist struggles of the time resulted in greater integration into a capitalist-led world economy. He also understood this to be partly the result of tensions between technocrats and 'red cadres' within socialist societies. Wallerstein, *The Capitalist World-economy*, 115. See also the excellent discussion in: Zeev Gorin, 'Socialist Societies and World System Theory: A Critical Survey', *Science & Society* 3 (1985): 332–366.

70 Gille, 'Global Postsocialist Condition?', 12.

71 See: Prasenjit Duara, 'The Cold War as a Historical Period: An Interpretive Essay', *Journal of Global History* 6, no. 3 (2011): 457–480, at 473; Nils Gilman, 'Modernization Theory: The Highest Stage of American Intellectual History', in *Staging Growth: Modernization, Development, and the Global Cold War*, ed. David Engerman, Nils Gilman, Mark Haefele and Michael Latham (Amherst: University of Massachusetts Press, 2003).

72 This began with the literature on 'convergence' that emerged from the European New Left and Marxist revisionists in the late 1960s; for this criticism of the similarity, see: Andre Gunder Frank and Marta Fuentes Frank, 'The Development of Underdevelopment', in *Tin Equity and Efficiency in Economic Development: Essays in Honour of Benjamin Higgins*, ed. Donald J. Savoie and Irving Brecher (Montreal: McGill-Queen's University Press, 1992), 341–392, at 357; this was also Mao's contention from the early 1960s. Contemporary views often hold that Soviet and Western concepts were both variants of an enlightenment legacy, see: Odd

Arne Westad, *The Global Cold War: Third World Intervention and the Making of Our Time* (Cambridge: Cambridge University Press, 2007).

73 Berthold Unfried and Eva Himmelstoss, *Die eine Welt schaffen: Praktiken von 'Internationaler Solidarität' und 'Internationaler Entwicklung'* (Vienna: Akademische Verlagsanstalt, 2012); for the contrast between West German and GDR developmental policies, see: Hubertus Büschel, *Hilfe zur Selbsthilfe: Deutsche Entwicklungsarbeit in Afrika 1960–1975* (Frankfurt: Campus, 2014). On differences and similarities, see Antonio Giustozzi and Artemy Kalinovsky, *Missionaries of Modernity: Advisory Missions and the Struggle for Hegemony in Afghanistan and Beyond* (London: Hurst, 2016).

74 On area studies, see Michael Kemper and Artemy M. Kalinovsky (eds), *Reassessing Orientalism: Interlocking Orientologies during the Cold War* (London: Routledge, 2015); Tobias Rupprecht, 'Schreibtischrevolutionäre: Die meždunarodnki als Bannerträger des sozialistischen Internationalismus in der späten Sowjetunion', in *Goldenes Zeitalter der Stagnation? Perspektiven auf die sowjetische Ordnung der Brežnev-Ära*, ed. Boris Belge and Martin Deuerlein (Tübingen: Mohr Siebeck, 2014), 231–249; Vladislav Zubok, 'Sowjetische Westexperten', in *Macht und Geist im Kalten Krieg*, ed. Bernd Greiner, Tim Müller and Claudia Weber (Hamburg: Hamburger Edition, 2011), 108–135; Apollon Davidson and Irina Filatova, 'African History: A View from behind the Kremlin Wall', in *Africa in Russia, Russia in Africa; Three Centuries of Encounters*, ed. Maxim Matusevich (Trenton, NJ: Africa World Press, 2007), 111–131; Pëtr Cherkasov, *IMEMO. Institut Mirovoj Ekonomiki i Mezhdunarodnych Otnoshenij. Portret na fone epochi* (Moscow: Ves Mir, 2004); Marie-Pierre Rey, 'Le Départment International du Comité Central du PCUS, le MID et la Politique Extérieur Soviétique de 1953 à 1991', *Communism* 74, no. 75 (2003): 179–215; Gerhard Duda, *Jenö Varga und die Geschichte des Instituts für Weltwirtschaft und Weltpolitik in Moskau 1921–1970. Zu den Möglichkeiten und Grenzen wissenschaftlicher Auslandsanalyse in der Sowjetunion* (Berlin: Akademieverlag, 1994).

75 Still very little is written on the exchange of Eastern and Western experts; one of few examples is: Paul Betts, 'The Warden of World Heritage: UNESCO and the Rescue of the Nubian Monuments', *Past and Present* 226 (2015): 100–125. The GDR, by contrast, understanding itself as a frontline Cold War state, often tried to isolate its experts from Western colleagues and the ideological contamination they represented.

76 Thanks to Christina Schwenkel for this information.

77 Sara Lorenzini, 'Comecon and the Global South in the Years of Détente', *European Review of History: Revue européenne d'histoire* 21, no. 2 (2014): 188.

78 Patrick Gutman, 'West-östliche Wirtschaftskooperationen in der Dritten Welt', in *Ökonomie im Kalten Krie*, ed. Bernd Greiner, Christian Müller and Claudia Weber (Hamburg: Hamburger Edition, 2010), 395–414.

79 Angela Romano and Frederico Romero, 'European Socialist Regimes Facing Globalisation and European Co-operation: Dilemmas and Responses – Introduction', *European Review of History* 21, no. 2 (2014): 157–164; Suvi Kansikas, *Socialist Countries Face the European Community: Soviet-bloc Controversies over East-West Trade* (Frankfurt: Peter Lang, 2014).

80 From the initial wave who noted this shift, see Frank, 'Long Live Transideological Enterprise!: 91–140, and André Gunder Frank, *Crisis: In the World Economy* (New York: Holmes & Meyer, 1980). More recently: Christopher Miller, 'From Foreign Concessions to Special Economic Zones: Decolonization and Foreign Investment in Twentieth-century Asia', in *Negotiating Independence: Decolonization and the Cold War*, ed. Leslie James and Elisabeth Leake (New York, London: Bloomsbury, 2015), 239–253; Pavel Szobi, 'Between Ideology and Pragmatism: ČSSR, GDR and West European Companies in the 1970s and 1980s', *European Review of History* 3 (2014): 255–269; Pál Germuska, 'Conflicts of Eastern and Western Technology Transfer: Licenses, Espionage, and R&D in the Hungarian Defense Industry during the 1970s and 1980s', *Comparative Technology Transfer and Society* 7, no. 1 (2009): 43–65.

81 Chen Jian, 'China and the Cold War after Mao', in *The Cambridge History of the Cold War Volume 3: Endings*, ed. Melvyn P. Leffler and Odd Arne Westad (Cambridge: Cambridge University Press, 2010), 181–200; Ezra Vogel, *Deng Xiaoping and the Transformation of China* (Cambridge, MA: Harvard University Press, 2011).

82 Thanks to Felix Wemheuer for this information.

83 Vámos, 'A Hungarian Model for China?'; Julian Gewirtz, *Unlikely Partners: Chinese Reformers, Western Economists, and the Making of Global China* (Harvard, MA: Harvard University Press, 2017).

84 Lea Shi, 'The Reinvention of Development Planning in China, 1993–2012', *Modern China* 6 (2013): 580–628; Sebastian Heilmann, 'Policy Experimentation in China's Economic Rise', *Studies in Comparative International Development (SCID)* 1 (2008): 1–26; Sebastian Heilmann, Lea Shiha and Andreas Hofem, 'National Planning and Local Technology Zones: Experimental Governance in China's Torch Program', *The China Quarterly* 216 (2013): 896–919; Sebastian Heilmann, 'The Rise of Industrial Policy in China, 1978–2012', *Harvard-Yenching Institute Working Paper Series* 1 (2013).

85 Martin K. Dimitrov (ed.), *Why Communism Did Not Collapse: Understanding Authoritarian Regime Resilience in Asia and Europe* (Cambridge: Cambridge University Press, 2013).

86 Duccio Basosi, 'An Economic Lens on Global Transformations: The Foreign Debt Crisis of the 1980s in the Soviet Bloc and Latin America', in *A Global 1989? Reflecting on Connections across Continents and Oceans in a Revolutionary World*, ed. Piotr Kosicki, Kyrill Kunakhovich, Jeremy Friedman and Stephen Kotkin (forthcoming). The Soviet Union did not have a financial centre such as Hong Kong through which international finance capital could operate.

87 Boyer, 'Big "1989," Small "1989"'.

88 Chris Saunders, '"1989" and Southern Africa', in *1989 in Global Perspective*, ed. Engel et al., 358–359. Adrian Guelke and Tom Junes, '"Copycat Tactics" in Processes of Regime Change: The Demise of Communism in Poland and Apartheid in South Africa', *Critique and Humanism Journal* 40 (2012): 171–192; Hal Brands, *Latin America's Cold War* (Cambridge, MA: Harvard University Press, 2010), 223–252.

89 Leslie Sklair, *Globalization: Capitalism and its Alternatives* (Oxford: Oxford University Press, 2002), 224. Also: C. H. McMillan, *Multinationals from the Second World-growth of Foreign Investment by Soviet and East European State Enterprises* (London: Macmillan, 1987); Wladimir Andreff (ed.), *Réforme et échanges extérieurs dans les pays de l'Est* (Paris: L'Harmattan, 1990); Eugène Zaleski, 'Les multinationales des pays de l'Est', in *Les multinationales en mutation*, ed. Alain Cotta and Michael Ghertman (Paris: Presses Universitaires de France, 1983), 195–213.Wladimir Andreff, 'The Newly Emerging TNCs from Economies in Transition: A Comparison with Third World Outward FDI', *Transnational Corporations (UNCTAD)* 12, no. 2 (2003): esp. 75–79.

90 Chris O'Malley, *Bonds without Borders: A History of the Eurobond Market* (Chichester: Wiley, 2015), 13.

91 Arne Westad, 'Was There a Global 1989?', in *The Global 1989: Continuity and Change in World Politics*, ed. George Lawson, Chris Armbruster and Michael Cox (New York: Cambridge University Press, 2010), 271–281, 273. On Soviet criticisms of Chinese reform, see Gilbert Rozman, *A Mirror for Socialism: Soviet Criticisms of China* (London: Tauris, 1985); Vámos, 'A Hungarian Model for China?'.

92 In this spirit, some work has been done on Soviet premier Alexey Kosygin, who failed to convince his fellow leaders to open the Soviet Union up to global forces in the early 1970s.

93 Johanna Bockman, 'The Long Road to 1989: Neoclassical Economics, Alternative Socialisms, and the Advent of Neoliberalism', *Radical History Review* 112 (2012): 9–42; Johanna Bockman, 'Scientific Community in a Divided World: Economists, Planning, and Research Priority during the Cold War', *Comparative Studies in Society and History* 50 (2008): 581–613. János Mátyás Kovács, 'Importing Spiritual Capital: East-West Encounters and Capitalist Cultures in Eastern Europe after 1989', in *The Hidden Form of Capital: Spiritual Influences in Societal Progress*, ed. Peter Berger and Gordon Redding (London: Anthem Press, 2010), 133–169.

94 Ther, *Die neue Ordnung*, 50–52; Sklair, *Globalization,* 224–227; on expert consensus-building and neo-liberalism, see Ágnes Gagyi, 'A Moment of Political Critique by Reform Economists in Late Socialist Hungary: "Change and Reform" and the Financial Research Institute in Context', *Intersections. EEJSP* 1, no. 2 (2015): 59–79. On workers' early support for neo-liberalism, see Don Kalb, 'Conversations with a Polish Populist: Tracing Hidden Histories of Globalization, Class, and Dispossession in Postsocialism (and Beyond)', *American Ethnologist* 36, no. 2 (2009): 211.

95 Cornel Ban, 'Neoliberalism in Translation: Economic Ideas and Reforms in Spain and Romania' (PhD diss., University of Maryland, Maryland, Washington, DC, 2011).

96 Tobias Rupprecht, 'Formula Pinochet: Chilean Lessons for Russian Liberal Reformers during the Soviet Collapse 1970–2000', *Journal of Contemporary History* 1 (2016): 165–186.

97 See David Lane, 'Eurasian Integration as a Response to Neo-liberal Globalisation', in *The Eurasian Project and Europe: Regional Discontinuities and Geopolitics*, ed. David Lane and Vsevolod Samokhvalov (Basingstoke: Palgrave Macmillan, 2015), 3–23.

98 Igiaba Scego, 'At Sea, Devoured by Our Indifference', *The Massachusetts Review*. Available online: https://www.massreview.org/node/443 (accessed 16 June 2015). On the valorization of the 'red passport' as giving greater sense of mobility than in the post-Cold War former Yugoslavia, see Stef Jansen 'The Afterlives of the Yugoslav Red Passport', *Citizenship in Southeast Europe* (2012). Available online: http://www.citsee.eu/citsee-story/afterlives-yugoslav-red-passport (accessed 12 January 2016).

99 Jiří Mareček, 'S vrtulníky to umíte, chválí Čechy NATO' ('You Sure Know How to Fly Helicopters, NATO Praises Czechs'), *Hospodarskenoviny*, 12 June 2012. Available online: http://archiv.ihned.cz/c1-56118760-s-vrtulniky-to-umite-chvali-cechy-nato?utm_source=mediafed&utm_medium=rss&utm_campaign=mediafed (last accessed 18 August 2017).

100 Christina Schwenkel, 'Rethinking Asian Mobilities', *Critical Asian Studies* 2 (2014): 235–258.

4

Russian Economic History in Global Perspective

Alessandro Stanziani

Russian economic history is constantly used to confirm our models and preconceptions instead of asking questions. This is often done by evoking the presumed 'specificity' of Russia (as a whole). The 'Mongol yoke', absolutism and serfdom; then communism and totalitarianism; and now, once again, the 'new Russian mafia' peril are among the most widespread notions historians and commentators use to explain Russian history. Notions of coercion, serfdom, failed reforms and communist economy are taken as being synonymous with 'backwardness'. Indeed, from the eighteenth century to the present, comparisons between Russia and the major European countries have formed part of a wider debate about 'backwardness'. The goal has been to create a comparative scale to account for both economic growth and so-called 'blockages'. Montesquieu's 'Asiatic Despotism', Voltaire's and Diderot's perceptions of Russia and Asia, and the so-called Asiatic mode of production described by liberal, radical and Marxist historiography in the nineteenth century are well-known examples. Then, in the twentieth century, the comparative and global analysis of Eurasia found its way into discussions of backwardness and underdevelopment, decolonization, the fate of communism and the Cold War as well as arguments such as Oriental despotism and Hayek's *Road to Serfdom*. Authors as different as Kula, Wallerstein and North agree on this: in early modern times, Russia and Eastern Europe responded to the commercial, agrarian and then industrial expansion of the West by binding the peasantries to the land and its lords.[1] It is interesting that even new approaches to world history such as Pomeranz's 'great divergence', while contesting Chinese backwardness and European ethnocentrism, still consider Russia the paradigm of unfree labour and lack of markets and, as such, opposed to both the Lower Yangtze and Britain.[2]

After the collapse of the Berlin Wall and Asia's return to world prominence, after the global crisis of the Western economies, the time has come to discuss these notions and stop using history to judge or to prove the superiority of the West in terms of economic efficiency or political organization. Of course, the point here is not to deny the differences between, say, Russia, China and England, but rather to study them from a more problematic perspective. A new historiography of Russia and of the Union of Soviet Socialist Republics (USSR) has developed in recent decades and contributed analyses and innovative solutions in all these areas. Curiously, those contributions have had trouble gaining recognition outside Russianist circles and conversely, Russian scholars, unlike specialists on China, India and Africa, have shown little interest in participating in global history debates, with a few notable exceptions of course – Lieven, Burbank and Morrison, among others – not to mention several forums on the topic in *Kritika* and *Ab Imperio*.[3] This back-and-forth exchange is indispensable but difficult, for indeed the comparative and/or globalizing approaches available to us accept a relationship between economic growth, on the one hand, and democracy, the absence of corruption, openness to minorities, innovative capacities and privatization on the other. However, this interpretation has a hard time accounting for Russia's history over the long run. How, despite several institutional changes, did Russia succeed in enlarging and later holding on to a vast territory from the seventeenth century until today? Why, despite its economic weaknesses and lack of democracy, has it not only continued to exist but maintained a leading role on the world stage?

Russia and economic backwardness

Alexander Gerschenkron is justly famous for *Economic Backwardness in Historical Perspective*. Yet these two terms – the notions of backwardness and historical temporalities – are hardly compatible. In reality, economic backwardness refers to logical time. From the eighteenth century to today, comparisons between the Russian economy and the economies of Europe's major countries have been part of a broader debate over the notion of 'backwardness'. It involves proposing a scale of comparison to account for economic growth as well as for so-called 'obstruction' factors. The framework of comparison is created by drawing up a list of elements based on a standard Western ideal. We will not recount the history of this model[4] here but simply mention its main components.

In this sense, Gerschenkron offers an excellent example of how the approach was applied to the case of Russia. Indeed, like Max Weber and others before him, Gerschenkron began by drawing up a list of Western characteristics on which his comparison would be based; he too emphasized cities, the bourgeoisie, markets and private property. Yet unlike Marx and to some extent Weber, he thought it was possible to arrive at industrialization (but not capitalism) without a bourgeoisie. In place of this component, 'backward' countries (to use the jargon of the 1960s and 1970s) such as Prussia and Russia had 'substituting factors', notably the state. This is a very clever solution to the problem raised by the need to reconcile particular features, historical specificities and general dynamics. If backwardness and diversity go together, then it is possible to conceive of alternative paths.[5]

One might wonder, however, if this solution really eliminates the confusion between historical time and logical time. Contrary to appearances, Gerschenkron does not compare Russia to England in specific historical contexts. Instead, he opposes an ideal image of the West (and of England in particular) to an equally ideal image of nineteenth-century Russia. English economic development is associated with the early introduction of a parliament, privatization of the commons and hence the formation of a proletariat available for agriculture and industry. In contrast, Russia is associated with market towns – and therefore with a bourgeoisie – as well as the presence of an absentee landed gentry living off serfdom. These interpretations stemmed from the research work on England and Russia available at the time Gerschenkron was writing, starting with more general works from Marx to Polanyi that stressed those characteristics in describing the English Industrial Revolution.

Soviet and Western historiographies also concurred on the limits of the 1861 Russian reforms (abolition of serfdom), the ensuing impoverishment of the peasants and the extent of tsarist industrialization.[6] Like these authors, Gerschenkron put great trust in the economic and statistical research produced in Russia between 1870 and 1930. Though these works do indeed contain a wealth of information, it is nevertheless important, as we have shown elsewhere, to understand the conditions under which it was produced. Our aim is not to invalidate turn-of-the-century Russian statistics, let alone 'correct' them in line with a given statistical history, but rather to take the empirical methods and the intellectual and political challenges of the period into account so their conclusions may be used later on.[7] In particular, the economic and social statistics produced in Russia at the turn of the century were, for the most part, the work of intellectuals, specialists and sometimes merely activists employed by the *zemstvo*, local self-government organizations. These authors were quick to reveal the inadequacies of the reforms, the limits of autocracy and the impoverishment of the peasantry. Above and beyond their considerable differences, 'Marxists' and 'populists' agreed on this point. They selected typical cases and variables to confirm their hypotheses. Kablukov, a professor of economics and statistics at the University of Moscow and in charge of statistics for the Moscow region in the early twentieth century, thus stated that a peasant should be classified as a *meshchane* (petit-bourgeois) as soon as he bought land for himself.[8] By definition, a peasant was someone who did not have enough land to satisfy the needs of his family.[9] These were the sources Gerschenkron used in his work, which were hence doubly decontextualized: he took out of context the turn-of-the-century sources, which in turn were the result of a particular empirical clarification.

At the same time, this approach completely dominated in the 1960s: a certain historical situation could fit into a more general pattern of economic development, drawing comparisons by analogy without worrying too much about the conditions in which the sources were produced. This explains how it eventually became possible to use Russian development and the debate between 'populists' and 'Marxists' from 1870 to 1914 in discussions about which type of development policies were best suited to Asia, Africa or South America during the 1960s.[10] The comparisons were not so much anachronistic as atemporal.

Russia and economic neo-institutionalism

Such approaches were not abandoned when colonialism and the Cold War came to an end; on the contrary, those historical processes even encouraged their use. The 'transition' to capitalism in the former Soviet bloc countries and in Latin America as well as in China and India became the inevitable outcome of an economic model considered to be valid everywhere. Neo-institutional economics, developed in the 1970s by Douglass North, among others, became the dominant paradigm in comparative economic history.[11] Instead of evoking an ideal competitive market, like liberal, neoclassical theory, neo-institutional thought seriously considered the criticism of those who viewed the market economy as a particular historical construction. It incorporated institutional phenomena into the neo-liberal approach, maintaining that institutions were efficient insofar as they offered a means to cope with 'market imperfections'.

According to this approach, the commons, which had been criticized since the eighteenth century as a source of inefficiency, were viewed as a safeguard against risk at a time when the markets were still so imperfect that they prevented rapid compensation for poor harvests in one region by using the surplus from other regions.[12] In this way, 'market imperfections' were the explanation for Russian peasant districts and even serfdom in Eastern Europe.[13] In other words, there was an economic explanation for every institution present in the history of humanity.

The only difference in relation to previous approaches was that henceforth the list of development factors was drawn up on the basis of one, and only one, criterion: efficiency and minimized transaction costs. The pattern has been applied to all sorts of historical experiments, including in Russia and the USSR. Using the theory of transaction costs and the information economy, Joseph Stiglitz, a Nobel Prize winner in economics, revealed the limits of free market equilibrium along with the distortions produced by the Soviet bureaucracy and by managed economies in general.[14] The same model is employed to talk about the market in nineteenth-century Africa, serfdom in Russia or fairs in Europe in the modern period: it is no accident that neo-institutional economics speak less about capitalism than about the market economy. This approach calls into question the classifications of economic systems proposed by traditional neoclassical and Marxist literatures (capitalism, peasant economy, feudalism, etc.). Instead we find a typology of organizations that evolve strictly in relation to the institutional context. Hence, the approach cannot explain the relationship between institutional changes and forms of market organization: are institutions the result or the source of economic behaviour?

In the case of the USSR, did economic weakness cause political decline or, on the contrary, did Soviet institutions close the market and thereby bring about its inevitable collapse? This question, which may seem innocuous to historians, was important for development policy insofar as the debate, especially in the 1990s, was focused on knowing whether it was first necessary to set up market institutions and a democratic political system in order to have a market, or conversely whether the market would give rise through its very development to adequate institutions. The issue appears to have been resolved since then because, contrary to the politically correct arguments that always sought to link capitalism to democracy, the experiences of China and Russia in recent years confirm that this equation is by no means obvious from the standpoint of either political philosophy or historical observation.

Russia and the great divergence

In a recent article, Gareth Austin took up the proposal put forward a few years ago by Kenneth Pomeranz and Bing Wong to develop a form of 'reciprocal comparison' in which Africa (Austin's case) and China (Pomeranz and Wong) would not be compared exclusively to the Western model as the exemplary scenario and exclusive yardstick.[15] The fundamental aim of these proposals was to break free from the 'Eurocentrism' underlying most economic history analysis. The solutions presented were arrived at in an unusual way in that the authors did not claim the 'specificity' of China or Africa in relation to the West. As Austin asserts, the point is not to reject any general model of economic development, but rather to widen the definitions of city, market and private property to include practices found in non-European regions.

In Pomeranz's approach, the 'Great Divergence' is mainly related to colonial expansion and related endowments: while Western Europe benefited from its American colonies, then from American markets and resources, Russian despotism and power limited Asian, mainly Chinese, expansion. Of course, as Pomeranz points out several times, we should not confuse global history, which focuses on broad yet determined spaces, with world history. If we accept this distinction, the next step is to grasp what these syntheses contribute when compared with comparative global history and conventional approaches. The problem lies in the difficulty of confirming these interpretations empirically; the environmental component and Europe's use of colonial resources correspond more to the colonizers' aims than to historical realities. Similarly, the history of Asia is punctuated with wars just as much as that of Europe.[16] In all these cases, the subsequent imperial constructions were often unexpected historical results that need to be explained. It is not by chance that much of the debate focused on the 'empirical proof' and data set. Authors such as Patrick O'Brien, Angus Maddison, Stephen Broadberry and Bishnupriya Gupta contest revisionist theories such as that of Kenneth Pomeranz, and show that the difference between European and Asian growth was significant as early as the sixteenth century, hence the role of colonies was less important.[17] These differences can be explained by the accumulation and spread of innovations as far back as the twelfth century, by the role of commerce and cities, and finally by English institutional reforms, in juxtaposition to the bureaucratic weight of China's predatory state. The debate in this sense has brought data and their measurement to the forefront of the discussion. In defence of Pomeranz, Robert Allen and especially Prasannan Parthasarathi emphasize that critics of the Great Divergence rely on

Maddison's estimates,[18] which were produced using data from the 1990s that were then extrapolated into the past. As these two authors show for China and certain regions of India respectively, the results would be profoundly different if the reference values were those from the mid-nineteenth century. In this case, the gap between Europe and the primary regions of Asia would be smaller, and Pomeranz's argument would be confirmed.[19] Thus it is true, as other authors such as Osterhammel[20] argue, that Russia was still suffering from famines in the 1890s; private property was still limited, democracy was weak if not nonexistent and corruption was widespread, along with repression; science had to fight against censorship; the army had few material resources, etc. Admittedly, the standard of living was constantly inferior to that of the Western powers, the great technological and scientific innovations came from elsewhere, and the rate of economic growth in Russia lagged behind that in the West. Yet these limitations never became so severe as to cause the collapse of the system. What are the reasons for this?

Thus, the question is not so much why Russia is not included in Pomeranz's analysis, but the reasons for and consequences of this. The reasons are that, while contesting China's backwardness and European ethnocentrism, Pomeranz still considers Russia the paradigm of unfree labour and lacking markets and, as such, as the country that stands in contradistinction to both the Lower Yangtze and Britain.[21] What if we escape from this ideal type of Russian economy?

Russia as the quasi-periphery of Europe and Asia?

One well-known argument borrowed from other authors by Wallerstein consists in showing that the expansion of Western capitalism was the cause of the second serfdom in Russia: increased demand for wheat in Europe prompted Russian lords to coerce peasants into producing the amount of wheat required for export. This was said to have resulted in an international division of labour: England produced textiles using wage labour, whereas Russia sold grain by resorting to serfdom. In reality, the situation was quite different. Russian serfdom was introduced in the fifteenth century in connection to the consolidation of Muscovite power; restrictions on peasant mobility were a factor in complex agreements and tensions between state elites and various categories of landowners.[22] The issue revolved around identifying which social groups should be allowed to own inhabited estates and transfer possession to their heirs. What was really at stake in the rules limiting peasant mobility was the social, political and institutional differences between old aristocracy and nobility resulting from state service, and later between these two categories and others (merchants, ecclesiastics, workers and peasants).[23] These transformations took place between the sixteenth and the seventeenth centuries, well before English industrialization, and had little to do with the West. The identification of social groups in Russia consequently was concerned with establishing state power in the Muscovite expansion to the steppes, on the one hand, and against Poland and Lithuania, on the other.[24]

The increase in labour service (*la corvée*) in the eighteenth century, so frequently mentioned by Wallerstein, therefore takes on a whole new meaning. According to the traditional analysis of serfdom, the rapid development of labour service was linked to a drop in commodity sales, causing the estates to fall back on their own resources and exert greater pressure on the peasants. The dynamics of Russian estates at the time do not confirm this argument. Most micro-economic studies focus on large estates[25] – even if some Soviet scholars like Koval'chenko exploited several estate archives. In part, such a focus creates a bias because large estates were more inclined to adopt modern techniques, and they tended to have higher yields and rates of commercialization than smaller units. Yet this bias does not invalidate our argument; rather, it confirms it. Despite the better performances of big estates, overall data reveal quite good outcomes for the Russian economy as compared with most Western economies,[26] and this occurred despite the well-known tendencies of statistics to underestimate products, yields and revenues. Proto-industrialization has long been considered an obstacle to modernization and industrialization – an approach that is firmly rooted in the hypothesis that large manufacturers and the 'British' way are the only paths to industrialization. More recently, this view has been strongly modified, stating instead that the continental European, Asian and Latin American paths, mostly anchored to small units, were the rule.[27] Recent analyses have also shown that, in contradiction to the first theories, guilds declined even without proto-industrialization (this was the case in most parts of England, Flanders and the Netherlands). Conversely, in many other parts of Europe (Bohemia, northern Italy), the seigneurial institutions, community and guilds remained strong despite the diffusion of proto-industry.[28] But to what extent does Russian history confirm or invalidate these issues?

In eighteenth-century Russia, agricultural prices continued to climb, rising by a factor of two and a half, which no doubt made service labour more profitable than quit-rent.[29] Wheat exports, which were relatively insignificant until the middle of the century, continued to rise and reached about 20 per cent of Russia's total exports in the late eighteenth century.[30] This growth did not take place at the expense of local and national markets, however. Beginning in the 1760s, growing demand for wheat in local and national markets pushed up prices, which in turn helped to integrate local channels in the national market.[31] The landed gentry sought to reverse the situation produced during the first half of the century, when urban merchants had taken over grain markets in the cities and the country. The noble landowners regained control over the sale of products from their estates and firmly took their place in urban markets. At the beginning of the 1760s, 413 of the 1,143 country fairs (36 per cent) still took place on noble estates; by 1800 the percentage had risen to 51 per cent (1,615 of 3,180 fairs).[32] This rapid development can be attributed not only to the nobles but also, and above all, to the peasants, who were increasingly involved in selling wheat and proto-industrial products.[33] Thus while 5 per cent of all private factories belonged to nobles in the 1720s, the percentage rose to 20 per cent by 1773. In 1725, 78 per cent of industrial activity was located in cities; that dropped to 60 per cent in 1775–78 and to 58 per cent in 1803.[34] On the whole, the second half of the eighteenth century saw a drastic increase in landlords entering the proto-industrial sector; the ruralization of proto-industry was not a symptom of demesne autarchy, but quite the contrary; it testified to the demesne's increasing commercialization. Both peasants and landlords entered the market in cereals, in addition to going in for proto-industrial activities and trade and transportation activities. Numerous 'serf-entrepreneurs' registered businesses or even proto-industrial and industrial activities – sometimes on behalf of the landowner and sometimes quite independently[35] – and they often employed workers in their proto-industrial activity. They came from the same villages or from neighbouring districts. During and after the mid-eighteenth century, peasants bought an important share of proto-industrial products while benefiting from increasing incomes.

Quit-rent declined on state-owned estates and on some private estates as well, while rising in the heartland (although this rise was generally moderate). Regional specialization also increased, with central and other industrial and proto-industrial areas tending to specialize, whereas agricultural areas lost non-agrarian activities. In particular, while factories shut down and proto-industrial activity was reduced in steppe and central 'black earth' areas,[36] the surface area of cultivated land expanded in the territory as a whole and in the main estates.[37] The main issue was that the use of *obrok* and the movements of peasants in the city and in neighbouring estates had intensified.[38] During the 1840s, in the northwestern and western agricultural and industrial regions of European Russia, passports and tickets granted to peasants included between 25 and 32 per cent of the male population.[39] By 1850, in the Vladimir province, 92.44 per cent of the state peasants were involved at least part-time in a non-agricultural occupation; in the Moscow province, the proportion was 89 per cent; in the Kostroma province, 86.5 per cent; in the Novgorod province, 80.5 per cent; in the Pskov province, 80 per cent; in the Iaroslavl province, 75.8 per cent; and in Nizhnyi-Novgorod, 65.7 per cent.[40]

To sum up, the economic dynamics of the eighteenth and first half of the nineteenth centuries in Russia cannot be explained by an increase in serfdom in response to European growth, but, on the contrary, by a relaxation of the labour constraints weighing on peasants and their gradual integration, together with noble landowners, in trade networks. These dynamics went beyond the official rules governing 'serfdom', which were increasingly overtaken by social and economic changes. It is just as hard if not harder to find confirmation of Russia's dependence on the West as it is in the case of India or colonial Africa. Finalism and historical determinism keep us from seeing the temporal dynamics specific to the Russian context.

Russian economic dynamics in comparative and global perspective

These outcomes confirm similar recent issues in the study of East European agriculture under serfdom.[41] For example, in Brandenburg-Prussia, by the turn of the nineteenth century, commutation payments increasingly eclipsed labour services. As in Russia, the government encouraged changes in the legal status of peasants;[42] however, before that date, increasing labour service in the seventeenth and late eighteenth centuries was not synonymous with a retreat from the market, as previously stated in the historiography, but, quite the opposite, commercialization of both peasant and demesne production (agriculture and proto-industrial products) quickly increased.[43] In contradiction to traditional historical literature on these matters (which conveyed the impression that East Elbian agriculture was a simple affair of cereal monoculture based on coerced labour), new detailed analyses based upon estates' archives reveal a complex picture of a large and expansive workforce and high commodity sales. This was true not only of Brandenburg, but also of other regions of East-Central Europe, including Poland. Peasant labour services here provided only 40 to 50 per cent of the demesne labour force required during the summer months and thus had to be supplemented by hired labour.⁴⁴ In all these areas, both peasants and seigneurs employed hired labour. There were also migrant day labourers who worked only during the harvest. In eastern Prussia, many of the day labourers lived in small towns, subsisting on wages earned during the peak season. Tracy Dennison and Sheilagh Ogilvie stress the strong similarities between Russia and Bohemia regarding serfdom and social relations. Peasant and seigneurial institutions interacted in both systems and strongly contributed to the social and economic dynamics.⁴⁵

Taken together, the experiences of Russia, Prussia, Lithuania and some parts of Poland lead to the conclusion that, on the whole, 'second serfdom' was not so much a form of slavery but, above all, a set of legal constraints on labour mobility. These rules were dictated much less by a scarcity of population than by increasing demand for agriculture produce and proto-industrial products. Labour and other institutions (seigneurial estate and justice, communes and guilds) were flexible enough to simultaneously guarantee a stable set of rules and the procedures to adapt them to the changing economic and social environment. Labour services were not opposed to market development; quite the contrary, the two enhanced each other. Proto-industry developed, and the specialization of some areas went along with the seasonality of proto-industrial activity for many peasants. Estate relations sometimes opposed proto-industry, but in some other cases they were favourable to it, which did not necessarily enhance or inhibit the proletarization of peasants and craftsmen (as asserted in Franklin Mendel's model, in which proto-industrialization slowed the growth of towns, confirmed by Jan De Vries).⁴⁶ Instead, agrarian development, proto-industry, demographic insights, and institutional and legal hierarchies varied from one estate to another, within the same country, in accordance with the specific relations among the landlord, the peasant community and the markets involved.

Like theories of dependence, comparisons made on the basis of ideal types or general models of historical economic development have trouble explaining historical dynamics, as the case of Russia shows. The fact that the dynamics did not correspond to those at work in England or France at the time in no way implies that they were incompatible with the development of markets and industry. Instead, it simply means that those results can be achieved by following different historical paths. Neither the formal status of Russian peasants nor common property was in itself a source of what the West sees as backwardness. These features help to explain the dynamics of the Russian economy after the abolition of serfdom.

Reforms and continuities in Russian history: The impact of the abolition of serfdom

The global trend of Russia between 1861 and 1914 hardly corresponds to the conventional images that Gerschenkron and many others paint. Revised population trends show, on the whole, lower mortality and birth rates and better living conditions in the eighteenth and nineteenth centuries than previously thought.[47] Thus, pauperization of the peasantry and frequent famines did not in fact take place,[48] and both agriculture and living standards experienced stable growth during the period from 1861 to 1914.[49]

Indeed, this revised trend is easy to understand when we put it into the broader and long-term perspective. Russian growth during the second half of the nineteenth century was important insofar as it had already been consistent during previous decades and as legal constraints on and bondage of the peasantry had already lessened before the official abolition of serfdom in 1861. As a consequence, during the second half of the nineteenth century and up to 1914, the rate of growth and commercialization of Russian agriculture was accelerated.[50] Between the 1880s and 1900, the grain trade spread capitalism to even the remotest corners of the empire[51] and Russia's wheat market was fully integrated into global markets.[52] Between 1861 and 1914, agriculture's contribution to the national income grew at a rapid pace, comparable to that of contemporary West European economies. As Gregory noted, Russia experienced rates of growth similar to those of Germany, France, America, Japan, Norway, Canada and the United Kingdom – 1.35 per cent average annual productivity growth in agriculture between 1883 and 1887 and 1909 and 1913, which was three-quarters of the industrial productivity growth rate and nearly equal to the economy-wide 1.5 per cent.[53]

Therefore, contrary to the common view, capital intensification took part in Russian growth; nevertheless, labour retained a dominant role. At the same time, the share of agriculture in the national income fell over the entire period (1881–1914) from 57 per cent to 51 per cent; but most of this decline occurred before Stolypin's privatization of common lands.[54] As opposed to the conventional view, the rates of growth of labour productivity in agriculture do not appear to have diverged significantly from the economy-wide average. In other words, if we look at the performance of agriculture and the main demographic index, recent estimations show that Russia was not falling behind most advanced countries but rather keeping pace with them.

Growth relied on the evolution of basic Russian institutions, for example the peasant commune. It is no accident that during the past twenty years, when the history of enclosures in Britain and agriculture in Europe was revisited,[55] the image of the Russian commune was contested as well.[56] Recent estimations made for Russia confirm the lack of any correlation between land redistribution and productivity.[57] Added to this revised view of Russian agriculture is that of industrialization. In contrast to traditional judgements, between 1881 and 1913 the share of industry in national income rose from 25 to 32 per cent. Industrial labour productivity was 28 per cent higher than that of agriculture.[58] This seems to confirm Olga Crisp's and more recently Borodkin's and Leonard's arguments that a lack of industrial labour was due not to internal passports or legal constraints on mobility, but to the strength of agriculture, its profitability and the interest that people had in staying in rural areas and alternating these stays with seasonal urban employment.[59]

If this is so, then, unlike Osterhammel's argument (Russia as an exception in Europe), the Russian specificity consisted in adopting extreme variations of Western solutions. Estate owners entered the proto-industrial and the cereal markets at the expense of urban merchants and producers and of occasional new 'bourgeois' estate owners. This outcome was politically relevant and specific in that it expressed an extreme defence of old agrarian aristocracies in a context of progressive transformation of the peasantry. In terms of economic growth, this solution was far from being catastrophic and confirms that markets and capitalism do not necessarily stand upon democracy and free labour. If this is true, then the place and role of Russia in global history requires a new basis. Which one?

Proto-industry developed in Western, Central and Eastern Europe from the end of the seventeenth century in response to market demand and demographic pressure.[60] It kept a central role all over Europe at least until the mid-nineteenth century. After that date, and only after, some areas declined and manufacturers and industries replaced the putting-out system.[61] However, this issue was far from being general, and in many European areas and districts, proto-industry retained a leading role during the second half of the nineteenth century and even in the twentieth century.[62]

This timing was even more relevant in Asia; authors such as Lee and Sugihara maintain that the 'industrious revolution' De Vries identified in Europe[63] was also present in some Asiatic areas.[64] As in Russia, in Japan and China too, the success of proto-industry, in particular of rural proto-industry, was at the root of a labour-intensive path of growth.[65]

In all these areas, as in most regions of Russia, agriculture did not turn into a simple supplier of produce and labour force for industry; quite the contrary, estates and peasants took part in the development of local and national markets, for both wheat and proto-industrial products. In Russia, as in Japan, and in Central Europe, the peasants' commercialization was not necessarily always 'forced' (by the landlords and/or the state); economic and legal dependence of many peasants was not in contradiction to the attraction the market exerted on many others.[66] As in many areas in Russia and Western Europe, in Japan increases in agricultural output and income led to a growth in demand for manufactured goods that was met by an expanding rural industry utilizing labour-intensive technology. The resulting growth in rural non-agricultural activity in turn generated increased incomes for rural households and hence increased demand for agricultural output.[67]

Similar results are now available concerning India; unlike the traditionally held view, which stresses the decline of cottage industry under British rule and the growing international markets, new research shows that 'traditional' labour-intensive techniques were well developed until the present day; thanks to their flexibility, these techniques allowed labour-intensive patterns of growth linked to family units integrated in both agriculture and industrial markets.[68]

However, such a persistent and global strength of agriculture and proto-industry had an unanticipated effect: urbanization and the supply of labour for urban manufacture were mostly seasonal.

Not only in Russia, Japan and France,[69] but also in Britain, until the mid-nineteenth century double employment (mostly in rural and urban areas) was the rule rather than the exception. This means that not only in Russia, but also in France and most other European countries, economic and industrial growth in the eighteenth and nineteenth centuries remained on a small scale and was labour intensive. Growth was mostly achieved through a movement along the same production function, the scope of which slightly moved upwards until the mid-nineteenth century.[70] There is evidence that a lot of productivity increase was not associated with specific innovations but with workers operating more machines.[71] The most often declared goal of these innovations was either improving the quality of the product or saving on capital, not labour. And if inventors were not particularly intent on saving labour, those who judged their inventions were even less so. In other words, economic actors did not wish to substitute labour with capital and the final outcome for the whole economy was an increasing demand for labour.[72]

- The collapse of those systems in the West was linked to a twofold process: increasing mechanization and decreasing prices of foodstuffs, colonial products and wheat; and stronger resistance from 'subaltern' groups. All of these phenomena, though occasionally present in the late eighteenth and early nineteenth centuries, took on decisive weight only in the last quarter of the nineteenth century. The second Industrial Revolution, the welfare state, the masses bursting onto the political scene and the decline of labour-intensive processes led to a disjunction between profitable production and coercion, at least in Europe and in many of its colonies. Free wage labour became more productive than coerced labour.
- However, this shift was far from universal; the accommodation between large-scale, intensive production and new forms of bondage returned to the fore with the First World War and its aftermath, as the revival of coercion in Africa and Nazi and Soviet Europe show. Soviet Russia was not only the land of coercion; more specifically, it marked an attempt to achieve the second Industrial Revolution using the methods and organization of the first, that is to say with increasing labour intensification, longer labour time and little attention to quality. The Soviet experience consisted in combining large-scale production and mechanization with labour intensification in terms of time and extremely unequal rights between working people and state masters. From this perspective, the main feature of Russia over the long run is not so much 'economic backwardness' as persistent, strong social inequalities inside an industrializing economy and society. The history of late tsarist and present-day Russia confirms that economic growth and markets are perfectly compatible with lacking democracy and unequal social rights.

Notes

1. Immanuel Wallerstein, *The Modern World-system: Capitalist Agriculture and the Origins of the European World-economy in the Sixteenth Century* (New York, London: Atheneum, 1974, 1976); Witold Kula, *An Economic Theory of the Feudal System* (London: New Left Books, 1976); Douglass North, *Structure and Change in Economic History* (New York: Norton, 1981).
2. Kenneth Pomeranz, *The Great Divergence* (Princeton, NJ: Princeton University Press, 2000).

3   Jane Burbank and Frederick Cooper, *Empires: A World History* (Princeton, NJ: Princeton University Press, 2010); Alexander S. Morrison, *Russian Rule in Samarkand 1868-1910: A Comparison with British India* (Oxford: Oxford University Press, 2008); Dominic Lieven, *Empire: The Russian Empire and its Rivals from the Sixteenth Century to the Present* (London: Pimlico, 2003).

4   See my 'Free Labour-forced Labour: An Uncertain Boundary? The Circulation of Economic Ideas between Russia and Europe from the 18th to the Mid-19th Century', *Kritika. Explorations in Russian and Eurasian History* 9, no. 1 (2008): 1-27.

5   Alexander Gerschenkron, *Economic Backwardness in Historical Perspective* (Cambridge, MA: Harvard University Press, 1962).

6   Just a few examples: Jerome Blum, *Lord and Peasants in Russia from the Ninth through the 19th Century* (New York: Atheneum, 1964); Richard Hellie, *Enserfment and Military Change in Muscovy* (Chicago, IL, and London: University of Chicago Press, 1971); Peter Kolchin, *Unfree Labour: American Slavery and Russian Serfdom* (Cambridge, MA: Harvard University Press, 1987); Daniel Field, *The End of Serfdom: Nobility and Bureaucracy in Russia, 1855-1861* (Cambridge, MA: Harvard University Press, 1976); Ivan Koval'chenko, *Russkoe krepostnoe krest'ianstvo v pervoi polovine XIX v.* (The economics of serfdom in Russia during the first half of the nineteenth century) (Moscow: Nauka, 1967).

7   Alessandro Stanziani, *L'économie en révolution: Le cas russe, 1870-1930* (Paris: Albin Michel, 1998).

8   Nikolai Kablukov, *Posobie pri mestnykh statistichekikh obsledovaniiakh* (Remarks for local statistical surveys) (Moscow, 1910), 8-10.

9   Alessandro Stanziani, 'Les enquêtes orales en Russie: 1861-1914', *Annales HSS* 1 (2000): 219-241.

10 Alexander Mendel, *Dilemmas of Progress in Tsarist Russia: Legal Marxism and Legal Populism* (Cambridge, MA: Harvard University Press, 1961); Paul Rosenstein-Rodan, 'Problems of Industrialization of Eastern and Southeastern Europe', *Economic Journal* 53 (1943): 202-211; Gunner Myrdal, *Economic Theory and Underdeveloped Regions* (London: Duckworth, 1956).

11 Douglass North and Robert Thomas, *The Rise of Western Civilization: A New Economic History* (Cambridge: Cambridge University Press, 1973).

12 Deidre McCloskey, 'The Open Fields of England: Rent, Risk, and the Rate of Interest, 1300-1815', in *Markets in History: Economic Studies of the Past*, ed. David Galenson (Cambridge: Cambridge University Press, 1989): 5-51; Randall Nielsen, 'Storage and English Government Intervention in Early Modern Grain Markets', *The Journal of Economic History* 57, no. 1 (1997): 1-33.

13 Tracy K. Dennison, 'Did Serfdom Matter? Russian Rural Society, 1750-1860', *Historical Research* 79, no. 203 (2003): 74-89.

14 Joseph Stiglitz, *Whither Socialism?* (Cambridge, MA: MIT Press, 1994).

15 Gareth Austin, 'Reciprocal Comparison and African History: Tackling Conceptual Eurocentrism in the Study of Africa's Economic Past', *African Studies Review* 50, no. 3 (2007): 1–28; Pomeranz, *The Great Divergence*, 8; Bin Wong, *China Transformed* (Ithaca, NY: Cornell University Press, 1997).

16 Stephen Broadberry and Bishnupriya Gupta, 'The Early Modern Great Divergence: Wages, Prices and Economic Development in Europe and Asia, 1500–1800', *The Economic History Review* 59, no. 1 (2006): 2–31; Patrick O'Brien, 'Ten Years of Debates on the Origin of the Great Divergence', *Reviews in History* (2010). Available online: http://www.history.ac.uk/reviews/review/1008 (accessed 17 August 2017).

17 Ibid.

18 Angus Maddison, *The World Economy: A Millennial Perspective* (Paris: Development Centre of the Organisation for Economic Co-operation and Development, 2001).

19 Robert Allen, *The British Industrial Revolution in Global Perspective* (Cambridge: Cambridge University Press, 2009); Prasannan Parthasarathi, *Why Europe Grew Rich and Asia Did Not: Global Economic Divergence, 1600–1850* (Cambridge: Cambridge University Press, 2011).

20 Jürgen Osterhammel, *The Transformation of the World: A Global History of the Nineteenth Century* (Princeton, NJ: Princeton University Press, 2014).

21 Pomeranz, *The Great Divergence*.

22 Hellie, *Enserfment and Military Change in Muscovy*.

23 Daniel Kaiser, *The Growth of Law in Medieval Russia* (Princeton, NJ: Princeton University Press, 1980); Dmitri Grekov, *Sudebniki XV-XVII vekov* (Precis of laws, 15th–16th centuries) (Moscow, Leningrad: Akademia Nauk SSSR, 1952).

24 Alessandro Stanziani, 'Serfs, Slaves, or Wage Earners? The Legal Statute of Labour in Russia from a Comparative Perspective, from the 16th to the 19th century', *Journal of Global History* 3, no. 2 (2008): 183–202.

25 Tracy Dennison, *The Institutional Framework of Russian Serfdom* (Cambridge: Cambridge University Press, 2010); Peter Czap, 'The Perennial Multiple-family Household, Mishino, Russia 1782–1858', *Journal of Family History* 7, no. 1 (2016): 5–26.

26 Carol Leonard, *Agrarian Reforms in Russia* (Cambridge: Cambridge University Press, 2011).

27 For a synthesis and a discussion, see Sheilagh Ogilvie and Markus Cerman (eds), *European Proto-industrialization* (Cambridge: Cambridge University Press, 1996); Pierre Jeannin, 'La proto-industrialization: développement ou impasse?', *Annales ESC* 35 (1980): 52–65.

28 Sheilagh Ogilvie, 'Guild, Efficiency, and Social Capital', *Economic History Review* LVII (2004): 286–333.

29 Boris Mironov, *The Social History of the Russian Empire*, 2 vols (Boulder, CO: Westview, 1999).

30 Boris N. Mironov, 'Eksport russkogo khleba vo vtoroi polovine 18 v.-nachale 19e v. (Exports of Russian wheat during the second half of the nineteenth century), *Istoricheskie zapiski* 93 (1974): 149–188; Boris Mironov, *Vnutrennyi rynok Rossii vo vtoroi polovine 18 veka-pervoi polovine 19e v.* (The Russian domestic market during the second half of the eighteenth century–first half of the nineteenth century) (Leningrad: Nauka, 1981).

31 Boris N. Mironov and Carol S. Leonard, 'In Search of Hidden Information: Some Issues in the Socio-economic History of Russia in the Eighteenth and Nineteenth Centuries', *Social Science History* 9, no. 4 (1985): 339–359.

32 Mironov, *Vnutrennyi rynok*: 153–154.

33 Alessandro Stanziani, 'Revisiting Russian Serfdom: Bonded Peasants and Market Dynamics, 1600–1800', *International Labour and Working Class History* 78, no. 1 (2010): 12–27.

34 Boris Mironov, 'Consequences of the Price Revolution in Eighteenth-century Russia', *The Economic History Review* 45 (1992): 465.

35 On serf-entrepreneurs, see Robert Rudolph, 'Agricultural Structure and Proto-industrialization in Russia: Economic Development with Unfree Labour', *The Journal of Economic History* 45 (1985): 47–69; L.S. Prokof'eva, *Krest'ianskaia obshchina v rossii: federal'naia renta c XVII-nachale XVIII v* (The private estates' peasants in Russia: the feudal rent in the seventeenth to early eighteenth century) (Leningrad: Nauka, 1981); Iurii A. Tikhonov, *Pomeshchic'i krest'iane v rossii: feodal'naia renta v XVII-nachale XVIII v* (The private estates' peasants in Russia: the feudal rent in the seventeenth to early eighteenth century) (Moscow: Nauka, 1974). On the urban activity of private peasants, I have consulted the following archives: RGADA, fond 294, opis' 2 and 3; fond 1287, opis' 3. TsGIAM, opis' 2, dela 31, 40, 82, 124, 146; RGADA, fond 210: razriadnyi prikaz; fond 248, Senat I senatskie uchrezhdeniia; fond 350: revizkie skazki po nizhegorodskoi gubernii, opis' 2, dela 1975 and 2056; fonds 615, krepostnye knigi, dela 526, 528, 529, 4753, 6654; fond 1209 (pomestnyi prikaz), opis' 1, delo 292; fond 1287 (Sheremetev), opis' 5 and 6; RGIA, fond 1088 (Sheremetev, opis' 3, 5, 10). See also Klaus Gestwa, *Proto-industrialisierung in Russland: Wirtschaft, Herrschaft und Kultur in Ivanovo und Pavlovo, 1741–1932* (Göttingen: Vandenhoek & Ruprecht, 1999).

36 Irina V. Ledovskaia, 'Biudzhet russkogo pomeshchika v 40-60kh godakh XIX v' (Estate owners' budgets in the 1840s–60s), in Akademiia Nauk SSSR, *Materialy po istorii sel'skogo khoziaistva i krest'ianstva SSSR*, vol. 8 (Moscow: Nauka, 1974): 240–245. David Moon, *The Russian Peasantry, 1600–1930: The World the Peasants Made* (London and New York: Addison Wesley Longman, 1999).

37 Ibid.

38 Koval'chenko, *Russkoe krepostnoe*: 394; Boris Gorshkov, 'Serfs on the Move: Peasant Seasonal Migration in Pre-reform Russia, 1800–1860', *Kritika: Explorations in Russian History* 1, no. 4 (2000): 627–656.

39 Nikolai M. Druzhinin, *Gosudarstvennye krest'iane i reforma P.D. Kiseleva* (The state peasants and the reforms of Kiselev), 2nd edn (Moscow: Nauka, 1958), 315, 321.
40 Ibid., 296–390.
41 For a deep revision of second serfdom in Central and Eastern Europe, see Markus Cerman, 'Social Structure and Land Markets in Late Medieval Central and Eastern Europe', *Continuity and Change* 23, no. 1 (2008): 55–100.
42 Hartmut Harnisch, 'Bäuerliche Ökonomie und Mentalität unter den Bedingungen der ostelbischen Gutsherrschaft in den letzten Jahrzehnten vor Beginn der Agrarreformen', *Jahrbuch für Wirtschaftsgeschichte* 24 (1989): 87–108.
43 William Hagen, *Ordinary Prussians: Brandenburg Junkersand Villagers, 1500–1840* (Cambridge: Cambridge University Press, 2002).
44 Robert Frost, 'The Nobility of Poland-Lithuania, 1569–1795', in *The European Nobilities in the Seventeenth and Eighteenth Centuries*, vol. II: *Northern, Central and Eastern Europe*, ed. Hamish Scott (London: Routledge, 1994).
45 Tracy Dennison and Sheilagh Ogilvie, 'Serfdom and Social Capital in Bohemia and Russia', *Economic History Review* 60, no. 3 (2007): 513–544.
46 Jan De Vries, *European Urbanization, 1500–1800* (London: Meuthen, 1984).
47 Steven Hoch, 'Famine, Disease and Mortality Patterns in the Parish of Boshervka, Russia, 1830–1932', *Population Studies* 52, no. 3 (1998): 357–368. Steven Hoch, 'On Good Numbers and Bad: Malthus, Population Trend and Peasant Standard of Living in Late Imperial Russia', *Slavic Review* 53, no. 1 (1994): 41–75. Steven Hoch, 'Serfs in Imperial Russia: Demographic Insights', *Journal of Interdisciplinary History* 13, no. 2 (1982): 221–246.
48 Stephen Wheatcroft, 'Crisis and Condition of the Peasantry in Late Imperial Russia', in *Peasant Economy, Culture and Politics of European Russia, 1800–1921*, ed. Esther Kingston-Mann and Timothy Mixter (Princeton, NJ: Princeton University Press, 1991), 101–127.
49 Elvira M. Wilbur, 'Was Russian Peasant Agriculture Really That Impoverished? New Evidence from a Case Study from the "Impoverished Center" at the End of the Nineteenth Century', *Journal of Economic History* 43 (1983): 137–144; Esther Kingston-Mann, 'Marxism and Russian Rural Development: Problems of Evidence, Experience and Culture', *American Historical Review* 84 (1981): 731–752; James Y. Simms, Jr, 'The Crisis in Russian Agriculture at the End of the Nineteenth Century: A Different View', *Slavic Review* 36 (1977): 377–398; James Simms, 'The Crop Failure of 1891: Soil Exhaustion, Technological Backwardness, and Russia's "Agrarian Crisis"', *Slavic Review* 41 (1982): 236–250.
50 Paul Gregory, *Russian National Income 1885–1913* (Cambridge: Cambridge University Press, 1982; paperback 2004); Alessandro Stanziani, *L'économie en revolution. Le cas russe, 1870–1930* (Paris: Albin Michel, 1998); Peter Gatrell, *The Tsarist Economy, 1850–1917* (London: Batsford, 1986).

51. Ivan Koval'chenko and L. Milov, *Vserossiiskii agrarnyi rynok, XVIII–nachalo XX v* (The Russian agrarian market, eighteenth–nineteenth centuries) (Moscow: Nauka, 1974).
52. Barry K. Goodwin and Thomas J. Grennes, 'Tsarist Russia and the World Wheat Market', *Explorations in Economic History* 35 (1998): 405–430.
53. Gregory, *Russian National Income*, 126–130; 168–194.
54. Serguei N. Prokopovich, *Opyt ischsleniia narodonogo dokhoda 50 gubernii Evropeiskoi Rossii v 1900–1913 gg* (Study of the national income of 50 provinces of European Russia, 1900–1913) (Moscow: Sovet Vserossiikikh kooperatvinikh S'ezdov, 1918), 67.
55. McCloskey, 'The Open Fields of England', 5–51.
56. Esther Kingston-Mann, 'Peasant Communes and Economic Innovation: A Preliminary Inquiry', in *Peasant Economy, Culture, and Politics of European Russia, 1800–1921*, ed. Esther Kingston-Mann and Timothy Mixter (Princeton, NJ: Princeton University Press, 1991), 23–51; Pavel' N. Zyrianov, *Krest'ianskaia obshchina Evropeiskoi Rossii 1907–1914 gg* (The peasant commune in European Russia, 1907–1914) (Moscow: Nauka, 1992); Judith Pallot, *Land Reform in Russia 1906–1917: Peasant Responses to Stolypin's Project of Rural Transformation* (Oxford: Clarendon Press, 1999).
57. Steven Nafziger, 'Communal Institutions, Resource Allocation, and Russian Economic Development' (unpublished PhD diss., Yale University, Yale, 2006).
58. Gregory, *Russian National Income*, 132.
59. Leonard, *The Agrarian Reform*.
60. William Hagen, 'Capitalism in the Countryside in Early Modern Europe: Interpretations, Models, Debates', *Agricultural History* 62, no. 1 (1988): 13–47.
61. Ogilvie and Cerman, *European Proto-industrialization*.
62. Charles Sabel and Jonathan Zeitlin (eds), *Worlds of Possibilities: Flexibility and Mass Production in Western Industrialization* (Cambridge, Paris: Maison des Sciences de l'Homme/Cambridge University Press, 1997).
63. Jan De Vries, 'The Industrial Revolution and the Industrious Revolution', *Journal of Economic History* 54, no. 2 (1994): 249–270.
64. Kaouro Sugihara, 'Labour-intensive Industrialisation in Global History', *Australian Economic History* 47, no. 2 (2007): 121–154; John Lee, 'Trade and Economy in Preindustrial East Asia, c. 1500–1800: East Asia in the Age of Global Integration', *The Journal of Asian Studies* 58, no. 1 (1999): 2–26.
65. Penelope Franck, *Rural Economic Development in Japan: From the Nineteenth Century to the Pacific War* (London, New York: Routledge, 2006).
66. Sugihara, 'Labour-intensive' Industrialisation.
67. Osamu Saito, 'The Labour Market in Tokugawa Japan: Wage Differentials and the Real Wage Level, 1727, 1830', *Explorations in Economic History* 15, no. 1 (1978): 84–100.

68 Tirthankar Roy, *The Economic History of India, 1857–1947* (New York: Oxford University Press, 2001); Frank Perlin, 'Proto-industrialization and Pre-colonial South Asia', *Past and Present* 98, no. 1 (1983): 30–95.
69 Gilles Postel-Vinay, 'The Di-integration of Traditional Labour Markets in France: From Agriculture and Industry to Agriculture or Industry', in *Labour Market Evolution: The Economic History of Market Integration, Wage Flexibility and the Employment Relation*, ed. George Grantham and Mary MacKinnon (London and New York: Routledge, 1994): 64–83.
70 Nicholas Crafts, *British Economic Growth during the Industrial Revolution* (Oxford: Oxford University Press, 1986).
71 Gregory Clark, 'Productivity Growth without Technical Change in European Agriculture before 1850', *Journal of Economic History* 47, no. 2 (1987): 419–432.
72 Christine MacLeod, *Inventing the Industrial Revolution: The English Patent System, 1660–1800* (Cambridge: Cambridge University Press, 1988).

5

Labour History Goes Global

Marcel van der Linden

Labour historians from Europe and North America frequently assert that their discipline is not in a healthy state. Unambiguously, they remind us of the boom in such studies during the 1970s, when, largely under the influence of the student movements, a mighty tide of monographs, dissertations and articles were written and published in their fields. It is, of course, undeniable that the interest in working-class history within the North Atlantic area declined following the end of the 1980s, if not earlier.[1] Many students have turned to other topics, and their teachers have also changed course, choosing new subjects that attract their interest or promise more in career terms. Likewise, many scholarly journals have changed or expanded their titles or subject matter, while others stick to the old profile and are losing subscribers. This is not an exact diagnosis, but we cannot ignore the general and relative decline in the fortunes of North Atlantic labour history writing.

Geographical extension

On the other hand, such a picture is a distortion, for the world is much larger than the North Atlantic: in various regions of South America, Africa and Asia, the historiography of workers and labour movements has made great strides in the last twenty to thirty years. That has led not only to an enormous number of publications, but also to institutional initiatives. Some examples:

- In 1996, the Association of Indian Labour Historians was founded in New Delhi. Since then, it has organized ten successful biannual conferences.
- In 2001, members of the Brazilian National Historians' Organization (ANPUH) formed a large section for the study of working-class history (Mundos do Trabalho).

- First conferences on labour history have taken place in South Africa (1978), Pakistan (1999), South Korea (2001), Indonesia (2005), Turkey (2011), Senegal (2012) and Bolivia (2012).

Labour and working-class history has gradually become a subject of research all over the globe. Therefore, one cannot really talk about a 'crisis' in the field, but must instead differentiate between continents and subcontinents. Many countries of the so-called periphery or semi-periphery have experienced a boom in labour history since the 1960s or 1970s. This development has probably been most spectacular in Latin America, where during the last forty years or so many studies have appeared, at first focusing on industrial labour, and soon after also on peasants, small businesses, indigenous peoples, the 'blacks' and the immigrants. South Africa, too, has seen an upturn in labour and working-class history; some of these new works deal mainly with trade unions and some have a broader perspective. Inspired by the British example, a South African History Workshop Movement began to flourish. In India, many of the first monographs were strongly traditional, even if some authors relatively early on began to link institutional aspects with the broad stream of social history. A special impulse emanated in the 1980s from the so-called subaltern studies, of which Ranajit Guha was the main protagonist. While this was a very politicized tendency that concentrated on the history of poor and landless peasants, it has produced some excellent work. A third current emerged alongside this new development, consisting of young historians interested in labour history, which distanced itself from subaltern studies and placed more emphasis on workers and their families. This third contingent showed more interest in infrastructural problems and also initiated the establishment of an archive for labour history.[2]

Substantive deepening

When labour history spread out over the world, it first maintained the traditional North Atlantic approach. Like their 'Northern' counterparts, the 'Southern' historians also focused primarily on mineworkers, dock workers or plantation workers, and neglected families and households and the work that took place there. They also mainly focused on strikes, trade unions and political parties; and, most importantly, they used the development of the North Atlantic as a model that peripheral working classes did 'not yet' match. Gradually, attempts were made to develop a less Eurocentric approach. Groundbreaking works included Walter Rodney's histories of the Upper Guinea Coast and of the Guyanese working people (1970 and 1981), Charles van Onselen's *Chibaro* (1976) on mine labour in Southern Rhodesia and the essays collected in Ranajit Das Gupta's *Labour and Working Class in Eastern India* (1994) on plantation workers, miners and textile workers in Assam, Bengal and elsewhere.[3] This 'globalization' in the study of labour history calls for a new type of historiography, one which 'overtakes' old-style labour history from North America and Europe by incorporating its findings into a new globally orientated approach. That is, indeed, an extremely ambitious project that has scarcely begun. Many of the goals of this new departure are unclear or need elucidation.

The concept of 'working class', which originated in nineteenth-century Europe, has been questioned more and more in the past decades. In the tradition of Karl Marx or Max Weber, workers, regardless of gender, were considered as (1) individuals who (2) live exclusively by selling their labour power to an employer for a wage and (3) conclude their contract with the employer voluntarily and for a limited period. In the so-called Third World, and, if one looks closer to home, in the highly developed capitalist countries as well, such 'labourers' are a rare species indeed. Workers are seldom isolated individuals but part of a family or a household that carries out different kinds of work and pools the wages paid for it. Furthermore, the workers, in order to survive, need reproductive labour produced by themselves or others, to enable them to spend their wages on rent for suitable accommodation, food, etc.

The borderlines between 'free' wage labour, self-employment and unfree labour are not clear-cut, and the opposition between urban and rural labour should not be considered absolute. The boundaries between the 'free' wage labourers and other kinds of workers in capitalist society are vague and gradual. Firstly, there are extensive and complicated grey areas full of transitional locations between the 'free' wage labourers and the slaves, the self-employed and the so-called lumpenproletariat. Secondly, almost all workers belong to households that combine several modes of labour. Thirdly, individual workers can also combine different modes of labour, both synchronically and diachronically. Finally, the distinction between the different kinds of workers is not clear-cut; for example, there are workers in Naples who work at night as thieves,[4] or the supposedly self-employed who work for one or two customers (in reality employers), or slaves-for-hire in Brazil and the Deep South of the USA performing classical wage labour. Besides such 'formal' deviations from the 'pure' status of wage labour, we find a series of implicit cases of exclusion from belonging to the working class: police officers, prostitutes, convict labourers or domestic servants, for example.

Complex reality, then, should encourage us to rethink the concepts of 'working class' or 'the workers'.[5] In searching for a new approach, we have to consider that in capitalism there *always* existed, and probably will continue to exist, several forms of commodified labour side by side. In its long development, capitalism utilized many kinds of work relationships, some based on economic compulsion, others with a non-economic component. Millions of slaves were brought by force from Africa to the Caribbean, to Brazil and to the southern states of the USA. Contract workers from India and China were shipped off to toil in South Africa, Malaysia or countries in South America. 'Free' migrant workers left Europe for the New World, for Australia or the colonies[6] and, today, sharecroppers produce an important portion of world agricultural output. These and other work relationships are synchronous, even if there seems to be a secular trend towards 'free wage labour'. Slavery still exists, sharecropping is enjoying a comeback in some regions, and so on. We can summarize by saying that capitalism could and can choose whatever form of commodified labour it thinks fit in a given historical context: one variant seems most profitable today, another tomorrow.[7] It is the historic dynamics of this 'multitude' that we should try to understand.

If this argument is correct, then it behoves us to conceptualize the working class as one (important) kind of commodified labour among others. Consequently, so-called 'free' labour cannot be seen as the only form of exploitation suitable for modern capitalism but as one alternative among several. We therefore need to form concepts that take account of more dimensions. As is well known, 'classical' analyses of the working class were based on the power relationships within the work process, a combination of three elements: '(1) purposeful activity, that is work itself, (2) the object on which the work is performed, and (3) the instruments of that work.'[8] The product of that work is the fourth element of Marx's analysis. A modified approach could incorporate these dimensions of classical Marxist analysis by distinguishing six important elements:

1. The relationship between the worker and his or her *capacity to work* (Does the worker have control over his/her body, or is it the employer or a third party?).
2. The relationship between the worker and his or her *means of labour* (Are these in possession of the worker, the employer or a third party?).
3. The relationship between the worker and what they *produce* (What portion of the yield or profit belongs to the worker, to the employer or to a third party?).

4. The relationship between the worker and the other persons in his or her household (What kind of social and economic dependence exists between the worker and the others in the household?).
5. The relationship between the worker and their *employer outside the immediate production process* (To what degree is the worker in the debt of his or her employer by virtue of the accommodation or the loans the employer provides?).
6. The relationship between *groups of workers within the work environment* (Are the workers subjected to forms of dependency on fellow workers?).[9]

Teleconnections

Through case studies and historical comparisons of cases, we can reconstruct the great diversity and logics of workers' experiences and actions; furthermore, the global interconnections between those experiences and actions also demand our attention. Such interconnections were already quite often recognized in the past, but they have been neglected equally often by labour historians to this very day.

We could call such connections *teleconnections*, after the example of geologists and climatologists who, since the beginning of the twentieth century, have demonstrated many linkages between regions located at a remote distance from each other. In reality, the immediate interests of workers in one part of the world can have direct repercussions for the immediate interests of workers in another part. Such entanglements emerge in all kinds of ways. A valid general analysis of them would require much more research, and a few examples must suffice here to illustrate what is at stake:

- *Labour processes in different locations can be linked via global commodity chains*. Luis Valenzuela, for example, shows how from the 1830s to the 1860s a very close nexus existed between Chilean copper miners and British copper smelters in Swansea (South Wales): 'Large quantities of Chilean copper and regulus arrived in the Swansea docks to be smelted and refined in the South Wales furnaces. On the other hand, Welsh coal and firebricks as well as other British produce were shipped from South Wales to Chilean ports close to the mines to pay for that copper and, incidentally, stimulating mining and smelting production.'[10]

- *Labour processes are themselves sometimes intrinsically international.* Transport workers such as seamen and dockers are 'natural' liaisons between regions separated by long distances. As early as the sixteenth and seventeenth centuries, and perhaps even earlier, they made logistical connections between workers in different continents. Seamen 'influenced both the form and the content of plebeian protest by their militant presence in seaport crowds' and 'used their mobility … to create links with other working people'.[11] Transport workers have figured prominently in the transcontinental dissemination of forms of collective action, as shown by the diffusion of the model of the Industrial Workers of the World from the United States to places such as Chile, Australia, New Zealand and South Africa. Moreover, in 1911 they were the first to organize transcontinental collective action, through simultaneous strikes in Britain, the Netherlands, Belgium and on the East Coast of the United States.[12]
- *Migrants can impart their experiences to other workers in the country of settlement* – as Indian workers did in the Caribbean and Southeast Asia, British workers did in Australia, Italian workers did in the Americas, and Chinese workers did in the Asian diaspora. Their presence in the new country could cause the segmentation of its labour markets, which might in turn lead to forms of ethnically segregated action. Also, returning migrants may import a repertoire of forms of collective action from their respective countries of origin.[13]
- *The employers' capital likewise realizes transcontinental entanglements.* The staff of multinational firms are mutually connected via corporate structures – a phenomenon that does not date from the last one hundred and fifty years, but is already at least four hundred years old.[14]
- *Consumption by workers of products produced by workers elsewhere* is another relationship. The increased use of sugar by workers in Europe in the eighteenth century influenced the activities of slaves in the sugar plantations of the New World. The inverse also seems to apply: Sidney Mintz suggests, for example, that sugar made the diet of workers in England more varied and richer, and therefore promoted the Industrial Revolution.[15]
- *The fate of workers can be mediated by state action.* The British campaign to abolish the slave trade (from 1807) had a major impact on labour relations in the Americas, Africa and parts of Asia. The introduction of immigration restrictions by nation states from the last decades of the nineteenth century is probably also bound up with the abolition of slavery, the emancipation of the serfs in Russia and other developments that promoted the mobility

of workers. Furthermore, the activities of the International Labour Organization (since 1919) have influenced workers' rights across the globe.[16]
- Last, but not at least, there are the *transnational waves of collective action*. In addition to instigating the first Russian Revolution in 1905, the Japanese victory over Russia, for instance, promoted nationalist and anti-colonial forces throughout Asia, and encouraged workers' collective action in many places. The second Russian Revolution starting in March 1917 and the Bolshevik seizure of power inspired an explosive increase of workers' collective action on all continents. The Hungarian uprising of 1956 was a 'powerful stimulus' for labour unrest in Shanghai in the following year.[17]

All such teleconnections cannot be viewed in separation from the ongoing class conflicts between employers and workers. Policies 'from above' followed collective actions 'from below', and vice versa. Beverly Silver shows that capital can respond to workers' unrest with a number of 'fixes', that is to say the reorganization of labour processes, shifting activities to other geographic locations, new product lines and banking or speculation.[18] Our broader concept of the working class enables us to add a variant, which we could call the 'labour modes fix': employers can, if they see their position threatened in one way or another, substitute one form of labour commodification for another, for example replacing 'free' wage labour with debt bondage or self-employment.

The connections and contradictions between different forms of labour commodification are of essential importance for global labour history. Marx already wrote in *Capital* that 'Labour in a white skin cannot emancipate itself where it is branded in a black skin.'[19] Robert von Pöhlmann summarizes the logic of this thought succinctly:

> How could the free working class, even if its members were well-organized, hope to influence wage-levels durably across the board, if a large part of the workers present were impervious to their influence because of their unfreedom, when the success of even the staunchest solidarity essentially depended on whether and to what extent the shortages caused by a strike could be compensated for with unfree workers?[20]

Also, obviously acute conflicts can emerge within individual segments of the workers. Often there are conflicts between better-paid and less well-paid groups of wage earners that are consolidated along ethnic, racial or gender lines.[21] Yet other allocative mechanisms assert themselves, even within one segment of the labour market in which workers have the same ethnic and religious background.[22]

A final word

These enlargements of the research terrain have far-reaching implications. To realize their broader approach, contacts between different subgroups of researchers should, I think, be significantly intensified. First, there should be more contact between labour historians in different regions. Second, a closer cooperation is desirable between the historians of wage labour and the historians of slavery, indenture and the peasantry. Initiatives in this direction are visible in parts of the Global South (Brazil, India and Southern Africa), but much more is feasible and desirable. Third, there is a significant overlap with economic, family, women's and legal history, and area studies, which could be better utilized. Finally, we should strive for more cooperation with other social scientists (anthropologists, sociologists, political scientists, geographers, etc.). In the terrain of traditional labour history, such cooperation already occurs, but it could be intensified. Anthropologists, for example, can make an important contribution to our insight into the incorporation of non-capitalist societies into the capitalist world economy.

Bridging these gaps presents great challenges. Historians concerned with slavery, for example, form a separate, rather extensive community, with their own periodicals (such as the excellent *Slavery and Abolition*), which are normally not read by labour historians. But, inversely, the historians of slavery do not usually concern themselves with the history of wage labour, and only seldomly read *International Labor and Working-class History* or the *International Review of Social History*. Initiatives aiming at cooperation between the historians of slave labour and wage labour originate mainly from Africa and Brazil; in recent times, they are finding cautious approval elsewhere as well. To make global labour history a success, much more of this kind of interaction will be necessary.

Notes

1   Overviews of North Atlantic labour history are given in Jan Lucassen, 'Writing Global Labour History, *c.* 1800–1940: A Historiography of Concepts, Periods, and Geographical Scope', in *Global Labour History: A State of the Art*, ed. Jan Lucassen (Berne: Peter Lang, 2006), 39–89, and in Lex Heerma van Voss and Marcel van der Linden (eds), *Class and Other Identities: Gender, Religion and Ethnicity in the Writing of European Labour History* (New York and Oxford: Berghahn, 2002). Informative too is Joan Allen, Alan Campbell and John McIlroy (eds), *Histories of*

Labour: National and International Perspectives (Pontypool: Merlin Press, 2010), with chapters on Britain, Ireland, the US, Canada, Australia and Germany as well as on India and Japan.

2   John D. French, 'The Latin American Labor Studies Boom', *International Review of Social History* 45, no. 2 (2000): 279–308; Jon Lewis, 'South African Labour History: A Historiographical Assessment', *Radical History Review*, no. 46-47 (1990): 213–235; Alan Cobley, 'Does Social History Have a Future? The Ending of Apartheid and Recent Trends in South African Historiography', *Journal of Southern African Studies* 27 (2001): 613–625; Partha Chatterjee, 'Subaltern History', in *International Encyclopedia of the Social and Behavioral Sciences*, vol. 22 (London: Elsevier Science, 2001), 15237–15241; Rana P. Behal, Chitra Joshi and Prabhu P. Mohapatra, 'India', in *Histories of Labour*, 290–314.

3   Walter Rodney, *A History of the Upper Guinea Coast, 1545–1800* (Oxford: Oxford University Press, 1970); Walter Rodney, *A History of the Guyanese Working People, 1881–1905* (Baltimore, MD: Johns Hopkins University Press, 1981); Charles van Onselen, *Chibaro: African Mine Labour in Southern Rhodesia* (Johannesburg: Ravan Press, 1976); Ranajit Das Gupta, *Labour and Working Class in Eastern India: Studies in Colonial History* (Calcutta: K. P. Bagchi, 1994).

4   Thomas Belmonte, *The Broken Fountain* (New York: Columbia University Press, 1979), 112–117.

5   On the same subject: Frances Rothstein, 'The New Proletarians: Third World Reality and First World Categories', *Comparative Studies in Society and History* 28 (1986): 217–238. Recent studies exploring the labour histories of previously neglected groups include Clive Emsley, 'The Policeman as Worker: A Comparative Survey c. 1800–1940', *International Review of Social History* 45, no. 1 (2000): 89–110; Erik-Jan Zürcher (ed.), *Fighting for a Living: A Comparative Study of Military Labour 1500–2000* (Amsterdam: Amsterdam University Press, 2013); Christian G. De Vito and Alex Lichtenstein (eds), *Global Convict Labor* (Leiden: Brill, 2015); Dirk Hoerder, Elise van Nederveen Meerkerk and Silke Neunsinger (eds), *Towards a Global History of Domestic and Caregiving Workers* (Leiden: Brill, 2015).

6   A magnificent overview is given in Dirk Hoerder, *Cultures in Contact: World Migrations in the Second Millennium* (Durham, NC: Duke University Press, 2002). It has now become clear that the nineteenth-century transatlantic migration circuit was in truth not larger than the contemporaneous migration circuits in South and Northeast Asia. See Adam McKeown, 'Global Migration, 1846–1940', *Journal of World History* 15 (2004): 155–189.

7   Recent studies supporting this contention include Marcelo Badaró Mattos, *Laborers and Enslaved Workers. Experiences in Common in the Making of Rio de Janeiro's Working Class, 1850–1920* (New York and Oxford: Berghahn, 2017); Sven Beckert, *Empire of Cotton: A New History of Global Capitalism* (New York: Knopf, 2014);

Rana P. Behal, *One Hundred Years of Servitude: Political Economy of Tea Plantations in Colonial Assam* (New Delhi: Tulika, 2014); Alessandro Stanziani, *Bondage. Labor and Rights in Eurasia from the Sixteenth to the Early Twentieth Centuries* (New York and Oxford: Berghahn, 2014).

8   Karl Marx, *Capital*, vol. I, trans. Ben Fowkes (Harmondsworth: Penguin, 1976), 284.

9   Naturally, dimensions may overlap. In the service sector, for instance, the means of labour and the labour product can be identical and in subcontracting the work team may consist of household members.

10 Luis Valenzuela, 'Copper: Chilean Miners – British Smelters in the Mid-nineteenth Century', in *World Development: An Introduction*, ed. Prodromos Panayiotopoulos and Gavin Capps (London and Sterling, VA: Pluto Press, 2001), 173–180, at 177.

11 Marcus Rediker, *Between the Devil and the Deep Blue Sea: Merchant Seamen, Pirates, and the Anglo-American Maritime World, 1700–1750* (Cambridge: Cambridge University Press, 1987), 294.

12 Marcel van der Linden, 'Transport Workers' Strike, Worldwide 1911', in *St. James Encyclopedia of Labor History Worldwide. Major Events in Labor History and Their Impact*, 2 vols, ed. Neil Schlager (Detroit, MI: Thomson Gale, 2003), 334–336.

13 See, for example, Chandra Jayawardena, 'Culture and Ethnicity in Guyana and Fiji', *Man*, New Series 15, no. 3 (1980): 430–450; Donna Gabaccia, 'The "Yellow Peril" and the "Chinese of Europe": Global Perspectives on Race and Labor, 1815–1930', in *Migration, Migration History, History*, ed. Jan Lucassen and Leo Lucassen (Berne: Peter Lang, 1997), 177–196; Prabhu Mohapatra, 'The Hosay Massacre of 1884: Class and Community among Indian Immigrant Labourers in Trinidad', in *Work and Social Change in Asia: Essays in Honour of Jan Breman*, ed. Arvind N. Das and Marcel van der Linden (New Delhi: Manohar, 2003), 187–230; Touraj Atabaki, 'Disgruntled Guests: Iranian Subaltern on the Margins of the Tsarist Empire', *International Review of Social History* 48, no. 3 (2003): 401–426.

14 Jan Lucassen, 'A Multinational and its Labor Force: The Dutch East India Company, 1595–1795', *International Labor and Working-class History* 66 (2004): 12–39; Giovanni Arrighi, Kenneth Barr and Shuji Hisaeda, 'The Transformation of Business Enterprise', in *Chaos and Governance in the Modern World System*, ed. Giovanni Arrighi and Beverly J. Silver (Minneapolis and London: University of Minnesota Press, 1999), 97–150; Alfred D. Chandler Jr and Bruce Mazlish (eds), *Leviathans: Multinational Corporations and the New Global History* (Cambridge: Cambridge University Press, 2005).

15 Sidney W. Mintz, *Sweetness and Power: The Place of Sugar in Modern History* (New York: Penguin, 1986), 183.

16 Marcel van der Linden (ed.), *Humanitarian Intervention and Changing Labour Relations: The Long-term Consequences of the Abolition of the Slave Trade* (Leiden: Brill, 2011). In recent years the historiography of the ILO has made great strides. See, e.g., Jasmien Van Daele et al. (ed.), *ILO Histories: Essays on the International Labour Organization and its Impact on the World during the Twentieth Century* (Berne: Peter Lang, 2010); Daniel Maul, *Human Rights, Development and Decolonization: The International Labour Organization, 1940-70* (Houndmills: Palgrave Macmillan, 2012); Sandrine Kott and Joëlle Droux (eds), *Globalizing Social Rights: The International Labour Organization and Beyond* (Houndmills: Palgrave Macmillan, 2013).
17 Klaus Kreiser, 'Der japanische Sieg über Russland (1905) und sein Echo unter den Muslimen', *Die Welt des Islams* 21 (1981): 209-239; Nader Sohrabi, 'Historicizing Revolutions: Constitutional Revolutions in the Ottoman Empire, Iran and Russia, 1905-1908', *American Journal of Sociology* 100 (1994-95): 1383-1447; Neil McInnes, 'The Labour Movement', in *The Impact of the Russian Revolution 1917-1967. The Influence of Bolshevism on the World outside Russia* (London: Oxford University Press, 1967), 32-133; Elizabeth J. Perry, 'Shanghai's Strike Wave of 1957', *China Quarterly* 137 (1994): 1-27, at 11. On international connections in working-class resistance, see also Steven Hirsch and Lucien van der Walt (eds), *Anarchism and Syndicalism in the Colonial and Postcolonial World, 1870-1940* (Leiden: Brill, 2013); Holger Weiss, *Framing a Radical African Atlantic: African American Agency, West African Intellectuals and the International Trade Union Committee of Negro Workers* (Leiden: Brill, 2014).
18 Beverly J. Silver, *Forces of Labor: Workers' Movements and Globalization since 1870* (Cambridge: Cambridge University Press, 2003).
19 Marx, *Capital*, I, 414.
20 Robert von Pöhlmann, *Geschichte der sozialen Frage und des Sozialismus in der antiken Welt*, 3rd edn, vol. 1 (Munich: Beck, 1925), 177. A striking example of such a connection is provided by Casanovas, who points out that until the 1880s 'free labourers in Cuba faced the constant threat of being replaced by forced labourers' and that therefore 'free labour co-operated increasingly with unfree labour in eliminating the combination of slavery and colonialism'. Joan Casanovas, 'Slavery, the Labour Movement and Spanish Colonialism in Cuba, 1850-1890', *International Review of Social History* 40, no. 3 (1995): 367-382, at 368-369.
21 Edna Bonacich, 'The Past, Present, and Future of Split Labor Market Theory', *Research in Race and Ethnic Relations* 1 (1979): 17-64. Bonacich's theory gains in explanatory power if it includes the role of states. See Yoav Peled and Gershon Shafir, 'Split Labor Market and the State: The Effect of Modernization on Jewish Industrial Workers in Tsarist Russia', *American Journal of Sociology* 92 (1986-87): 1435-1460.

22 In the 1880s, for example, indentured Muslim labourers from British India in Trinidad were divided over the question of whether, during prayer, they should face towards the East or to the West. See: Prabhu P. Mohapatra, '"Following Custom"? Representations of Community among Indian Immigrant Labour in the West Indies, 1880–1920', in *India's Labouring Poor: Historical Studies c.1600–c.2000*, ed. Rana P. Behal and Marcel van der Linden (New Delhi: Foundation Books, 2007), 173–202.

6

Towards a Transnational and Global History of Demographic and Migratory Processes and Discourses

Attila Melegh

Introduction

Fifty years ago, due to a focus on national frameworks and national political communities, there were strong arguments against making demography a global science. Alfred Sauvy – the famous French demographer and author of the term 'Third World' – argued that without a world government, or any similar entity, and the related social solidarity, it makes no sense to speak about 'world population'. Therefore, he settled on the study and the management of national populations.[1] At that time, demographers had just started to think about an international policy and organizational framework that would foster global governance in demographic processes. First, in the 1930s and 1940s, there were ideas concerning demographic transitions that portrayed global development as a hierarchical process. The texts by Thompson, Laundry and Notestein argued that other regions should follow the pioneering West and, most importantly, Western Europe. From the point of view of hierarchy, dividing lines were drawn across Europe, thereby making the regional variation of Europe very significant. Such ideas were coupled with the opinion that in the 'East' (whatever that meant) there was no time to wait in reducing fertility and changing reproductive behaviour. This led to a 'family planning industry', as coined by Demény, and a related creation of global databases on fertility, mortality and nuptiality.[2] By the 1960s, there were monumental and systematic efforts and, most notably, an institutional framework to create strategies and policies for global family planning.[3]

During the same period, within history writing, owing to various authors, including John Hajnal, European divisions and the comparison with non-European areas became consolidated as well-established research areas of demography and historical demography (see, for instance, the Cambridge Group for the History of Population and Social Structure).[4] While this research focus is still prevalent today, the creation of global, macro- and micro-level databases led to the dismantling of the original ideas, as we will see below. Moreover, as the ideas of different regions were often based on differential fertility, the dramatic convergence of fertility by the early 2000s questioned the significance of regional variations in this respect.

The new interest in global demographic history is also related to the demographic shrinking of Europe and the so-called West. In 1950, Europe represented almost 30 per cent of the world population. By the early 2000s, this percentage was 10 points, or even 15 in some cases, lower (with the countries of Europe overall returning to eighteenth-century levels). However, the overall control of wealth – with the exception of Eastern Europe and the former Soviet Union, which lost half their share in global gross domestic product – only fell a few percentage points (Demény and McNicoll 2003). Due to the global and differential decline of fertility and nuptiality, Europe has reached comparatively very low levels within both, and in the framework of global competitive capitalism, it has become even more concerned with gaining more migrants in order to maintain various sectors of the economy. Furthermore, the current restructuring of the world economy and the related crises of various regions, together with the massive outflow of people, also remind us that processes are interrelated and that there is a need to build global databases on demography as well as migration.

These circumstances, in turn, lead to the need for a new global history of demographic change. New (post-family planning) global, migration-population strategies and policies will shape not only global, or transnational, research in historical demography but also the history of migration. In further contrast to the 1940s and 1950s, in present-day migration, for example, we already have a rapidly developing set of international laws and organizations that clearly aim at controlling national and/or bloc-type processes within the European Union, the North American Free Trade Agreement, the Southern Common Market, etc. We also have a complex set of laws guiding spatial movement of people within and at the external borders within the blocs, such as in the European Union. The need to understand global processes will only increase, as is exemplified by the post-2013 refugee crisis affecting the entire

Mediterranean and West Asian region as well as Europe. Such developments of globalization will further influence global history writing.

Global databases and the collapse of Malthusian ideas

In addition to the factors affecting the emergence of global governance in demographic processes, the construction of databases and scientific developments all advance a more global and more integrative story of demographic change. Within historical demography from the 1960s, and most importantly from the 1980s, there have been major efforts to deconstruct ideas of demographic transitions based on a mechanic sequence of changes in, mortality and family formations. During these decades, historical demographic analyses of larger-scale population processes debated the validity of uniform and traditional demographic regimes. These analyses questioned the hierarchical, simplistic and modernization type of demographic models concerning the first and the second demographic transitions and/or migration transitions. They concluded that behind the similarities, we find somewhat specific historical processes with multiple social, economic and cultural factors in the background or we find seemingly differing processes related in terms of causes.[5] Here the point is not the findings of the 1970s and 1980s that so-called traditional family models varied quite substantially, but rather that spreading fertility control, for instance, could be linked to largely different micro-social and cultural structures and that stages of transition did not follow each other according to a unified logic.[6] These factors appear only when scales of investigation can shift from the macro to the micro level, which allows a glimpse into actual behavioural motives and micro-structures among historical populations. Furthermore, it has also become clear since then that regionally on a mezzo level there are stable longer-term migratory and demographic structures or developmental models that, apart from social discontinuities, followed stable trajectories without any uniform 'transition' character. A case in point, in East and Southeast European population processes, certain migration and demographic patterns even survived the dramatic political and economic transitions of the twentieth century.[7]

Beyond the deconstruction of transition theories, available empirical data have also become much more global in scope. First of all, for the period after the 1950s we have a rather systematic global data set not only on population size, fertility (crude rates, total fertility rate, etc.), mortality, and age composition on the basis of censuses, but also for the period after the 1960s on migration as well as on migration matrices (migratory links) for all the countries in the world. These databases, which are at the United Nations (e.g. World Population Prospects) and the World Bank (e.g. migration matrices since 1960), are often just estimates based on censuses and population registers, and even sometimes estimates based on estimates (like the Wittgenstein method, which estimates migration flows from migration stock matrices since 1960, also containing a large number of estimates).[8] But regardless of the observations in the national sphere, these databases are systematic on a global level not seen before. We already have more than sixty years of data to look at on a global level and this greatly improves our chances of writing a global demographic history of the recent past and of constructing hypotheses concerning previous developments.[9] Concerning the use of such data, Wilson argues:

> Of all the data collection and production tasks carried out by the various organizations of the United Nations, none is more helpful to a demographer seeking to assess long-term trends than the regularly revised World Population Prospects.[10]

However, recent databases have not only improved, there are now extensive computerized databases concerning a large number of communities relating to demographic trajectories, family history and other aspects of historical demography going well back into the nineteenth and even the eighteenth centuries.

One of these endeavours is the Eurasia Project on Population and Family History, which has combined 2.5 million longitudinally linked individual records on a micro level in over a dozen locations across Eurasia, allowing a historical examination of events between 1700 and 1900 to be undertaken. Between 2005 and 2014, the project published some key award-winning books that altered our comprehension of global demographic change in the early modern and modern periods.[11] The project provides a substantially more detailed understanding of historical trajectories of population change – that is to say, not just historical, reported 'narratives' on demographic behaviour – in different parts of Eurasia. It could, additionally, provide local empirical evidence to refute the workings of Malthusian positive and preventive checks in early modern European communities, which were supposed to maintain a balance between the growth of the population and that of the economy. This theory resurfaced during the 1960s and 1970s.[12] On a micro level, the Eurasia Project on Population and Family History found new ways to explain how marriage decisions were related to economic structures and status, which once again avoids the Malthusian linkage between late marriage and economic independence. Also strengthening the earlier claims of the historical anthropologist Jack Goody,[13] the project found a large number of similarities between Europe and Asia. Such findings undermine the East-West dichotomy as a crucial macro-regional dividing line in historical demography, which has existed ever since Thomas Malthus wrote his famous treatise on global population development and made a global-historical scaling of demographic progress from areas influenced by famine, disease and war towards areas free of such constraints.[14]

The problems of Malthusian checks also come up in Gráda's 2009 global history of famine.[15] This relatively short global history treatise also argues rather convincingly that the first famines were due to multiple causes, including civil and external wars, bad crops, environmental shifts and colonialism. Altogether, these causes cannot be put into a Malthusian framework of positive checks. The 'Third Horseman' was the result of random causes: 'Thus the evidence is mixed, both the role of contingency in human behaviour and the strong randomness in natural and ecological occurrences.'[16]

With the above statements, we are arriving at the end of a long period during which Malthusian frameworks have been predominant. This revision is also advanced by the increasing significance of global migration, which cannot be forced into a single form of reasoning or hierarchical developmental models.

The need for developing theories of global change in migration processes

The global history of migration is becoming a significant issue for the interpretation of the current global condition and even the sociology of migration runs into major problems when interpreting and explaining global changes in migration. Regardless of dramatically growing interest in these changes, there is a lack of any systematic theory of change. The warning put forward by McKeown (presented below) still remains valid, and he is right that we have to combine various elements when analysing the complex mechanisms behind migration and we need more comparisons:

> At the most obvious level, attention to global migration will provide more grist for comparative micro- and macrostudies about the operation of migration networks, the causes of migration, migration's relationship to economic and demographic change, the role of gender, and integration into local societies.

But serious work in this direction will be undertaken only once it is clear that global migrations are broadly comparable, an assumption that is still not well established in migration history. Even scholars who are aware of migration beyond the Atlantic tend to characterize it as directly subject to European expansion and not generated by the same impulses that shaped transatlantic migrations.[17]

Without doubt the Eurocentric focus of migration history is going to fade away, and the roles of non-European processes are going to be key issues. But before this occurs, it is worth showing that historical sociology has not been able to produce systematic theories that can explain some turning points in migration processes, or simply provide a modernization version of linear transition theories, which have become very problematic concerning other processes in demography itself.

Classical and neoclassical macro and micro migration theories seek to discern mechanisms based on wage differentials and labour market processes without a proper historical perspective, without which no theory of migration is able to provide a sound interpretative framework. Structural-historical and world-system theories have arrived at the clear postulation according to which transition from rural to non-rural economies and world capitalist intrusion create a scenario for massive emigration. From the theoretical perspective of intervention and the break-up of 'traditional' systems, scholars following this approach also argue that colonial or historically established connections matter. Notwithstanding, they give no systematic analysis of longer-term developments beyond the specific periods leading to substantial social transformation or establishing specific links.[18]

Network theory and cumulative causation theories are also relevant in understanding historical change because they help to explain why and how established migration flows continue and how they are maintained. Nonetheless, these theories are not adequate as they cannot explain why such flows might dwindle, become less intensive or become cyclical. Furthermore, these theories offer little insight into the ways in which transitional or intermediary countries are integrated into global flows and how this mode of global integration might transform in the long run.

Concerning longer-term and more empirical approaches to the question of how migratory integration of countries and regions varies over time, we have only a few hypotheses and even these are not supported by systematic evidence or statistical modelling. This is all the more astonishing as clearly these processes can modify longer-term developmental trajectories of countries and regions. For example, without receiving larger flows from outside the region itself, Eastern Europe has become a labour reservoir for other parts of Europe. Up until now, global history and historical sociology have provided little help in perceiving and grasping these changes because they are far more complex than many other demographic changes, such as fertility decline.

The concept of migration transition has gained some prominence, as developed by the geographer Wilbur Zelinsky, who modelled historical change after the idea of demographic transition as established in the United States and Europe during the 1930s.[19] Zelinsky argues that, following an increase in emigration because of socio-historical processes, countries with large-scale emigration gradually become countries of net immigration within the framework of a fairly linear development. This model was revised recently by Fassmann and Reeger, who conceptualize this transition from emigrant to immigrant status as 'migration cycles' based on a combination of demographic dynamics, labour market structures and (short-term) economic cycles.[20] In order to avoid the pitfalls of previous modernization theories (openly evoked by phrases like 'take-off'), these cycles are not identical and they are embedded in temporal and spatial contexts. While even these models fail, they raise very important points concerning, for example, business cycles and migration policies, which have also been identified in the global history of migration.[21]

The theories mentioned above are related to migration hump, or migration curve theory, according to which countries may move over time and with rising income levels from increasing to decreasing flows of emigration and then to an immigrant country (Ziesemer 2008; Faini and Venturini 2008).[22] In other words, upon reaching a certain level of economic wealth, countries produce more migrants as the migrants, or potential migrants, are actually able to finance and organize moving to countries that are better off. In contrast, an increase in wealth actually reduces the incentive for massive emigration. Although this is a non-linear idea of progress that may serve as a compelling starting point to understand migration better, migration hump theory only focuses on one transition and lacks a complex approach to the integration of various groups and/or territorial units into a global flow of people. Such an approach must combine not only wealth differentials but also related historical processes of economic integration into the world economy. Moreover, as there have been reverse or cyclical processes of migration, the premise of a gradual move towards an immigrant status is actually inaccurate with regard to many countries.

The task now is to start reflecting upon the above-mentioned sociological theories and historical studies themselves. This interaction has been rather poor and often major works are ignored on both sides as Jan Lucassen, Leo Lucassen and Patrick Manning argue:

> In short, we argue that the basis of contemporary optimism or pessimism regarding migration movements and settlement processes has been built on a weak understanding of the past, and thereby of the nature of these phenomena. This is explained by the fact that – as historians tend to stress – much of their research is neglected by the general public and policymakers, but also by a lack of systematic historical knowledge on global connections and processes as such.[23]

In addition to some comprehensive typologies of migration epochs, such as those developed by Manning,[24] there are quite a large number of descriptive analyses on the history of migration mainly concerning the time around the nineteenth and early twentieth centuries. While these analyses may be very informative and sometimes brilliant in capturing historical problems, they are either very specific in time and enquiry or actually too broad, showing that there was an increase in connections around the world mainly towards North America and within and around Europe. The latter point is aptly criticized by McKeown.[25] In addition to limited geographical scope, previous scholarship has been interested in dividing up migration according to various social and legal types of migration, particularly free and forced migration, thus creating various subfields, although we know today that these categories cannot be completely separated.[26] To a large extent, due to West-centric perspectives, a lack of cross-disciplinary discussions and immense difficulties concerning comparative sources, statistical historians have failed to give a systematic and theoretically well-founded analysis of how countries and macro- and mezzo-regions in various historical epochs have been integrated into a global flow of people and how these integration modes have changed.[27]

One excellent example of how decade-long efforts in the constructing of specific databases can help theoretically sound, systematic and cross-disciplinary analysis of specific global migratory processes and their consequences is the slave trade database established by a large number of scholars working on the 'Black Transatlantic'.[28] The constructed estimates are based on various sources, including ship records for each African port or reports on the ethnic identities of slaves that were shipped from Africa. The examination of the long-term consequences could serve as a model for analysing the impact of exporting non-forced labour even in an 'Age of Migration'.[29]

There are also very important initiatives that focus on specific historical periods and specific spaces. These initiatives include studying border management as complex social and political practices in Eurasia, most importantly the works of Sabine Dullin and Etienne Peyrat in transnational history writing.[30] From such studies, we learn how borders were constructed around the Soviet Union, for instance, providing insight into connections, international relations and migration. They further show that borders have always been crossed and that conflicts related to such crossings had the ability to lead to various forms of migration. Nevertheless, from a migration history point of view, these processes only represent certain angles. As a result, we need to combine these angles with the analysis of how longer-term structures and policies influence migration.[31]

A similar argument can be made concerning the in-depth study of certain empires, together with the collapse of those empires, as being terrains of 'internal' and 'external' migration processes, the 'actors' in which deserve global attention. Among a long list of studies, there is the research by Ursula Prutsch on the identities of migrants coming from the Habsburg monarchy to Brazil and the rest of Latin America. Or there is the work of Brunnbauer on Southeastern Europe between the late 19th century to the 1960s brilliantly analyzing the interplay between migrants, diasporas, state and society. There are also new studies on a two fold dynamic of migration history and decolonization studies that show how previous colonizer societies and the newly liberated colonies transformed due to massive migration taking place during and after decolonization.[32]

Migration and the global history of labour

In the area of labour history, there are particularly compelling studies that might alter our perspectives on migration. In fact, migration is certainly too broad a category; accordingly, there might be some very strong arguments in favour of dividing this category up into migrant groups and of having a global history of specific groups. As shown above, a focused study has already been made in the case of the slave trade. But other types of unfree labourers or domestic workers and caregivers can also be considered such groups. As there are already some critical theories concerning these groups, this focus might provide some very fruitful research areas in the coming years.[33]

During the period of 'early globalization' – the period when new (and unequal) global social spaces were created via new forms of trade and special relationships between emerging companies, the colonizing and colonized states – there were also massive flows of free and unfree labour, soldiers, sailors and other related groups. In current research, the social patterns and mechanisms of desertion have gained some momentum in the study of (forced) migration, free and unfree work of sailors, soldiers and slaves.[34] Such studies fit into the longer-term research on global labour history, including such projects as the Global Collaboratory on the History of Labour Relations 1500–2000, an international research project for the statistical analysis of all kinds of labour relations organized by the International Institute of Social History.[35]

Concerning unfree labour migration, one recently published volume deserves special attention because it provides a reflective theoretical framework for comprehending the global history of domestic and caregiving workers.[36] After a decline of global domestic work in the 1970s, by the 1990s this form of migration became a leading engine in global and even intra-European migration and a key gendered terrain of global inequality mechanisms. A new book by Hoerder, van Nederveen Meerkerk and Neunsinger endeavours to link demographic research with labour history, post-colonial studies and feminist critiques. In addition to historically specific case studies of countries such as Chile, Yemen, Austria and Morocco, there are excellent global historiographical chapters analysing the development of research perspectives during the last half-century. These chapters show how family history, historical demography of households and family life cycles were, or were not, incorporated into Marxist and feminist labour history or even migration history. The volume argues that especially in the light of current efforts concerning the protection of domestic workers by international organizations, like the International Labour Organization, there is a great necessity to write the integrated comparative history of how domestic workers tried to protect their rights and entitlements, how they became integrated into the fluid and changing systems of family economies and familial groups, and how gender aspects were connected to migration (which requires much greater attention). Accordingly, we must also improve upon the databases of today, which often lack variables concerning not only the historical periods but also the social status and social characteristics of migrants. Without such improvement, we are unable to have a global history of specific migrant groups, especially those hidden behind the 'privacy' of privileged groups and embedded into hierarchically organized global care chains.

Global and transnational history of demographic discourses in the twentieth century

Interest in the comparative history of demographic discourses and policies began to grow extensively from the late 1980s and early 1990s onwards. This situation was both related to a shift towards new forms of control and a rewriting of specific policies of repressive regimes; it was also partially related to the use of the archives of various international organizations like the Population Council of America. From the 1990s onwards, this comparative history was also extended to previous socialist state countries and this focus led to excellent works on gender inequality, anti-abortion policies and various other forms of repression. Altogether, we can claim that right now we see the emergence of a transnational and global history of demographic policies and discourses.

Up until the early 2000s, comparative histories of population policies revealed how demography was a method for social engineering, how it greatly contributed in varying ways to the selective control of the population inside and outside Europe, and how it was embedded into global and national ideological and geopolitical debates.[37] Of great importance was a growing interest in the global history of population conferences and international societies, revealing the global interactions they facilitated.[38] There were pioneering endeavours based upon popular beliefs and attitudes concerning population policies as well as ideas concerning demographic change and/or migration among non-elite groups for various regions.[39]

Specific histories of population and eugenic policies and discourses concerning South and Southeast European societies, for instance, reveal the substantial interaction between scholars and policymakers following international developments before the Second World War, during state socialism and after the rise of new regimes. These histories also explain that state socialism saw somewhat varied population policies despite shared similarities.[40]

From a gender perspective, critical historical sociology and critical global history developed in relation to social and reproductive policies, utilizing various methods of research in order to reveal the micro- and macro-ideological mechanisms of control; repression over families, women and their bodies; and forms of resilience. These studies, accordingly, embedded the analysis of demographic discourses into gender-power relations. While these studies also showed changes under state socialism and especially after it, they also demonstrated very resilient structures of gender suppression.[41]

In order to avoid mechanical national and ideological comparisons, there are groundbreaking endeavours to write a transnational history of demographic thinking; nevertheless, we need to work out the methods and interpretative frameworks for writing a truly global history.[42] In their very recent study, Hartmann and Unger promote the writing of a transnational history of demography – in other words, the history of 'transnational demographics'. They argue that the constant politicization of demographic discourses and how they were used to construct new forms of population policies in the twentieth century have to be taken into account. In this analysis, we must link local, national and global dimensions of demographic discourses to see how global demographic knowledge interacted with local practices in analysing and regulating local populations.

If we perform a systematic comparative analysis of demographic thinking in terms of producing, transferring and discussing, an analytical perspective can be found within the context of discursively constructed global and local hierarchies.[43] Exactly in the same way as Unger and Hartmann claim the necessity to understand the construction of population by comparison, the book by Baloutzova on demography and nation in Bulgaria, for example, argues that 'Population numbers were interpreted differently at different times and in different cultures and their reading was legitimated by the perception of the country's international position.'[44]

Thus, discursively constructed global and competitive hierarchies of nations framed population ideals and helped in formulating programmes to show how nations could be 'revitalized', made 'healthy' and 'normal', or could be advanced with regard to other competitors. In a comparative framework, it seems that certain discourses saw changes in social conditions as essential tools for transforming 'unfavourable' population developments; others *directly* disciplined the behaviour of local social groups. Even a shared pronatalist consensus could be divided up into subcategories and demographic nationalisms could work in different ways according to the society versus population debate.[45] Concerning Hungary, where there was a pronatalist consensus between the two world wars, Turda not only shows that, as opposed to populist social reformers demanding assistance for peasants, Hungarian governmental policies were much closer to the ideal of a eugenic state promoted by Germany. Turda also shows how the internationally circulating knowledge of genetics and population statistics were utilized in various political conflicts.[46]

Turkey is another important example of a country that altered perspectives several times within the same demographic nationalism.[47] Following the study of Thornton,[48] who demonstrates the spread and describes the mechanism of the spread of hierarchically understood demographic development around the globe, Serap Kavas argues that pronatalist family values and norms were promoted by the Turkish government in the early years of the republic and this changed only later during the 1950s. Thus, there were shifting policies to push the country to the level of advanced countries, employing a demographic disciplining process in various ways.

The shift from pronatalism to family planning in the early 1960s happened within a context of a paradoxical relationship between the Turkish government and American agents of the global family planning industry.[49] In the developing global policy of family planning, Turkey played an important role in the movement for a period of time. International expertise was utilized to analyse fertility intentions (the famous Knowledge, Attitude and Practices (KAP) surveys) and to develop social policies helping to reduce fertility. But the initially smooth interchange was soon confronted by questions over national sovereignty. Consequently, while US experts pushed towards family planning interventions, such efforts were partially rejected and local experts and government officials pushed for national control and tried to reframe the problem in terms of health care and health services. Thus, local-global interplay changes the focuses of such programmes.

Kenya provides another very compelling example when considering these shifts and interactions. After the liberation of Kenya from a brutally repressive colonial regime, the country was seen as an area of demographic growth regardless of having very little actual and reliable data.[50] This belief in a population growth that was too high was guaranteed by the hegemony of the demographic discourses, according to which Third World countries were supposed to create imbalances due to being backward countries experiencing demographic transitions.[51] However, the efforts made within the global family planning industry were deconstructed after the Population Studies and Research Institute was established. It is noteworthy nonetheless that the World Bank did not stop demanding such policies until the 1980s.

Another important case for the relative autonomy of local developments is Poland.[52] Interestingly, in Polish scholarly circles, being part of a continuous interaction between local and international actors, the concerns over fertility and migration not only led to the foundation of the Polish Institute for the Scientific Investigation of Population Problems, but also rather systematic and very autonomous research activities. As opposed to other East European demographic nationalisms, the main characteristic of the Polish demographic thinking of this time was its concern about 'overpopulation' and the agrarian character of its demographic patterns. Moreover, we can see that this concern over a growth that is too rapid was not understood in terms of Malthusianism, but as the result of changing social structures.[53] Thus, even in certain global historical eras and regional tendencies, the variation of demographic ideas and discourses was far higher than expected and we need to create complex frameworks to see the transnational and structural linkages.

Conclusion

The historical research on demographic and migratory change is at a turning point and within the next decades new global theories will emerge that can take into account the methodological and data developments that came before. New global data, new types of comparisons and the focus on new methods have led to the dismantling of historical geographic models and frameworks of demographic transition theories. After the dramatic convergence of fertility behaviour throughout the world, the field of migration will certainly be a key field for future research, especially because we have to understand migrant labour history and the connections with changing global macro- and micro-structures. The way areas and groups were integrated into the global flow of people will be a main focus of database constructions. They are important not only because of the recent changes in historiography, but also because various political and economic actors will ask us how we can account for the relevant structural conditions of such processes. In order to answer the relevant questions, a much closer collaboration between sociologists and historians is needed owing to the fact that migration, with its very complex composition and causal linkages, cannot be grasped via recent historical or even sociological methods as explained above.

The transnational and global history of demographic discourses will also provide new insights, considering that no structural change can be understood without such cognitive patterns since they are fundamental autonomous actors of change. This interplay has once again become very apparent as emerging refugee waves, for instance, strengthen such discourses in the space of a few months; these discourses might even reconstruct political developments completely in the long run. Thus, we must systematically link demographic processes and discourses in the near future in order to show our readers how social communities prepare the ground for future possibilities in the regulated patterns of birth, death and migration, which are key elements of the entire social reproduction process.

Notes

1. Paul Demény and Geoffrey McNicoll, *Encyclopedia of Population* (New York: Macmillan, 2003), 3.
2. Paul Demény, 'Social Science and Population Policy', *Population and Development Review* 14, no. 3 (1988): 451–479.

3   For example, Myron Weiner and Michael Teitelbaum, *Political Demography and Demographic Engineering* (New York and Oxford: Berghahn Books, 2001); Michael Teitelbaum and Jay M. Winter (eds), *Population and Resources in Western Intellectual Traditions* (New York and Cambridge: Cambridge University Press, 1989), 102–121; Michael Teitelbaum and Jay M. Winter, *A Question of Numbers: High Migration, Low Fertility and the Politics of National Identity* (New York: Hill & Wang, 1998); Maria Sophie Quine, *Population Politics in Twentieth Century Europe* (New York: Routledge, 1996); Alison Bashford, 'Nation, Empire, Globe: The Spaces of Population Debate in the Interwar Years', *Comparative Studies in Society and History* 49 (2007): 170–201; Alison Bashford, *Global Population: History, Geopolitics, and Life on Earth* (New York: Columbia University Press, 2016).

4   John Hajnal, 'European Marriage Pattern in Perspective', in *Population in History: Essays in Historical Demography*, ed. D. V. Glass and D. E. Eversley (Chicago, IL: Aldine Publishing Company, 1965).

5   One of the early critiques: Ansley J. Coale and Susan Cotts Watkins (eds), *The Decline of Fertility in Europe* (Princeton, NJ: Princeton University Press, 1986). Newer critiques: Noriko O. Tsuya, Feng Wang, George Alter and James Z. Lee (eds), *Prudence and Pressure: Reproduction and Human Agency in Europe and Asia, 1700–1900* (Cambridge, MA: MIT Press, 2010); Christer Lundh and Satomi Kurosu (eds), *Similarity in Difference: Marriage in Europe and Asia, 1700–1900* (Cambridge, MA and London: MIT Press, 2014); Tommy Bengtsson, Cameron Campbell and James Z. Lee (eds), *Life under Pressure: Mortality and Living Standards in Europe and Asia, 1700–1900* (Cambridge, MA: MIT Press, 2005); Adam McKeown, 'Global Migration, 1846–1940', *Journal of World History* 15, no. 2 (2004): 155–189; on the transition theories, see: Attila Melegh and Péter Őri, 'A második demográfiai átmenet' (The Second Demographic Transition), in *Család és népesség itthon és Európában* (*Family and Population in Hungary and Europe*), ed. Zsolt Spéder (Budapest: Századvég, 2003).

6   For the 1970s among other pieces, see: Peter Laslett, 'Family and Household as Work Group and Kin Group: Areas of Traditional Europe Compared', in *Family Forms in Historic Europe*, ed. Richard Wall, Jean Robin and Peter Laslett (Cambridge: Cambridge University Press, 1983), 513–563. Alan Macfarlane, *The Origins of English Individualism: The Family, Property and Social Transition* (Oxford: Blackwell, 1978).

7   Corrado Bonifazi, 'The Evolution of Regional Patterns of Migration in Europe', in *International Migration in Europe: New Trends and New Methods of Analysis*, ed. Corrado Bonifazi, Marek Okólski, Jeannette Schoorl and Patrick Simon (Amsterdam: Amsterdam University Press, 2008), 107–128; France Meslé, 'Mortality in Central and Eastern Europe: Long-term Trends and Recent Upturns', *Demographic Research, Special Collection* 2 (2004): 45–70; Tomáš Sobotka, 'Ten

Years of Rapid Fertility Changes in the European Post-communist Countries: Evidence and Interpretation', *University of Groningen, Population Research Centre, Working Paper Series* 02-1 (2002); István Horváth and Remus Gabriel Anghel, 'Migration and its Consequences for Romania', *Südosteuropa* 57 (2009): 386–403; Zsolt Spéder and Balázs Kapitány, 'Failure to Realize Fertility Intentions: A Key Aspect of the Post-communist Fertility Transition', *Population Research and Policy Review* (2014): 393–418; Heinz Fassmann, Elisabeth Musil, Ramon Bauer, Attila Melegh and Kathrin Gruber, 'Longer-term Demographic Dynamics in Southeast Europe: Convergent, Divergent and Delayed Development Paths', *Central and Eastern European Migration Review* 3, no. 2 (2014): 150–172; Attila Melegh, 'Net Migration and Historical Development in Southeastern Europe since 1950', *Hungarian Historical Review* 1, no. 3–4 (2012): 144–182.

8 Guy J. Abel, 'Estimating Global Migration Flow Tables Using Place of Birth Data', *Demographic Research* 28 (2013): 505–546; Çagar Özden, Christopher Parsons, Maurice Schiff and Terrie Walmsley, 'Where on Earth Is Everybody? The Evolution of Global Bilateral Migration, 1960–2000', *World Bank Economic Review* 25, no. 1 (2011): 12–56.

9 For the use of the databases, World Population Prospects in particular, see: Chris Wilson, 'Understanding Global Demographic Convergence since 1950', *Population and Development Review* 37, no. 2 (2011): 375–388.

10 Ibid., 156.

11 Lundh and Kurosu, *Similarity in Difference*; Noriko et al., *Prudence and Pressure*; Robert C. Allen, Tommy Bengtsson and Martin Dribe (eds), *Living Standards in the Past: New Perspectives on Well-being in Asia and Europe* (Oxford: Oxford University Press, 2005).

12 For example, Anthony Wrigley and Richard Schoefield, *The Population History of England. 1541–1871: A Reconstruction* (Cambridge, MA: Harvard University Press, 1981).

13 Jack Goody, *The East in the West* (Cambridge: Cambridge University Press, 1996); Jack Goody, *The Development of the Family and Marriage in Europe* (Cambridge: Cambridge University Press, 1983); Jack Goody, 'Women, Class and Family', *New Left Review* 219, no. 1 (1996): 199–132.

14 Thomas Robert Malthus, *An essay on the principle of population: A view of its past and present effects on human happiness; with an inquiry into our prospects respecting the future removal or mitigation of the evils which it occasions* (1826; Cambridge: Cambridge University Press, 1992); Attila Melegh, 'Biopolitics, Regions and Demography', in *European Regions and Boundaries A Conceptual History*, ed. Diana Mishkova and Balazs Trencsényi (New York: Berghahn Books, 2017).

15 Cormac Ó Gráda, *Famine, a Short History* (Princeton, NJ, and Oxford: Princeton University Press, 2009).

16 Ibid., 39.
17 McKeown, 'Global Migration', 168.
18 Douglas S. Massey, 'Why Does Immigration Occur? A Theoretical Synthesis', in *The Handbook of International Migration: The American Experience*, ed. Charles Hirschman, Philip Kasinitz and Josh DeWind (New York: Russel Sage Foundation, 1999), 34–52; Alejandro Portes and Jozsef Böröcz, 'Contemporary Immigration: Theoretical Perspectives on its Determinants and Modes of Incorporation', *International Migration Review* 23, no. 3 (1998): 606–630; Saskia Sassen, 'Foreign Investment: A Neglected Variable', in *The Migration Reader: Exploring Politics and Policies*, ed. Anthony M. Messina and Gallya Lahav (London: Lynne Rienner Publishers, 2006), 596–608.
19 Wilbur Zelinsky, 'The Hypothesis of the Mobility Transition', *Geographical Review* 61 (1971): 219–249. Hein de Haas, 'Migration Transitions: A Theoretical and Empirical Inquiry into the Developmental Drivers of International Migration', *DEMIG Project Paper, International Migration Institute Working Papers Paper* 24 (2010). Available online: http://www.imi.ox.ac.uk/publications/wp-24-10 (last accessed 11 April 2019).
20 Heinz Fassmann and Ursula Reeger, 'Old Immigration Countries in Europe: The Concept and Empirical Examples', in *European Immigrations: Trends, Structures and Policy Implications*, ed. Marek Okólski (Amsterdam: Amsterdam University Press, 2012), 65–90; Fassmann et al., 'Demographic Dynamics'.
21 McKeown, 'Global Migration'.
22 Thomas Ziesemer, 'Growth with Endogenous Migration Hump and the Multiple, Dynamically Interacting Effects of Aid in Poor Developing Countries', *Working Paper Series United Nations University–Maastricht Economic and Social Research and Training Centre on Innovation and Technology* 57 (2008); Riccardo Faini and Alessandra Venturini, 'Development and Migration: Lessons from Southern Europe', *ChilD Working Paper* 10 (2008).
23 Jan Lucassen, Leo Lucassen and Patrick Manning (eds), *Migration History in World History. Multidisciplinary Approaches* (Leiden and Boston: Brill, 2010), 5.
24 Patrick Manning, *Migration in World History* (New York and London: Routledge, 2005).
25 McKeown, 'Global Migration'.
26 Lucassen et al., *Migration History*, 6–10.
27 Ibid.; Manning, *Migration*; Sassen, 'Foreign Investment'; Charles Tilly, 'Migration in Modern European History', in *The Migration Reader: Exploring Politics and Policies*, ed. Anthony M. Messina and Gallya Lahav (London: Lynne Rienner, 2006).
28 Just a few works: David Eltis, David Richard, Stephen Behrendt and Herbert S. Klein, *The Atlantic Slave Trade. A Database on CD-ROM* (Cambridge: Cambridge University Press, 1999); Patrick Manning, *Slavery and African Life: Occidental, Oriental and African Slave Trades* (Cambridge: Cambridge University Press, 1990);

Nathan Nunn, 'The Long Term Effects of African Slave Trades', *The Quarterly Journal of Economics* 123, no. 1 (2008): 139–176. John Thornton, *Africa and Africans in the Making of the Atlantic World, 1400–1800*, 2nd edn (Cambridge: Cambridge University Press, 1998).

29 Stephen Castles, Hein de Haas and Mark J. Miller, *The Age of Migration: International Population Movements in the Modern World* (London: Palgrave, 2013).

30 Sabine Dullin, 'L'entre-voisins en période de transition étatique (1917–1924): La frontière épaisse des bolcheviks à l'Est de l'Europe', *Annales. Histoire, Sciences Sociales* 69, no. 2 (2014): 383–414.

31 de Haas, 'Migration Transitions'; Hein de Haas, 'The Determinants of International Migration. Conceptualizing Policy, Origin and Destination Effects', *DEMIG Project Paper 2, International Migration Institute Working Papers*, Paper 32 (2011).

32 Among others, see the work of Lori Watt, *When Empire Comes Home: Repatriation and Reintegration in Postwar Japan* (Cambridge, MA: Harvard University Asia Center, 2009); Christoph Kalter, 'Shared Space of Imagination, Communication, and Action: Perspectives on the History of the "Third World"', in *The Third World in the Global 1960s*, ed. Samantha Christiansen and Zachary A. Scarlett (New York: Berghahn, 2013), 23–38; Klaus J. Bade (ed.), *Enzyklopädie Migration in Europa* (Paderborn: Ferdinand Schöningh/Wilhelm Fink, 2007). See also Ulf Brunnbauer, *Globalizing Southeastern Europe: Emigrants, America, and State since the Late Nineteenth Century* (Lanham, Md.: Lexington Books, 2016).

33 See, for instance, Rhacel Salazar Parrenas, *Servants of Globalization* (Stanford, CA: Stanford University Press, 2001).

34 See, for instance, the work of Matthias van Rossum, 'Claiming Their Rights? Indian Sailors under the Dutch East India Company (VOC)', in *Law, Labour, and Empire Comparative Perspectives on Seafarers, c. 1500–1800*, ed. Maria Fusaro, Bernard Allaire, Richard Blakemore and Tijl Vanneste (London: Palgrave, 2015), 263–277; Gopalan Balachandran, *Globalizing Labour? Indian Seafarers and World Shipping, c. 1870–1945* (New Delhi: Oxford University Press, 2012).

35 See 'The Global Collaboratory on the History of Labour Relations 1500–2000' available online: https://collab.iisg.nl/web/labourrelations (accessed 23 August 2017), and works like Karin Hofmeester, Jan Lucassen and Filipa Ribeiro Da Silva, 'No Global Labor History without Africa: Reciprocal Comparison and Beyond', *History in Africa* 14, no. 1 (2014): 249–276.

36 Dirk Hoerder, Elise van Nederveen Meerkerk and Silke Neunsinger (eds), *Towards a Global History of Domestic and Caregiving Workers* (Leiden and Boston: Brill, 2014).

37 For example, Myron and Teitelbaum, *Political Demography*; Teitelbaum and Winter, *Population and Resources*; Teitelbaum and Winter, *A Question of Numbers*; Quine, *Population Politics*; Bashford, 'Nation, Empire, Globe'; Bashford, *Global Population*.

38 For example, Robert Cliquet and Kristiaan Thienpont (1995), *Population and Development: A Message from the Cairo Conference* (Dordrecht, Boston and London: Kluwer Academic Publishers, 1995).
39 For example, Arland Thornton, *Reading History Sideways: The Fallacy and Enduring Impact of the Developmental Paradigm on Family Life* (Chicago, IL: University of Chicago Press, 2005); Arland Thornton, 'International Family Change and Continuity: The Past and Future from the Developmental Idealism Perspective', in *Marriage at the Crossroads: Legal, Social, and Policy Perspectives*, ed. Elizabeth S. Scott and Marsha Garrison (Cambridge: Cambridge University Press, 2012); Charlotte Höhn, Dragana Avramov and Irena Kotowska, *People, Population Change and Policies: Lessons from the Population Policy Acceptance Study – Volume 1* (New York and Berlin: Springer, 2008); Dragana Avramov, *Acceptance of immigrants in Europe? Viewpoints about immigration and expectations towards foreigners in the Czech Republic, Germany, Estonia, Hungary, Austria, Poland, Slovenia, and Finland* (Berlin: Schriftenreihe des Bundesinstituts für Bevölkerungsforschung Sonderband, 2008).
40 For example, Maria Bucur, 'Remapping the Historiography of Modernization and State-building in Southeastern Europe through Health, Hygiene and Eugenics', in *Health, Hygiene and Eugenics in Southeastern Europe to 1945*, ed. Christian Promitzer (Budapest: Central European University Press, 2010), 429–445; Marius Turda and Paul Weindling, *Blood and Homeland: Eugenics and Racial Nationalism in Central and Southeast Europe, 1900–1940* (Budapest and New York: Central European University Press, 2007); Marius Turda, *Modernism and Eugenics* (New York: Palgrave Macmillan, 2010); Svetla Baloutzova, *Demography and Nation. Social Legislation and Population Policy in Bulgaria, 1918–1944* (Budapest and New York: Central European University Press, 2011).
41 Dorottya Szikra, 'Eastern European Faces of Familialism: Hungarian and Polish Family Policies from a Historical Perspective', in *Selektive Emanzipation: Analyse zur Gleichstellungs- und Familienpolitik*, ed. Diana Auth, Eva Buchholz and Stefanie Janczyk (Opladen and Farmington Hills, MI: Verlag Barbara Budrich, 2010), 239–254; Susan Gal and Gail Kligman, *The Politics of Gender after Socialism: An Historical Comparative Essay* (Princeton, NJ: Princeton University Press, 2000).
42 For example, Heinrich Hartmann and Corinna R. Unger, *World of Populations. Transnational Perspectives on Demography in the 20th Century* (New York: Berghahn, 2014).
43 Bashford, 'Nation, Empire, Globe'; Bashford, *Global Population*; Attila Melegh, *On the East/West Slope. Globalization, Nationalism, Racism and Discourses on Eastern Europe* (Budapest and New York: Central European University Press, 2006); Attila Melegh, 'Between Global and Local Hierarchies: Population Management in the First Half of the Twentieth Century', *Demográfia English Edition* 53, no. 5 (2010): 51–77; see also the review: Attila Melegh, 'Review of Svetlana Baloutzova,

Demography and Nation: Social Legislation and Population Policy in Bulgaria, 1918–1944', *Continuity and Change* 27, no. 3 (2012): 481–486.
44 Baloutzova, *Demography and Nation*, 7–8.
45 Amartya Sen, 'Population: Delusion and Reality', *The New York Review of Books* 41 (1994).
46 Marius Turda, 'In Pursuit of Greater Hungary: Eugenic Ideas of Social and Biological Improvement, 1940–1941', *The Journal of Modern History* 85, no. 3 (2013): 558–591.
47 Serap Kavas, 'Discourses of Demographic Change and Population Policies in Turkey in the Twentieth Century', *Demográfia English Edition* 57, no. 5 (2014): 91–112.
48 Thornton, *Reading History Sideways*.
49 Heinrich Hartmann, 'Twofold Discovery of Population. Assessing the Turkish Population by its "Knowledge, Attitudes and Practices," 1962–1980', in Hartmann and Unger, *World of Populations*, 178–201.
50 Maria Dörnemann, 'Seeing Population as a Problem. Influences of the Construction of Population Knowledge on Kenyan Politics (1940s to 1980s)', in Hartmann and Unger, *World of Populations*, 201–215.
51 Melegh, 'Biopolitics, Regions and Demography'.
52 Morgane Labbé, '"Reproduction" as a New Demographic Issue in Interwar Poland', in Hartmann and Unger, *World of Populations*, 36–57.
53 Sen, 'Population'.

7

The Idea of Africa in History: From Eurocentrism to World History

Catherine Coquery-Vidrovitch

Introduction

This chapter intends to demonstrate – by way of a very brief historical overview of the centrality of Africa since the beginning of humankind – that throughout all successive historical globalizations, Africa south of the Sahara (we may roughly take it as a geographical subcontinent) was neither more nor less significant than other 'worlds' (e.g. the Indian Ocean world, Mediterranean world, Far East Asia, Europe, etc.). Although Europeans have built 'their' idea of Africa, which they believed – and still believe – that they 'discovered', they were in fact almost the last ones to do so. Africa and Africans had developed a long history before Europeans interfered in their continent, disrupting its relations with the rest of the world. Moreover, Africans had played a prominent role at different stages of world globalization before Western intervention.

Geographically, Africa is located at the centre of three worlds, and has facilitated their connections to one another: the Mediterranean world (from ancient times), the Indian Ocean world, and only later the Atlantic world. Accordingly, from the beginning of ancient history, Africa has played a major role worldwide: it is needless to say that humankind began in Africa and diffused from Africa all over the world.

For a long time, Africa was the main provider of gold, either to the Indian Ocean world (from Zimbabwe) or to the Mediterranean and European worlds (from the Western Sudan). It served as a main provider of labour, sending slaves to the rest of the world, including to the Muslim world, India and the Americas. With the Industrial Revolution, Africa became a crucial provider of raw materials for the industrialization of Britain and France; and today, Africa is again a leader in sources of energy (gas) and precious metals and minerals. Gold from South Africa, for example, coming from ancient gold streams, provided 60 per cent of the world's gold in the twentieth century.

The point is not so much to demonstrate what might (and should) be relatively well known, but to understand why these facts were left aside, forgotten or even denied. We may (negatively) assert, as expected, that others confiscated African gold, African men and African raw materials. Nevertheless, it may also be instructive to (positively) consider the process by which Africa generated so much wealth and so many products, without which other continents would not have been able to develop. Africa was necessary for world development, and Africans were actors as well as constantly adapting partners that should be studied as such and not just be reduced to passive victims. For example, plantations could only develop with planters as well as with African slaves; industry could only develop with industrial discoveries and steam engines, and it could only produce with African raw materials.

Why was only Africa's place in the world denied, being turned into a 'periphery' according to Western knowledge when Europeans believed they had 'discovered' Africa? Let us rather say that Africans 'discovered' Europeans, long after they had already met Arabs, Indians and even the Chinese. Africa was not marginal to capitalism: like others, it was a major prerequisite for world development, that is to say for the making of world capitalism.

African history rediscovered

The history of Africa is extensive and has been ignored for too long.[1] The reason for this is known: Eurocentrism produced social sciences during the beginning of modern times, the Enlightenment and, above all, the nineteenth century. Unfortunately, Africanist or Asiatic knowledge, including history and ethnology, began to emerge at the time when political and cultural European supremacy over the rest of the world reached its highest point. For a long period (too long a period) the European observer's viewpoint was supposed to be universal. It was only at the end of the 1970s that this postulation began to be discussed by Indian and Palestinian researchers under the name of *subaltern studies*. Before this time, Africa, beginning with African geography, became a topic that was studied precisely at the moment when European scientists dominated the study of societies.[2]

During antiquity, the Mediterranean world ignored Africa as a continent. South of Egypt, unknown or little-known spaces were called either Nubia, or Ethiopia, or Libya. The term *Africa* appeared with the Romans, who used the name only for Carthage's hinterland (the senator who defeated Punic Carthago was nicknamed *Scipio Africanus*). Later, Arabs restored the name *Ifriqiya*. *Africa* was only used for the whole continent when, at the very end of the fifteenth century, Portuguese navigators sailed around the cape in 1498, changing its name from the Cape of Tempests to the Cape of Good Hope. Modern Africa was born from portolans and cartography. From the sixteenth century onwards, European writings described Africa, building their idea of Africa from the tales of traders, missionaries, explorers and any other kinds of travellers and slave traders.

In the early 1980s, two books written by the Congolese scholar Valentin Mudimbe deconstructed *Africanism*.[3] Surprisingly, these books were not translated into French, while Edward Said's deconstructing *Orientalism* was translated only two years after its English version was published.[4] Similarly, and at the same time, with *Black Athena*, Martin Bernal wanted to deconstruct both Hellenism and Egyptology as, at least partly, European constructions. While Said's or Mudimbe's enterprises were well accepted, at least in the English-speaking world, Bernal's books were globally rejected amid endless controversies. Why? Because Said and Mudimbe dealt with non-Western spaces, which were of little interest to most Western scholars, while Bernal attacked head-on white knowledge concerning what is supposed to be its Western cradles: Egypt and Greece. He was often provocative, but he also proposed common-sense statements that were unfairly denied. Western scholars, implicitly or explicitly, made the 'Greek miracle' an Indo-European production; they also thought of Egypt, studied from the eighteenth century onwards, as the 'mother' of Western culture, completely excluding sub-Saharan Africa. In addition to Bernal being recognized as a specialist neither of Egypt nor of Greece, he dared to interconnect both worlds. His linguistic speciality allowed him to compare and connect both Egyptian and Greek cultures, a comparison rarely made before. This was considered an inappropriate assertion, similar to when, twenty years before in France, Cheikh Anta Diop had proposed the Egyptian origins of sub-Saharan culture.[5] Wim van Binsbergen is right to state that many of Bernal's ideas are today confirmed by recent discoveries. Like Said and Mudimbe, Bernal was a talented precursor whose contribution helped to reject a Eurocentric vision of world history.[6]

Being myself a specialist in African history south of the Sahara, I focus my chapter on this area. The questions are as follows: why did European scientists behave for so long as if Africa, and especially African history, did not exist, although the sub-Saharan continent had played such an important part from the very beginning of humankind; and why was sub-Saharan Africa so long marginalized, forgotten and even rejected?[7]

This denial of Africa has a long history.[8] A negative image of Africa emerged when the Atlantic slave trade began on the western side of continent. Although Muslim Arabs had developed, from the ninth century onwards, other African slave trade routes towards the Mediterranean Sea and the Indian Ocean, the Atlantic slave trade specifically connected blackness and slavery. From the seventeenth century, and especially from the eighteenth century onwards, an Atlantic slave was only black, and all black people were thought of as slaves. In French, in Diderot's famous *Encyclopédie*, negro (*nègre*) is synonymous with black slave.

At the turn of the nineteenth century, when slavery was discussed by philosophers and condemned by humanitarian thinkers, black people's inferiority became a racial target. Linné, then Buffon, proposed a 'scientific' differentiation between inferior races (the lowest one being black) and the superior race (of course, the white one). This paradigm was developed throughout the nineteenth century to become a 'scientific truth' by the last third of the century. Despite slavery disappearing in European colonies due to the growing emancipation of slaves, this paradigm was a logical result of previous slave trading and was useful in maintaining black people's low social status.

With emerging colonial imperialism, all Western people, the USA included, were convinced of the incapacity of Africans to develop by themselves. Racialism grew progressively stronger over the century. This racialism can be seen in missionary and colonial literature: former travellers were curious and even admired the people they discovered. In time, European writings became more and more severe. At the end of the nineteenth century, most of them called for colonial conquest to suppress the African slavery that their recent ancestors had contributed so much to develop. Out of a few hundred assimilated citizens, colonialism made 'natives' (in French: *indigènes*) out of former slaves, thereby creating a legal status of inferiority. In short, racism emerged and remained very strong at least until the mid-twentieth century. Only in 1946, in French African colonies, was the so-called *statut de l'indigénat* finally abolished.

Western heritage is heavy. Today, Western opinions are fed by this cumulative anti-black, anti-African contempt. Africans were pagans turned into slaves, and then slaves turned into natives. In present-day France, this contempt resulted in a scandalous opposition between French citizens allegedly rooted in the country (the ultra-right militant Le Pen nicknamed them *de souche*), and French immigrants, especially blacks coming from south of the Sahara or Muslim Arabs coming from the Maghreb. This nationalistic movement finally resulted in a recent aberration: a dreamed-up concept of *national identity* that only includes continental hexagonal France and is praised by a national romance (*roman national*). It led to a disastrous speech by former French president Nicolas Sarkozy, delivered at Cheikh Anta Diop University in Dakar in July 2007, in which he publicly declared to an audience of Senegalese professors that 'Africans had not yet entered history enough'.[9]

For centuries, Africanist research was distorted by a number of prejudices reinforced by most colonial historians, ethnologists and anthropologists. Recently, *post-colonial studies* has demanded that Western researchers consciously get rid of this Eurocentric heritage. This may also apply to a number of African researchers who were taught, as others, what Valentin Mudimbe nicknamed the 'colonial library', that is to say, the inherited biased Western literature used by all researchers across the world. Moreover, colonial heritage has made Africans suffer from an inferiority complex, doubting their ability to ever equal Western knowledge, as Achille Mbembe rightly underlines.[10]

Africa, a mother of the world

Notwithstanding the issues above, in a similar way to other parts of the world, Africa and Africans brought a lot of creative wealth to foreign worlds. Africans, like others, may be proud of their historical legacy throughout history, rather than insisting on all that was taken out, plundered and lost. No more and no less than other parts of the world, Africa was at the core of world culture and wealth.

It is necessary to remind ourselves that humankind began in Africa. Several times during the last millions of years, prehistoric people left Africa (specifically Eastern and Southern Africa) to spread out all over the world. For a time, it was thought that our common ancestor was Lucy, who lived in Kenya some 9 million years ago. Now Toumai, discovered in northern Chad and thought to be a common ancestor, is considered to be 13 million years old. Again, around 200,000 years ago, Homo sapiens, our direct ancestor, was born in Africa.

Why, when actual history begins, between 7,000 and 4,000 years ago, do Africans stay at home on their continent for centuries to come, only to leave it by force and slave trading? This is probably because this very large continent was, for diverse reasons, a satisfactory place for expansion, particularly concerning agriculture. That being said, Africans did not isolate themselves. Not only was Africa south of the Sahara frequently located in the middle of the known world at the time, but it also ensured multilateral connections between other worlds coming to Africa. European cartography places Europe in the middle of the map; the Chinese do the same for China, and Americans for the Americas. Place Africa in the middle of the map (which is seldom done) and at once you understand that Africa is a crossroads for three worlds:

- The Afro-Asiatic Mediterranean world, probably the oldest connection;
- The Indian Ocean world, mainly between the fifth and the sixteenth centuries;
- The Atlantic world, the last to appear, only at the end of the fifteenth century.

Considering that African history had begun centuries before, Europeans did not 'discover' Africa, but only discovered *their* Africa.

Connections played their part on both sides: foreigners (Indians, Chinese, Arabs, Portuguese, other Europeans and Americans) successively or at the same time interfered in Africa and its relations with the rest of the world. Such interference was very profitable for them; as a result, their respective histories were influenced by and evolved because of Africa. This influence and transformation occurred in Africa as well, resulting in cultural, political and economic hybrids. Africans were not simply passive partners of traders from abroad. New streams, new actors and new contacts constantly emerged: sultans monopolizing gold mines, slave traders and trade entrepreneurs were instrumental both inside and outside Africa. This is not a surprise, it is normal history. We may compare this situation with European history, when, often, external events were important factors for change. Such was the discovery of the Americas for Europeans. Let us take only a French example: Roman conquest; North-South medieval competition between people of Oil and Oc languages; pre-modern wars against Spain and England in the seventeenth and eighteenth centuries; Napoleonic adventures in the nineteenth century; and three wars against Germany, two of them world wars in the twentieth century – all these contacts with others were impulses for change.

Therefore, there is no reason why African history would be a mere epiphenomenon when compared to other histories. Just because technological improvements started later than in other places, this did not hinder historical internal processes. Only Eurocentric history made African history peripheral. For Africans, other people were peripheral. A few historical processes may help to explain this.

Gold and Africa

From ancient times, and during the Middle Ages and pre-modern history, gold, a rare and precious metal, was a condition for financial prosperity in both Europe and the Indian Ocean world. Where did gold come from before the beginning of the sixteenth century? Before then, only a little gold had been discovered in the Caribbean islands (Mexico and Peru primarily mined silver), and afterwards gold was mostly mined in Brazil in the eighteenth century. Accordingly, except for remote mines in the Ural Mountains, gold was mainly produced in the Western Sudan where mines were located near the upper Senegal River, and in the hinterland of the coast that the Portuguese nicknamed early on 'gold coast' (*costa do oro*). While a Byzantine historian, Maurice Lombard, describes this as early as 1947, he only once alludes to 'Sudanese gold'.[11] He first thought that Byzantine gold came from plundering ancient Egyptian tombs or from Nubian gold in the upper Nile. In addition to confusing 'Sudan gold' and 'Muslim gold', he does not speak of sub-Saharan African producers and brokers. He only describes a closed cycle circulating between Byzantium, the Muslim world and Western Europe, without questioning where the gold comes from in spite of a well-known history of Western Sudan's medieval empires – Ghana, Mali and Songhai – which built their power upon gold trade.[12] Al-Bakri at the end of the eleventh century and Al-Idrisi at the end of the twelfth century both describe a Ghana Empire of gold.[13] Ibn Khaldun tells the story of Kankan Musa, king of Mali, and his splendid pilgrimage to Mecca.[14] He went across the desert with 12,000 slaves and many camels, carrying so much gold to Cairo that inflation exploded.

Africans exchanged gold for Saharan salt. For them, salt was a biological necessity because there were very few salted leguminous plants south of the Sahara. This trade is extremely old. The first source to mention it is the Greek historian Herodotus (fifth century BC), who describes it as a 'mute trade' beyond 'Hercules columns' (the strait of Gibraltar) between gold and salt traders: the former (Phoenician traders) brought salt and retired, while the latter (African ones) came to determine whether or not the salt was enough to exchange for their gold.[15] The game was repeated for as long as necessary. This practice still existed in the fifteenth century, when the first Portuguese or Italian traders (such as Venetian Alvide da Cà da Mosto) described it (1445–57).[16]

African gold was necessary for European development before the discovery of America. It began early: in Rome, one cannot understand why Septimius Severus, an African born in Leptis Magna (now 60 miles east of Tripoli), was made emperor (third century AD) without realizing that this harbour was the final point of a central trans-Saharan road. To become emperor, an African needed not only power but also wealth, and a city so large and splendid as Leptis Magna cannot be explained, as is usually done, just by its production of olive trees and wheat fields, which was the usual case all around the Mediterranean Sea. Put simply, gold arrived there.

African gold was known by ancient Greek and Roman people, and was also known in the Middle Ages. Around the Mediterranean Sea, Arabs preferred using silver for their currency, but they predominantly used gold to get involved in the West European world. Western Europe needed gold to exchange with Eastern Asia. European caravans travelled across the Asiatic continent as far as India and even China, eager to collect silk cloth, precious stones and spices. It is no exaggeration to suggest that African gold (rather than Byzantine gold) allowed Marco Polo to finance his ships and supplies and travel to China as early as the end of the thirteenth century.

The same occurred with the gold in Southern Africa. The Zimbabwe kingdom was prominent in gold production between the eleventh and fifteenth centuries. Only one century later had the Portuguese heard of the Monomotapa kingdom, which developed after Zimbabwe vanished. Gold from Zimbabwe supplied the Indian Ocean traffic. A great deal of Chinese pottery has been discovered in Zimbabwean sites, located 200 miles, in the hinterland, from Sofala, an important port on the Indian Ocean.[17] The same is true for the huge amounts of gold consumed in ancient Egypt, which was not a gold producer but imported it from mines located south of Egypt.

Africans were rather ignorant of the gold value on the world market at the time. They thought that a salt bar was as valuable as a gold ingot. Nevertheless, thanks to their gold, Western and Southern Africa played a significant part in the making of the Western world. Without their gold, and without the active political and economic roles played by major African gold empires, modern pre-capitalism would not have emerged. Medieval African gold was conducive to development in a way similar to Johannesburg gold when it was discovered at the end of the nineteenth century in 1886. During most of the twentieth century

(1917–90), because of the break between the East and the West, South Africa produced 80 per cent of the gold used as a standard currency by the Western world (and 60 per cent of the world's gold production). For centuries, Africa provided the world with its primary financial tool.

Slaves and Africa

Sub-Saharan African slaves were sent to almost every part of the world: towards the Mediterranean Sea, across the Sahara and from Egypt; towards the Indian Ocean by the Omani and Zanzibar sultanates; and towards the Atlantic Ocean. An internal slave trade also developed widely inside Africa, where plantations were created on the eastern coast, on the western coast and in the upper Congo. An actual 'Slave Mode of Production' expanded over the whole of Africa in the nineteenth century, which was similar in some ways to the cotton plantations in the US South[18] with networks of slave trade roads covering the entire continent. Sugar cane and cotton plantations expanded in the Americas, while clove, cotton and sisal plantations developed in Africa. African slaves worked everywhere across the world, not only in the Americas, but also in Arabia, India and Indonesia, and even in China. Black Africans were not only used as producers on pre-modern plantations but were also incorporated inside the capitalist system, above all in the United States when cotton fed the textile industry. It was a significant impulse for the first Industrial Revolution, on the eve of the nineteenth century. In other words, African slaves and Africa were at the core of what Marx explains was a major force of production. For centuries, Africa provided the world with its labour force.

Raw materials and Africa

A third moment is the pre-colonial nineteenth century, when the Atlantic slave trade declined. The English Industrial Revolution needed more and more raw materials,[19] not only cotton produced by American slaves, but also oil seeds needed to oil machines, to give light to workshops before the invention of electricity (end of the century), to make soap (the formula of which had just been discovered) and to dye cloth before the invention of chemical dye (end of the century). Palm oil mainly came from West African coastal areas, peanuts came from Senegal[20] as well as India, and copra oil came from Eastern Africa; dye came from plants (indigo, kola nuts) and red and yellow trees from rainforests. Zanzibar was the only clove producer and exporter. At the end of the century, wild rubber was collected in equatorial forests, in Africa as well as in Brazil until the establishment of Indonesian and Malaysian plantations in 1911. South African gold was flooding the world. Again, sub-Saharan Africa was essential for Western capitalism, with political and social African systems adapting to new markets. Inside Africa, both production and slave labour increased. New local and regional political entities emerged: empires of conquest, warlords, jihadi leaders and planters. Long before colonial conquest was completed, the internal political configuration of Africa had already been transforming.[21]

The independence era again forced Africa to provide the world with its wealth. A familiar process is still at work today, with Africa probably possessing the richest mineral resources in the world (diamonds, gold, copper, cobalt, uranium, rare minerals, etc.). In other words, Africa provided, and continues to provide, the Western world with a growing amount of raw materials and minerals demanded by European production, industrialization and equipment.

International politics and Africa

The European Berlin Conference (1884–85) was proof that Africa was instrumental in international affairs. For the first time, the European great powers met (the Ottoman Empire included) to not only conclude peace once war was over (as a number of them had done many times before, notably in 1815 at the Congress of Vienna, which put an end to Napoleonic expansion). In Berlin, it was different: they met to avoid war.[22] The only topic discussed was Africa, proclaiming the rules of the game to avoid conflict.

Almost total colonization was achieved in the early 1900s (the establishment of the Morocco protectorate in 1912 was the final step in the conquest of Africa). For a moment, between the two world wars, Africa was taken away from the rest of the world. It was used as a reserve by European mother countries because of the economic depression starting in Europe in 1931. Africa nearly disappeared as an issue in world affairs. It was a short parenthesis: from the beginning of the Second World War to the end of the Cold War (1939–89), Africa was again a critical military battlefield that then turned into a diplomatic one. First, it was used as a battlefield against Nazi troops by British and Free French armies. General de Gaulle asserted he was in France in 1940 in Brazzaville (Congo), and again with the Brazzaville conference in 1944. Congo and Cameroon were points of departure for the French army in reconquering southern Italy and France. After the Second World War, Africa became a strategic and diplomatic arena of the Cold War, midway between the East and the West. Africa began to make claims for its own self-rule and development when the Third World emerged as an international actor with the Bandung Conference in 1955 and the non-alignment movement from 1956 onwards.

In the 1960s, independence reinforced the African voice: soon forty-five African states (today fifty-four states, including islands) voted at the United Nations assemblies. The Organisation of African Unity was created in 1963, thereafter making efforts to help late colonies fight for their independence. Looking at a map makes things clearer: Africa was a buffer zone between the USA and Western Europe on the one side, and the Soviet Union and China on the other. African states were courted by both parties; they themselves were torn between liberal and socialist options (called the Monrovia and Casablanca groups).

Since the fall of the Berlin Wall, interest in Africa has not decreased. The end of the Cold War instead brought about new opportunities because it did not mean the end of arms trading. A part of the African continent is now a major consumer of armament production from the West. It has resulted in tragic internal political histories. It would be fraudulent to assert that this is only a result of the incompetence of African powers. This may be partly true, but politics nowadays is a worldwide affair, increasingly involved with economic globalization. Africa, for example, is taking the lead in oil production, and in many other precious metals and minerals. Once more, the African continent is necessary for the world.

Conclusion: A future for Africa?

Therefore, from the beginning of history, Africans were located, no more and no less than any other country, in any time, at the core of world history. Like others, they were necessary for the whole to develop. Africa has played a major part producing irreplaceable raw materials as well as precious metals and minerals as well as providing a huge labour force (yesterday's slaves and today's migrant workers). Nevertheless, the subcontinent remains less industrialized as well as lacking a large consumer market. This is why others think that Africa is 'peripheral' to their own worlds. However, this is untrue for multiple reasons, including economic factors as well as strategic, demographic, cultural and human ones.

How to get rid of this infernal cycle that makes people inferior, defamed and victimized? True, African history encompasses an upsetting series of trials that benefited outsiders who took advantage of these misfortunes. We now have to reject this symbolic representation and to accept the realities of today: others decided that Africa was a periphery. Africans themselves have to prove that it is untrue. They have to be positive, remembering not so much what others took from them but how much the world was endowed with what they provided to others. African capacities are huge. Africans may be confident knowing that they were able to resist so many assaults over the centuries. The youth is large in number as well as dynamic, and inventive; productive resources are enormous. Made possible through an exponential rise in schooling, in spite of so many drawbacks, culture is flourishing and social and political trends are moving forward. Since the 1990s, a strong desire for democratization has been expressed, with popular national conferences multiplying once more in spite of many obstacles. Civil and political society has become increasingly differentiated, and the majority of the population has also become urban. Middle classes are developing all over the continent which increasingly reject dictatorial powers. Unfortunately, social change is a slow process. From time to time, it may stop and even regress due to patrimonialism and corruption. Nevertheless, it cannot be ignored even though the international media still often maintains an Afro-pessimist view of a continent condemned to remain peripheral. This is contradicted by exploding information and communication processes (mobile phones, the Internet, computerization, etc.), and also by an impressive GDP acceleration average in spite of the worldwide crisis.

Africa should now aim at building a global political force able to compete with other international powers. Prominent individuals as well as influential and well-known African groups are working towards such a goal. African political and philosophical literature, including francophone literature that not so long ago emphasized *françafrique*, now insists on the necessity for Africans to 'count on their own force'.[23] We, the Western world, have to let these forces evolve instead of despising or ignoring them.

Notes

1   On the traditions of writing African history and on the formation of a genuine African historiography, see, among many others, Catherine Coquery-Vidrovitch, 'African Historiography in Africa', *Revue du Tiers Monde* 216, no. 4 (2013): 111–127.

2. Immanuel Wallerstein, *Unthinking Social Science: The Limits of Nineteenth-century Paradigms* (Cambridge, MA: Polity Press in association with B. Blackwell, 1991); Immanuel Wallerstein, *Open the Social Sciences: Report of the Gulbenkian Commission on the Restructuring of the Social Sciences* (Stanford, CA: Stanford University Press, 1996).
3. Valentin Yves Mudimbe, *The Invention of Africa: Gnosis, Philosophy, and the Order of Knowledge* (Bloomington: Indiana University Press, 1988); Valentin Yves Mudimbe, *The Idea of Africa* (Bloomington: Indiana University Press, 1994).
4. Edward Said, *Orientalism* (New York: Vintage Books, 1978).
5. Cheikh Anta Diop, *Nations nègres et culture* (1965; Westport, CT: Lawrence Hill, 1974).
6. Wim van Binsbergen (ed.), *Black Athena Comes of Age: Towards a Constructive Re-assessment* (Berlin: Lit Verlag, 2011); Martin Bernal, *Black Athena: The Afroasiatic Roots of Classical Civilization. Volume 1: The Fabrication of Ancient Greece, 1785–1985* (London: Free Association Books, 1987); Martin Bernal. *Black Athena: The Afroasiatic Roots of Classical Civilization. Volume 2: Archaeological and Documentary Evidence* (New Brunswick, NJ: Rutgers University Press, 1987).
7. Catherine Coquery-Vidrovitch, *Petite histoire de l'Afrique: L'Afrique au sud du Sahara de la préhistoire à nos jours* (Paris: La Découverte, 2011).
8. William B. Cohen, *The French Encounter with Africans: White Response to Blacks, 1530–1880* (Bloomington: Indiana University Press, 1980); Catherine Coquery-Vidrovitch, 'Le postulat de la supériorité blanche et de l'infériorité noire', in *Le livre noir du colonialisme. XVIè-XXIè siècle: De l'extermination à la repentance*, ed. Marc Ferro (Paris: Robert Laffont, 2003), 646–685.
9. Adame Ba Konare (ed.), *Petit précis de remise à niveau sur l'histoire africaine à l'usage du président Sarkozy* (Paris: La Découverte, 2008).
10. Achille Mbembe, *On the Postcolony* (Berkeley: University of California Press, 2001).
11. Maurice Lombard, 'Les bases monétaires d'une suprématie économique: L'or musulman du VIIe au XIe siècle', *Annales* 2 no. 2 (1947): 158–159.
12. Maurice Lombard, *L'islam dans sa première grandeur* (Paris: Flammarion, 1971).
13. Muhammad Idrisi, *Géographie d'Édrisi*, trans. Amédée Jaubert (Paris: L'Imprimerie Royale, 1836).
14. Ibn Khaldun, *The Muqaddimah: An Introduction to History* (Princeton, NJ: Princeton University Press, 1980).
15. Herodotus, *The Histories* (Oxford: Oxford University Press, 1998).
16. Alvide da Cà Da Mosto, *Relation des voyages à la côte occidentale d'Afrique 1445–1457* (Paris: E. Leroux, 1895).
17. Peter Garlake, *Great Zimbabwe* (New York: Stein and Day, 1973).
18. Frederick Cooper, *Plantation Slavery on the East Coast of Africa* (New Haven, CT: Yale University Press, 1977); Claude Meillassoux, *The Anthropology of Slavery:*

The Womb of Iron and Gold (Chicago, IL: University of Chicago Press, 1991); Paul Lovejoy, *Transformations in Slavery: A History of Slavery in Africa* (New York: Cambridge University Press, 1983).

19 Colin Newbury, *Western Slave Coast and its Rulers: European Trade and Administration among the Yoruba and Adja-speaking Peoples of South-western Nigeria, South Dahomey and Togo* (Oxford: Clarendon Press, 1961).

20 Andre Vanhaeverbeke, *Rémunération, du travail et commerce extérieur: Essor d'une économie paysanne exportatrice et termes de l'échange des producteurs d'arachide au Sénégal* (Louvain: Centre de recherches des pays en développement, 1970).

21 Catherine Coquery-Vidrovitch, *Africa and the Africans in the 19th Century: A Turbulent History*, trans. Mary Becker (Oxfordshire and New York: Routledge, 2009); Coquery-Vidrovitch, *Petite histoire de l'Afrique*.

22 Henri Brunschwig, *Le partage de l'Afrique noire* (Paris: Flammarion, 1971).

23 For example, Souleymane Bachir Diagne, Amina Mama, Henning Melber and Francis B. Nyamnjoh, *Identity and Beyond: Rethinking Africanity* (Uppsala: Nordiska Afrikainstitutet, 2011); Célestin Monga, *Nihilisme et négritude* (Paris: Gallimard, 2009); Moussa Konaté, *L'Afrique noire est-elle maudite?* (Paris: Fayard, 2010).

8

Global and Regional Comparisons: The Great Divergence Debate and Europe

Eric Vanhaute

The 'global turn', the shift to writing global and world history, is the most significant historiographical development of recent decades. The Great Divergence debate has been a driving force in this shift; it centres on the question of why the Western world emerged during the nineteenth century as the most powerful and wealthy world civilization of all time, eclipsing long-standing empires such as Qing China, Mughal India, Tokugawa Japan and the Ottoman Empire. Until recently, the core of the Great Divergence debate has been the comparison between early modern Great Britain and Qing China.[1] The main instigators of this debate were proponents of the so-called California school. They included Kenneth Pomeranz, Roy Bin Wong, Jack Goldstone, Dennis Flynn and Arturo Giráldez, Robert Marks and others. Basically, they turned the traditional argument of 'the rise of the West' as a long-term and internal European process on its head. They claimed that until the eve of the Industrial Revolution in Great Britain, there were many 'surprising resemblances' between the most advanced economies of Eurasia and that these economies were more or less on a par. The Great Divergence took place quite late, together with industrialization, and it was quite sudden and contingent.[2] This theorem and the subsequent debates triggered a wave of comparative research aimed at reciprocal analysis of structures and processes in distinct Eurasian societies and regions.

The Californians' call for 'reciprocal' and 'encompassing' comparisons drew historians' attention to pivotal questions of timing and spacing. What are relevant chronological and spatial scales that allow the discerning of meaningful differences and resemblances? The continuing debates on the Great Divergence have made it clear that it is important to be precise when it comes to place and time, even and especially in world-historical comparisons. The rise of world history has deconstructed the state as an exclusive unit of analysis, as well as dismantling overall categories like 'the West' and 'the Rest'. When constructing new global narratives, they simply do not work. The more regions are studied in a comparative and interconnected way, the more it becomes clear that differences within Europe, Asia or other so-called 'world regions' have continually been significant. Long before industrialization, parts of Europe were already wealthier than other European and Eurasian regions. Industrialization and modern economic growth in Great Britain and Western Europe were not sudden and inevitable contingencies. They can only be understood by their particular historical and regional stories. The Great Divergence debate showed us how regional perspectives can sustain new global comparisons by integrating knowledge of other regions of the world, in terms of comparison and connection. As Peer Vries justly concludes in his recent essay on the Great Divergence debate, 'that is enormous progress'.[3]

In this chapter, I question the premise of global comparisons – as such a contradiction in terms – by stressing the regional perspective. Global comparisons create new narratives of multi-scaled regional trajectories of social change. They include both the small, regional scale, and the larger supra-regional and inter-regional dimension. Through a world-historical lens, regional stories can only be understood in relative, interconnected and systemic terms. This chapter reviews the impact of the Great Divergence debate on the practice of broadscale or global comparisons. It covers four major arguments: 1) The Great Divergence was the single most important debate in recent world and global history, which both enlarged and redirected the long-standing convergence/divergence dispute in social sciences. It unlocked new fields of research, introduced new approaches and created new data and knowledge. 2) The dynamics within the Great Divergence debate push it to go beyond its own terms and to transcend its own limits. Perspectives and methods tested within the Great Divergence debate challenge more general interpretations of the history of global capitalism. 3) World-historical research on the processes of integration and hierarchy of global capitalism needs to adopt a multi-layered systems perspective. Systems analysis incorporates comparisons and connections in an integrated, hierarchical frame and it allows for the development of a combined structural, top-down (geometry) and agency-driven, bottom-up (frontier processes) approach. 4) I conclude with some reflections on how a re-evaluation of the regional perspective can sustain broadscale, global comparisons, creating new narratives of multi-scaled regional trajectories of social change.

Explaining the Great Divergence: From the West to the East and back

World history took a different course after 1750. Great Britain and other industrializing nations made the successful transition from an organic to a mineral-based, fossil fuel economy, releasing the Prometheus of technology-based and capital-intensive growth.[4] This pushed their productive and military strength to unprecedented heights, resulting in an unparalleled, worldwide economic and geopolitical dominance around 1900. This process has been coined in different iconic terms, including 'The Rise of the West', 'The European Miracle' and 'The Great Divergence'.[5] Soon after 1900, Max Weber wondered 'to what combination of circumstances the fact should be attributed that in Western civilization, and in Western civilization only, cultural phenomena have appeared which (as we like to think) lie in a line of development having universal significance and value'.[6] For a long time, the Weberian research programme was framed within Eurocentric paradigms. Whether one researched the origins of the industrial take-off primarily in Western European societies, like Max Weber or Karl Marx, or found it in the imperial space that Great Britain commanded, like Eric Williams, almost all research started from and circled back to Europe. The problem with Weber's approach was that it left many hypotheses regarding the technological, institutional, social, political or geographical conditions within Great Britain, Europe or the West unchecked. It lacked a genuine comparative and systemic framework that would help identify which conditions were, in retrospect, necessary or sufficient to set Europe on its perceived industrial Sonderweg.

Recently, new tendencies in global and world history have fundamentally altered the contours of and the dynamics within this vibrant research field. In this context, numerous scholars have reoriented themselves, to use the expression of the late Andre Gunder Frank. They started looking across the Eurasian landmass in order to compare the European experience with that of China, East Asia or South Asia. The debate about the remarkable rise of global inequalities in the last few centuries was, to a large extent, instigated by publications from the above-mentioned California school. Although these authors' views often oppose one another, they generally agree on a rough comparability in economic performance between China and Europe (or between the Yangzi Delta, China's most developed region, and Britain and Holland) until sometime in the 1700s. Some of them have also argued that Western Europe's subsequent leadership owed much to its relations with areas outside Europe, which provided far greater relief from the ecological pressures created by early modern growth than East Asian core areas could gain from their peripheries.[7]

This intellectual return to the East is primarily motivated by the observation that the scientific and economic development of China in the centuries prior to the divergence makes it all the more puzzling as to why industrialization and the subsequent rise to global power took place in the West. The second trigger has been that since the late twentieth century, the economic and geopolitical dominance of Europe or the West seems much less self-evident. The subsequent economic growth spurts of Japan, the Asian Tigers and China, combined with the latter's growing geopolitical importance, begs the question of whether we are witnessing 'The Rise of East Asia' and to what extent this rise also implies the 'Descent of the West'. Perhaps it points to a 'Great Convergence', a catch-up process in economic and political development between the two sides of the Eurasian landmass, or between 'the West' and 'the Rest'?

This general research interest has mostly been framed in economic terms: what are the causes of the wealth and poverty of nations? What induced the emergence of a new kind of sustained and substantial accumulation of wealth and growth? Why did this create new and unprecedented regional inequalities? In a recent overview of the debate, Peer Vries examined a wide range of explanations proposed by economic growth theorists and economic and global historians alike: natural resources, geography, labour, consumption, capital accumulation, trade, conquest, institutions, legislation, culture and religion, state actions, science and technology.[8] He stresses that none of the factors he studied can act as the one and only cause of the Great Divergence. There are just too many different factors acting in conjunction in different ways over time: 'The Industrial Revolution and modern economic growth were neither foreseen, nor predicted or planned. It would be a major error to look at pre-Great Divergence history as a race between countries, which one would industrialize first.'[9] Still, this begs the question: what is the historical story behind this remarkable global transformation? Was the great transformation mainly an internal European process with roots in its own history? Should the causes be sought in global shifts? Did coincidence play a major role? Moving beyond the discussions about the one and only 'prime mover', there is a growing opinion that the rise of the West was a 'contingent' (conditional, not required) process, a process that was not inevitable and could possibly not have happened. On the other hand, this change in the course of world history was not just random, it could not have occurred just anywhere. It was the result of a unique cumulative process, with roots inside and outside Europe.

Within a wide array of literature, three models of explanation can be discerned. The first, and clearly the most long-standing tradition, has a distinctly Eurocentric character. It chiefly evaluates the rise of Europe as a largely autonomous process resulting from internal changes. Since the 1990s, a new school points to Asia's age-old predominance and recognizes many similarities between Western and Eastern societies until the nineteenth century. This model seeks an explanation for the divergence in a non-predestined and even accidental concurrence of circumstances. A third tradition distances itself both from the classic Eurocentric and the (sometimes referred to as) Asia-centric explanations. It departs from an increased interaction between the West and the East, from which European countries were able to gain the most benefit after 1500. Thanks to several comparative advantages, this increased interconnection enabled them to strengthen their position in the areas of trade, knowledge and state power.

The founding literature on 'The Miracle of the West' sketches the rise of Europe essentially as an internal process. As a consequence of key differences in social and cultural life, Europe was able to break away from other regions in the world. Europe's position in the global system changed dramatically between the fifteenth and nineteenth centuries, when it became the absolute dominant power in the new global system. This important change is the result of a new internal dynamism within the European world, contrary to an assumed stagnant Eastern society. This explanatory model relies on Max Weber's research programme, which asserts that the West distinguishes itself via a steady and systematic rationalization of thoughts, actions and institutions. The differences between Europe and the non-West grew increasingly large. Industrialization seems to flow automatically out of this Western dynamism. This vision is shared by disciples of Max Weber (rational state), Adam Smith (market economy) and Karl Marx (capitalist production relations) alike. For many who adhere to the Weberian premise, culture makes the difference: for example, the development of new, Western cultural patterns related to labour, discipline, freedom, knowledge, etc. The West was the first area to develop modern, rational institutions – a modern state system, a modern bureaucracy and an efficient military apparatus – while also promoting individual property rights and a more-or-less efficient and 'free' market economy. Within this framework, strong arguments have been made for a range of prime movers, such as Europe's extraordinary drive for invention and innovation and openness to borrowing ideas from others (David Landes, Carlo Cipolla); the fundamental shift in European values, such as the rise of individualism (Alan Macfarlane), and the rise of bourgeois values (Deirdre

McCloskey); the unique set of institutions and property rules (Douglass North); and an unprecedented marriage of science and technology (Joel Mokyr).

Within the last two decades, new and comparative data sets undermined the image of Europe's gradual lead in the centuries before 1800. According to these comparisons, the Asian continent created at least 60 per cent of the world's wealth in the eighteenth century while containing 66 per cent of the world's population. According to some estimations, the per capita income in East Asia (without Japan) was comparable with that of Western Europe around 1700. So the gigantic reversal of fortunes mainly occurred after 1800. Studies that distance themselves from a Eurocentric approach perceive the world until the eighteenth century as a place of major similarities. Due to China's dominant position in the early modern world economy, comparisons usually concentrate on Europe versus China. Just like West European countries, China developed productive arable farming and intensive industrial and commercial systems. The organization of property rights and markets was not inferior to Europe, nor was their political organization less developed. Like other commercial societies in those days, growth was limited by the boundaries of organic agricultural systems. Assuming what they call a reciprocal comparative perspective, these authors made the compelling claim that it can no longer be taken for granted that European states, centuries before the Industrial Revolution, experienced exceptional economic, legal, institutional and political frameworks, allowing for the formation, integration and operation of more efficient markets.

Some authors have further minimized Europe's rise as a short-term interlude within the long-term dominance of Asian civilizations due to a combination of sheer luck and downright violence (Andre Gunder Frank, John M. Hobson). Kenneth Pomeranz made the most compelling case for not considering the European path as a 'normal' outcome of history. Commercial capitalism and the Industrial Revolution did not arise as the result of a long, progressive process; they arose from necessity.[10] Contrary to China, which could profit from its large and united empire, the European continent gradually stalled in an ecological bottleneck: scarcity of energy and scarcity of raw materials. The responses to this bottleneck (coal and industrial technology, colonization) gave Europe a considerable advantage afterwards: more efficient technical knowledge and a network of colonies (an Atlantic trade system). Until the nineteenth century, models of social and economic development in the main centres of development around the world remained based on agrarian, organic energy economies that did not create huge regional inequalities. Why one eventually triumphs over the other is not the result of providence; it is a concurrence of circumstances in which coincidence plays a major role.[11] Recent publications have labelled the revisionist image of the world before 1800 – a world of striking similarities – as too one-sided or even simply wrong.[12] While they do not advocate a return to former Eurocentrism, they argue that major imbalances in economic and political power were not coincidental; they sprang from a different social organization between the West and the East. In his recent book, Vries diverges both from neoclassical growth theories and the revisionist writings of the Californians: 'Whatever the outcome of that debate, it simply is a myth that the economic history of early modern Europe would be the history of the rise of a Smithian market ... Actually it goes for all major countries that ever took off.' He adds: 'The coming of modern economic growth was not a natural continuation of previous economic history, be it on a different scale: it was quite unnatural. It was not something that was bound to occur if only certain blockades would disappear.' The revisionism of the California school is, in turn, 'very salutary, but I think there are very good reasons to claim that revisionism went too far'. Instead of a world of remarkable similarities, Vries sees 'a world of striking differences'.[13]

The question remains as to what extent Europe's changing global position can be explained from an internal dynamism. Since the Late Middle Ages, contacts with the outside world changed Europe's position on many levels. First, its own capitalistic trade system gradually incorporated other parts of the world in such a way that the fruits of this system chiefly served the core. Second, Europe created a unique knowledge system via accumulation, imports and adaptation. This knowledge system was the breeding ground of industrial acceleration in the nineteenth century. Third, Europe applied this knowledge and technology to the development of strong state systems and of previously unseen military strength. The result was near absolute political and military dominance in the nineteenth century. A wide range of explanatory stories have aimed to understand Europe's changing role within a global perspective and have stressed different external key factors: geography and climate, making Eurasia, and Europe in particular, the most favourably endowed regions in the world (Jared Diamond, Eric L. Jones); interactions with societies in Eurasia, instigating Europe's recovery since the Late Middle Ages (William H. McNeill, Janet L. Abu-Lughod); and European imperialism, enabling its states to dominate peoples and resources beyond their shores (e.g. the use of African labour: Joseph E. Inikori; Eurasian invasion of flora and fauna: Alfred Crosby; a globalizing Europe-centred division of labour: Immanuel Wallerstein). The rise of the West completely upset relations on a world scale. The convergence of internal societal transformations and external expansion beyond its old borders propelled Europe from the periphery to the centre of global events.

Comparisons, connections, systems: understanding convergence and divergence

Researching the Great Divergence has triggered a wide array of research, including different sets of data, research strategies, scopes, scales and units of analysis. The central question is whether these units – regions, states or the world economy – permit meaningful comparisons as well as to what extent the units of comparison are connected within broader webs or systems of interaction. Using multiple spatial frameworks has tended towards more narrative approaches, and transregional comparisons have retained spaces of varying sizes and definitions alongside nations and global systems as units of analysis. Regardless of how the Great Divergence debate fares in future research, it has influenced and stimulated work on various other areas and periods. This impact is clear in the way it avoids the sharp categorical distinctions central to other approaches within modernization and globalization studies. It does not a priori deduce a place's prospects from its location within global networks. Instead, it suggests the possibility of multiple paths of development, stresses several continuous, rather than dichotomous, variables, and makes global ties influential, but not decisive by themselves. It stresses that regional units of various kinds and sizes remain important to the story of global economic history.[14]

This tension between diverging scales of analysis – between comparison and connection – prompts one of the most fundamental debates within the field of world and global history. How can we understand processes of regional convergence/integration versus divergence/hierarchy in the 'modern world' within a global framework? How do we relate tensions of divergence within a context of increased connections? This debate goes to the core of the social sciences. Over the past two centuries, the social sciences have developed a dominant view that the modern world shows a pattern of more-or-less linear development, in which all positive trends over time converge into a more homogenized world.[15] By and large, the left and right shared the same belief in the inevitability of progress and the linear upward pattern of social processes. This ideology of ultimate, positive convergence of all states and peoples reached an apotheosis in the three decades after the Second World War. At the same time, a number of analysts began to contest this linear model, arguing that the modern world was also one of heterogenization and polarization.[16]

Analysing the social world, the linear versus polarizing models of historical development became a debate about whether the various zones or countries would converge, and, in turn, lead to an approximately equal standard of economic, political and cultural structures. Despite the many ways in which there has been convergence, a global perspective shows that there has been simultaneous and strong polarization. Much of this can only be observed if different scales of analysis are interconnected, if regions are not analysed as self-contained units, and if the global is not seen as an undifferentiated macro process. The need for a global and historical perspective instigated three, interrelated research strategies that facilitated multi-layered and multi-focal frames of analysis. The first compares individual cases in a 'two-way mirror', making both sides of the comparison equal (reciprocal comparative analysis). The second strategy analyses the interactions and interconnections between societies or systems, and considers how those patterns of contact shift (network analysis, translocal/ transregional/transnational analysis). The third takes human systems, in which various societies and their mutual contacts are given shape, as the central unit of analysis. Examples include economic systems (the current world-system), migration systems, ecological systems (climate, disease) and cultural systems. Human societies are always linked together by several of these systems and they act in reaction to these systems (systems analysis).

The debate about the Great Divergence has yielded large-scale comparative studies on differences in geography, ecology, population, resources, wages, institutions, state-building, and so on. Key issues in comparative history are 1) what is comparatively being measured and how, and 2) how does one avoid explanatory reductionism, methodological nationalism and analytical synchronism? Scholars of the California school have made a strong case for the method of reciprocal comparisons precisely to avoid approaching non-Western histories from the stylized facts of European history and to turn away from predetermined world views.[17] The method of reciprocal comparison can give historical research more analytical rigour by forcing researchers to formulate problems, ask questions, look for answers and develop explanations in a more structured and systematic way. The questions about methodology and sources remain intensively debated: which units are fit for comparison and why? Which assumptions and models underlie any comparison with a global ambition?[18] Moreover, historians making comparisons often face the challenges of lacking data and scholarly work to create comparable accounts from widely differing sources, compiled under very different assumptions and purposes.[19] Some collaborative networks responded to this challenge by compiling large-scale sets of quantitative economic data over time and space, such as prices, wages and estimates of GDP (the Global Price and Income History Group; the Madison Project). However, GDP estimates preceding the nineteenth century are tentative at best, and useless at worst.[20] Wage-based proxy for living standards remains perilous since wage labour outside Western Europe, until late in the twentieth century, represented a small minority and took different positions in different societies. Still, if carefully contextualized in regional stories, these data can serve in reciprocal comparative analyses. For example, recent historical research on Asia has produced some partial and regionally specific evidence to suggest that standards of living in Western Europe and maritime provinces of China and South India may not have noticeably differed before the late eighteenth century.[21] Accordingly, comparative research explicitly raises the question of spatial dimensions.

By definition, world-historical research challenges conventional chronological and geographical frames. It stresses both areal integration and differentiation.[22] Much historical work continues to be done at a local, regional or national level in order to achieve control over information and sources. This tension can regenerate national frameworks and essentialize features of a nation's history. This is clear in some efforts to re-propel institutions as main drivers of unequal development. For Daron Acemoglu and his associates, economic performance is largely explained by a country's institutions, and in many cases these stem from early colonial choices. While settler colonies, for example, usually created a liberal property rights regime that promoted growth, in other colonies Europeans reinforced or introduced coercive institutions. This 'reversal of fortunes' argument posits a single critical intervention and one dichotomous variable (good or bad property rights), ignoring any effects of subsequent global connections.[23]

A wide range of recent world-historical studies has favoured a network perspective. Moving away from comparative histories brings up a whole new set of questions and subjects about connectedness, entanglement, reciprocity and circulation. New metaphors, such as flows, networks, webs and chains, and new epithets, such as trans, inter, cum and meta aim to translate the experience of border-crossing interconnections. This includes topics like human and labour migration, chains and networks of commodities, and long-distance trade, including methods of navigation, finance, tariffs and price movements, and price convergence. This angle explicitly questions spatial frameworks, creates decentring narratives and gives agency to the parties involved. It can also favour horizontal stories of entanglement, which risk levelling out history.[24] Connections of whatever kind are created and redefined in a world that is not flat. Stratification and inequality define the direction and the impact of networks. Societal relations configure the world on different levels or scales. In order to understand how they influence each other, a global framework has to integrate connections and networks within (overlapping) scales and (overarching) systems. Over time, these societal systems have grown from small to large, from mini-systems such as chiefdoms, to meso-systems such as civilizations, to the world-system of today. They have become larger, more complex, more hierarchical and more intertwined, reconfiguring connections and networks time and again.

Over the last two decades, cross-regional comparative and interconnective research has gained a wealth of new knowledge about the 'birth of the modern world'. In order to understand why processes were similar or different – why interactions went one way and not the other – one needs to understand the systemic logics that combine those patterns. A systems perspective does not narrow the lens to focus on the macro-boundaries; it aims to understand how the different scales or frames of time and space within the system tie together, forming a multitude of 'worlds'. A 'world' is not a constant; it is bound by nested human activity. It refers to social change that can only be understood in specific contexts of space and time. For that reason, no single delineation can be absolute. On the contrary, choosing a space and time perspective (where? when?) is linked to an intrinsic substantive choice (which social change?). Consequently, a global or world perspective cannot apply exclusive frameworks of space and time nor can it draw fixed boundaries. Neither do worlds consist of fixed scales; they overlap from small to large. Interactions between external boundaries or internal scales create zones of contact and interaction that we call frontiers. This is where different scales and social systems come together.

Scales and contact zones or frontiers are central concepts of analysis in contemporary world history and global studies.[25] Rather than reducing an entity to the properties of its parts, a systems perspective focuses on the arrangement of and relations between the parts that connect them to a whole, thereby creating a 'world'. Systems have a strong internal cohesion, but they are also open to, and interact with, their external environments, resulting in continual evolution. World-systems are open systems with operational closure, reproducing the very elements of which they are composed.[26] From the moment these patterns of reproduction have become irreversible (and the factors that can prevent deployment have become too weak or are no longer present), a system is functioning and has replaced former systems. Systemic interactions between communities and societies are two-way, necessary, structured, regularized and reproductive. 'Worlds' refer to these nested interaction networks, whether these are spatially small or large. Until recently, world-systems did not cover the entire surface of the planet. Only capitalism could transform itself from 'being a world' to 'the historical system of the world'. A comparative world-systems perspective is a strategy for explaining social change that focuses on whole, interpolity systems rather than single societal units. The bulk of world-systems analysis has been engaged with the so-called modern world-system: historical capitalism.[27]

Historical capitalism combines a globalizing economic unity (based on extensive trade and exchange relations and a hierarchical division of labour) with a multitude of political entities (states, bound together in an interstate system) and a multitude of cultures (civilization traditions such as world religions and state-bound, group-bound, class-bound and gender-bound identities, tied together by a universalistic geo-culture). Research into systemic processes of convergence and divergence should be based on three basic and interrelated questions. One: what makes the system? What are the factors of internal coherence and integration? Two: how does the system reproduce internal hierarchies and stratifications? Three: where are the boundaries of the system? What makes its frontiers? A research strategy of incorporating comparisons turns away from the search for invariant hypotheses based on more-or-less uniform cases. Its goal is to give substance to historical processes through comparisons of its parts, conceptualizing variations across time and space.[28]

The geometry and the frontiers of historical capitalism

The Great Divergence is part and parcel of the chronology and geometry of historical capitalism. Capitalism, as a social system, developed as an integrated complex of stratified time, stratified space and stratified social power relations. There is a persistent perception, in both scholarly communities and popular opinion, that the recent rise to power of an array of non-traditionally powerful countries is inverting an age-old trend of global divergence. This rhetoric of globalization and global convergence by and large obscures long-term global stratification – the reproduction of hierarchies in global power relations – together with the emergence of new inequalities.[29] A structural-historical view contends that the processes associated with globalization tend to reproduce stratification and hierarchy in the capitalist system and that 'globalization' as a concept mainly serves to legitimize neo-liberal 'modernization'.[30] A global and historical systems analysis reveals the insistent multi-dimensional nature of global capitalism. Cycles of global expansion contributed to the political upward mobility of a limited number of non-core countries, while states in the core remained politically and economically dominant.[31] A considerable body of academic research confirms that the stratified structure of the world-system has remained remarkably stable over time, despite (varying levels of) upward and downward mobility.[32] The processes associated with global growth do not benefit all countries equally. In contrast, they contribute to the reproduction of hierarchy and stratification in the system.

In order to untie global processes of divergence and convergence, we need to map and understand the interaction between short-term fluctuations and long-term change in global capitalism. A dominant focus on 'massive and large-scale change' in the short term still leads to a large body of scholarly research that disregards long-term continuity and stratification in the global system of power relations. Structural stratification remains one of the – if not the – most defining features of the global system of power relations today.[33] The work of the Italian-American political economist and sociologist Giovanni Arrighi is a challenging attempt to reconcile the political economy of capitalism with the call of global history to understand convergence and divergence, integration and hierarchy beyond established core-periphery relations.[34] His work shows in a comparative, incorporated and historical way how modes of production, circulation, consumption and distribution are organized, and how they created and transformed modes of reproduction. Since this perspective has no meaning outside the system-bound world-historical coordinates, it rejects both abstract localism and abstract globalism.[35] Internal logics and transformations are formative to the system as a whole: 'The globalization of historical capitalism must instead be represented as involving fundamental structural transformations of the spatial networks in which the system of accumulation has been embedded.'[36]

Since historical capitalism goes through cyclical phases of expansion and contraction, it continuously creates and recreates zones of contact or frontier zones. It is frontier-making through the recurrent waves of geographical expansion and socio-ecological incorporation of nature, land and labour. This coercion to put human and extra-human natures into the service of capital accumulation has gradually extended the zones of appropriation. Quoting Jason

Moore, these zones create 'cheap natures' in the form of labour, food, energy and raw materials in order to encounter capital's rising costs of production.[37] Capitalist incorporation and expansion is fuelled by the opening of the 'Great Frontier', a metaphor for an interconnected set of shifting frontiers. Frontier expansion provided an astounding wealth of nature that reduced production costs and increased profitability for centuries to come. For example, each successive food regime

> has particular conditions for cheap food, and each relatively stable set of relationships are expressed in a world price governing production, circulation and consumption of food ... The food regime is premised on forms of enclosure across time and space. This dimension is critical because enclosure alters ecological relations: substituting world-extractive for local-extractive processes, thereby foreclosing local futures for a capitalist future driven by variable and unstable markets, rather than socio-ecological needs.[38]

Frontiers generate shifting sets of 'localized' activities to secure access to labour and land for 'globalized' commodity production (primarily agricultural, forest and mining goods). The sites where this happens become frontier zones. Frontiers connect the expansion of global commodity chains with the creation of unequal geographical and social spaces. As Beckert states in his fascinating story about global cotton:

> The geographical rearrangement of economic relations is not just a noteworthy element of capitalism or an interesting aspect of its history; rather the shifting recombination of various systems of labor, and various compositions of capital and polities is the very essence of capitalism ... These frontiers of capitalism are often to be found in the world's countryside, and the journey through the empire of cotton reveals that the global countryside should be at the centre of our thinking about the origins of the modern world.[39]

Frontier expansion has often been associated with problems of social, economic and ecological sustainability. This results in the apparent need for these frontiers to be continually shifting towards new areas. Frontiers embody historical processes of both incorporation and differentiation that create and reorganize spatial settings. Frontier zones do not vanish after incorporation; they are permanently replicated by convergent and dialectical processes of homogenization (the reduction of frontiers) and heterogenization (the creation of new frontiers). Analytically, a frontier perspective can grasp the imbalances of incorporation processes, emphasizing the role of the margins and friction zones. Due to the incomplete nature of incorporation, frontier zones are the prime locus of negotiation processes regarding socio-economic commodification and socio-cultural assimilation. This frontier focus requires research into similarities and differences, into connections and into systemic changes. Frontiers determine exclusion and inclusion; they enforce new rules while giving space for resistance. Frontier zones have been the locus of both confrontation (war, resistance, lawsuits, intolerance, plunder, extraction, sabotage, ecological degradation, segregation) and cooperation (biological symbiosis, marriage, economic partnership, political bonds and treaties, celebration, conversion, gifts). Constant renegotiation forms a fundamental process in the shaping of ongoing, accelerating, retreating or stagnant incorporation processes. 'Peripheral' agents, such as peasant and indigenous movements, act within these 'fault lines'. Frontier processes create concrete spatial settings, structured by asymmetrical power relations.[40] It is not the finiteness of frontier processes – the prevailing idea of a homogenizing world (convergence) – but rather their permanence, the constant reproduction of instances of heterogenization (divergence), that must be questioned in world history.

Global and regional comparisons

This chapter questions the 'global turn' in historiography through the subsequent redefinition of frames and scales of time and space. Up to now, it has addressed three major arguments: 1) the Great Divergence debate, the single most important debate in recent world and global history, both enlarged and redirected the long-standing convergence/divergence dispute in social sciences. It unlocked new fields of research, introduced new approaches and created new data and knowledge. 2) The dynamics within the Great Divergence debate push it to go beyond its own terms and to transcend its own limits. Perspectives and methods tested within the Great Divergence debate challenge more general interpretations of the history of global capitalism. 3) Global research into the processes of integration and hierarchy of global capitalism need to adopt a multi-layered systems perspective. Systems analysis incorporates comparisons and connections in an integrated, hierarchical frame and it allows for the formulation of a combined, structural, top-down (geometry) and agency-driven, bottom-up (frontier processes) approach. I conclude with the question of how a re-evaluation of the regional perspective can sustain broadscale, global comparisons, thereby creating new narratives of multi-scaled regional trajectories of social change.

The Great Divergence debate has sharpened discussions on the potentials and limits of a global or world-historical perspective. It has opened up fixed narratives that universalize specific, space-time bound experiences. However, it also risks recreating new particularistic histories embedded in a multitude of regional specificities. The only way to avoid new, fixed master narratives or re-emerging essentialist regional/national stories is to continuously query new knowledge from regional research within a comparative, interconnected and systemic perspective. The Great Divergence debate has compelled us to rethink some fundamentals of historical research. It shows how a change of perspective can change the whole story. World historians are forced to invent and reinvent geographical schemes, to question the limitations of regional frames and to debate how to connect and integrate the various spatial scales. Regions in a world-historical perspective are not a given; that is why they lack the spatial precision of countries. They are also multi-dimensional and overlapping, from the big Afro-Eurasian ecumene, maritime regions, border areas and rim zones, to small-scale social, rural or urban systems. Within a given region, people share clusters of traits or connections that are different from those that they have with people beyond that region. Interacting regional histories make the world economy; a developing world economy also remakes regions. In addition, it urges historians to contextualize, rethink and sometimes reject concepts forged within Western social sciences. This is illustrated by unceasing debates about the nature of (capitalist) economy, states, formal and informal institutions, useful knowledge, property rights and so on.

A global perspective is, by definition, highly ambitious. It investigates processes of 'world-making' – of social change – in a broad time-space context. It compares; it connects; it incorporates; it systemizes. Global history and world history deconstruct world-making processes and construct new world-making narratives. That is why the global perspective is inclusive. It includes outer worlds and outer times in our world; it includes 'us' in our narrative. However, it has to be aware that patterns observed in a global frame are often as much the outcome of geographical and historical contingencies as they are of historical necessity. World history does not reconstruct a singular march of humanity towards modernity; it portrays messy worlds and a multitude of historical experiences. It constructs visions of the past that are capable of accounting for both fragmentation and integration on multiple levels (local, regional, national, continental and global). It builds frameworks that permit historians to move beyond the issues that have been dominating social sciences since the nineteenth century: cultural distinctions, exclusive identities, local knowledge and the experiences of individual societies and states. It facilitates the study of large-scale, border-crossing comparisons, processes and systems.[41] This ambition includes the use of multiple spatial scales. Global comparisons do not erase regional frames, they reinvent them. Interacting regional histories make the world economy; a developing world economy remakes regions.

We, moreover, need more bottom-up, regionally focused research that includes all world regions. This perspective also re-evaluates Europe's position in the world. Europe's history is taking its own global turn, not by presenting a new singular encompassing story or by stressing the uniqueness of Western civilization[42] but by creating regional stories in comparative, connected and systemic frames. European historians have always been aware that there was no such thing as Europe as a single unit of analysis.[43] In economic terms, they have been discussing for a long time the division between East and West – with the East becoming less developed at least since the end of the Middle Ages – and between North and South – the so-called 'Little Divergence', with the North becoming more wealthy from the end of the Middle Ages.[44] Robert Allen has stressed the divergence in European wages and prices from the Middle Ages to the First World War, substantiating the existence of remarkable differences in wealth between different regions in Europe.[45] Britain's Industrial Revolution is explained by exactly its different structure of wages and prices compared to the European continent and Asia. Research on markets (of labour, goods, capital) has shown time and again that it was only in the nineteenth century that the geographical constraints for European market integration became less important.[46] Geography, in particular access to the sea, rather than political borders determined their location and size. Coastal markets tended to be larger and had greater scope for advancement than land-locked markets. North-western Europe, specifically, reached comparatively high levels of integration earlier than any other region.[47]

Comparing regional growth paths within Western Europe has been the central ambition of the Comparative Rural History of North-Western Europe (CORN) network. Using the concept of regional agro-systems, these historians analyse differences and similarities in rural societies from a long-term comparative perspective.[48] Historians of pre-industrial Europe have recently published new work on regional income and wealth disparity before the Industrial Revolution.[49] Regional labour regimes are the central focus of the Global Collaboratory on the History of Labour Relations in the period 1500–2000, coordinated by the International Institute of Social History in Amsterdam. This project aims to map all types of labour relations worldwide, varying from slavery, indentured labour and sharecropping, to free wage labour and self-employment from 1500 up until today. Global labour history is not a matter of stages but of differing combinations.[50] The emergence of a comparative regional perspective with a strong focus on Europe, within a long-term world-historical frame, and starting from a bottom-up research strategy, is also evident in a selection of new collaborative research projects: 'Success and failure of Western European societies in coping with rural hazards and disasters, 1300–1800' (B. Van Bavel, Utrecht), 'The historical dynamics of industrialization in North-Western Europe and China, 1800–2010' (B. Van Leeuwen, IISH Amsterdam), 'Economic growth and inequality: Explaining divergent regional growth paths in pre-industrial Europe (Late Middle Ages–19th century)' (E. Thoen, Ghent University), 'Global capitalism and commodity frontiers' (U. Bosma, IISH Amsterdam, S. Beckert, Harvard, E. Vanhaute, Ghent) and 'Analyzing famines in historical contexts' (T. Myllyntaus, Turku, and G. Jonsson, Iceland). By bringing intra-European variety into global debates, these projects deconstruct the primacy of the scale of world regions and refute the argument of England, or Great Britain, as a *pars pro toto* for European developments. The Northwestern European path towards capitalism can only be understood through its variety of interconnected, regional stories.

Bringing regional stories into a world-historical perspective urges us to rethink the classic micro–macro division. As De Vito has pointed out in his essay about global history and micro-history, the key is to avoid conflating the level of analysis (macro/micro) and spatial scope (global/local) of these two approaches.[51] 'World' or 'global' are mindsets that do not necessarily imply the study of world-scale phenomena. There is no such thing as a comparison of global events; the concept of global comparisons is built on regional perspectives. It does not preclude an exclusive macro-analytical perspective based on predefined concepts and categories, nor does it support a hegemonic view on globalization as a fundamentally homogeneous process bringing world economy and world society together. A regional, bottom-up perspective is a spacial approach that overcomes the global/local divide. Limiting comparisons to macro-regions risks downplaying the importance of in-depth studies based on primary sources, creating or regenerating ethnocentric perspectives and obscuring alternative or competing categories, concepts and connections.[52] By definition, a world-historical view questions temporal and spatial subdivisions and relations, not as hierarchical but as contingent processes.[53] A frontier perspective and/or regional-systemic research urges comparison and connection (of individuals and groups, objects and goods).[54] The 'spatial' is constructed out of the multiplicity of social relations across all scales. In this perspective, the units to be compared are no longer taken for granted; rather, the issues and the ever-changing configurations are selected according to great historical questions and through the intensive study of primary sources. In the same way, Potter and Saha argue that

> connected histories of empire grounded in specific places and concerned with particular individuals might help us avoid the simplifications encouraged by the planetary scale of analysis that absorbs many Global historians … But we need to avoid the planetary simplifications of some brands of Global history, and indeed we need to push the agenda of scalar revisionism further by acknowledging the varied experiences of particular regions within different empires and within different colonies.[55]

We can expect that this reorientation will change the practice of historical research over time, for example with more collaborative as well as more decentralized research outside established hierarchical structures of knowledge. This research will appeal to different academic traditions, multiple languages and plural social groups. It will raise the need for awareness about the implication of historical research for each local community and the construction of its memory and self-representation, and ultimately the necessity of strong cooperation with non-academic institutions and groups within each context.[56]

Notes

1   Peer Vries, *Escaping Poverty: The Origins of Modern Economic Growth* (Vienna: Vienna University Press, 2013), 39.
2   Peer Vries, 'What We do and do not Know about the Great Divergence at the Beginning of 2016', *Historische Mitteilungen der Ranke Gesellschaft* 28 (2016): 294.
3   Ibid., 297.
4   David Landes, *The Unbound Prometheus: Technological Change and Industrial Development in Western Europe from 1750 to the Present* (Cambridge: Cambridge University Press, 1969); Edward A. Wrigley, *Continuity, Chance and Change: The Character of the Industrial Revolution in England* (New York: Cambridge University Press, 1988).
5   William Hardy McNeill, *The Rise of the West: A History of the Human Community* (1963; Chicago, IL: University of Chicago Press, 1992); Eric Jones, *The European Miracle: Environments, Economies, and Geopolitics in the History of Europe and Asia* (Cambridge: Cambridge University Press, 1981); Kenneth Pomeranz, *The Great Divergence: Europe, China and the Making of the Modern World Economy* (Princeton, NJ: Princeton University Press, 2000).

6. Max Weber, *Protestant Ethic and the Spirit of Capitalism* (1930; New York: Dover Publications, 2003), 13.
7. Daniel Little, 'Eurasian Historical Comparisons: Conceptual Issues in Comparative Historical Inquiry', *Social Science History* 32, no. 2 (2008): 235–261.
8. Vries, *Escaping Poverty*; also: Jonathan Daly, *Historians Debate the Rise of the West* (London and New York: Routledge, 2015).
9. Vries, *Escaping Poverty*, 55.
10. Pomeranz, *The Great Divergence*.
11. Robert B. Marks, *The Origins of the Modern World: A Global and Ecological Narrative from the Fifteenth to the Twenty-first Century*, 2nd edn (Lanham, MD: Rowman & Littlefield Publishers, 2006).
12. Vries, *Escaping Poverty*; Vries, 'Great Divergence'; Eric Vanhaute (ed.), 'Escaping the Great Divergence? A Discussion about and in Response to Peer Vries's Escaping Poverty: The Origins of Modern Economic Growth', *Tijdschrift voor Sociale en Economische Geschiedenis* 12, no. 2 (2015).
13. Vries, *Escaping Poverty*, 47, 401, 433.
14. Kenneth Pomeranz, 'Writing about Divergences in Global History: Some Implications for Scale, Methods, Aims and Categories', in *Writing the History of the Global: Challenges for the 21st Century*, ed. Maxine Berg (Oxford: Oxford University Press, 2013), 117–127.
15. Immanuel Wallerstein (ed.), *The World Is Out of Joint: World-historical Interpretations of Continuing Polarizations* (Boulder, CO, and London: Paradigm Publishers, 2015).
16. Ravi Palat, 'Convergence before Divergence? Eurocentrism and Alternate Patterns of Historical Change', *Summerhill: Indian Institute of Advanced Study Review* 16, no. 1 (2010): 42–58; Ravi Palat, 'Dependency Theory and World-systems Analysis', in *A Companion to Global Historical Thought*, ed. Prasenjit Duara, Viren Murthy and Andrew Sartori (Chichester: Wiley-Blackwell, 2014), 369–383.
17. Roy Bin Wong, *China Transformed: Historical Change and the Limits of European Experience* (Ithaca, NY: Cornell University Press, 1997); Pomeranz, *The Great Divergence*; Gareth Austin, 'Reciprocal Comparison and African History: Tackling Conceptual Eurocentrism in the Study of Africa's Economic Past', *African Studies Review* 50, no. 3 (2007): 1–28; Parasannan Parthasarathi, 'Comparison in Global History', in *Writing the History of the Global: Challenges for the 21st Century*, ed. Maxine Berg (Oxford: Oxford University Press, 2013), 69–82.
18. Jan De Vries, 'The Great Divergence after Ten Years: Justly Celebrated yet Hard to Believe', *Historically Speaking* 12, no. 4 (2011): 10–25.
19. Maxine Berg, 'Global History: Approaches and New Directions', in *Writing the History of the Global Challenges for the 21st Century*, ed. Maxine Berg (Oxford: Oxford University Press, 2013), 1–18.

20 Patrick O'Brien and Kent Deng, 'Can the Debate on the Great Divergence be Located within the Kuznetsian Paradigm for an Empirical Form of Global Economic History?', *Tijdschrift voor Sociale en Economische Geschiedenis* 12, no. 2 (2015): 63–78.
21 Bozhonng Li and Jan Luiten Van Zanden 'Before the Great Divergence? Comparing the Yangzi Delta and the Netherlands at the Beginning of the Nineteenth Century', *The Journal of Economic History* 72, no. 4 (2012): 956–989.
22 Martin W. Lewis, 'Geographies', in *The Oxford Handbook of World History*, ed. Jerry H. Bentley (Oxford: Oxford University Press, 2011), 36–53.
23 Daron Acemoglu and James A. Robinson, *Why Nations Fail: The Origins of Power, Prosperity and Poverty* (New York: Crown, 2012).
24 Jan De Vries, 'Reflections on Doing Global History', in *Writing the History of the Global: Challenges for the 21st Century*, ed. M. Berg (Oxford: Oxford University Press, 2013), 32–47.
25 Eric Vanhaute, *World History. An Introduction* (London and New York: Routledge, 2013); Hanne Cottyn, 'A World-systems Frontier Perspective to Land: Exploring the Uneven Trajectory of Land Rights Standardization in the Andes', *Journal of World-systems Research* 23, no. 2 (2017): 515–539.
26 Astrid De Wachter and Pieter Saey, 'Trajectories of Regions and Spatial Integration in the Worldsystem', *Tijdschrift Voor Economische en Sociale Geografie* 96, no. 2 (2005): 165–166.
27 Immanuel Wallerstein, *World-systems Analysis: An Introduction* (Durham, NC, and London: Duke University Press, 2004). Chase-Dunn C., H. Inoue, T. Neal and E. Heimlich (2015), 'The Development of World-Systems', *Paper Institute for Research on World-Systems 86, University of California, Riverside*, http://irows.ucr.edu/papers/irows86/irows86.htm.
28 Philip McMichael, 'Incorporating Comparison within a World-historical Perspective: An Alternative Comparative Method', *American Sociological Review* 55, no. 3 (1990): 385–397; Christopher Chase-Dunn and Thomas Hall, *Rise and Demise: Comparing World-systems* (Boulder, CO: Westview, 1997).
29 Michael Cox, 'Power Shifts, Economic Change and the Decline of the West?', *International Relations* 26, no. 4 (2012): 369–388; Daniel Flemes, 'Network Powers: Strategies of Change in the Multipolar System', *Third World Quarterly* 34, no. 6 (2013): 1016–1036.
30 Giovanni Arrighi, Beverly J. Silver and Benjamin D. Brewer, 'Industrial Convergence, Globalization, and the Persistence of the North-South Divide', *Studies in Comparative International Development (SCID)* 38, no. 1 (2003): 3–31; Shalendra S. Sharma, 'The Many Faces of Today's Globalization: A Survey of Recent Literature', *New Global Studies* 2, no. 2 (2008): 1–27; Eric Vanhaute, 'Historicizing Global Studies: About Old and New Frontiers of World-making', *'Potentials and*

Challenges of Global Studies for the 21st Century', *Global Europe, Basel Papers on Europe in a Global Perspective Institute for European Global* Studies, *Universität Basel*, no. 105 (2014): 50–59.

31 Rob Clark, 'World-systems Mobility and Economic Growth', *Social Forces* 88, no. 3 (2010): 1123–1152.

32 Jeffrey D. Kentor, *Capital and Coercion: The Economic and Military Processes That Have Shaped the World Economy, 1800–1990* (New York: Garland Publishing Inc., 2000); Salvatore Babones, 'The Country-level Income Structure of the World-economy', *Journal of World-systems Research* 11, no. 1 (2005): 29–55; Matthew C. Mahutga, 'The Persistence of Structural Inequality? A Network Analysis of International Trade, 1965–2000', *Social Forces* 84, no. 4 (2006): 1863–1889.

33 Giovanni Arrighi and Jessica Drangel, 'The Stratification of the World-economy: An Exploration of the Semiperipheral Zone', *Review (Fernand Braudel Center)* 10, no. 1 (1986): 9–74; Christopher Chase-Dunn and Bruce Lerro, *Social Change: Globalization from the Stone Age to the Present* (Boulder, CO, and London: Paradigm Publishers, 2014).

34 Giovanni Arrighi, *The Long Twentieth Century: Money, Power, and the Origins of Our Times* (New York and London: Verso, 1994); Giovanni Arrighi, *Adam Smith in Beijing: Lineages of the Twenty-first Century* (New York and London: Verso, 2007); Jan-Frederick Abbeloos and Eric Vanhaute, 'Cutting the Gordian Knot of World History: Giovanni Arrighi's Model of the Great Divergence and Convergence', *Journal of World Systems Research* 12, no. 1 (2011): 89–106.

35 Philip McMichael, *Food Regimes and Agrarian Questions* (Halifax and Winnipeg: Fernwood Publishers, 2013), 12.

36 Giovanni Arrighi, 'Spatial and Other "Fixes" of Historical Capitalism', *Journal of World-systems Research* 10, no. 2 (2004): 538.

37 Jason W. Moore 'Transcending the Metabolic Rift: A Theory of Crises in the Capitalist World-ecology', *The Journal of Peasant Studies* 38, no. 1 (2011): 1–46; Jason W. Moore, *Capitalism in the Web of Life. Ecology and the Accumulation of Capital* (London and New York: Verso, 2015); Thomas D. Hall, 'Incorporation into and Merger of World-systems', in *Routledge Handbook of World-systems Analysis*, ed. Salvatore Babones and Christopher Chase-Dunn (London and New York: Routledge, 2012), 37–55.

38 McMichael, *Food Regimes*, 9.

39 Sven Beckert, *Empire of Cotton: A Global History* (New York: Vintage, 2014), 440–441.

40 Saskia Sassen, 'When the Center No Longer Holds: Cities as Frontier Zones', *Cities* 34 (2013): 67–70.

41 Jerry H. Bentley, 'The Task of World History', in Jerry. H. Bentley (ed.), *The Oxford Handbook of World History* (Oxford: Oxford University Press, 2011), 1–16.

42 Ricardo Duchesne, *The Uniqueness of Western Civilization* (Leiden: Brill, 2011).

43 Vries, 'Great Divergence', 268–270.
44 Paolo Malanima, *Pre-modern European Economy One Thousand Years (10th–19th Centuries)* (Leiden and Boston: Brill, 2009).
45 Robert C. Allen, *The British Industrial Revolution in Global Perspective* (Cambridge: Cambridge University Press, 2009).
46 Roman Studer, *The Great Divergence Reconsidered: Europe, India, and the Rise to Global Economic Power* (Cambridge: Cambridge University Press, 2015).
47 Victoria Bateman, *Markets and Growth in Early Modern Europe* (London: Pickering and Chatto, 2012); Bas van Bavel, *The Invisible Hand? How Market Economies Have Emerged and Declined since AD 500* (Oxford: Oxford University Press, 2016).
48 Erik Thoen, '"Social Agrosystems" as an Economic Concept to Explain Regional Differences: An Essay Taking the Former County of Flanders as an Example (Middle Ages–19th Century)', in *Landholding and Land Transfer in the North Sea Area (Late Middle Ages–19th Century)*, ed. Bas van Bavel and Peter Hoppenbrouwers (Turnhout: Brepols, 2004), 47–66; Rural Economy and Society in North-western Europe, 500–2000, 4 vols, 2010–16, CORN-Series (Turnhout: Brepols, 2010–2016).
49 Guido Alfani and Wouter Ryckbosch, 'Growing Apart in Early Modern Europe? A Comparison of Inequality Trends in Italy and the Low Countries, 1500–1800', *Explorations in Economic History* 62 (2016): 143–153.
50 Alessandro Stanziani, *Bondage: Labor and Rights in Eurasia from the Sixteenth to the Early Twentieth Centuries* (New York and Oxford: Berghahn, 2014).
51 Christian G. De Vito, 'Micro-spatial History: Towards a New Global History' (paper presented at the 'Connections. Global and Transnational History' seminar, Fundação Getulio Vargas, Centro de Relações Internacionais, Rio de Janeiro, 8 May 2015), 1.
52 Ibid., 5–6.
53 Anne Gerritsen, 'Scales of a Local: The Place of Locality in a Globalizing World', in *A Companion to World History*, ed. Douglas Northrop (Chichester: Wiley-Blackwell, 2012), 213–226.
54 Matthias Middell and Katja Naumann, 'Global History and the Spatial Turn: From the Impact of Area Studies to the Study of Critical Junctures of Globalization', *Journal of Global History* 5, no. 1 (2010): 149–170; Glenn Adamson and Giorgio Riello, 'Global Objects: Contention and Entanglement', in *Writing the History of the Global Challenges for the 21st Century*, ed. Maxine Berg (Oxford: Oxford University Press, 2013), 177–194.
55 Simon J. Potter and Jonathan Saha, 'Global History, Imperial History and Connected Histories of Empire', *Journal of Colonialism and Colonial History* 16, no. 1 (2015) (e-print). Available online: http://eprints.whiterose.ac.uk/89866/5/Potter%20Saha%20Connected%20Histories%20FINAL.pdf (accessed 1 June 2016).
56 Vanhaute, 'Historicizing Global Studies'; De Vito, 'Micro-spatial History', 33. This text has been completed and submitted in the summer of 2016.

Index

Abbas, Mahmud 90
Ab Imperio 8, 116
Abu-Lughod, Janet L. 189
Accra 22, 88
Acemoglu, Daron 192
Adamov, Arthur 74
Addis Ababa 99
Afghanistan 84
Afghanistan War 99
Africa 12, 15, 18, 39–42, 57, 72, 83, 85, 88, 89, 91, 93, 95–7, 99, 100, 116, 118, 119, 120, 129, 137, 140, 142, 144, 156, 169, 170, 171, 172, 173, 174, 177, 178, 179, 180
Africa south of the Sahara, sub-Saharan Africa 14, 169, 171, 172, 174, 178
   colonial Africa 124
   East, Eastern Africa 39, 173, 177
   North Africa 7
   postcolonial Africa 88
   South Africa 11, 17, 90, 97, 138, 140, 142, 170, 177, 178
   Southern Africa 144, 173, 176
   Western Africa 176, 177
Afrocentrism 40
Aksum 39
al-Assad, Hafiz 90
Al-Bakri 39, 175
Alexandria 33
Algeria 43, 50, 53
Algeria War 50
Al-Idrisi 175
Ali Khamenei 90
Allen, Robert 120, 199
America
   North America 3, 4, 6, 12, 56, 81, 137, 139, 150, 156
   South America 53, 118, 137, 140
the Americas 10, 142, 169, 174, 177
Amsterdam
   International Institute of Social History (IISH) 9, 158, 199, 200

Andalusia 39
Angola 84, 87, 89, 90, 91, 99
Annales school 14, 25
Antwerp 55
Apollinaire, Guillaume 68
Arabia 177
Archivo General de Indias 7
Armenia 58
Armitage, David 3
Arrighi, Giovanni 195
Asia 10, 12, 14, 34, 35, 65, 83, 85, 93, 115, 116, 118, 120, 121, 127, 137, 142, 143, 153, 184, 185, 187, 192, 199
   Central Asia 32, 84, 91
   East Asia 19, 86, 88, 96, 176, 186, 188
   South Asia 185
   Southeast Asia 14, 32, 38, 89, 95, 96, 99, 100, 142
   West Asia 151
Asian diaspora 142
Asiatic mode of production 115
Association of Indian Labour Historians 138
Athens 36
Atlantic Ocean 177
Atlantic world 169, 170
Auber, Daniel-Esprit 64
Austin, Gareth 8, 9, 120
Australia 10, 14, 31, 53, 140, 142
Austria 53, 158
Austria-Hungary 57

Bachelet, Michelle 90
Baggesen, Jens 34
Balzac, Honoré de 49
Bandung Conference 179
Barcelona 51, 62
Basel 64
Baudelaire, Charles 62
Bavaria 33, 50
Bayly, Susan 90
Beckert, S. 200
Beckett, Samuel 74

Belgium 11, 53, 56, 58, 142
Bellagio 23
Bentley, Jerry 199
Berlin 7, 9, 34, 36, 43, 48, 50–3, 55–6, 60–1, 63, 75, 99, 178
  Centre of Modern Oriental Studies 7
Berlin Wall 87, 116, 179
Bernal, Martin 40, 171
Bertrand, Romain 30, 39
Bin Wong, Roy 120, 183
Bizet, Georges 64, 65
Black Athena 40, 171
Black Transatlantic 156
Bloch, Marc 30
Bockman, Johanna 91
Bohemia 62, 122, 125
Boldini, Giovanni 62
Bolivia 138
Böll, Heinrich 72
Borodkin, Leonid 127
Boschetti, Anna 71
Bosma, U. 200
Bossuet, Jacques-Bénigne 30
Botswana 89
Bouffon, Georges Louis Leclerc de 172
Boulanger, Georges 70
Brandes, Georg 34
Braudel Centre, Binghampton 23
Braudel, Fernand 25, 30, 74
Brazil 17, 31, 139, 140, 144, 157, 175, 178
Brazilian National Historians' Organization (ANPUH) 138
Brazzaville conference 178
Bright, Charles 2
Britain 41, 58, 115, 121, 127, 128, 142, 169, 185, 199
  Great Britain 4, 183–5, 200
British Empire 14
Broadberry, Stephen 120
Brussels 55, 63, 67, 75
Bucharest 91, 99
Budapest 11, 25, 51
Buenos Aires 22
Bulgaria 41, 57, 160
Burbank, Jane 116
Buzzatti, Dino 72
Byzantium 34, 175

Cairo 39, 66, 175
California School 183, 185, 189, 191

Cambodia 84, 100
Cambridge Group for the History of Population and Social Structure 150
Cameroon 178
Camus, Albert 74
Canada 14, 57, 126
Cape of Good Hope 171
Cape Matapan 33
Cape of Tempests 171
capitalism 17, 75, 81–6, 88, 92, 98, 100, 101, 117–19, 121, 126, 127, 140, 150, 170, 176, 178, 184, 188, 194–6, 198, 200
Caribbean 72, 140, 142
  islands 175
  universities 14
Carné, Marcel 59
Carthage 171
Casanova, Pascale 71, 72
Cassatt, Mary 62, 68
Catherine II 34
Ceaușescu, Nicolae 87
Césaire, Aimé 41
Chad 173
Chagall, Marc 62
Charle, Christophe 5, 16
Charles X 74
Charpentier, Gustave 65
Che Guevara, Ernesto 92
Chicago economists 81
Chile 90, 98, 141, 142, 158
Chimènes, Myriam 64
China 8, 31, 32, 38, 42, 53, 72, 81, 83–5, 89, 91, 94, 96, 97, 116, 118–21, 127, 140, 174, 176, 177, 179, 183, 185, 186, 188, 192, 200
  Chiang Ching-kuo (Nikolay Elizarov) 89
  Chiang Kai-shek 89
  Communist Party Politburo 89
  Guomindang 89
  Qing era/dynasty 38, 183
Chopin, Frédéric 64
Cipolla, Carlo 187
civilization
  Asian 188
  Egyptian 39
  European 39
  French 56, 61
  Greek 39

Modern 95
  Western 183, 185, 199
Clinton, Bill 87, 104
Cold War 8, 11, 82–6, 90, 94, 99, 100, 115, 118, 179
  Global Cold War 16
colonialism 5, 11, 87, 118, 153, 172
  British 14
  early modern 9
  Spanish 7
colonies 8, 41, 57, 63, 120, 140, 157, 179, 188, 192, 201
  European 120, 172
  French 172
  settler 192
Comecon 90, 93, 96–7
Comité International des Sciences Historiques (CISH)
  Congress Jinan 12
  Congress Oslo 12
communism 84, 88, 97, 115–16, 118
  Soviet communism 87
Comparativ 9
Comparative Rural History of North-Western Europe (CORN) Network 199
comparisons 29, 115–16, 118, 125, 153, 183, 188, 190–1, 194, 200
  border-crossing 199
  cross-cultural 5
  global 183–4, 197, 199, 200
  historical 141
  national, ideological 159
  reciprocal 191
  regional 183, 197
  transregional 190
  types of 162
  world-historical 184
Conan Doyle, Arthur 59
Congo 41, 99, 177–8
Congress of Vienna (1815) 178
conquest 186
  of Africa 178
  colonial 172, 178
  Roman conquest 174
Constantinople 33
Coquery-Vidrovitch, Catherine 18
Courbet, Gustave 62
Crisp, Olga 127

Crosby, Alfred 189
Cuba 58, 83–5, 87, 89, 91, 99
cultural history 25, 33, 36, 37
  transcultural history 32
cultural transfers 2, 15, 16, 30, 31, 35, 36, 42, 67, 68, 71
Cyprus 85
Czechoslovakia 90

da Cà Mosto, Alvide 176
Dalí, Salvador 68
D'Annunzio, Gabriele 60, 73
Das Gupta, Ranajit 139
Debussy, Claude 65
De Camões, Luís 30
de Gaulle, Charles 178
Delacroix, Eugène 61
Delaunay, Robert 62
Demény, Paul 149, 150
Dennison, Tracy 125
De Vito 200
de Vries, Jan 125
Diamond, Jared 189
Diaz, Delphine 71
Dickens, Charles 59
Diderot, Denis 47, 115, 172
Diop, Cheikh Anta 39, 40, 171
Döblin, Alfred 60
Donizetti, Gaetano 64
dos Santos, José Eduardo 90
Dostoievsky, Fedor M. 60
Dresden 11, 12, 25, 29
Dreyfus affair 67, 74
Duda, Andrzej 98
Dullin, Sabine 157

East
  Far East 65, 90, 169
  Middle East 56, 83, 91
Eastern bloc 16, 87, 88, 90–3, 95, 97, 98, 101
East Indies 53, 66
Eckermann, Johann Peter 47, 75
Eco, Umberto 72
Egypt 41, 57, 66, 85, 90, 91, 171, 175–7
Engels, Friedrich 70
England 17, 38, 50, 51, 116, 117, 121, 122, 125, 142, 174, 200
Enlightenment 37, 38, 69, 75, 170

entanglements 4, 9, 13, 15, 30, 85, 100–1, 141, 142, 192–3
Ernst, Max 68
Espagne, Michel 15, 68, 71
Ethiopia 39, 84, 87, 91, 99, 171
   Derg 91
Eurasia 35, 99, 115, 152, 156, 183, 184, 185, 186, 189
Eurasian Customs Union 85
Eurasianism 34
Eurasian Project on Population and Family History 152
eurocentrism 8, 19, 21, 120, 138, 154, 169, 170, 171, 173, 175, 185, 187, 188, 189
Europe 5, 6, 8, 10, 12, 13, 17–19, 33–7, 38, 41, 43, 46, 48–50, 56, 59, 64, 65, 70, 71, 74, 81, 83, 93, 98, 116, 119–22, 127, 129, 137, 139, 140, 142, 149–51, 153, 155, 156, 159, 169, 174, 175, 178, 183–90, 199, 200
   Central Europe 42, 51, 65, 84, 127, 128
   East Central Europe 8, 11, 124
   Eastern Europe 17, 43, 56, 83, 84, 86–9, 90, 94, 96, 97, 98, 103, 115, 119, 127, 150, 155
   industrial Sonderweg 185
   Northern Europe 65
   North-Western Europe 8, 19, 200
   Southeast Europe 56
   Southern Europe 56, 97
   Western Europe 18, 34, 120, 127, 128, 149, 175, 176, 179, 184, 185, 188, 192, 199
European Berlin Conference 178
European Community 96
European History Quarterly 25
European Network in Universal and Global History (ENIUGH) 11, 12, 13, 25, 29
   Congress Budapest 11
   Congress Dresden 11, 12, 25, 29
   Congress Leipzig 11, 29
   Congress London 11, 29
   Congress Paris 11–15, 39, 43
European Union 150

Fallmerayer, Jakob Philipp 33
Fanon, Frantz 41
Fantin-Latour, Henri 61
Fauvelle-Aymar, François-Xavier 39
Febvre, Lucien 14
Félibrige 48
Ferrer, Francisco 71
Fichte, Johann Gottlieb 34
First and Second International 70
First, Second and Third World 17, 82, 83, 87, 90–4, 91–3, 139, 149, 161, 179
First World War 6, 15, 41–3, 58, 67, 82, 129, 160, 164, 178, 199
Flanders 122
Florence 4
   European University Institute 4
Flynn, Dennis 183
Fondation Biermans-Lapôtre 58
Fondation Deutsch de la Meurthe 58
Fondation Nuber Pacha 58
Fondation Rosa de Abreu-Grancher 58
Fontane, Theodor 60
France 7, 9, 11, 13, 14, 15, 33–6, 38, 40, 41, 43, 48, 50, 51, 55, 56, 58–60, 63, 64, 67, 69, 71–6, 86, 125, 126, 128, 169, 171, 173, 178, 179
   Bourbon Restoration 75
   First Empire 69, 73
   Second Empire 49, 61
   Third Republic 49, 50, 51, 55, 61
   Vichy era 67
Frank, André Gunder 8, 185, 188
French Revolution 38, 46, 67, 69

Gabon 11
Gatti, Armand 74
German Democratic Republic (GDR) 90
German National Congress of Historians 12
Germany 4, 5, 7, 11, 13, 22, 30, 33, 34–6, 38, 41–3, 50, 51, 53, 56, 57, 62, 64, 74, 126, 160, 174
   Academy of Science 7
   East Germany 5, 7 (*see also* German Democratic Republic (GDR))
   West Germany 5
Gerschenkron, Alexander 116–18, 126
Geyer, Michael 2
Ghana 39, 99, 175
Ghent 18, 55
Gibraltar, strait of 175
Giráldez, Arturo 183

Global Collaboratory on the History of
    Labour Relations 1500–2000 158, 199
global condition 2, 153
globalization 2, 3, 19, 41, 53, 65, 81–9, 91,
    92–4, 97, 98, 100, 139, 151, 169,
    190, 194, 195, 200
  alternative globalization 99
  capitalist 85, 88, 93
  divided globalization 82
  early globalization 157
  economic globalization 86, 92, 179
  historical globalization 169
  modern globalization 99
  red globalization 23, 86
  socialist globalization 89, 91, 95, 96,
    99, 101
Global Price and Income History Group
    192
Global South 17, 83, 87, 88, 90, 92, 94, 95,
    99, 101, 144
Goethe, Johann Wolfgang von 47, 49, 75
Goldstone, Jack 183
Goody, Jack 153
Gounod, Charles 64, 65
Gráda 153
Grandner, Margarete 10
Grass, Günter 72
Great Depression 82
great divergence 8, 18, 115, 120, 184–6,
    190–1, 194
Great Divergence debate 8, 183–4, 190–1,
    197–8
Greece 32, 33, 36, 40, 56, 57, 85, 171
Gregory, Paul 126
Gris, Juan 68
Guadalajara 22
guest workers
  Angolan, Cuban, Mozambican,
    Vietnamese 89
Guha, Ranajit 138
Gupta, Bishnupriya 120
Guyana 90

Habsburg monarchy 157
Hajnal, John 150
Hamburg
  Global and Area Studies Institute 7
Hannover
  Zeitschrift für Weltgeschichte 9
Hanoi 88

Hartmann 159
Havana 88
Hayek, Friedrich 115
Hegelianism 3, 39
Heine, Heinrich 47, 67
Hellenism 171
Helsinki Accords 94
Herodotus 175
Hervé, Louis-Auguste-Florimond Ronger,
    called 64
Hobson, John M. 188
Hoerder, Dirk 158
Høffding, Harald 34
Holland 34, 53, 62, 185
Holy Alliance 74
Honduras 90
Hong Kong 11, 112
Hugo, Victor 60, 69, 70
Hungarian Academy of Science 22
  Journal of World History 22
Hungary 13, 18, 93, 96, 98, 99
Huntington, Samuel 87
Hussein, Saddam 99

Ibn Khaldun 30, 175
Iceland 200
Ifriqiya 171
India 17, 39, 81, 116, 118, 121, 124, 128,
    138, 140, 144, 169, 176, 177, 183
  Mughal India 183
  South India 192
Indian Ocean 172, 176–7
Indian Ocean traffic 176
Indian Ocean world 169, 174–5
Indochina 53
Indonesia 88, 138, 177
Industrialization 17, 19, 89, 117, 122, 127,
    129, 169, 178, 183, 184, 186, 187, 200
  proto-Industrialization 17, 122, 125
Industrial Revolution 129, 142, 169, 177,
    183, 186, 188, 199
Industrial Workers of the World 142
Inikori, Joseph E. 189
Institute of World History. *See* Russian
    Academy of Science
intercultural transfers 14–16
International Committee of Historical
    Sciences 25
International Labor and Working-Class
    History 144

International Labour Organization 143, 158
International Review of Social History 144
Ionesco, Eugène 74
Iran 90
Iraq 41
Iriye, Akira 103
Iron Curtain 11, 94, 95, 98
Israel 11
Italy 11, 38, 41, 53, 57, 64, 74
  Northern Italy 122
  Southern Italy 179
Itinerario 9

Jagdeo, Bharrat 90
Japan 4, 11, 38, 42, 43, 53, 57, 72, 74, 81, 83, 96, 126–8, 183, 186, 188
  Tokugawa Japan 183
Java 66
Jellinek, Ellfriede 72
Johannesburg 176
Jones, Eric L. 189
Jonsson, G. 200
Journal of Global History 9
Journal of Modern European History 25
Joyeux-Prunel, Béatrice 63

Kablukov, Nicolai 118
Kandinsky, Wassily 62
Kankan Musa 175
Karady, Victor 55
Kaspi, André 71
Kazakhstan 11
Kenya 173
Klenze, Leopold 33
Korea 42
Koselleck, Reinhart 38
Kossok, Manfred 21, 23, 103
Koval'chenko, Ivan 122
Kritika 116
Kula, Witold 115
Kundera, Milan 72
Kupka, František 62

Labour History 137, 138, 139, 143, 144, 157, 158, 162
  global labour history 9, 17, 143, 144, 158, 200

Lamprecht, Karl 5, 29
Landes, David 187
Laos 84
Latin America 12, 57, 58, 83, 88, 96, 97, 99, 118, 122, 138, 157
Laundry 149
League of Nations 41
Lebanon 57
Le Coq, Charles 64
Le Coq, Hervé 64
Lefebvre, Georges 102
Leiden 10
Leipzig 9–12, 19, 29, 35. *See also under* universities; European Network in Universal and Global History
  Institute for Universal History 11–13
Leningrad 91
Leninism 87, 89
Leonard, Carol S. 127
Le Pen, Marine 14, 173
Leptis Magna 176
Libya 171
Lieven, Dominic 116
Linné, Carl von 172
Liszt, Franz 64
Lithuania 122, 125
Liverpool 53
Livorno 62
Lombard, Maurice 175
London 7–11, 14, 22, 25, 29, 45, 48–50, 52–4, 59, 60, 75
  Global Economic History Network 8
  Institute of Historical Research 8
  School of Oriental and African Studies (SOAS) 7
London School of Economics 9
Louis XIV 64
Lucassen, Jan 156
Lucassen, Leo 156
Ludwig I 33, 36
Lviv 42
Lyon 55

Macfarlane, Alan 187
Maddison, Angus 120–1
Madison Project 192
Madrid 48, 49, 51, 75
Maghreb 173
Malaysia 98, 140

Mali 90, 175
Malthus, Thomas 153
Manning, Patrick 4, 156
Man Ray, Emmanuel Radnitsky, called 68
Maoism 91
Mao Zedong 83
Marco Polo 176
Marès, Antoine 71
Mark, James 16
Marks, Robert 183
Marseille 55
Marxism 5, 8
Marxism-Leninism 97
Marx, Karl 70, 117, 139, 140, 143, 177, 185, 187
Massenet, Jules 65
Maupassant, Guy de 49, 59
Mazlish, Bruce 3, 21, 23, 146
Mbeki, Thabo 90
Mbembe, Achille 173
McCloskey, Deirdre 188
McKeown, Adam 153, 156
McNeill, William H. 189
McNicoll, Geoffrey 150
Mecca 175
Mediterranean Sea 172, 176
Mediterranean world 169, 171, 174
Megali Idea 33, 34
Melegh, Attila 18
Mendel, Franklin 125
Mercure de France 63
Merrill, Stuart 68
Mexico 175
Meyerbeer, Giacomo 64
Mintz, Sidney 142
Miró, Joan 68
Modigliani, Amedeo 62
Mogadishu 99
Mokyr, Joel 188
Molière, Jean-Baptiste Poquelin, called 47
Monde(s) 9
Mongolia 83
Monomotapa 176
Monrovia and Casablanca groups 179
Montesquieu, Charles de Secondat, baron de 115
Moréas, Jean 68
Morocco 158
Morocco protectorate 178

Morrison, Alexander S. 116
Moscow 22, 51, 53, 63, 75, 85, 89, 104, 118, 124
Moulin, Raymonde 64, 76
Mozambique 84
Mubarak, Hosni 90
Mucha, Alfons 62
Mudimbe, Valentin 171, 173
Munch, Edvard 62
Munich 36, 50, 63
  'Athens of the Isar' 36
Musil, Robert 60
Muslim Arabs 172–3, 176
Muslim world 169, 175
Myllyntaus, T. 200

Nafplio 33
Nancy 48
Naples 139
Napoléon I 51, 74
Napoleonic expansion 178
  wars 42
Netherlands 9, 11, 13, 122, 142
Network of Organizations in World and Global History (NOGWHISTO) 12
Neunsinger, Silke 158
Neva 34
New Delhi 22, 138
New International Economic Order 92
New Zealand 10, 14, 142
Nicaragua 84–5
Nile 175
Nolte, Hans-Heinrich 9
non-alignment movement 92, 179
Nordic Countries 56, 57
North, Douglass 115, 118, 188
North Atlantic Free Trade Agreement (NAFTA) 87, 150
North Atlantic Treaty Organization (NATO) 99
North Korea 84, 99
Norway 126
Notestein 149
Nubia 171

O'Brien, Patrick 8–10, 120
Offenbach, Jacques 64, 65
Ogilvie, Sheilagh 25
Orbán, Victor 85, 98

Organisation of African Unity (OAU) 179
Organization of the Petroleum Exporting Countries (OPEC) 94
Oriental despotism 115
Ortega, Daniel 85
Oslo 12, 65
Osterhammel, Jürgen 4, 5, 7, 121, 127
Ottoman Empire 32, 42, 178, 183

Pakistan 11, 138
Palestine 42
Paparrigopoulos, Constantine 33
Paris 7, 11–17, 19, 22, 29, 30, 34, 35, 39, 43, 45–76
    Académie française 67
    Association des écrivains et artistes révolutionnaires (Association of Revolutionary Writers and Artists) 71
    Centre National de la Recherche Scientifique (CNRS) 7
    Cité universitaire internationale (International University Campus) 58
    Collège de France 15
    École des Beaux-Arts 60, 62
    École des Hautes Études en Sciences Sociales 7
    École Nationale Supérieure (ENS) 15
    Institut du Monde Arabe 7
    International Congress of Writers for the Defence of Culture 71
    International Peace Congress 69
    International Socialist Workers' Congress (1889) 70
    La Revue blanche 63
    Revue de synthèse 29
    Revue d'histoire moderne et contemporaine 25
    Salon d'Automne 61, 62
    Société des artistes français 61
    Société Nationale des Beaux-Arts 61
Paris Commune 51, 70
Parsons, Talcott 87
Parthasarathi, Prasannan 120
Pasler, Jann 64
Pasolini, Pier Paolo 72
Pericles 33
Persia 42, 57
Peru 175

Peter I, 'the Great' 34
Peyrat, Etienne 157
Picabia, Francis 68
Picasso, Pablo Ruiz 62, 68
Pinochet, Augusto 98
pipeline, Druzhba oil, Soyuz gas 90
Pöhlmann, Robert von 143
Poland 35, 93, 98, 122, 124, 125, 161
Pomeranz, Kenneth 8, 115, 120, 121, 183, 188
Population Council of America 159
Portugal 30, 57
postcolonial history 40, 88
    studies 158, 173
postcolonialism 41
Potter, Simon J. 201
Prague 99
Prussia 50, 117, 124, 125
    Eastern Prussia 125
Prutsch, Ursula 157
Putin, Vladimir 85, 98, 100
Pyongyang 88

Reagan, Ronald 104
Reicha, Anton 64
Renaissance 38, 60
re:work Centre 9
Rodney, Walter 139
Romania 56, 87, 88, 93
Rome 22, 34, 45, 60, 66, 69, 75, 99, 176
    Académie de France 60
    Third Rome (*see* Russia)
Rossini, Gioachino 64
Rupprecht, Tobias 16
Russia 17, 34–7, 41, 43, 51, 56, 57, 60, 62, 64, 85, 87, 98, 100, 104, 115–22, 124–9, 142, 143
    European Russia 124
    Third Rome 34
Russian Academy of Science 22
Russian Revolutions (1917) 143

Sachsenmaier, Dominic 4
Saha, Jonathan 201
Said, Edward 171
Saint Petersburg 35, 60, 63, 75
Saint-Saëns, Camille 65
Sanchez-Sibony, Oscar 86–7
Santiago de Chile 88
Sapiro, Gisèle 71, 72
Sargent, John Singer 62

Sarkozy, Nicolas 14, 173
Sartre, Jean-Paul 74
Sauvy, Alfred 149
Saxony 35, 50, 99
Scandinavia 7, 34, 36, 73
Scego, Igiaba 99
Schmidt, Helmut 104
Schnitzler, Arthur 60
Schwenkel, Christina 100
Sciascia, Leonardo 72
Scipio Africanus 171
Scotland 51
Scribe, Eugène 64
Second World War 6, 7, 16, 34, 42, 43, 63, 93, 159, 160, 164, 178, 179, 190
Senegal 11, 89, 138, 177
Senegal River 175
Septimius Severus 176
Seurat, Georges 62
Seven Years War 2
Seville 7
Signac, Paul 62, 63
Sihamoni, Norodom 90
Singapore 11, 96, 98
Sino-Soviet split 91
Sisley, Alfred 68
Sklair, Leslie 97
slavery 17, 40, 125, 140, 144, 172, 199
Slavery and Abolition 144
slaves 40, 139, 140, 142, 156, 158, 170, 172, 173, 177
slave trade 142, 156, 157, 171, 172, 174, 177
Smiley, Xan 104
Smith, Adam 188, 189
Smyrna 33
socialist camp 16, 82, 83, 94
    countries 16, 84, 91
    economies 87
    globalization 8, 91, 93, 95, 96, 99, 101
    internationalism 16, 94
    revolutions 83
    states 82, 84, 86–8, 91, 94–6
    systems 83
    world 81–101
Sofala 176
Songhai 175
Sosa, Porfirio Lobo 90
South African History Workshop Movement 138
South Caucasus 85
Southern Common Market 150
South Korea 96, 98, 138
South Wales 141
South Yemen 99
Soviet Union 6, 16, 82, 83, 86, 89, 90, 94, 97, 112, 150, 157, 179. *See also* Union of Soviet Socialist Republics (USSR)
Spain 11, 42, 57, 64, 70, 174
Spontini, Gaspare 64
Sri Lanka 84
Stalin, Joseph 89
Stanziani, Alessandro 17
Stiglitz, Joseph 119
Stockholm International Peace Research Institute (SIPRI) 7
Stokes, Gale 87
Stolypin, Piotr Arkadievich 126
subaltern studies 41, 138, 170
subalterns 17, 129
Sudan, Western 169, 175
Sue, Eugène 60
Sultanates, Omani, Zanzibar 177
Swansea 141
Sweden 11, 34, 95
Switzerland 11, 13, 53, 55–7
Syria 85, 90

Taiwan 89
Tanzania 88
Tanzania-Zambia railway 91
Tashkent 91
Terk, Sonia, m. Delaunay 62
Thailand 11
Thatcher, Margaret 104
Thoen, E. 200
Thompson 149
Tiersot, Julien 65
Timbuktu 39
Tirana 99
Togo 11
Tokyo 22
Totalitarianism 115
Touré, Amadou 90
Trinidad and Tobago 11
Tripoli 176
Tunisia 53
Turkey 11, 41, 57, 138, 160, 161
Turku 200

Ukraine 99
Unger 159
Union of Soviet Socialist Republics (USSR) 87, 90, 116, 119, 129. *See also* Soviet Union
United Kingdom (UK) 8, 9, 11, 13, 14, 53, 57, 86, 126
United Nations 42, 179
  Red Cross 82
  Olympic Committee 82
United Nations Commission for Trade and Development (UNCTAD) 92
United Nations Educational, Scientific and Cultural Organization (UNESCO) 14
United Nations Industrial Development Organization (UNIDO) 92
United States 4–6, 9, 11, 14, 32, 38, 41, 43, 46, 63, 65, 74–5, 83, 86, 92–3, 139, 140, 142, 155, 172, 177, 179
Universal History 3, 5, 29, 30, 31
Universities
  Berlin University 55
  Cheikh Anta Diop University, Dakar 173
  Columbia University 58
  Friedrich-Wilhelm University, Berlin 56
  Ghent University 18, 200
  Harvard University 58, 200
  Humboldt University, Berlin 56
  Leipzig University 5, 50
  Munich University 50
  Sorbonne, Paris 56
  University of Athens 33
  University of Moscow 118
  University of Oxford, Centre for Global History 9
  University of Warwick, Global History and Culture Centre 9
Ural 89, 175
Utrecht 200

Valenzuela, Luis 141
Vallès, Jules 49
Van Bavel, B. 200
van Binsbergen, Wim 171
van der Linden, Marcel 17
Van Dongen, Kees 62
Vanhaute, Eric 18, 19, 200
Van Leeuwen, B. 200
van Nederveen Meerkerk, Elise 158
van Onselen, Charles 139
Vasco da Gama 30
Venezuela 85, 100
Venizelos, Eleftherios 33
Verlaine, Julie 64, 76
Versailles 75
Viellé-Griffin, Francis 68
Vienna 48, 51, 60, 63, 75, 178
Vietnam 32, 41, 50, 84, 85, 87, 89–91, 95, 99
  War of liberation 43
Vietnam War 50
Voltaire, François Marie Arouet, called 30, 47, 115
Vries, Peer 10, 184, 186, 189

Wagner, Richard 64
Wallerstein, Immanuel 115, 121, 122, 189
Warsaw 22, 42
Washington 22
Washington Consensus 93
Weber, Max 117, 139, 185, 187
Weber, William 64
Weimar 56
Werner, Michael 15
Westad, Odd Arne 89
Westernization 98, 101
Whistler, John Mc Neill 62, 68
Wilfert, Blaise 71–3
Williams, Eric 185
Wilson, Woodrow 41
Wittelsbach family 33
World Exhibition (1867) 51
World Exposition (1889) 62
world history 3–7, 43, 95, 115, 120, 169, 171, 179, 183–6, 193, 197–8
World History Association (WHA) 10
Wundt, Wilhelm 29

Yangtze/Yangzi Delta 8, 115, 121, 185
Yemen 158
Yugoslavia 98

Zanzibar 88, 178
Zimbabwe 89, 169, 176
Zola, Emile 59, 60, 62

THE THAMES AND I

The Japan Society
Founded 1891

The Thames and I

A MEMOIR OF TWO YEARS AT OXFORD

———□———

by

Prince Naruhito
CROWN PRINCE OF JAPAN

With a Foreword by
HIS ROYAL HIGHNESS, THE PRINCE OF WALES
and a Preface to the English edition by
HIS IMPERIAL HIGHNESS, THE CROWN PRINCE

English translation by
SIR HUGH CORTAZZI

GLOBAL ORIENTAL

THE THAMES AND I
A MEMOIR OF TWO YEARS AT OXFORD

Originally published in 1993 in Japanese by Gakushūin Kyōyōshinsho,
Tokyo, under the title *Thames no tomo ni*
© Prince Naruhito, Crown Prince of Japan

First published in 2006 by
GLOBAL ORIENTAL LTD
PO Box 219
Folkestone
Kent CT20 2WP
UK

www.globaloriental.co.uk

English edition © Global Oriental Ltd 2006

ISBN 1-905246-06-4

All rights reserved. No part of this publication
may be reproduced or transmitted in any form or by any
electronic, mechanical or other means, now known
or hereafter invented, including photocopying and
recording, or in any information storage or retrieval
system, without prior permission in writing from
the Publishers.

British Library Cataloguing in Publication Data
A CIP catalogue entry for this book is available
from the British Library

Set in Garamond 11.5 on 13pt by Servis Filmsetting Ltd, Manchester
Printed and bound in England by Antony Rowe Ltd, Chippenham, Wilts

CLARENCE HOUSE

It gives me great pleasure to introduce this enjoyable and perceptive Memoir, which The Crown Prince of Japan wrote in 1992 and which has now been translated into English. The book shows a keen eye, a delicate sense of humour, an enviable desire to be involved in a wide variety of activities and a power of description which gives the reader interest and enjoyment.

There is a close friendship between the United Kingdom and Japan, which is reflected in the solid bond between the Imperial and Royal Families. It always gives us pleasure to welcome members of the Emperor's Family to the United Kingdom and it is marvellous that so many of them have chosen to attend British Universities.

Prince Naruhito clearly enjoyed his time at Oxford, and I thank His Imperial Highness for sharing so much with us in this very readable memoir.

Charles

PREFACE TO THE ENGLISH EDITION

I am very pleased that an English translation of my memoir has now been published. It is twenty years since I left Oxford but I recall fondly the days I spent there as if they took place yesterday. I feel that what I learned whilst I was studying in England during those brief two years has enriched my life a great deal. I shall be pleased if English readers find something of interest in this account of my experiences and impressions.

I am most grateful to Prince Charles, the Prince of Wales, for the interest which he has shown in my book and for the warm message which he has written for the English publication of this memoir. I also wish to express my appreciation for the efforts of all concerned, which enabled this translation to be published. I thank in particular Sir Hugh Cortazzi, the translator, for the zeal and efforts he has put into this project. I would also like to express my appreciation for the help and advice given by others over this publication, especially my mentors Professor Mathias and Dr Highfield.

I hope that this book may contribute even if only in a small way to mutual understanding between Britain and Japan and bring our two countries closer together.

Naruhito

CONTENTS

———□———

Photographs taken by HIH The Crown Prince facing page 50

Foreword by HRH The Prince of Wales	v
Preface to the English edition	vii
Preface to the Japanese Edition	xii
Translator's Note	xiii
The Gakushūin	xiv

1. Ten Days in the Japanese Ambassador's Residence: 1
    Arrival in London   1
    Life in the ambassador's residence   2
    First visit to Oxford   4
    Excursion by the Thames   5

2. Life in Colonel Hall's House: 7
    I move to Colonel Hall's   7
    Studying English   8
    Life in the Hall household   12
    Second visit to Oxford and call at Professor Mathias's house   16
    Visit to Scotland   18
    Last month at the Halls   20

Contents

3. Entering Oxford: 24
   Arrival at Merton 24
   Before matriculation 27
   University Entrance ceremony 30

4. About Oxford: 32
   'Dreaming spires' 32
   'Town and Gown' – A brief history of Oxford University 33
   College system 35
   Education at Oxford and regular activities in the
      University 38
   Merton 41

5. Daily Life at Oxford: 46
   In the mornings 46
   Middle Common Room (MCR) 48
   Shopping and the English character 50
   Draughts and baths 54
   Dinner 54
   High table 57
   Weekends 60
   Family visits 62
   With Oxford students 64

6. Cultural Life at Oxford: 73
   Films, theatre and music 73
   Enjoying chamber music 77
   Visits to places associated with musicians: England and
      music 82

7. Sport: 85
   Rowing 85
   Tennis and squash 86
   Jogging, climbing, skiing and other sporting activities 92

Contents

8. Life as a Research Student at Oxford:	98
Why I decided to do research on the Thames as a highway	98
Professor Mathias	100
Visiting record offices	111
Dr Highfield	115
Preparing my thesis	123
Canals past and future	127
9. Travels in Britain and Abroad:	129
Weekend drives in the countryside and around Oxford	129
Trips in Britain involving overnight stays	131
Travelling round Europe and meeting European Royal Families	135
10. Looking Back on My Two Years' Stay:	137
The English people as I saw them	137
On leaving Britain	141
Postscript	144
Bibliography	146
Index	147

PREFACE TO THE JAPANESE EDITION

I was at Oxford from the end of June 1983 to early October 1985 and my stay in Britain thus came to roughly two years and four months. I had so many experiences during this time that I cannot recount them all here. It is seven years now since I left Oxford and the precious memories of my younger days there come flooding back across the years. I need hardly say how valuable they have been to my way of life today.

However, as my supervisor at Oxford during my studies there, Professor Peter Mathias, wrote in the preface to the Japanese translation of his book *The First Industrial Nation* 'In preparing this preface to a new edition of my book I am writing for Japanese readers about what must seem to them the other side of the world', I too, in recording memories of my two years at Oxford, am writing in Tokyo which is on the other side of the world to Oxford. In writing this preface the thoughts, which race through my mind, are all about my enjoyable life as a student at Oxford. It was, of course, impossible in the brief two years that I lived in Oxford to grasp the whole picture of the university with its diversity and long history. However in the short period that I was at Oxford I had had an unforgettable experience. I have tried, as best I can, within the limits of what a single individual can absorb, to describe what I saw, did and thought and I hope that it will contribute to better understanding.

I want to dedicate this account of my two years in Oxford to my parents who made this stay possible. Without their help and support I would not have been able to enjoy to the full the life of a student abroad.

Winter, 1992

TRANSLATOR'S NOTE

Thames to tomo ni, was originally published in Japanese by Gakushūin Kyōyōshinsho in Tokyo in 1993. Her Imperial Highness, The Crown Princess Masako, had long planned to produce a translation of this book, but owing to her many commitments was unable to do so before the present translation was submitted to His Imperial Highness Crown Prince Naruhito. When the Prince was at Oxford he was the elder son of the then Crown Prince Akihito who became the Heisei era Emperor in 1989 on the death of the Shōwa era Emperor (Hirohito).

This translation has been made from the Japanese by Sir Hugh Cortazzi. He wishes to record his thanks for all advice received from the Crown Prince's Household and for the valuable suggestions made by Lady Bouchier (Dorothy Britton) and Ms Akiko Machimura on the best way to translate this text. He is also grateful to Professor Mathias, Dr Roger Highfield, Colonel Tom Hall and Dr Carmen Blacker for reading the text and suggesting amendments. Any remaining errors are his responsibility.

A very small number of minor modifications have been made in translating the text to reflect the facts as known to the translator who has added a few explanatory footnotes.

Permission for this translation to be made was given by the Japanese Imperial Household in late 2004.

THE GAKUSHŪIN

The Prince makes various references in the text to the Gakushūin where he had studied in Japan. The Gakushūin University traces its origin to the 'Old Gakushūin' which was established in 1847 in Kyoto as the educational institution of the Imperial Court. The name Gakushūin is made up of three Chinese characters meaning 'to be taught', 'to learn' and 'institution'. In 1877, after the Meiji Restoration, it was re-established in Tokyo as a school for the nobility and was popularly referred to as the Peers School. In 1884 entry to the school was opened to children from outside the ranks of the nobility. In 1947 the Gakushūin became an entirely private school to which anyone could gain entry if they passed the entrance examinations. In 1949 the Gakushūin University was established. The university now has some 9,000 students and fourteen departments divided into four separate faculties. It also has a graduate school comprising six separate schools and fourteen specialist courses.

CHAPTER 1

TEN DAYS IN THE JAPANESE AMBASSADOR'S RESIDENCE

―――――□―――――

Arrival in London

I arrived at London's Heathrow airport before dawn on 21 June 1983. I do not remember much about what I could see of London from the aircraft, perhaps because I was sleepy and nervous. The sky in the foreign country in which I was to live for two years looked dull and cloudy and although it was supposed to be summer it felt unexpectedly chilly. I was greeted by Ambassador Hirahara, Mr Elliott, the head of the Far Eastern Department at the British Foreign Office, and one of my cousins who was working in Japan Airline's London Office Mr Mibu Motohiro and others. After a few minutes in an airport room I was taken by car to the ambassador's residence where I was to stay for ten days.

This was not my first visit to London. I had spent a short time there on my return from visits to Belgium and Spain in 1976. Because I was changing planes I had little time to see London and my memory of that visit was limited to seeing Windsor Castle and the river Thames flowing past, and eating roast beef at a nearby restaurant. I was impressed by Windsor Castle but I was not much impressed by the Thames or the taste of the roast beef. I had a clear memory of looking at the Thames while crossing over it on an old bridge and seeing rubbish floating in dirty water. The taste of the roast beef seemed plain and nothing special.

Now seven years later, as I abandoned myself to the comfortable motion of a motor car, I felt that the curtain was quietly lifting and that I was about to begin an unprecedented two-year stay in a foreign country and the drama of an unknown yet exciting experience as a foreign student. Looking out of the car windows I thought that London had a solemn atmosphere and that the buildings looked impressive and serene. The environment of the Ambassador's residence was tranquil and impressed me very favourably. After taking a rest in the morning I went out again in the afternoon for a drive around the city. This gave me a second chance to see the Thames. Looking at the river up close, with buildings such as the Houses of Parliament, Big Ben and St Paul's Cathedral providing a backdrop, I realized for the first time what an important part the river plays in the London scene. The River Thames – from my former image of it as a rather dirty river, to its existence as a necessary, vital element in the London scene – rapidly began to captivate my mind. And at that point I had no idea that the Thames would become the theme of my studies and research while I was in Britain.

Life in the ambassador's residence

My stay in the residence, thanks to the arrangements made by Ambassador and Mrs Hirahara, was a very pleasant one. This was a good opportunity for me to learn more about Britain.

On 22 June, the day after my arrival, I was able to watch the opening of parliament. The solemn ceremony took place in the House of Lords in the presence of Her Majesty Queen Elizabeth and her consort Prince Philip, Duke of Edinburgh. The ceremony began with the formal entry of the Queen and Prince Philip into the chamber where the peers dressed in their resplendent robes were waiting. In due course the Queen's messenger proceeded to the House of Commons and speaking in a loud voice knocked on the door of the chamber. After he had twice been refused entrance, on the third occasion the door was opened and the members of the lower house proceeded as a body to the upper house. I realized that the historical rationale behind the opening of the door of the House of Commons at the third summons and the whole proceedings lay in the puritan revolution, when the House of Commons achieved its independence from the crown and became the central organ of government. Soon, the members of the lower house dressed in their ordinary clothes made their appearance. I noted among them Mrs Thatcher, the Prime Minister. The Queen read out the speech setting out the policies of the second Thatcher administration. The ceremony ended after about thirty minutes. This was the first occasion for me to appreciate that Britain was indeed a land of tradition.

That evening I called at her invitation on Princess Alexandra at St James's Palace. This was the first time I had met the Princess but she made me feel very much at home by the informal and friendly way in which she received me. The following day I was to call at Buckingham Palace where I had been invited to tea by Her Majesty the Queen. Prince Andrew and Prince Edward were present and I had a pleasant time in a relaxed atmosphere. The Queen asked what I was going to do in Britain and spoke among other things about her visit to Japan. Prince Andrew spoke about his service in the navy and Prince Edward about his life as a student. Of course I felt rather nervous but the conversation was very informal and enjoyable. I wondered how 'Tea' was served in England, but the Queen kindly poured the tea herself. I also noted that sandwiches and cakes were served with Tea. On the 24th I was invited to lunch by Princess Anne at her house in Gloucestershire. I made a courtesy call on Princess Margaret and signed the book at the Queen Mother's. I was very fortunate to be able to meet so many members of the Royal Family so soon after my arrival. I was also able at this time to meet the relevant British Foreign Office officials, the Earl and Countess of Mansfield from Scotland who were my personal guarantors, Colonel Tom Hall, with whom I would be staying for three months to study English before entering the university, Sir Rex Richards, the warden of Merton College at Oxford where I would be studying, and Professor Peter Mathias from All Souls, who would be my academic supervisor. My meeting with these latter two gentlemen before I had even entered the university increased my expectations of life at Oxford. Sir Rex Richards struck me as a courteous English gentleman and Professor Mathias seemed a typical scholar. I also benefited from briefings about Britain which members of the Embassy in turn gave me over breakfast.

The Thames and I

First visit to Oxford

I first went to Oxford on 24 June. I still have a clear recollection of that visit. I went by car along the M40 to Oxford which lies some 90 kilometres to the North West of London. In the countryside, which looked as if it was covered by a green carpet, I occasionally saw sheep grazing. I spent a peaceful hour contemplating this poetic and bucolic scene. Soon after turning off the main road, we were driving along a narrow country road and passing through villages with rows of stone buildings. Suddenly, I caught sight of the tower of Magdalen of which I had seen a photograph. Soon we reached Merton. There Sir Rex Richards, whom I had met on the previous day, was waiting for me and he showed me round the various college buildings. While looking at this diverse group of old buildings where I would be studying in the future I was moved in an inexplicable way. During our tour Sir Rex introduced me to a scholarly person with white hair and thick spectacles. He seemed to be deeply absorbed in the study of some book, but as soon as Sir Rex spoke to him he jumped up and shook hands. He was Dr Roger Highfield, the scholar, who would be my tutor at Merton. My first impression of him was that he was rather frightening. Sir Rex no doubt introduced us at this time as he wanted us to get to know one another. Dr Highfield soon returned to his desk and his books. For some reason he left a deep impression on me.

The warden also showed me the 'real tennis' court nearby (for an explanation of 'real tennis' please see the chapter on sports). I was also shown the room which I would be using during my two years at the college, but it was under repair and I could see that there were holes everywhere. Although the college was on holiday I saw various students wandering around. As we passed the warden spoke to each of them. He seemed to know them all by name and through this I began to recognize the merits of the college system. This was probably due in part to the warden's character but also reflected the size of the college which allowed him to remember each student. Although my visit to Merton was a short one I felt greatly attracted by the atmosphere of Oxford and the college. As I was driven back in the car and looked out at Christ Church and the various other colleges on the High Street, I felt very fortunate that I would be able to spend two years here.

I should explain how it came about that out of Oxford's many colleges I entered Merton. It had been left to the British government to decide both the university and college where I was to study. I heard that after some deliberation Merton had been chosen. The reasons were that Sir Rex Richards, the respected vice-chancellor of the University, was the warden of Merton, which was among the oldest colleges in Oxford, it was small enough to enable me to make friends easily and had a good academic reputation. Everyone takes a favourable view of his own college, but looking back nine years later I am convinced that Merton was indeed the right choice. I also heard that the presence at Oxford of Professor Mathias had been an important factor in choosing Oxford rather than Cambridge.

Excursion by the Thames

On 25 June, the day after my visit to Oxford, I made a trip to see various sights on the Thames some half-way between London and Oxford. I lunched that day with Ambassador Hirahara and other Embassy officials at a hotel at Goring-on-Thames. It was the right weather for a walk; so we went out into the hotel garden after lunch and followed a footpath by the river. There were many boats on the Thames that day. The white boats sailing on the river seemed to go so well with the brick-coloured bridge not far off while the blue of the river in the sunshine created a truly attractive scene. And I loved the sight of the various groups sitting on the river bank chatting and laughing.

We went on to Henley-on-Thames. There I learnt that Henley was famous as the place where the Royal Regatta was held, but I was particularly impressed by the beauty of the colours of the façades of the houses by the river. At one place on the river, where there is a wooden bridge, I gazed out over the river and realized how different the Thames is to Japanese rivers. The Thames does not have a dry flood plain[1] and flows calmly between the banks which are part of

---

[1] As many Japanese rivers do

The Thames and I

the land beside the river unlike Japanese rivers with their concrete embankments.

The next place we visited was Marlow. From *'The Compleat Angler' Hotel* where we stopped for tea I enjoyed another fantastic view of the Thames with its suspension bridges, the churches across the river and the many flowers which added to the charm of the scenery. Thus, as I came into contact with the river I began to feel a strong affection for the Thames and the image of a dirty river which I had had in the past was completely dissipated.

In addition, while I was staying at the ambassador's residence I was taken on excursions in the South of England, to Brighton, the white cliffs of Beachy Head, Hastings, famous for the battle of the Norman Conquest of 1066, as well as to Canterbury.

CHAPTER 2

LIFE IN COLONEL HALL'S HOUSE

―――□―――

I move to Colonel Hall's

My twelve days at the ambassador's residence passed quickly. On 3 July I moved to Colonel Hall's house at Chiselhampton outside Oxford. The scenery on the way was familiar as I had travelled this route before on my visit to Oxford, but as I was rather nervous and facing a long 'home-stay' I did not have much inclination to enjoy the scenery. Fortunately, this was not my first experience of a 'home-stay'. In my third year at middle school I had made my first visit overseas to Australia where a 'home-stay' had been part of the trip, but I could not disguise my apprehension in facing a long three-month 'home-stay'.

Colonel Hall's house was a splendid three-storey brick building and it seemed somewhat oppressive. The porch was not far from the gate, but I soon recognized that a spacious garden lay behind the house. I was greeted at the porch by Tom Hall, his wife, Mariette, and their three children, Lucy, Edward and John. I was struck by the size and height of the entrance hall which went up to the second floor. There were various books on the hall table; on one side there was a piano and around the hall were Hall's work-room, the sitting-room, and the dining-room. After we had exchanged greetings Mrs Hall showed me to my room on the first floor. The room had its own bathroom and WC. On the walls there were decorated plates and pictures of birds. From the window I could see the large farm managed by Hall where a number of cows were grazing peacefully and green fields stretching as far as the eye could see. When I came out of my room I looked straight down onto the front hall. Soon, lunch was served. In addition to members of the Hall family, Ambassador Nakagawa who had been appointed to accompany me to Britain, Ambassador Hirahara, Counsellor Fuji who had been given the task of looking after my affairs during the whole of my stay as a student in Britain, and officials from the Japanese Embassy were present. As it was a warm day the table had been laid outside on the terrace. This, my first experience of British home cooking, exceeded all my expectations.

After lunch, I received representatives of the Japanese press in the garden. According to the record which I have the correspondents took pictures of me looking at the horses brought by acquaintances of Colonel Hall and of my taking a walk. After the meeting with the press was over Ambassadors Nakagawa and Hirahara and the others departed and I was left alone in the Hall household. In the evening Colonel Hall invited me to swim in the heated pool in the garden and John showed me how to play croquet, which is similar to the Japanese game of 'gate ball'. At this time of year it is light in Britain until quite late and it was still light when the evening meal was served at 7.30. During the meal Colonel Hall suggested that I look outside. There I saw a fox. Sadly, I do not recall anything about the conversation at dinner that evening except the fox. However, Colonel Hall, his wife and children seemed good people who treated me kindly and I thought I would be able to get by during the three months ahead of me. The first day in the Hall household had seemed rather long, but when I went upstairs to go to bed the Colonel took me to my room and said: 'Good night Hiro,[1] Welcome to our home.' I then realized that the day had ended without mishap and I felt a surge of relief.

Studying English

One of the main purposes of my stay with Colonel Hall before entering university was to improve my English. Colonel Hall, who had been an honorary ADC to the Queen,[2] ran a language school

---

[1] Hiro was the personal name which the Prince used while at Oxford.
[2] Colonel Hall has told me that he was not an ADC to the Queen, but was for eighteen years a Gentleman at Arms in the Queen's bodyguard. Hugh Cortazzi.

Life in Colonel Hall's House

and had established a school in Japan. The reason why the British government had recommended that I study with him before I went to Oxford was probably because he managed a language school and this meant that I could study at his home. My language teachers were Mr and Mrs Corcos who taught at Colonel Hall's school and had had experience of teaching in Japan. I met them on the day after my arrival and I had a very favourable impression of them.

The arrangements were for me to receive two hours tuition in the mornings and in the afternoons with each of them in turn. The lessons were held in the basement. At first, to learn practical expressions used in daily life in England an English conversation book was used. To improve my understanding of spoken English I listened to the BBC morning news and to help my reading ability emphasis was placed on understanding newspaper articles. At the beginning, I could hardly understand at all the BBC news on the radio, but I had less difficulty with television news and depending on the subject matter was able to grasp the meaning straight away. After listening to the news on the radio and watching it on TV I had to answer questions, sometimes orally and sometimes in writing, about what I had heard and seen. The same arrangements applied to newspaper articles. As homework I had to keep a diary in English about what I had been doing that day. The first task on the following day was to read through and correct what I had written; the appropriate expressions were explained to me and grammatical errors pointed out. This was very helpful to me in learning how to express my thoughts in English. This was not all that my lessons consisted of. All sorts of materials were used from time to time. On the ground floor tea was served in between lessons. This was poured by the teachers but I noticed that Diana [Corcos] was better at this than her husband Philip [Corcos]. It only consisted of putting a tea bag in the teapot and pouring on boiling water, but Philip almost always managed to scald himself or do something else untoward.

In addition to lessons inside there were occasional lessons outside. One day, we visited the prehistoric monuments at Stonehenge and Salisbury cathedral. While looking round these sites I studied the pamphlets describing their history and found them very helpful in learning the relevant vocabulary. On the following day, I was

The Thames and I

questioned in English about the visits; this was useful practice in describing what I had seen. Stonehenge is a collection of huge, ancient stones which look as if they had suddenly appeared in the middle of the grassy plain. One could not help but wonder why and who had built it. Salisbury cathedral, not far away, towers over Salisbury plain; it has the highest and most beautiful spire in Britain which was completed in the middle of the fourteenth century and I was overwhelmed by its impressive appearance. The cathedral is an example of English Gothic. In recent years, there has been speculation about 'mystery circles'[3] in this area.

One of my tasks during my outside lessons was to explore Oxford with the help of a booklet explaining the history of the city. In St Mary's Church I tried my hand at brass-rubbing. It entailed placing a sheet of paper on the ancient relief portraits carved into the brass plaques on the graves of those buried there and rubbing black wax onto the paper so that the image appeared on the sheet. Although the plaques were not the real thing but small size copies for tourists I found the process of brass-rubbing a fascinating one.

Among the many other places which I visited were the Museum in Oxford, the Royal Observatory at Greenwich and the Canal Museum at Northampton. I learnt a good deal of basic information about canals from seeing actual things in the museum.

Colonel Hall took me to buy stamps in a shop nearby and I learnt how they were sold. I was also taught how to order beer in a pub. To digress, I should like to describe my first experience in a pub. That day Colonel Hall drove me and his elder son Edward to three pubs in the neighbourhood. Colonel Hall guessed that, after I had gone up to Oxford, I would occasionally visit a pub, and thought that it would be useful for me to learn how to order beer and sample the atmosphere of an English pub. I was taught that in an English pub you did not just ask for a glass of beer but asked either for bitter or lager. Bitter is a traditional English beer with a bitter taste and brown in colour. Lager beer is the type normally drunk in Japan. I learnt that one normally ordered beer by the pint (equivalent to 0.57 litres).

---

[3] The Prince was probably referring to the crop circles which appear each year.

Life in Colonel Hall's House

A pint is rather less than there is in a bottle of Japanese beer. So in ordering beer one said: 'A pint of bitter, please!' or 'Half a pint of lager, please!'. Still, I had to summon up some courage to give an order. All went well at the first pub we visited. At the second pub the landlord gave me a look implying 'who is this fellow?' The third pub, which lay beside the Thames and had a thatched roof and white walls, was very pretty. It had a pleasant atmosphere and I visited it after I had joined the university. At first, I did not much care for the taste of bitter, but on my first visit ever to a pub I liked the atmosphere very much.

The river Thames provided material for my study of the English language. Of course at that time I had not yet decided to make the study of transport on the Thames the subject of my university thesis. I only decided on this after I had joined the university. But various items of information about the Thames which I gleaned while staying with Colonel Hall were useful to me in my future studies. One of these was a book by John Gagg[4] about canals, which I read with Mrs Corcos. As one of the objectives of my lessons was to improve my ability to read English I would read a section of the book in advance of the lesson and would then answer questions from Mrs Corcos about what I had read. For someone like myself who knew absolutely nothing about canals in Britain this was a very good introduction to understanding the subject.

In addition to knowledge gained from reading, I had the new experience, while I was staying with Colonel Hall, of actually going on the river. One way of going on the river was punting. Punting is used at both Oxford and Cambridge and consists in moving a boat called a punt, which has a flat bottom and a square prow, by using a long pole; the boat can carry about four people and the pole is made of metal. According to my diary the first time I went punting was on 28 July when I had an enjoyable time with Mr and Mrs Corcos punting on the Cherwell which is a branch of the Thames. We boarded the punt at the Cherwell boathouse restaurant. This was the

---

[4] John C.Gagg is the author of two books about canals published in the1970s. One published in London in 1973 was entitled *5000 Miles, 3000 Locks*, the other published in Princes Risborough in 1971 was entitled *250 Waterway Landmarks*.

easy part; I soon found that it was difficult to prevent the boat turning round and round in a circle and I had difficulty in getting it to move forwards. Moreover, the metal pole was heavy to lift and got stuck in the mud at the bottom of the river. So I was in trouble. I noted that some of the boats going in the opposite direction had expert punters while others had novices like me. When going under a bridge one punter had inadvertently lifted his pole so that it struck the arch of the bridge and the pole fell into the river. I was surprised to see a group jump into the river to pull it out.

I did a return trip one day, although not by punt, from Abingdon, some nine kilometres South of Oxford, to Clifton Hampden, a distance of about eight kilometres. En route at a place called Culham we came to a lock and I was interested to see how it operated. A lock is a mechanism to raise or lower a boat on a steeply flowing river or on a canal; this was a small version of the locks on the Panama Canal. The lock gates being opened and shut mechanically we asked the lock-keeper to open the lock for us and with the boat tied to the bank we were able to observe the rise and fall of the water in the lock and how boats passed through. Although there were four other boats waiting at Clifton lock the transit was effected without a hitch. At Clifton Hampden we had lunch in the open air at the *Barley Mow Inn* and got back to Abingdon at about 5 o'clock. The fact that I can recount all this ten years later is because I wrote about my experiences at the time as part of my homework for Mrs Corcos.

Life in the Hall household

Apart from the two-hour sessions of English-language tuition in the mornings and afternoons there was no fixed routine on weekdays and my activities varied from day to day. I got up in the morning before 8 o'clock and had breakfast with the Hall family. I was impressed to see that in addition to toast there were a variety of cereals from which to choose. In addition to cornflakes there were all sorts of other products made from various types of grains. Colonel Hall and Mrs Hall would generally read the newspaper at breakfast and would sometimes summarize the contents for me in an easily understandable way. After breakfast they would go about

Life in Colonel Hall's House

their daily business and I would return to my room to prepare for my lessons; I would soon go down to the basement. Although it was a basement it was fairly light, quiet and suitable for studying. After my lesson it was time for lunch. The menu differed from day to day. When roast lamb was served Colonel Hall would himself do the carving and dish it out on the plates. In English homes it is customary for the host to carve and serve the meat. With lamb, mint sauce and red currant jelly are served. I recall that on most days lunch was soon over but we had pleasant conversations over the meal. After lunch I returned to my lessons. When these were over my free time began. In the summer weather I enjoyed swimming and tennis and generally relaxed in the sitting-room. Mrs Hall enjoyed classical music. One of her favourite pieces was a Schubert quintet which I liked very much and on many occasions we had lively conversations about it.

In the evenings the Halls would often invite people they knew and I would join them at table. On the evening after my arrival a Dutch couple and their son came round: I had a great deal of difficulty on this occasion in following the conversation. They seemed a very pleasant family but sadly we could not communicate adequately. Later, when I visited Holland, I met them again as they were acquaintances of Queen Beatrice. Fortunately, their son was also studying at Oxford and we were occasionally able to meet. Colonel Hall having been in attendance on the Queen, among their acquaintances was someone who had done work connected with the Queen's horses[5] and whose wife had been lady-in-waiting to the Queen Mother. Also living in the neighbourhood was the younger sister of the Queen of Sweden and her husband. German, American and Canadian friends also called.

During dinner at the Halls' house I would be asked how my English lessons were going and from time to time they would question me about Japan and the Japanese language. Colonel Hall had been to Japan on many occasions in connection with his language school there and all the family were very interested in Japan. I was, for instance,

---

[5] Colonel Hall has explained that the Queen's stud manager was Sir Michael Oswald.

asked about the relationship between the Chinese and Japanese languages and the use of the same characters in both languages, as well as about the Japanese pronunciation of Chinese characters, and the difference between Chinese characters and *hiragana*. I would then write Chinese characters on scraps of paper and explain how they were constructed. It is not easy to explain phrases which are commonplace in Japanese and at first I had some difficulty, but drawing on written materials I gradually learnt to cope. For instance, I showed how a tree was written and explained how to understand how characters were put together, with two trees together meaning a wood and three trees a forest. Colonel Hall had his own seal with two characters reading '*tomi*' and '*horu*'[6] to represent his name Tom Hall. After drinking strong coffee which kept us awake, eating chocolate mints and having an after-dinner drink we used to go on talking late into the evening.

Some evenings we visited the houses of some of the Halls' acquaintances. On the day after I arrived in the Hall household we visited the house of a Mr Barclay, a neighbour, swam, played tennis and had tea. On 14 July there was a barbeque supper at the same house. This was the first time I had been to a dinner outside the Halls' except to the house being used by Counsellor Fuji. The Halls, the Barclays, their son and daughter and the latter's friends were present. The barbecued meat fresh from the grill tasted really delicious and the evening was most relaxed and enjoyable. I was soon asked about Japan and in particular its mechanical industries. I did my best to reply in my broken English but it was hard work. Nevertheless, I found the conversation with the other guests of about my age interesting. The Barclays said to me: 'English is not easy at first' and were most kind. I felt that I had had a glimpse of English hospitality.

As I enjoy tennis Colonel Hall occasionally arranged what he called tennis parties. Fortunately, he had a wide circle of acquaintance in the area and I got to know many people through tennis. While staying with the Halls I had other opportunities which I had

---

[6] In Japanese *tomi* means wealth and *horu* dig.

not anticipated to meet new people. For instance, at one of the tennis parties at a neighbour's house I got to know a former Davis Cup player. On his invitation I had the good fortune of being able to play on one of the courts at Wimbledon. At Oxford in 1991 I ran into one of those whom I had met at the first of these tennis parties.

While I was staying with the Halls, apart from studying the English language, I got to know a good deal about England and English life. They did all they could to help me in this. The following are some of the things I remember learning from Hall or his children and which naturally helped me greatly to understand Britain.

On 9 July the Halls' youngest son John was due to graduate from Cheltenham College, an English public school in Gloucestershire and the Halls took me with them to the 'speech day' at the school when the families of the boys who were leaving that term could wander freely around the grounds. I was guided around the grounds by John and his friends. It may well be interesting and enjoyable to live a communal life at a boarding school, but I felt that because school discipline was strict life there must have been quite hard and difficult at times. I also saw the rooms which the boys used. The muddy shirts and socks and old worn desks which I saw seemed typical symbols of dormitory life. However, I was interested for the first time in my life to see what a public school was like. We enjoyed a picnic lunch, which the Halls had brought with them, at a table set up in one corner of the spacious garden. Other tables appeared to be occupied by the families of other leavers while nearby young girls wearing smart straw hats were wandering by. It was indeed a peaceful scene.

A particularly vivid memory is the village fête which was held not far from where the Halls lived. That day Colonel Hall arranged for me to be accompanied by his elder son Edward. As the word 'fête' suggests it was a happy occasion: there were various games, and food and drink were on sale. But I made a frightful blunder at the fête in a game involving throwing Wellington boots. The game in England is called 'Wellington' whereas the similar game in France is called 'Napoleon'. Perhaps because I threw the boot with too much energy it flew sideways across a wall. The bystanders who probably regarded me as some strange oriental burst out laughing. I heard later that the boot had grazed a farmer working in a field. Edward, who usually called me Prince Hiro at home, conscious of the circumstances and not wanting to embarrass me, on this occasion tactfully just called me Hiro.

Very recently, I met someone in Tokyo who said he had met me at Oxford. He was the owner of the place where the fête had been held. I had totally forgotten this, but he had not known who I was that day and had asked me 'Where are you from?' I had replied 'From Tokyo'. He then asked me 'From where in Tokyo?' and when I had replied 'From the centre of the city' he had guessed who I was. Even so it had been a good day. It would be impossible in Japan to go to a place where hardly anyone would know who I was. It is really important and precious to have the opportunity to be able to go privately at one's own pace where one wants.

Second visit to Oxford and call at Professor Mathias's house

On 26 July, I was invited by Professor Mathias to lunch at All Soul's where he was a fellow. This was the first time that I had ever had a meal in college and sitting next to Professor Mathias I felt rather nervous. The dining hall at All Soul's is not very large. The other members of the college seemed to be happily enjoying their meal. Among them I noticed one or two who looked like Japanese and who might have been university teachers. I was able to choose from the menu and ordered first a bean soup followed by a meat dish which looked tasty and was recommended by Professor Mathias. It turned out to be liver and had a strong smell. I should have taken notice when Professor Mathias had told me that it was liver. While I was eating two scholars who sat opposite to us and whose names I remember well were Professor Needham and Dr Simmonds. Professor Needham who spoke a good deal and was wearing a Merton tie seemed to be very attached to the college. Dr Simmonds, on the other hand, was rather taciturn and I was lost for words after greeting him with the words 'how do you do?' At this stage it could not be expected that I should be able to converse fluently. When I had been introduced to Dr Simmonds by Professor Mathias, he had explained that my grandfather was the Emperor of Japan. This seemed to strike a bell with him and when we had coffee after the meal Dr Simmonds sure enough produced a photograph out of his pocket. This was of my grandfather on the occasion of his visit to Oxford.

A date was fixed for me to visit Professor Mathias's home in Gloucestershire. This was an attractive simple stone-built house. After a delicious lunch with his wife and daughter, the Professor took me on a guided tour of Chedworth Roman Villa where the bath and house built in Roman times had been preserved. I knew that the Romans were accustomed to taking baths but I was surprised to discover that hot-water and cold-water baths were separated. The method of heating the water was ingenious. Professor Mathias politely and kindly explained each feature of the villa and I had a most enjoyable day.

While I was staying with the Halls I took part in various public functions. I shall not forget the day when I was invited to a garden party at Buckingham Palace. This was held on 19 July which was a hot, sunny day. Men wore either black or grey morning coats and grey top hats. Perhaps because it was summer there were a few more grey than black morning coats and the vast majority had grey top hats. The ladies' clothes were gorgeous. There were a number of people among the diplomatic corps and royal household whose faces I recognized. When the Queen, the Duke of Edinburgh, Prince Charles, Princess Diana and other members of the Royal Family came onto the terrace the national anthem was played.

When the national anthem was over paths were opened up through the crowd and the Queen and members of the Royal Family made their way slowly towards the Royal Tent speaking to various people on the way. In the Royal Tent raspberries and other fruits were served with tea and cake. After the Royal Family reached the tent I was asked by members of the household to wait my turn to be called to meet the Queen. Eventually, I was able to exchange greetings with the Queen and the Duke of Edinburgh. After I had told her that I was enjoying my stay in Britain, the Queen said that she had recently attended the opening ceremony of the NEC factory near Edinburgh. She had been much impressed by having to wear an overall which looked like a space suit. The Duke of Edinburgh asked me in a humorous tone why I had chosen to go to Oxford rather than Cambridge. This was probably because he was Chancellor of Cambridge University.

Visit to Scotland

Towards the end of August, about half-way through my stay with the Halls, I went on a visit of a few days to Scotland. On 28 August I went from London to Edinburgh and stayed very comfortably with the Earl of Haddington and his family at Tyninghame castle. At lunch in the dining-room, which was decorated with the portraits of Haddington's ancestors, the visit to the castle twenty-one years ago by Princess Chichibu was mentioned. That evening we went to hear a concert which was part of the Edinburgh Festival. This consisted of a performance by Pinchas Zuckerman of a Brahms Violin sonata and a Brahms Viola sonata. He had chosen to play these pieces as this was the 150th anniversary of the birth of Brahms. This fine concert performance provided an excellent opportunity to appreciate the different tones of the two instruments, violin and viola. On returning to the Haddington's I danced a Scottish reel with members of the family. There were only a few who knew the correct way of dancing the reel. But with the men and women forming a circle and dancing holding hands it was great fun. Lord Haddington who was approaching his eightieth birthday also seemed to enjoy the dancing.

On the following day, I went with the family to visit a ruined castle nearby. From the ruins on the edge of a cliff we had a wonderful view over the sea. In the afternoon, we went into Edinburgh and visited Edinburgh castle and the palace of Holyrood. Looking at these beautiful, attractive and magnificent buildings and fine city I was overcome by solemn feelings as I thought of the dark and sad episodes of Scottish history, memories of which seem to persist silently and even show signs of going on forever. At the same time I felt for a moment the underlying discord even today between England and Scotland. We went on to look down over Edinburgh from a nearby hill. Through the haze we could see the various spires and shapes of the buildings which made up the city of Edinburgh

Life in Colonel Hall's House

and I realized why Edinburgh is called the pearl of the British Isles. That evening, accompanied by Lord Haddington's grandchild, I enjoyed another concert in the same hall as on the previous evening. The programme this time consisted of a Mozart Violin Concerto and Mahler's *Das Lied von der Erde*.

On the following morning, Lord Haddington showed me his garden with its profusion of beautiful flowers, and part of his estate. To call it an estate does not convey its size. It was huge, covering about seventy per cent of the area bounded by the Yamanote line in Tokyo. At lunch, students of Edinburgh University, known to Lord Haddington, joined us for a barbeque at a log cabin-type cottage by the sea. That evening I put on a dinner-jacket (tuxedo in Japanese) and went again to Edinburgh castle to see the military tattoo. Various spectacular events were put on in the square in front of the castle. I was particularly impressed by the performance of the bagpipers. A single piper suddenly appeared at the highest point on Edinburgh castle and in the silence which followed we heard the sound of the bagpipes. It was a phantasmic scene.

On the following day, the 31st, I went to Scone Palace in Perthshire, the home of Lord Mansfield, where I was received by the Earl and Countess of Mansfield and their two children. I was shown around inside the palace by Lady Mansfield who spoke with much good humour and elegance and explained everything in an easily understandable way. Among the many historical objects in the house she showed me was a tree-planting spade, which my parents had used during their visit to Scone Palace in 1976. I could imagine how much they had enjoyed their few days with the Mansfields. Lord Mansfield was a Minister for Northern Ireland when I came to study at Oxford. If he had not had this post I would probably have had my 'home-stay' before going up to Oxford with the Mansfields. Although I only had half a day including lunch with the Mansfields at Scone Palace, thanks to the warm reception they gave me, I had a most relaxing and enjoyable time. In the evening, I went back to the Haddingtons and putting on a dinner-jacket attended a formal dinner. After dinner there was more Scottish dancing and Scottish songs were sung with Haddington's grandchild playing the flute and Counsellor Fuji playing the piano. I remember especially the singing of *Loch Lomond*. At the end, all present joined arms and sang *Auld Lang Syne*.[7] The last night at the Haddingtons was a lively and nostalgic one.

During my three days with the Haddingtons the Earl and his wife, despite the fact that they were getting on in years, accompanied me everywhere and their son and grandson did all they could to entertain me. During my short stay in Scotland I was overwhelmed by the hospitality of my hosts, including the Mansfields. On 1 September, full of fond memories, I left the Haddingtons and went on by car to the Lake District in the North of England. As we came nearer to our destination we were increasingly surrounded by hills. I had not felt deprived of anything while staying with the Halls, but the generally flat landscape made me long for the mountains. I was not 'homesick' but rather 'mountain-sick'. On this trip to Scotland I had not been into the Highlands with their many mountains, but the Lake District, combining both lakes and mountains, cured my 'mountain-sickness' and a night in a hotel by a lake provided a chance to rest and relax. That evening perhaps I was too much affected by once more being in the mountains: at any rate, when I was in the corridor after leaving my room, I suddenly realized I had left my key behind. I faced the distressing situation that I was locked out, but I managed to find the manager and borrowed the master key. One could say that this was an extension of my practical language lessons with Mr and Mrs Corcos. Next day, we went round various lakes and visited Wordsworth's cottage. This brought to a close my tour of Scotland and the Lake District and I returned to Oxford by train from Lancaster.

Last month at the Halls

With the arrival of September the days gradually got shorter and there was a feeling of autumn in the air. I only had another month with the Halls. The flowers, which had been blooming in profusion when I had arrived, were getting fewer and the days became quite

---

[7] *Hotaru no hikari* (light of the fireflies) in Japanese.

Life in Colonel Hall's House

chilly. The pace of my lessons in English quickened and became more difficult, but I clearly needed a good knowledge of English to pursue my studies and live a full life at Oxford. So I studied as hard as I could. During the month, as part of my education, in addition to studying English, I was given the opportunity of seeing how English justice worked through a visit to the Royal Courts of Justice in Oxford. I also went to Stratford-on-Avon to see Shakespeare's *Henry VIII*.

Colonel Hall and Mr and Mrs Corcos accompanied me to the Royal Courts of Justice. After a chat with the judge I went into the court-room. I was fortunate enough to be seated beside the judge and was able to see from beginning to end part of a case involving arson. The black robes and wig of the judge made me realize that the old traditions were still being maintained. There were many points in the case and in the defence which I had difficulty in following, but it was a good experience to be able to see how the court operated and I found it a valuable addition to my studies.

Mr and Mrs Corcos accompanied me to Stratford-upon-Avon. Among the many Tudor houses in the town we visited the house where Shakespeare was born and the church where he was buried. We then went to the Royal Shakespeare Theatre. Fortunately, as I had studied a summary of the play with Mr and Mrs Corcos, I was able to follow the plot but the play was long and gloomy. I was greatly moved by being able for the first time to visit Shakespeare country and see one of his plays in his home town.

When I look back on my three-month stay with the Halls I think that my experiences can be divided into four important elements. The first element consisted of language study. While I still felt that English was really difficult to learn and had many depths, I thought that in the time since I had first come to stay with the Halls it had become much easier for me to converse in English as well as to read and write English. I owe this to the help I received from Mr and Mrs Corcos and everyone in the Hall household. The second element consisted in meeting all sorts of people not only in the Hall household but also outside. I learnt a good deal from the hospitality which I received about how to entertain and give pleasure to other people. This will be very useful for me in future in entertaining others. The third element is related to the second. I began to have a better understanding of English life as a result of living with the Halls and visiting other houses. The fourth element lay in learning to enjoy country life. I was told that the dream of every Englishman and woman was to be able to live in the country. As circumstances allowed they would try to leave the city for the country where they might do a bit of farming and with their livestock pass the time in peace and tranquillity.

Soon after I arrived to live with the Halls I suffered from hay fever for the first time in my life. Taking meals in the open air and wandering around farms caused slight discomfort. Then when I thought that my hay fever was getting better my nose would be afflicted by the smell of manure. When I first mentioned this to Mrs Corcos she dismissed it with the words 'good country smell' and as I got used to it I also decided that it was a good thing. Because we lived in the country I was able to enjoy the fresh vegetables and jam from the Halls' farm and breathe good country air in such green and pleasant surroundings. I cannot find a better expression than to say that my three months with the Halls was a very peaceful time. I am deeply grateful to the Halls for receiving me so warmly into their home and the happy memories I have from this time.

My stay with the Halls ended on 3 October and in preparation for entering Merton on the following day I moved to Counsellor Fuji's house outside Oxford. Counsellor Fuji's house was an old rectory which he had rented for two years not far from Abingdon in the village of Besselsleigh. Fuji lived here with his wife, two children and niece and did various work connected with my stay at Oxford. I should explain that Counsellor Fuji had been chamberlain to the Shōwa Emperor and Empress since 1970 and had studied at Copenhagen University in Denmark. He had obtained his doctorate for a study of sea urchins and was an expert Viola player. In this connection he served as Vice-Chairman of the Viola Study Association. Fuji had had much experience of living abroad but this was the first time his wife and children had experienced such a lengthy stay overseas. I greatly appreciated the fact that they had so readily accepted this appointment.

Fuji's house was a two-storey simple building. Behind it there was

Life in Colonel Hall's House

a square-shaped garden of about the size of four tennis courts. which looked out on to farmland. The dining-room and sitting-room, with fireplaces, led off the entrance hall; at the back there was a room with a piano, which could be used as a music room. My room was upstairs at the back with a view of the garden. I used to stay here from time to time after I had entered college, for instance, during vacations and when the college was shut for conferences or other events. It was a very comfortable residence. I was nervous that night before I entered college but I felt at home in the congenial company of the Fujis.

CHAPTER 3

ENTERING OXFORD

―――――□―――――

Arrival at Merton

On 4 October I left Counsellor Fuji's house to spend two years at Merton; my feelings were a mixture of anticipation and anxiety about the new life I was beginning. Perhaps it was due to the nervousness which I felt, but the brief fifteen minutes it took by car from the Fujis' house, where I had slept the previous night, to Merton seemed particularly long. The sounds of the vehicles passing along the cobbled streets, which always used to please me, sounded oppressive that day.

Sir Rex Richards, the warden, whom I had already met during my stay in London, was there to greet me in front of the college gates. I was immediately asked, as is the custom at Oxford, to sign the register of new students which was presented to me at the porter's lodge. I was so nervous that my hand holding the pen shook and when I wrote my name Naruhito in roman letters my writing looked quite awful. This was the first official action of my stay at Oxford.

Having signed the register and received the key of my room the warden introduced me to two other students. One of them was the chairman of the Middle Common Room to which, as a graduate student, I would belong. The other was the chairman of the Junior Common Room, to which undergraduates belong. The chairman of the Middle Common Room was an American called J. He was tall and, at close range, his face, on which a magnificent beard sprouted,

Entering Oxford

looked rather off-putting. He was a very gloomy-looking person, but his eyes showed that he was also gentle and kind. On the other hand, the chairman of the Junior Common Room was an English girl called M who had a very pretty face.

In the Front Quad I met representatives of the English and Japanese media. I was asked various questions by the representative of a local radio station, but the only question I can now remember was 'Do you want to join in all student activities including going to the pub?' I replied in words which I intended to mean that I probably would want to do so. Sir Rex interposed and said: 'As the Prince has only just arrived and is nervous, the questioning should now stop' and the meeting with the media was brought to a close. At that time I really was anxious about the life that lay ahead of me and about what I could do while I was at Oxford. I simply did not have enough ability in English at that time to explain how I then felt.

Carrying a suitcase I made my way up the stone stairs to my rooms on the second floor which was the top floor. My rooms were at the end and consisted of two adjoining rooms, a study and a bedroom. My bathroom lay across a different corridor on which was the room for my police guard. That corridor led to the small second floor landing, and had a door which was closed at night. From my study which was the size of about eight *tatami* mats[1] I had the view which I had hoped for – south over Christ Church Meadow, while from my bedroom I could look down on the peaceful garden of the college. With such a good and quiet outlook I could not have had a better set of rooms.

My desk was big enough to provide ample space for any number of papers. Within easy reach of my desk there was a wooden revolving bookstand and facing the desk there was a bookcase with three shelves. The top of the bookcase was too high for me to reach, but the bookcase by my desk and the revolving bookstand were within easy reach when I was studying, as I could take up any book I wanted without having to move round too far. There were chairs and a table

---

[1] *Tatami*, which are mats made of straw, usually measure about 6.0 x 3.0 feet, but the size varies slightly in different parts of Japan. They are about 2.4 inches thick. Room sizes in Japan are usually described as consisting of a given number of *tatami* mats.

The Thames and I

in the middle of the room and a sofa by the wall. In addition, there were two upright armchairs by the door and an electric fire. In the bedroom, apart from the bed, there was a wardrobe; adjoining this was a wash-basin which had doors to it so that it could be closed off from the rest of the room when not in use. There was also a chest of drawers with three large drawers. And the window above the bed had a curtain so unreliably flimsy it looked as if it would tear at any minute.

It was good to have rooms which I could use as I wanted. I only had one suitcase but I spent some time deciding by trial and error where to put my various things. The light fades early in England in October and by the time I had set my things out it was already getting dark.

Shortly afterwards, as I had promised J, I went down to the bar. Attracted by the smell of beer I soon found myself in the bar and was greeted in the dingy light by a number of curious students. I joined J and M at a table in the middle of the room and some students gathered round. The first girl, to whom I was introduced, was wearing a straw hat, despite the fact that we were indoors, and had a silver star on her forehead. I wondered what sort of a strange place I had come to. So I was relieved to see that some of the others were typical undergraduates such as I had imagined them to be. I can still remember that it was at this moment sitting in the midst of the aroma of the beer and watching the forms and gestures of the students in the gloom that I realized I was in Oxford so far away across the sea.

Invited by J to accompany him I went into hall for my first meal in college. Helping myself to soup and a meat dish at the door we took our seats. J sat opposite me at the long, old and worn dining-table. The benches we sat on were uncomfortable. Looking round, all I could see in the darkness were the faces of the students lit up by the lamps set on the tables. Each had different features and different coloured hair. It was all something I was seeing for the very first time. An enormous number of portraits of people I did not know hung on the walls around the hall. Above was almost total darkness, but I could just make out the shape of the beams in the dizzyingly high ceiling. J, guessing that I was feeling overwhelmed by the atmosphere, assumed an especially kind expression. It was a flurried meal.

Entering Oxford

In my confusion I have forgotten whether I drank the soup and ate the meat and do not remember anything about the conversation. All I recall is that I gave a sigh of relief when the meal, which was better than I had expected, was all over.

Once again, J said, 'Let's go and have our coffee in a friend's room' and so we went up another stone staircase in a different part of the college. The occupant of the room was a girl who was a friend of M's rather than of J's. The room was much the same size as mine, but as there was a bed in the room I realized that it must be a combined bedroom and living-room. A number of others came in including the girl with the silver mark on her forehead. There clearly were not enough chairs to go round. So the newcomers sat on the carpet. As I was standing there with a blank look on my face I was offered a chair that looked as if it was ready to collapse. We chatted sitting in a circle and mugs of coffee were handed round; everyone spoke freely. Unfortunately, while I understood that they were chatting about the joys and troubles of student life I had no opportunity to contribute to the conversation. But I began to understand how they spent their time after dinner and I was happy just to be there. This was also the first time I saw my fellow students nonchalantly putting their mugs on the floor.

In this way my first day at Merton came to a close. Saying goodbye to all present I returned to my room and prepared for bed. I buried myself beneath my three blankets. It was a quiet night and I did not hear a sound from anywhere round about.

Before matriculation

My life at Merton really started from the following day. To get from my room to hall I had a few minutes walk as this was in a different building. Despite the fact that it was only early October it felt chilly that first morning at Merton. This was the second time I had been in hall. I was surprised to see how different it looked in the morning light. One reason for this was the small number of students there, but I was again astonished by the fine beams criss-crossing in the high ceiling. I was rather afraid that it would be cold in hall in winter.

Although I had joined the college this did not mean that the formalities for entering the university would follow immediately. The university entrance ceremony did not take place until 15 October. Before that there were various college and university ceremonies to be held. On the morning of the 6th I put in an appearance at a meeting in the JCR to which I had been invited. In the afternoon J invited various members of the MCR including myself to tea in his room and I went along. They seemed a very nice group of students. One student, who wore glasses and had a beard, seemed particularly voluble. While holding pieces of cake we began to introduce ourselves and spoke about what we were planning to do. Looking back now I realize that most of those I met at tea that day were the ones with whom I developed particularly friendly relations during my two years at Oxford. This tea turned out to be an unexpected opportunity to meet new people.

That evening there was a college admission ceremony in hall. The new students entered hall one by one as their names were called out. After greeting the warden we entered our names in the register. This was a very brief ceremony but the atmosphere was most congenial. Afterwards, there was a dinner to welcome the new students, attended by various senior students and members of the teaching staff of the college. I was placed next to Dr Highfield. I had already met him and greatly enjoyed the dinner. At the end of the meal Sir Rex Richards, the warden, struck the table with a mallet and gave a short speech to close the ceremony mentioning that we should not keep the domestic staff too long. I felt that I was now really a member of the college.

On the 7th we were given general advice about things we needed to know about college life, such as how to get in touch with the doctor responsible for treating members of the college, and other important points to note. After listening to these instructions we moved to the Examinations Schools building, where exams took place as well as lectures, and were given an introduction to the club activities in the University as a whole. I was surprised by the variety; there were so many different facilities including sports clubs, the union where debates took place, cultural circles as well as places where we could enjoy meals. In the evening, I attended a party in the

Entering Oxford

MCR to welcome newcomers to the college. I was impressed by the way the students were able to relax and mix freely and how they were good at socializing. Here I was able to find many valuable friends.

There were no particular ceremonies on the 8th and I went to a cinema in the town to see the film *Gandhi* directed by Richard Attenborough. It was a long but well-produced film and faithfully reflected Gandhi's philosophy and desire for peace. At the end of the film, the fact that more than half the audience did not immediately get up to go attested to its excellence.

In the morning of the 9th there was a lecture by Dr Highfield about the history of the college, which was attended, as I remember, by a large number of new students. This was followed by a mini-tour to see the places he had mentioned. In the evening I was invited to a party of the Oxford Music Society probably because they knew that I played the viola.

In the afternoon of the 10th I attended a history seminar. Professor Howard's lecture to students, who were going to study history, was relatively easy to follow. In the evening, I took part in a drinks party to welcome new students to Merton where I had the good fortune to be able to talk with members of the teaching and college staff. I went on to a party for students particularly interested in the history of the college. This was a good chance to meet other students and a most enjoyable party, but I was in some difficulties because, when I was asked about my particular field of research, I could not answer as I had not yet decided what this would be.

My first week in Oxford thus came to an end with a round of parties. I think they were very relevant for my future time at Merton. I met a large number of students at these parties which were not just occasions for drinking and boisterousness. The prime purpose of these important social occasions was to enable people to meet others and converse informally with a glass in one hand. We Japanese tend to get together in groups of people we already have connections with. I did not see that sort of thing at Oxford. I felt that everyone was delighted to talk and exchange views with anyone. As for dress, people either dressed informally or, surprisingly frequently, put on dinner-jackets. While I was at Oxford I always had a dinner-jacket ready in my room.

The Thames and I

There are all sorts of parties, as I once found to my chagrin. It was after the entrance ceremony. I thought that parties always involved a meal, so I did not have any supper before going to an evening party where there was nothing to eat except crisps and nibbles!

University Entrance ceremony

The 15th, the day of the university entrance ceremony, soon came round. It was a really chilly day with light drizzle. At nine o'clock the new entrants to the college met in the front quad. My name was first called out as 'Mr Naruhito'. This was greeted with a burst of laughter from the other students and my name was corrected to 'Prince Naruhito'. The stiff atmosphere relaxed and having replied 'yes' to my name I went along with the other new entrants to the Sheldonian Theatre where the ceremony was to be held. It was arranged that while I was at Oxford I would simply be called 'Hiro' by staff and fellow students. I thought that 'Hiro' was much easier for people to remember than 'Naruhito' and I liked the sound of 'Hiro' as a name.

Since I had already joined Merton and started going to lectures, some readers may wonder what was meant by the term 'entrance ceremony'. The ceremony that day was actually the 'Matriculation Ceremony' where the term 'matriculate' means permission to enter the university. Dress on this occasion for men consisted of a white shirt, white bow tie and suit under a black gown (which was actually a simple piece of black cloth with holes for the arms) which was also worn on other ceremonial occasions and at formal meals, with a mortar board on the head. This is similar to the headgear of students at Waseda University without the brim. The gowns worn by graduate students, which hang down below the hips, are longer than those worn by undergraduates, which only stretch as far as the hips. Women students wore white blouses with a black ribbon and a gown on top. Led by a representative of the college we began a procession to the place where the ceremony was to be held. We passed along the cobbled pavement of Merton Street into the narrow High Street and across over Radcliffe Square into the Sheldonian Theatre. Fortunately, an English girl who was studying Japanese and a young student from the Philippines whom I had met soon after entering

Entering Oxford

Merton were walking comparatively near me and there was another English student in our group who took it upon himself to look after me. As we passed in front of the Japanese camera crews I shall not forget his face as he said the single word 'Smile!'

As I walked through the medieval-looking streets of modern Oxford, wearing a gown and a white bow tie, I thought I am really now an Oxford man. Simply taking part in the procession to the Sheldonian theatre made it a memorable day for me, but the ceremonies inside the hall were overwhelming. The beautiful round theatre had been designed by the famous English architect Sir Christopher Wren who also designed St Paul's Cathedral in London. Apart from matriculation ceremonies the theatre was used for the conferment of degrees. The proceedings began at 9.45 with solemn music played on the organ. Latin was the language used throughout and the only words I understood were 'sit down, please' which were said by the vice-chancellor in English. I followed the ceremony by reading the translation on the leaflet which I had in my hand. During the ceremony the persons who had led us from our colleges declared 'We introduce our students to the University'. To this the vice-chancellor responded formally: 'Everyone of you should be conscious of the great expectations placed on you by the community and the nation and the hope that you will study hard, as hard as you can, while you are here.' The ceremony lasted a mere fifteen minutes, but it made me realize the weight of tradition here in Oxford. I was relieved that I could now regard myself as a member of the university.

CHAPTER 4

ABOUT OXFORD

'Dreaming spires'[1]

I should like to give a brief introduction to Oxford. The modern city of Oxford has a population of over 100,000. It lies some ninety kilometres to the northwest of London on the middle reaches of the Thames. The name Oxford derives from the two words 'ox' and 'ford' meaning a river which an ox could walk across. In England there are many place names ending in 'ford' such as Stratford and Bradford where there were shallow places at which a river could be crossed fairly easily. The Oxford crest naturally shows an ox crossing a river. The centre of Oxford and the main street in the city is the High Street which runs east to west. The main buildings of the city are ranged on either side of the High Street to the north and south.

In the north of this central area are St Mary's Church, All Souls, Queen's, Brasenose and a number of other colleges as well as the Bodleian Library and its annex Radcliffe Camera. To the north and facing on to Broad Street is the Sheldonian Theatre while on the south side of the High Street are University College and Oriel together with shops and restaurants. Going west from the High Street you come to Carfax crossroads which is the busiest spot in Oxford. Turning north you then come to the Cornmarket which is a shopping street: if you turn south you come into St Aldate's street

---

[1] From Mathew Arnold's poem *Thyrsis*: 'And that sweet City with her dreaming spires, She needs not June for beauty's heightening.'

About Oxford

where you can see the tower of Christ Church. Going further south you reach a bridge over the Thames. Suburbs of the city lie south of the river and of Christ Church Meadow which is a large field by the river. To the north there are various green spaces including University Park while to the east is the Cherwell, a branch of the Thames, which flows under a bridge by the side of Magdalen.

For a view of the city in its entirety you should go towards Headington and South Park in the north-east of the city and climb the gentle green slope. The old college buildings, churches and towers will appear one by one as you look back. While I was studying at Oxford I went many times to this spot and enjoyed the view. It was best towards sunset. I can never forget the moment when silhouettes of the spires of Oxford one by one caught the evening light and seemed to float above the mists. This mystical sight, which has aroused so much admiration, is called Oxford's 'Dreaming Spires'. Going on from South Park down a gentle slope you soon come to a junction where there is a dual carriageway to the left, but if you go straight on to the right you will see the spire of Madgalen College Chapel which seems to mark the entrance to Oxford. Passing by Magdalen there is a slight curve in the High Street and Queen's, All Souls, St Mary's Church and other ancient buildings of the University appear one by one in a really dramatic way. If you are lucky you will see some students in their gowns among the throng walking up and down the High Street. The term 'town and gown' means the citizens of Oxford and the university students.

'Town and Gown' – a brief history of Oxford University

It is not entirely clear why a university was established at Oxford. According to a leading source, in the twelfth century King Henry II banished Thomas à Becket, the Archbishop of Canterbury, to the continent and in order to prevent contacts between the Archbishop and English students studying at the University of Paris, King Henry summoned the students to return home. The students who came home and other students who were unable to pursue their studies at Paris took up their abode in Oxford and the university was born. It is not clear when the university was formally established, but documents have been preserved which show that soon after 1100 there were students at Oxford and it is said that up to about 1300 Oxford had some 1,500 students. Oxford was probably chosen because it was a place where routes crossed in the centre of England and it was easy for people to congregate there. There are not many documents which describe what Oxford University was like in those early days and such accounts, as there are, are not necessarily accurate, but it seems that the teachers and students lived in rooms which they rented from local people and that teaching was carried out in the teachers' rooms, in churches or in the cloisters of monasteries. In the Middle Ages a university was where teachers and students lived a communal life. It did not have to have buildings of its own.

For this reason, and when from time to time students did not pay their rent, petty quarrels occurred between students and townsfolk and sometimes led to brawls when weapons were used on both sides. This was the origin of the popular term 'town and gown'. In 1209 when one student wounded and killed an Oxford woman the trouble led to a court case and the university was forced to close. Many students and teachers left the town and, it is said, moved to Cambridge, leading to the beginning of the university there.

The antagonism between town and gown was at its most violent in 1355. The disturbance in that year was said to have resulted from a row caused by several students over the quality and stinginess of the wine served in *Swyndlestock Tavern* in the centre of town. The citizens and the students gathered respectively in the neighbourhood of St Martin's Church in the area of Carfax and in St Mary's Church. The disturbances lasted two days and resulted in many dead and wounded. The incident was brought to an end by the expulsion of the students from the city. The university used this occasion to petition the king and request the strengthening of their privileges while the town had to pay compensation to those injured.

As an aside, I might add that I was advised to avoid going out alone at night in town wearing a gown. I was surprised to discover that the antagonism between town and gown still lingers to this day.

In order to stop these quarrels a number of students got together to rent a house and thus began the system whereby the students

About Oxford

selected their own leader and began to live in a community of their own. The houses, which were called 'halls', were granted legal status by clerics, aristocrats and others and became colleges.

I think many readers will know that in the Middle Ages university scholars had a special status as members of a guild. At that time students spent seven years living together as pupils under a chief whom they called 'master' in the same way as craftsmen served as apprentices under masters in their trade. Relics of these practices can be seen from the use of the terms 'master', 'doctor', and 'professor'. The word 'masterpiece' originates from an apprentice making a work of art in order to become a 'master'.

When walking around Oxford one occasionally met tourists who asked: 'Where is the University?' It was not only Japanese who were puzzled in this way. The question can be said to reflect a special feature of Oxford. There is no single building which can be described as 'Oxford University': there are thirty-five colleges in Oxford today, including four colleges[2] which only take women and seven which are for postgraduates and research students. These are all independent institutions but together they form Oxford University. The head of the University is the Chancellor, but this is an honorary post and responsibility for the administration of the university falls to the vice-chancellor. While I was at Oxford the Chancellor was former Prime Minister Harold Macmillan who had become the Earl of Stockton. Like the departments in Japanese universities Oxford has various faculties and students invariably belong both to a college and to a faculty. I belonged to the Faculty of Modern History. While I was at Oxford there were some 12,400 students (7,600 men and 4,800 women) in the university, including 1,850 overseas students.

College system

Any account of Oxford University must cover the college system. Let me explain briefly the special characteristics of the system. Colleges are in essence places where students studying different

---

[2] Now two,

subjects live a communal life together. Some colleges are exclusively for women, but most colleges take both men and women. Women were only admitted to Oxford comparatively recently. The largest colleges have some 500 students and the smaller ones about 150. The colleges are of all sizes but the average number of students in any one college is about 300. In the average college, in addition to the students' rooms, there are usually a chapel, library, dining-hall, office, common-room, teachers' rooms and bar. Undergraduates should in principle live within a radius of six miles of Carfax and graduate students within a radius of twelve miles. As a result, students either rent a flat in the city or live in college. At Merton, of which I was a member, there were some 300 students, half of whom lived in college. It was obligatory for undergraduates to spend the first year of their three-year degree course in college.

Colleges are administered by the head of the college and the fellows. The colleges use different titles for their head. Merton, for instance, is headed by a warden, Balliol by a master, Exeter by a rector, Magdalen by a president, Worcester by a provost, Brasenose by a principal. The fellows who are teachers and researchers are informally referred to as 'dons'. One of the fellows in charge of the accounts is the bursar; internal administration comes under the domestic bursar, finance under the financial bursar and college property under the estates bursar. It may be surprising to speak of college estates, but in fact many colleges own large areas of land and are accordingly landed proprietors. Scouts, who are college servants, clean the rooms except at weekends. According to college gossip, they also keep their eyes and ears open and observe what is going on in the students' lives, checking for instance whether someone of the opposite sex is staying in a room and that rooms are tidy and being used for their proper purpose.

The college system is said to have been started around the thirteenth century. There is still some dispute about which is the oldest college – Merton, University College or Balliol. Merton was the first college to receive its charter in 1264 (University College received its charter in 1280 and Balliol in 1284). Merton has some of the oldest buildings still in use; one part goes back to the end of the thirteenth century. University College is said by some to have been founded by

About Oxford

King Alfred the Great, in the ninth century, but there is no documentary proof of this, although it is known for a fact that in 1249 William of Durham supplied funds to provide for a large number of students. There is no doubt that these funds were increased and became attached to the college, although it is not clear whether a college existed at that time. There are records which show that in 1266 a number of scholars got together under John de Balliol; on this basis Balliol College claims that it dates back to 1263. On the basis of the date on which it received its charter and on having the oldest extant buildings in Oxford, Merton is the oldest of all the colleges. University College was the first to receive a financial donation and Balliol was the first college known to have scholars. It is not easy to reach a conclusion on this issue; we need to consider not only the various formal documents but also the actual facts and to take note of the way in which the colleges have grown over the years, but we can say that colleges had been established by the thirteenth century. Exeter, Oriel and Queen's were established in the fourteenth century. The establishment of New College needs to be dealt with separately.

In 1379 the bishop responsible for the University was William of Wykeham. He established New College near the north wall of the city with the aim of educating candidates for the clergy whose numbers had been greatly decreased by the plague which had been prevailing at that time. The adjective 'new' in New College does not just indicate that as compared with existing colleges it was new; it applied to various other aspects of the college. For example the college plan provided for the first time for a quadrangle (called 'quad' in Oxford and 'court' in Cambridge). Generally speaking at Oxford the quad consists of a square garden covered in grass and surrounded by buildings. The oldest quad in Oxford is claimed to be 'Mob Quad' in Merton. This was by chance a square. In the case of New College the quad, designed by William of Wykeham himself, is surrounded by the main buildings of the college, namely the chapel, the library, the lodging for the head of the college and the fellows' rooms. This was the first purpose-built quad in Oxford and it became the pattern for other colleges founded later. New College had more fellows and larger buildings than any of the colleges established previously. In educational terms the college did not confine itself to the education of graduates who already had a master's degree but also took in undergraduates who were to live in college with the fellows. As I explain below this was the beginning of the unique tutorial system. In these ways New College had a major impact on the development of later colleges.

In the fifteenth century three additional colleges were established. These were Lincoln, All Souls and Magdalen. All Souls was established solely for research and is different from every other college in Oxford in that it does not cater for any undergraduates.

I cannot comment further here on every college, but here is a list of the other later colleges in the order of their foundation: sixteenth century: Brasenose, Corpus Christi, Christchurch, Trinity, St John's; seventeenth century: Wadham and Pembroke; nineteenth century and later: Keble, Manchester, Somerville and others.

As I have explained, Oxford consists of numerous colleges with some dating back to the thirteenth century. Many have historically interesting buildings. Sadly, many of these were remodelled in the Victorian era, but some still remain as they were. I think that the college system lies at the heart of Oxford University's educational philosophy.

Education at Oxford and regular activities in the University

I do not have space to enumerate here all the reasons why I consider Oxford's education so excellent. I shall refer to some of these below but I should like to mention in particular the tutorial system (called at Cambridge 'supervision'). The tutorial system means the teaching on a one-to-one basis by a teacher who has been appointed to look after a pupil who meets with his tutor once a week. The student presents for discussion an essay which he has prepared and lists problems he has encountered in his research. The tutorial lasts about an hour during which the tutor sets the theme of the essay to be prepared for the following week's session and gives the student a list of books and documents to be consulted in its preparation. This is generally very long and more than anyone can absorb in the time available. Depending on the individual student he may be asked to join in a tutorial for another student; he may also have two tutorials in one week if he is studying two different subjects. Graduate students generally have two supervisors, one within the college and one outside. In my case the tutor with whom I had one-to-one sessions was Professor Mathias of All Souls and the thesis I wrote while at Oxford was assessed by him.

My tutor within Merton was Dr Highfield. He helped me with the essays which Professor Mathias asked me to prepare and I was able to discuss with him any problems which cropped up in my research. Dr Highfield's position was that of 'moral tutor' or 'in college tutor'. He acted essentially as a tutor in the same way as Professor Mathias and to distinguish them I called the latter my supervisor. The role of a tutor is primarily to give guidance in study and research, but the tutor is also available to give advice on any problems or stress that the student may encounter. The experience of studying and living together promotes mutual understanding and respect and leads to the development of close relationships. This system of close contacts between pupils and teachers encourages students to develop opinions of their own and is an excellent way of training them to construct logical arguments, although some people think that the views of teachers are too strongly reflected in the opinions of students.

According to the book entitled *Igirisu Shakaikeizaishi no tabi* (A journey through English Social Economic History) by Ugawa Kaoru, the tutorial system developed from the building of rooms intended for both study and living. Thus, at New College, which was established in the fourteenth century, large rooms were built in which four students were to study and live together. The eldest of the four was responsible for supervising the study of the other three. This is said to have been the origin of the system of individual tuition in English universities.

The tutorial system has an important role in education at Oxford. Lectures are primarily an aide to the preparation of essays for tutorials. For a student reading history as a main subject lectures lasting an hour began at 9.0 in the morning while seminars generally took place in the afternoon from 5.0 or later.

I shall now comment briefly on Oxford University activities. Every year there are three university terms lasting eight weeks.

The Thames and I

The first term, called Michaelmas term starts in early October. As I have explained, the first ceremony of the term is that of matriculation. The actual day on which the ceremony takes place varies from year to year. When I went to Oxford the ceremony was held on 15 October. In addition, at the beginning of the academic year, all the university clubs and associations organize introductory parties to welcome new members. The first term ends in the middle of December. During the vacation the college may be used for conferences and other purposes and undergraduates have to vacate their rooms. Graduate students depending on the nature of their research can generally make arrangements to stay in college and many do so.

The second term, called Hilary, lasts from mid-January to the end of March. I do not recall any particular ceremonies during this term, but around the end of the term the Oxford and Cambridge boat race takes place on the Thames and attracts a great deal of attention. The race is watched by crowds lining the river bank and is broadcast on television. (See chapter below on sports.)

The third term, called Trinity, lasts from the end of March to roughly the end of June. The weather is better during this period and this is the season for all sorts of sports and outside activities. At 6.0 o'clock on the first of May the choir climbs up to the top of Magdalen tower and the ceremony of singing 'May Morning' takes place. Despite the early hour large numbers collect on Magdalen Bridge from where the tower can be seen. This ceremony is said to date back to the early sixteenth century. Perhaps because it was still rather dark and chilly and I was quite sleepy the voices gave me a mystical feeling. The pubs were allowed to open at this early hour on this day and after I had listened to the song I went with friends, who had come out with me, and enjoyed an early glass of beer at a pub.

In June, I recall the good weather when I could see students lying down on the college lawn reading books, and chatting. This was the time when all sorts of sports competitions, especially in rowing, were held between the colleges. I was fortunate enough to be chosen as one of the college tennis team and was able to join in competitions with other colleges every week.

In May, popular dance parties called 'May Balls', a special feature of Oxford, take place. Students who usually wore jeans all the time would dress up in dinner-jackets and go to the balls with their partners in evening dress and other finery. Not all colleges had May Balls, but Merton's was very popular; it began about 10.0 o'clock and went on until about 6.0 the following morning. One problem was the rather high price of the tickets. In the course of the evening supper was served. A lot went on; a jazz band and a string quartet provided music, there was a disco and there were jugglers and other performers. This ball came at the end of Trinity Term which marked the end of the academic year; the undergraduates then left Oxford and the university had a long four month vacation.

Merton

I have referred quite often to Merton but I should like to add a brief guide to the college. Merton was founded in 1264 in the middle of the thirteenth century by the Lord Chancellor Walter de Merton, later Bishop of Rochester. The college has had a chequered history since its foundation. It was a Royalist centre during the puritan revolution in the seventeenth century when Charles I was executed. The college today contains a room reputed to have been used by Queen Henrietta Maria, consort of Charles I. While the Queen was taking refuge in Merton the King lived in Christ Church. According to one story, in those days Merton and Christ Church were connected by an underground passage-way. At the time of the puritan revolution one of the few natural scientists was appointed at the King's request to be warden of the college. He was William Harvey (1578–1657) who discovered the principles governing the circulation of the blood. In later years, two other doctors of medicine held the post of warden. While I was at Merton the warden, Sir Rex Richards, was a chemistry scholar and I was surprised to hear that he was the first warden since 1750 to have been a scientist.[3]

Based on the map overleaf let us take a walk round the college. The college faces the cobbled Merton Street. Going in through the gateway you come to the relatively broad front quad. Standing in the corner you willl see ahead of you the dining hall, and looming

---

[3] In recent years scientists have often replaced theologians and classicists as heads of colleges.

MERTON COLLEGE, OXFORD

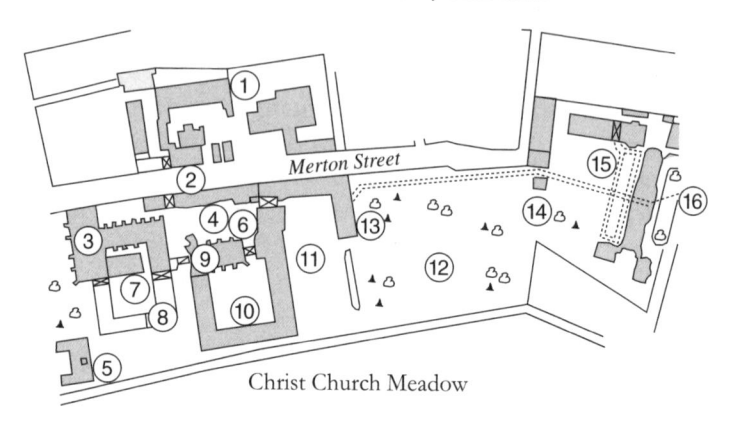

1. Real Tennis Court
2. Main Gate
3. Chaple
4. Poter's lodge
5. Grove
6. Front quad
7. Mob quad
8. Library
9. Hall
10. Fellows quad
11. St Alban's quad
12. Fellow's Garden
13. My rooms
14. Summer House
15. Warden's residence
16. Rose Lane

large to the right Merton College Chapel, while to the left you can see the entrance to the fellows' quad. The dining hall was built in the latter part of the thirteenth century but most of it was rebuilt in the late eighteenth and nineteenth centuries. Part of the massive iron entrance door to the hall with its convoluted decoration is said to date from the time when the college was established. The fellows' quad was put up at the beginning of the seventeenth century when Henry Savile was the warden; this was the first quad in Oxford to have three-storey buildings. Crossing the front quad and moving left you come to the undergraduates' rooms in St Alban's Quad.

The undergraduates' rooms and the library are next to the chapel. Passing through the narrow passage between the chapel and the hall you come immediately to Mob Quad. As I have already explained, this is the oldest quad in Oxford. By chance, I got to know a student who had a room in one corner of Mob Quad. When I visited his room I found that the windows were small and the room was rather dark. The walls had an ancient medieval appearance and I felt that I was back in olden times. The library on the first floor, which even today suggests its fourteenth century origins, is one of the oldest in England. Among its many important treasures is the first printed version of the bible in Welsh. A particularly interesting item is a chained book. This dates from the Middle Ages when books were sometimes attached to chains to prevent them from being stolen. At Merton, until the end of the sixteenth century, important and rare books were attached to chains and placed on desks between the windows. These books and a number of books in the library, which were passed on to the library by fellows of the college, are part of the college's inheritance. As a result of the purchase at the end of the sixteenth century of a quantity of printed books the number of desks in the library was no longer sufficient and the first staffed library in England was created. I understand that the custom of chaining books lasted in Oxford until the end of the eighteenth century. It is said that a ghost may appear in the library, but I never had a chance of meeting it while I was studying at Merton and the existence of this phantom has not been confirmed.

Going from Mob Quad you soon come to the entrance to the chapel. Parts of the chapel go back to the end of the thirteenth century. An interesting feature of the building is that although it should have had the shape of a cross it lacks the end part of the cross and is thus in the form of a T. According to one theory, the end part could not be built because of shortage of funds. As a result, Merton College Chapel is the first example among Oxford College chapels which is constructed in the shape of a T. In addition to the normal church services concerts were occasionally given in the chapel. Merton's Kodály Choir gives a concert in the chapel once a year. The choir was founded by a pupil of the Hungarian composer Kodály who spent a number of years at Merton and this was how its name originated. In the year I joined the university, perhaps due to the good acoustics and fine singing, I was much moved by the performance of Handel's *Messiah*. The chapel has some rare old stained glass dating from about the fourteenth century with images of various saints; facing them there are a number of images in stained glass of the same person. He is reputed to be the donor of the glass, Maunsfield,[4] who had been Chancellor of the University and who perhaps wanted future generations to see his portrait and be aware of his achievements. There were in all twenty-four images of him. Dr Highfield kindly took me to see the chapel tower built in the middle of the fifteenth century. From the top the view of Oxford was as good as one could wish. However, while going up and down the spiral staircase, my clothes became covered with the dust of ages.

Returning to the front quad and going in the direction of St Alban's quad you see the building containing the students' rooms with the bar for the exclusive use of the JCR in the basement. Especially at dinner time the smell of beer comes wafting out. On the first floor there is the MCR common-room. There is also a room with a large television screen and a so-called games room. Most of those who live in St Alban's quad are students, but there are also some rooms which are used by the teaching staff for tutorials. St Alban's was once an Oxford Hall which became part of Merton at the end of the nineteenth century. This was where I lived while I was at Oxford. This quad is surrounded by buildings on three sides; on the fourth side there is an iron gate through which the college garden can be seen. The ridges of the buildings make them look as though they are all connected, but in fact they are all separate buildings and if you want to go from one to another you have to go down to the ground floor and go outside. Passing from the quad between the buildings you come to the back garden. This is the much beloved Fellows' Garden which has a large fine lawn on which it is tempting to lie down. In good weather the students gather here to chat and enjoy themselves. In the early spring great numbers of crocuses and daffodils spring up as if they are encircling an old tree. The back garden is separated from Christ Church meadow by the medieval city wall marking the southern edge of Oxford. From the wall above the back garden there was a pleasant place provided with a seat from

---

[4] Henry de Maunsfield, also spelt Maunnesfeld, Mammesfeld or Maymysfeld who died in 1328 was a fellow of Merton. He was Chancellor of the University in 1309 and again in 1311. He became Dean of Lincoln in 1316. According to the DNB (OUP, 1997) 'In 1283 ... he filled with glass at his expense all the side windows of the chancel of the old collegiate church of St John the Baptist in Merton College, putting his monogram on several of them.'

About Oxford

which there was a good view of the meadow. In one corner of the garden there was a small and attractive single-storey white music room called the Summer House.

Following the city wall and going towards the west you come to the spot where through an iron gate you can see St Alban's Quad. From here you have a good view of all the buildings around the quad. You can also see from here my rooms on the second floor. Going on from here you pass behind the fellows' quad and come to the south side of Mob Quad and the chapel. This area is called the Grove and there are a number of buildings containing students' rooms. In front behind an iron fence is a narrow road leading to Christ Church meadow. Most readers will probably have heard the name of Irvine, the mountaineer, who disappeared with Mallory in their 1924 climb of Mount Everest. He had been an undergraduate at Merton and had climbed the chapel wall many times. There is a monument to the memory of this mountaineer standing inconspicuously in the Grove as if it symbolizes his death in Mallory's shadow. This takes us to the end of our tour of Merton.

There are also student rooms in the area called Rose Lane to the east next to the botanical garden as well as many outside the college in Holywell Street. When I was at Merton there were, according to the records, which I have by me, 230 undergraduates and 80 graduate students as well as 50 research fellows. About half of the research fellows were teaching fellows who gave tutorials. Candidates wanting to enter Merton were encouraged to take up the study of subjects for which there were specialist tutors at the college. In my time at Merton there was the comparatively large number of twelve students reading modern history. There were seven students in each of the groups reading classics, physics, chemistry and mathematics. There were six reading law, five English, physiology, biochemistry, modern linguistics, and music. Among them were students reading the three subjects of philosophy, politics and economics (commonly referred to as PPE) as well as others reading both history and modern linguistics or history and economics. I shall now move on to write about my life at Oxford.

CHAPTER 5

DAILY LIFE AT OXFORD

In the mornings

My day at Oxford started with breakfast in hall which began at 8.15. There were far fewer students at breakfast in hall than at lunch or dinner. Usually, only around twenty turned up at breakfast so that even if I was a bit late I could easily find a seat and did not have to worry that there would be nothing left. Toast and an egg dish were always on the menu plus, varying from day to day, ham, bacon or sausage etc; it was all self-service. Coffee and tea were, of course, also available. Interestingly, perhaps because of the old religious custom of serving fish on fast days, kippers were served on Fridays. I tried a kipper once but found it difficult to remove the bones and I did not care for the taste. My breakfast generally consisted of a slice of toast, some cereal, such as corn flakes, and tea. When there were boiled eggs on the menu I usually took one. Tea and coffee were obtained from urns by the door. The tea was very strong and the same colour as the coffee. The dining hall was only open for breakfast for half an hour. Anyone who overslept could, however, get a late breakfast from the undergraduates' bar.

After breakfast I used to go to the college office where, if I was in for lunch and dinner, I put my name in the book. If by chance one forgot to do this and was stopped by the steward at the door of the dining hall one was usually allowed in. At dinner on Wednesdays and Fridays Merton students could bring up to three guests and entertain them to dinner in the first floor lobby where the guest table was

Daily life at Oxford

situated. This was a popular place to dine as the food at the guest table was a good deal better than in hall. On mornings when bookings were taken for the guest table during the following week there was usually a long queue of students wanting to register, but many of them had to put their names on the waiting list. There were, however, generally some cancellations and they might be lucky in securing places.

I would then go and collect my mail and newspaper from my pigeon hole. When I first entered college I had lots of invitations to parties and events as well as letters from people in Britain and abroad. There might be messages from Dr Highfield or Professor Mathias or from other Merton students, some scribbled on scraps of paper. On Valentine's Day there were cards from various unknowns. There were also occasional messages from Japanese tourists who had visited Merton. Among them were some from students who had just graduated from the Gakushūin and who had apparently called at the college during a tour to Europe during the spring vacation. The porters were most assiduous in looking after my mail and as a result I never encountered any problems. Now that I come to think of it my mail box in college was the most important way for me to develop social contacts. Every morning *The Times* was delivered to my mail box. I ordered it from the shop nearest to the college and paid for it in advance. When the newspaper did not appear one day I realized that my subscription must have run out. So I went round to the shop, bought that day's paper and renewed my subscription.

After this I returned to my room and usually drank some coffee while glancing through the newspaper. I had bought a kettle in Oxford after I had joined the university to make hot water for my coffee; it turned itself off automatically once the water had boiled.

Meanwhile, the scout came, removed any rubbish I might have and gave the rooms a simple clean. Once a week she went over the rooms with a vacuum cleaner and some scouts used to chat a lot, too, which I enjoyed. In my first year the scout responsible for my rooms was married to a policeman and was someone the college had specially engaged for me. My second year scout was always startled whenever she inadvertently touched an alarm clock I had brought with me which spoke the time when you touched it. She complained one day that MacDonalds had opened a branch in Oxford and when I said that there was a MacDonalds near the university where I had studied in Tokyo, she expressed great surprise and advised me 'you should do without those sorts of American things!' The scout cleaned the room but did not do the washing which I had to do for myself.

When my scout had left it was time for me to get down to my studies. Some mornings I had lectures to attend or had to collect documents from the library or public record office, but generally I spent the time in my room preparing my essays. Lunch was from 12.45. In addition to Merton students, students from other colleges used to come for lunch; as a result, there tended to be a long queue outside the hall. On particularly crowded days the queue stretched as far as the college office; it was especially cold waiting on winter days, but I practically never saw anyone attempt to jump the queue. As one entered step by step into the hall, one was hit by the warmth inside. At lunch, which was self-service, there was a choice of three or four dishes. One dish might be a meat stew; another might be spaghetti with a meat sauce and a third a meat pie. Having collected a plate for the main dish you held it out in front of you and the person in charge gave you, as you indicated, potatoes and cooked vegetables such as Brussels sprouts or green peas. If you did not ask for only a little your plate would be piled high. When I first entered college and did not know the form or when I was late in saying 'only a little please' I had the unfortunate experience of having my main dish smothered in vegetables. But Merton food was good and there was never anything I could not eat. After lunch I generally went to the graduates' common-room, the MCR.

Middle Common Room (MCR)

The MCR had been built in the thirteenth century as the warden's residence and remains much the same today. In particular, the fine old beams are still there. As I have explained above, the first time I was in the MCR was when I was introduced by the warden to J, the chairman, on my arrival at Merton. J had then introduced me in his room to other members of the MCR and invited me to drinks in the

Daily life at Oxford

common-room. In a short time, after I had joined Merton, I had got to know most of the other members.

One of my main joys at Merton was to go up to the MCR after lunch, drink coffee and spend a short time there with the other members. The MCR was, of course, at its most lively immediately after lunch and dinner. However, after lunch most members could not dally very long and after some thirty minutes would say: 'I must get back to work.' Nevertheless, these moments with my fellow students, brief as they were, were very important for me. Coffee was freely available in the MCR and one or other of the members would pour it out into the cups provided. It was fairly strong coffee, but the conversation while we were drinking it was most enjoyable. It usually covered a wide variety of topics, but occasionally it focused on a single topic. I remember some of these. One topic, which led to a heated controversy, was whether as a result of the reduction in government contributions to university costs the decision not to award an honorary degree to Prime Minister Thatcher was right. Some students thought that the university's decision was natural in the circumstances while others argued that in view of her achievements and as she had graduated from the university she deserved the award. I refrained from taking sides and listened to the arguments which became heated; inevitably, the debate ended without any conclusion being reached. Another subject of discussion was the rights and wrongs of the introduction at Wimbledon of the system adopted at that time of judging by sound whether a service was in or out. One student laughingly suggested: 'With such thick glasses as are worn by the umpire it is surely very difficult to determine whether a service is in or out when the ball is travelling at such speed.' But another argued forcefully that Wimbledon did not need such a 'sound' system.

There was a notebook at the bar close to the door to the MCR; in this the server of coffee or someone else noted down the names of those who took coffee and the amounts owing were collected later. The same system applied to drinks from the MCRs minibar. At first I was unaware of this system and only after some time did I realize that I had been taking coffee and drinking liqueurs without paying up. I now realize and regret my error. I was surprised that the coffee cups, which were washed in lots of washing-up liquid, were not rinsed properly, but I gathered this was always the case in England. I do not know whether this is true or not.

Occasionally, when I went to the MCR, there would be nobody there. I would then glance through copies of *The Times, The Economist* and *Newsweek* which were laid out in the common room and I might spend some time looking at the leaflets announcing events in Oxford. Sometimes, I would lounge in a dilapidated armchair and just contemplate the white ceiling with its fine beams.

Each term there was an MCR dinner to which guests could be invited. Men would wear dinner jackets if they had them and ladies would come in evening dresses and other finery. The dinners were usually held in the Savile Room next to the dining hall while aperitifs would be served in the MCR. After a brief chat the party would move to the Savile Room. Port would be served at table and after the toast to the Queen was announced all joined in the toast saying 'The Queen!'. After coffee the party returned to the MCR where the conversation continued. I liked the general 'at home' atmosphere of these dinner parties and usually went to the dinners each term while I was at Oxford. In addition to members of the MCR various post-graduate students from outside the college attended these dinners and as a result I got to know a number of very interesting individuals.

I learnt about events sponsored by the MCR from printed notices or more often from colleagues after lunch. There were various events apart from the dinners such as theatre performances and excursions on the river.

After coffee in the MCR I often had more studying to do. Of course, on some days I had work to do until dinner time. In the intervals when I felt the need for exercise I would play tennis and go jogging to work up a sweat. I would also go into town to buy books and everyday articles.

Shopping and the English character

I would now like to write briefly about my shopping expeditions. In addition to notebooks, index cards and card cases required for my studies, and with help from my police escort, I also bought such daily necessities as drinks and fruit. When I had invited anyone to join me

1 Oxford colleges along the High Street, looking from St Mary's Church towards Magdalen

With fellow students

Daily life at Oxford

at the guest table I would buy wine and sherry at a shop nearby. Readers may perhaps have heard of William Morris (1877–1963), the founder of Morris Motors, later British Leyland (not to be confused with the famous artist also called William Morris.) Before he began to make motor cars he had worked in a bicycle shop. His bicycle shop had become the shop where I bought wine. (I wonder what has happened to it since.) I also went frequently to the newsagent's where they stocked lots of different magazines. They had a large variety of magazines relating to leisure pursuits and I often bought issues with information about canal tours which were relevant to my studies.

My regular paper was delivered every morning to my letter box in college, but if there had been some major event or I felt that I wanted to read another point of view I would look at a different newspaper. When I first went to Merton I was not used to English money. When I was told by the shop assistant that my purchases came to so many pounds or pence, I did not always hear properly what was said and either had to ask again or handed over the wrong sum. Another problem was that until I got accustomed to British money I used too many notes and collected too many heavy coins. On one occasion they all fell out of my purse. I was rather flustered but my police escort and people around, without making the slightest fuss, joined in picking up the coins. I recognized that I had made a blunder but as a result of this incident I was also struck by the kindliness of English people and I went back to college feeling relieved.

I appreciated the way in which English people after passing through a door would wait and keep the door open for the person behind. I can hardly remember any occasion when a door was closed in my face. When I was shopping I also noted that British people were good at forming queues and keeping their positions in the queue. I often saw long queues before the college dining hall and at bus stops. When I thought I was joining the end of a queue I was sometimes told that was not the end of the queue and I would take more care in future. Sometimes in a shop someone would ask 'Is this the end of the queue?' and I realized that there were established ways of forming queues. When I dropped my coins from my purse I was in a hurry to make my payment as there was a queue behind me.

The Thames and I

However, in England it is rare to be hustled by people behind one in a queue even if one is taking rather a long time to pay; so perhaps I did not have to feel rushed.

The following was another blunder I made. There is a large covered market on the High Street and Cornmarket. Before I knew much about Oxford I went into the market and had difficulty in finding the way out among the maze of stalls selling everything from clothes to food and trinkets. Meat and fish could also be bought here. I was surprised to see a pheasant outside a stall which sold game and realized that in England shooting game was a popular sport. In one corner there was a shop selling fresh coffee. When I went there first and ordered some ground coffee the man behind the counter asked me whether I wanted it 'fine' or 'medium'. I did not understand what he meant and did not know how to reply. I managed to get by on this occasion and thus added some more words to my English vocabulary. There was also a pet shop in the market where, over a number of days, I saw the same parrot in a cage. I felt sorry for the bird which had not found a buyer. It was interesting to see so many different types of pets.

I took lots of photographs while I was at Oxford. When I went to look up documents in the library and public record office I always had a camera in the bottom of my bag. I never knew when I would be able to take a good shot in the town. There were three camera shops which I used to visit where my face was known and I would either be asked: 'Working hard?' or 'Are you enjoying your time at Oxford?' When I took in films for developing, normally I would be asked my name and address. But in one shop where I had been many times in the past and where the assistants knew my name and address these would be written on the envelope in which the films were sent up for developing without my needing to say a word. There was one assistant, who reminded me of someone who used to work for us. One day shortly before I was due to leave Oxford I went as usual to this shop and a young assistant on duty said to me: 'This is Ms ——'s last day in the shop and we are all having tea upstairs, won't you join us?' This was so unexpected and sudden an invitation that I hesitated for a moment before replying. I guessed that the assistant might be referring to the older lady I have mentioned and as she had been so

Daily life at Oxford

helpful I thought that this would be a very good opportunity of expressing my thanks and accordingly joined the party. As I had surmised correctly the tea was in her honour. Many other members of the staff were present and we all enjoyed a lively conversation all about photography.

I enjoyed visiting shops selling new books as well as second-hand bookshops. I often went to Blackwell's and to Parkers'. At one second-hand book store in the High Street, where I bought etchings of Oxford, I was surprised to see many *Ukiyo-e* (Japanese prints). I saw at the top of one print of an exotic place the word '*Miyako*' (meaning capital i.e. Kyoto, the old capital) and the proprietor whom I knew asked me if it was of Japan. One day, passing by chance by the shop, I saw in the window an old map showing the route of the Thames; first thing on the following morning I went to the shop and bought it. I still have the map by me now and often refer to it. One day, in the antiquarian book corner in Blackwell's I came across some books which I needed for my studies but which I did not think I would ever be able to find. I clapped my hand with joy and bought them there and then. I also enjoyed buying records, CDs and music.

This has nothing to do with shopping, but when I was at Oxford I had my first experience of going into a bank. The reason was that I had been out of England visiting various other countries and wanted to change the foreign currency which I had acquired into English pounds. This might be my first and last experience of being in a bank. I also used a credit card to buy in Oxford shops, but I do not suppose I shall have the chance to shop in this way in the future. I used a barber's shop in the town to get my hair cut. The first time they looked at me rather oddly and my hair was cut rather roughly, but when I went there a second time I was greeted in a very friendly fashion with a warm 'Good Morning, Sir' and my hair was carefully trimmed. My haircut this time lasted about twice as long as on the first occasion. The barber chatted to me saying 'I saw an interesting television programme about Japan' and asked 'Do you like Oxford?' After this I always went to the same barber's shop while I was at Oxford. Over in England the barbers do not wash your hair unless you specially request it and I used to go back to college and wash my hair in the bath.

The Thames and I

Draughts and baths

I must record that I suffered a bit in my daily existence from the cold including while taking a bath. The draughts were one cause of discomfort. There was no central heating in my rooms and the only source of heating was an electric heater in my study. So when I went to Merton I bought another electric heater for my bedroom, but the draughts coming through the cracks round my bedroom window were very cold. When we parted Colonel Hall had given me an electric blanket and told me to use it at Oxford; it had much use! With Mrs Fuji's help I managed to stop up the cracks. Another of my memories of the cold was in the bathroom. There was usually one bath on each floor in the college. I was fortunate enough to have my own separate bathroom in an adjoining room to which I could get without being seen by others, but when I half-filled the bath tub with hot water, the tap would run cold and I never had enough hot water for a really good hot soak! As there was no shower over the bath, when I washed my hair, I had to make do by filling the bath only a third full and rinse my hair in the basin into which I poured the remaining hot water. From this experience I realized why English people are not accustomed to lingering in the bath. To be honest, I began to long for a Japanese bath. I had realized from visiting Chedworth Roman Villa with Professor Mathias that the Romans had liked hot baths. Did the custom of enjoying hot baths leave Britain with the Romans? Be that as it may, I must say that now I feel a certain nostalgia for both the baths and the draughts. How to cope with them was one of the things I learned at Oxford.

Dinner

There were two sessions at dinner in Merton, perhaps because of the size of the hall. An informal dinner was served from 6.30 and a formal dinner from 7.30 and students could choose which one they wanted to go to. At the first session those attending could wear what they liked and it was a self-service meal. At the formal dinner you had to wear a gown and a tie. Any student who was incorrectly dressed or arrived late had to pay a forfeit and swallow a beer at

Daily life at Oxford

one go. At the formal dinner the fellows sat at a high table on a dais at one end of the hall. When a mallet was struck on the table a representative of the students would come forward and recite a grace in Latin. In the British film *Chariots of Fire* one scene shows a college hall. Although this was at Cambridge, the scene at Merton was much the same. At dinner (informal or formal) the menu was the same, namely soup, meat and desert; coffee was not included. At the informal dinner you received a plate and a dish at the entrance and went on to the counter where the food was dished out on to your plates. Gravy and cooked vegetables were placed separately on the tables and you helped yourself as they were passed round. I particularly liked the almost over-cooked sprouts and I always took a large portion. Once an English friend sitting beside me asked how I could like such stuff so much! At the formal dinner you were served by the dining-room staff. Students were permitted to bring their own drinks into hall. Most either drank water or beer which was served to them at the door. There were stands just inside the door for coats and jackets which I sometimes used. Occasionally I forgot that I had left a garment there and would not collect it for some days, but it was generally where I had left it. It was very rare for any item to be stolen.

Twice a week guests could be invited if places had been reserved at the guest table. On these occasions students could bring in wine and enjoy leisurely chats with their guests. Apart from the enjoyment of looking down from the lobby onto the diners below the guests were able to enjoy specially prepared gourmet dishes. I asked Ambassador Hirahara and others from the Embassy to dine as my guests; they seemed pleased with the setting and the cuisine.

I should like to mention another aspect of dinner in hall. Every year there was a 'Brown Rice Week' which lasted a whole week. In order that a contribution could be made to the relief of famine in Africa and for assistance to refugees, at the formal dinner during this week only brown rice was served. Students taking dinner paid the same amount for their food as at other times and the difference between the costs of the normal menu and of brown rice was given to charity. I thought this an excellent scheme as it increased the understanding of students for those who were suffering. In the Michaelmas Term in 1983 £321 (the pound at that time was worth

348 yen) was contributed to the 'Save the Children Fund'. I went a number of times during 'Brown Rice Week' to formal dinners and found that brown rice alone left me feeling rather hungry, but I had the satisfaction of having performed a good deed. According to one student, the day on which I only had brown rice, the rice was the worst that week.

According to my records, while at Merton, the cost of breakfast was 43 pence, lunch 78 pence and dinner one pound. A student who took all meals in college naturally saved on his expenses. At Oxford, students were encouraged to take their meals in hall, but some wanting to save only took breakfast and dinner in college. Meals in colleges were not all equally good. Fortunately, while I was at Merton the college was reputed to have the best food in Oxford. This reputation dated back to the time when one undergraduate, deploring the poor quality of the food, contributed funds for the employment of a good chef. According to student gossip, a certain college had the worst food humans could eat.

Meals in college provided the best opportunity to get to know other students. Soon after I joined the college I noted that students sitting next to one another at table would introduce themselves and shake hands. I got to know many other students at meals in college. As I explain later it was through meeting someone at breakfast that I was able to form a string quartet. There were no fixed places for seating at meals. So I met many other students whose lively conversation ranged over a wide range of topics. These included, of course, the world scene, politics, economics, theatre, music, sports and other topics. I was asked about Japan and my researches and this led me to learn about many things which I had not known about before. When I went to Merton and was spoken to for the first time by a number of people one after the other I had a hard time, but as I began to make friends conversation became much easier. Meal times became an important element in my life. When students, who are studying a variety of different subjects, are living and taking meals together, they meet other students outside their own field with wide knowledge of other subjects. Conversations with them are an invaluable opportunity to widen one's own knowledge. This may be the reason why the university encouraged students to take meals in hall. Before

Daily life at Oxford

I left for Oxford my mother urged me to take meals in hall as often as possible, and to buy a good umbrella. I realize now what wise advice it was, and I am tremendously grateful.

Most students got through their meals quickly and speedily emptied their plates conversing all the while. I would often find that I was the only one who still had a full plate! I was struck by the fact that other students could eat so quickly while talking. The way in which students conversed with all and sundry around them was quite different from what happens in Japanese universities.

High table

While I was at Oxford I was fortunate in having many opportunities of taking meals at high table both at Merton and at other colleges.

I should like to explain more about high table and will base my remarks on my experience of high table at Merton. Sherry is served as an aperitif in the senior common room. Then, after some conversation, the group moves downstairs to the high table in the dining hall for the meal. I have already related how the dinner begins. The first time I sat down at high table at Merton I was astonished by the array of silver. I did not examine each piece, but at one college I noticed a piece of silver with a hallmark for 1624. When I first dined at high table at Merton I did not know most of the staff at the table other than Dr Highfield. Sitting opposite me was someone who looked a typical Oxford don; he said to me abruptly: 'Japanese drive on the left as we do in Britain, don't they?' I promptly replied: 'yes, that's the case' and then he turned to the don sitting next to him and said: 'but until quite recently there was one part of Japan where they drove on the right; that was on the island of Okinawa'. To be frank, I was astonished. I had expected that at Merton the conversation might turn to Japan, but I did not think the subject would be broached in quite that way.

The next thing that surprised me was that the food at high table was so much better than that served to the students. Unfortunately, I do not have by me the menu for that day, but I do remember that we began with smoked salmon and we had a full-course dinner including dessert. For students it was an honour to be invited to dine at high table, but it was a bit of an ordeal to eat with the dons. Later, one student said to me: 'Everyone seems to have problems talking with the dons at high table. The trouble is that the dons know too much.' I nodded, but in fact I always enjoyed being invited to join the dons at high table and I managed to get by in conversation with them.

I will now say a few words about occasions when I was invited to the high table in other colleges. Professor Ugawa Kaoru of Rikkyo University once arranged for me to be invited to the high table in Somerville as the guest of Dr Harvey, a scholar of medieval history. I asked her many questions about her special field of study and her replies were, of course, valuable for my research. But I remember noticing that there were many men among the students. Somerville, which only took women students, was Prime Minister Thatcher's college. So I asked the principal of the college by whose side I was sitting: 'Since when has the college admitted male students?' She promptly replied: 'The reason why there are so many men here tonight is that this is a guest evening and the students have brought along their boyfriends.' What a silly question to have asked her, I thought, and still blush at the memory.

I was also privileged to be invited to the high tables at colleges such as Exeter, Brasenose, Worcester, Magdalen and New College.

Magdalen College (which, curiously, is pronounced 'Maud-lin') has a very odd custom for their high-table guests. I was introduced to Magdalen by a musical friend who had connections with the college and was invited by the master to join the high table. As at other colleges aperitifs were served in a separate room but the way we went to the dining hall was different. We all went along the roof of the cloisters and I remember that the guests who had been invited for the first time, having signed their name in the guest book, were then asked to weigh themselves on an old weighing machine in the form of a chair. The weights were calculated in stones (one stone equals 6.4 kilograms) as is the custom in Britain.

Invitations I received were issued by the authorities of the colleges where I had got to know the dons or the master or in the case of Somerville through the intervention of a friend. At St John's I was invited by a student, whom I had come across and who was studying Japanese, to join the students' table. At one seminar at the

Daily life at Oxford

Nissan Institute of Japanese Studies, which had been established at St Antony's as a result of a gift from the company, I got to know one of the fellows of St John's and was invited as a guest to dinner in the senior common room. St John's was, apart from Merton, the only college at Oxford where I dined at both the students' table and the fellows'. I thought that the food was rather better at Merton, but it was not bad at St John's.

I enjoyed dining with fellows at all the colleges and it was interesting to observe the students. There were colleges where it was not necessary to wear gowns. While in some colleges, the hall was so small that students had to sit squashed together on forms close to the walls. When someone had finished eating and wanted to leave, it was impossible to get out unless one climbed up onto the table and walked along it, which some students did, in their shoes! At another college, where so few people attended meals I asked why, and was told that students kept away because the food was so poor. It may not seem to matter greatly whether the food was good or not, but the fact that the food at Merton was good attracted students to eat in hall, thus encouraging them to get to know one another and learn a lot from one another. There are various arguments about English food. One friend of mine said: 'The English don't pay much attention to food. They prefer to concentrate on improving their houses and put their energies, for example, into painting their house. In France the opposite applies. They concentrate on the food and don't bother about their house.' What do readers think? Is this assertion fair?

After-dinner drinks and fruit are served in a separate room. Port is usually the first choice, but Madeira (a red desert wine from the island of Madeira, a Portuguese possession) and a sweet white wine (usually Sauterne from the Bordeaux area) are also available. The way in which port is served is interesting. Each person pours the port into his own glass and passes the port on to his neighbour. The port must be circulated in the clock-wise direction. When I first took port I apparently made a mistake in passing the wine; seeing the looks of horror on the faces of the dons I realized that I must have passed the wine in the wrong direction. When I enquired whether this was the case, most of the dons said 'That is the custom in England'. On the other hand, one Merton fellow who specialized in law gave a different reply: 'It is done to fool the witches.' I thought this explanation made sense because during the Middle Ages witches were regarded as abnormal beings. Dr Highfield explained to me that, when a table plan is prepared, the host (usually the warden or the master) has the chief guest on his right and the port is passed from the chief guest to the host and so on clockwise. English people are mostly right-handed and the port glass is thus placed in front of the guest on the right side. Port is normally served in a fairly heavy decanter and it is easier to take hold of the decanter with the right hand. I learnt that the reason why English people like port so much is because at the time of negotiations between Methuen, the British Envoy to Portugal, and the Portuguese government at the beginning of the eighteenth century it was agreed that the tariff on port should be decreased thus favouring port as against French wines. I need hardly add that the name port comes from Oporto, the harbour from which port was exported from Portugal.

There were various ways in which I passed the time after dinner. When I was under pressure to prepare for tutorials or absorbed in my research I would generally spend the time in my room. On other occasions I might visit friends in their flats or have visitors in my rooms or I might go to concerts or pass the time in the MCR. In the past it was a special feature of Oxford that if you stayed out late and missed the curfew when the college gate was shut you had to climb over the college wall when you came home. Merton's gate was closed at midnight in term time and at 11 o'clock in the vacations, but students could get a key to the wooden gate at the back of the college and anyone who was late and had a key could get back into college without climbing the wall. Similar arrangements must have been made in other colleges.

Weekends

At weekends I played tennis or music or visited the houses of friends, but I also enjoyed myself very much by taking photographs in Oxford and driving around the neighbouring countryside. I shall write about these drives later. One of my biggest tasks at weekends was doing my washing. Fortunately, there were three washing

Daily life at Oxford

machines and a drier, with a drying room attached, in the basement of the building in St Alban's quad. When I joined Merton I was told how to use these machines and when the weekend came round I used them. All I had to do was put my washing in the machine, pour in the appropriate quantity of detergent and insert the money, but as I was not used to the procedure it was a bit of puzzle for me. The first time I used the machines I made a major mistake. As instructed I put in my washing, the detergent and the money. I gathered that the washing would be ready in forty minutes; so I went back to the basement forty minutes later, only to find that there were soap suds all around. When I looked carefully I discovered that soap suds had clearly come from the machine I had been using. There was another student looking fed up near the machine who asked: 'Is this yours? The soapsuds have over-flown.' I had overloaded the machine with washing. I apologized to him and did my best to get over the difficulties I had caused. I still have a good laugh at my mishap. The other student turned out to be a German called H who was a member of the MCR whom I got to know as a result of this incident.

When the washing was finished all I had to do was to put it in the drier. It was a delicate matter to get the timing right. If a lot of students were using the machines and you were a bit late in collecting your washing you might find it displayed on top of the machine. This was because when a student wanting to use the machine found that the previous man's washing had dried, he would take it out and replace it with his own. This happened to me on several occasions, but I never lost anything as a result. After they had been dried, shirts had to be ironed. Immediately after I began at Oxford I went into the city and bought an iron and an iron-stand. I learnt how to use the iron from one of my police escorts. I did not find it too difficult to learn and while I was studying at Oxford I did all my own ironing. This was one of my Oxford experiences.

I have already often mentioned my police escorts: I must say a little more about them. During my two years at Oxford I was provided with two police officers from the Metropolitan Police who were responsible for my safety. One was called Roger Bacon; it is rather difficult to describe him, but he was very much an Englishman. The other was called Bruce Ayer, a charming man, who spoke

English with a Scottish accent that was easy to understand. They were opposite in character but both good men. They took it in weekly turns to occupy the room next to mine and to provide round the clock protection. As far as I was concerned they did more than provide protection. They were excellent guides to English life. They made all sorts of arrangements for me and helped me with my understanding of documents which were difficult to read. I also got them to read letters for me and they did all sorts of administrative tasks as well. Whenever I went out one of them would always go with me, but they were never obtrusive. Roger Bacon's name will lead some readers to recall that of the famous English philosopher Roger Bacon (1214–94) who lived in the neighbourhood of Folly Bridge in Oxford and carried out astronomical observations from a building there which at a later time was rebuilt at vast expense. It is said that people called a building which looked absurd a 'folly' and that is why the bridge is called 'Folly Bridge'. There is also a narrow street in Oxford called 'Roger Bacon Lane'. When Roger, my police offer, came across it he was delighted. The favourite phrase of Bruce, the other officer, was 'Oh dear!' When anything happened these were the first words he uttered. During the two years they were with me I never had any unpleasant moments. They provided me with every possible help during this time and I shall never forget all they did for me.

Family visits

During my time at Oxford visits from my family gave me a great deal of pleasure. In the second half of February 1984 my parents made a tour of Africa and stopped off in Belgium. His Majesty the King of the Belgians very kindly invited me to come over to Brussels so that I could meet my parents, whom I had not seen for some time, and we were able to have an enjoyable time together. The King and Queen and my parents had had a long-standing friendship and I greatly appreciated this unexpected opportunity to meet them again. My parents were also able to pay a short visit to London on their way back from Africa that April and I was able to give them a tour of Oxford. On the way to Oxford we called at Colonel Hall's home where we all had tea with him and his family and my parents were able to see where

Daily life at Oxford

I had lived for three months. I had told them in my letters about my life there, but there is a real difference between what you can learn from letters and what you see for yourself. They were shown around Merton by Sir Rex Richards and Dr Highfield and they were able to meet some of my close friends. Sir Rex gave a lunch for them in the senior common room and invited Professor Mathias, Dr Highfield and several Merton students to join us for lunch. For lunch that day the Merton College chef, whose face I recognized, grilled the meat near the door of the common room. The meal was one of the best meals I had at Merton. I was very pleased by the care and consideration for my parents, who had come from so far away, shown by Sir Rex, the college chef and others at Oxford who were present.

In the afternoon I showed them round Oxford. We went first to St Mary's Church, from whose tower we had a good view over the city of Oxford, and I pointed out the main sites. I also took them to University and New Colleges. My father had visited Oxford in 1953 when at the age of nineteen he had attended the coronation of Queen Elizabeth and had stayed with the master of University College. On that occasion he had planted a cherry tree; he was delighted to find that it had grown into a big tree in the thirty-one years since he had been in Oxford. The room in which my father had slept had changed a good deal in the interim but I shall not forget the nostalgic look on my father's face when he saw it once again. From University College we crossed the High Street and went on to All Souls where I had my tutorials. Guided by Professor Mathias we went into his room where he sat on a sofa, asking me to sit beside him, thus re-enacting one of my tutorials.

From Oxford we went on to visit Broughton Castle where Lord and Lady Saye and Sele and their son William received us warmly. It was a most enjoyable family gathering and we were all able to relax together. I had discussed with the ambassador and members of the staff of the Japanese Embassy in London plans for them to visit Oxford and Broughton Castle. So it was rewarding to see that my parents could relax after their long, tiring and anxious journey. That evening we were able to enjoy some music and played a trio. Lady Saye and I both played the viola while my mother played the piano. It was a long time since we had played together.

The Thames and I

In July of that same year my younger sister Princess Sayako [Nori no Miya] visited Oxford after a few days 'home stay' with Colonel and Mrs Hall. I showed her round Merton and Oxford and accompanied her to the pretty village of Broadway some forty kilometres north-west of Oxford, where we enjoyed a fine view of the countryside from a nearby hill. She liked best the views of Christ Church Meadow and of the country near Broadway. In March 1985 my younger brother Prince Akishino visited Oxford. I took him up the chapel tower at Merton and to Christ Church Meadow. From the top of the chapel tower Dr Highfield pointed out to him the main buildings in Oxford. In the evening, I took my brother to a Chinese restaurant which I had been to a number of times before. He was able to converse with the restaurant staff in Chinese, a language which he had studied at university. He later also became a student at Oxford and I hope that his visit proved useful in that connection. Thus, in my two years at Oxford all my close family visited me. It was a real joy to be able to show them around.

With Oxford students

1. VISITING STUDENTS' FLATS AND GOING OUT

At Merton the best time to enjoy talking with one's friends was in the evenings after dinner. I should now like to write briefly about the friends I made chiefly at Oxford.

Shortly after I went up to Merton I got to know a very pleasant couple. The man had come up to Oxford at the same time as I had and was reading English Literature at Merton. The girl was doing research at a different university but they were always together and no one doubted that she was also at Merton. P and his fiancée were very kind to me while I was at Oxford and they greatly helped to make my stay at Oxford so enjoyable. I got to know P at the first MCR dinner after term began. Thereafter they often came to my rooms for a chat. P was learning to play the *shakuhachi* (a Japanese five-holed bamboo wind instrument) and his fiancée was interested in Japanese design. They both showed great interest in Japan. One day, they asked me what was the word for 'lazy' in Japanese. I told them that the appropriate translation was *'namakemono'*. P immediately memorized

Daily life at Oxford

the word and pointing to his fiancée called her *'namakemono'*. They still use some Japanese words when they write to me these days. They also asked me what was the Japanese for 'Your Highness'. I explained that the word was *'denka'* and said that this should not be confused with the electric light in the ceiling to which I pointed and which was called *'denki'* in Japanese. Afterwards, I regretted saying this but it was too late and thereafter the two of them teased me by referring to me as *'denki'* and pointing at the light said that it was *'denka'*. One day P came round with his *shakuhachi* and persuaded me to blow into it, but I could not get a peep out of it. He then produced some good sounds from the instrument and declared in his typical way, as he blew into the instrument, 'I am Samurai!'

They were not the only ones whom I entertained in my rooms. Another was J, the girl who had walked beside me when we went to the matriculation ceremony at the beginning of the first term. She was studying Japanese and had visited Japan; we often spoke of the difficulties which Japanese had in learning English. I used to serve *senbei* (rice crackers) to students who visited me. I was interested to find why some liked *senbei* covered in seaweed and others did not. English people seem to have an antipathy to seaweed. When, later on, I visited Wales someone in a speech declared: 'We Welsh people eat seaweed in the same way as you do in Japan.' The implication was that Welsh people when eating seaweed were closer to Japanese than English people.

I often went to pubs with P and his fiancée. One pub which we frequented was the *Turf Tavern*, which I shall refer to later when discussing music at Oxford. They taught me the meaning of the term 'pub crawl'. I gathered that it involved going to at least ten pubs and drinking a pint of beer at each. True or false it was an interesting piece of information for me. On their recommendation I also tried various types of beer in a pub. I found that there were all sorts of bitter as well as many kinds of lager. Talking of pubs I found that there were a number of pubs on the banks of the Thames set in beautiful scenery. At a pub in the north of Oxford called *The Perch* (a perch is a type of fresh water fish) meals were served at tables with chairs in the garden. From there one could walk along a stretch of promenade by the river. It was a good place to spend the middle of

The Thames and I

the day in the summer. The *Trout Inn* was not far from there along the river bank. From the *Trout* you could hear the water flowing over a weir and see a Chinese-style wooden bridge; this gave an exotic flavour to the scene of the pub and the river. Accompanied by my police escort I once cycled from Merton and visited all three pubs in the area, *The Perch*, *The Trout* and *The White Hart*.

I also went with my friends to restaurants as well as to pubs. There were no Japanese restaurants in Oxford, but there were Chinese, Indian, Italian and French restaurants as well as others serving the food of the countries from which the proprietors came. I generally found the food at Merton appetising and did not often long for Japanese cuisine. But Chinese food and curry did not cost much and made me think of Japan. We also often went to pizza and spaghetti places as well as to fish-and-chip shops where we bought cod, herring, plaice or some other white fish with chips doused in vinegar and wrapped in newspaper. As fish and chips at the time of the industrial revolution were an important source of protein for workers, this was one of the tastes which I found relevant to the period of my studies.

I was also invited by members of the MCR to go to wine bars which served cocktails. We did not know one cocktail from another; so we each ordered different ones and, though this was rather bad behaviour, sampled by drinking through straws those ordered by others. I also went to a disco in the city to see what it was like. Here I made a real blunder. I remember that it occurred on a Saturday evening. I went with another man who was a member of the MCR and who apparently liked discos. We were stopped at the door and when I asked why I was told that on that evening people in T shirts and jeans were not admitted. As usual I was in jeans and my companion was wearing a T shirt. The door-keeper pointed to my police escort who was behind us and said 'You will do!' He was not wearing a tie but he was wearing a blazer and thus apparently qualified. While I was at Oxford I tried as far as possible to be like other students and certainly did not explain who I was. So I gave up and went weakly away. I learnt through this experience some new information, namely that at discos in Oxford at the weekend a certain standard of dress was required.

While I was at Oxford I generally wore informal clothes such as jeans when I went out. When Japanese tourists saw me thus garbed

Daily life at Oxford

they looked as though they could hardly believe their eyes. When some young Japanese girls saw me in jeans one day they spluttered 'It's a lie' (i.e. I can't believe it!). Not knowing what they meant by 'a lie' I did not know how to respond. My first attempt to visit a disco having ended in failure I went on the next occasion in a mixed group of men and girls from the MCR to a different disco. As this was my first time in a disco I felt overwhelmed by the noise in the hall. On the dance floor I saw young people dancing all sorts of steps. So I joined them doing my own kind of dance steps and finding myself face to face with a girl from the MCR. I was not in the least bored. It was two o'clock in the morning before we left. Perhaps this was the first and the last disco I would go to in my life.

I should like to add a few words about visits to friends' flats. One day, I went to C's flat, the MCR treasurer who was a vegetarian. C and a friend made a vegetarian dish for us. I recall that it was a bit unique although not much to my taste, but we had an interesting conversation. C was very keen on films, so much so that he made his own films. We had a really varied discussion and of course we talked that evening about films we had enjoyed. Those who lived outside college generally had flats with kitchens so that they could cook their own meals. In my second year I was invited to a wine-and-cheese party by M, the American who was chairman of the MCR. His fiancée was a French woman and I was surprised by how many different sorts of cheeses there were at the party that evening. There were quite a few members of the MCR present and I learnt a lot from them about cheese and wine.

M was also very fond of films. M and C arranged for videos they had chosen to be shown in the MCR after dinner. When I said that I had not seen many Hitchcock films they immediately borrowed some. I thought *Psycho*, *The Birds* and *Rear Window* were particularly good films. When members of the MCR sat round and watched Visconti's film *Death in Venice* on television it was so exciting that I had difficulty in getting to sleep that night. M or C kindly let me know when there was something worth watching and C always brought me a glass of Chartreuse while I was watching the programme. Only afterwards did I realize that he had treated me to these drinks.

I visited a number of other flats. I was invited to the home of a foreign student from Oman to a meal where his state's cuisine was served. I was also asked to lunch by a student from Singapore who was a member of another college and we had a good meal which resembled Japanese '*shabu-shabu*'. On another occasion I was invited to his house by K, an American student, to join him for a meal. We were joined by K's brothers and cousins who were also studying at Oxford. We had a noisy evening and ended up with an enjoyable concert on the banjo. K's elder brother R was teaching at New College and invited me to the high table there. R was later appointed to the staff of Princeton while I was at Oxford. In 1985 at the end of my time at Oxford I went home via America and was able to stay a night at his home in West Virginia. When I visited Princeton where he was then teaching he arranged for me to be introduced to Brook Shields the American film star.

2. Various group activities at Oxford

There are all kinds of groups at Oxford. The groups with which I was directly involved were the Oxford Japan Society (OJS), the karate and judo groups and the dramatic society. I was either honorary president or an honorary member of these groups. The OJS was made up of students studying Japanese and of Japanese students at Oxford. The Society contributed to the understanding of Japan by organizing lectures on Japanese culture and society, putting on Japanese films, arranging tea ceremony demonstrations and showing how to prepare and cook Japanese food. Each term the OJS circulated a printed programme of their activities and whenever I could I went along to any of their meetings which I thought would be interesting. I was able to see famous productions directed by Ozu Yasujiro and Mizoguchi Kenji and to have my fill of Japanese films while I was in England. Of course, Japanese films were shown with English subtitles. At OJS demonstrations Japanese dishes and beer could be sampled and these were particularly popular occasions. I also attended Japanese dinners and *koto*[1] performances. As a result, I got to know many students who were deeply interested in Japan as well as many Japanese students at the university.

---

[1] A *koto* is a form of Japanese zither used from early times.

Daily life at Oxford

I should add a few remarks about a Japanese language lecture which I observed. There was a conversation class that day, in the course of which there was a discussion in Japanese about how to learn Japanese and the advantages and disadvantages of various methods. The main theme was about the role of Chinese characters (*kanji*) in the Japanese language. Would it be a good idea to do away with Chinese characters? Some suggested that this would greatly reduce the problem of reading Japanese and increase the amount of time available for the study of other languages. I was asked to comment. As far as I remember, I pointed out that Chinese characters were ideograms and thus made it possible to absorb sentences quickly. Moreover, there were many words in Japanese with the same sounds but different meanings and *kanji* made it possible to distinguish between words with the same sounds. For instance, if you say '*kami wo kiru*' where '*kiru*' means 'to cut', '*kami*' can mean both 'paper' and 'hair'. One of the students at this class is engaged these days in research into Japanese art. He was an undergraduate at St John's and invited me to dinner in his college. I was glad to note that all those who were studying Japanese were good students. I expect that they will all be playing major parts in Anglo-Japanese relations.

My connection with the karate club came about because one of the members of the MCR belonged to the club. He invited me to watch a practice. I never learnt how to do karate, but I was interested to learn what induced Oxford students to take it up and how karate was practised at the club. A Japanese karate expert who was teaching in the USA happened to be in Oxford at that time and was coaching members of the club. I was, therefore, able to observe carefully how karate was practised at the club. Shortly after this I was asked to become an honorary member of the club and on some occasions I went along to the club to watch training sessions. I noted that Japanese terms were invariably used and that it came naturally to the students to refer to the teacher as '*Sensei*'. On one occasion after the session I had a leisurely chat and a beer with members of the club. I was impressed by the fact that many of the members, who included a number of women, had taken up karate with the aim of building up their strength of mind. As I was only made an honorary member of the judo club shortly before I left Oxford I did not have a chance to see them training. However, I asked a number of members of the club to tea in my rooms and we were able to have a chat. As a result of this meeting I was able last year to meet a number of Oxford judo players while they were in Tokyo. I shall comment on the Oxford dramatic society later.

3. CONTACTS WITH OXFORD UNDERGRADUATES AND DONS

Oxford University students generally work hard. This is due to a large extent to the tutorial system, but it is also relevant that each term undergraduates have to take examinations, popularly called 'collections', and undergo regular tests of their academic abilities. Students express their own opinions clearly in various debates and seminars and in their everyday conversations. The dons expect students to express their own opinions in the essays which they present at tutorials. I was surprised by the wide education of Oxford students. Whenever they got together they never had any difficulty in starting up a conversation, finding a subject in which all present were interested and pursuing the topic. In a word, they were experts in social intercourse. They were never reserved and shy at parties. To celebrate my birthday I gave a party at Merton and invited a large number of fellow students to it. As host I did not have to worry about how the party would go; the guests made it go with a swing. My only concern was that my guests who were not used to drinking Japanese saké might enjoy it too much. As I feared, a number suffered from a bad hangover.

The interest of Oxford students in Japan was primarily in Japanese science and technology and the Japanese economy. With some exceptions they did not seem to know much about Japanese culture. Thus, they knew what such and such a company produced and its special characteristics, but some did not know whether Japan lay to the north or the south of the equator. Even so, however, I was pleased to find that a lot of them knew about origami and bonsai.

Another characteristic of Oxford students was that they dressed simply and frugally, but you could not miss the fact that there was a wide variety in what they wore. They were quite content to appear in torn jeans and sweaters with darns but it was interesting to observe how their individual preferences were shown in the mixture of colours in what they wore. In the evening I saw many students going

Daily life at Oxford

to parties wearing dinner jackets. The women who wore drab or sober colours during the day would appear in all their finery in the evenings as there seemed to be many spots in Oxford where this was expected. It seemed to me that possibly the confidence gained from knowing how to dress to perfection must have made their ordinary clothes seem unimportant to them.

Most students at Oxford had their own bicycles. There are many one-way streets in Oxford and parking is not permitted in most streets in the city centre. This made it inconvenient to go around by car and one saw lots of students cycling to and from the library or research facilities. On the first day on which I rode a bicycle in Oxford, one student called out to me: 'I see that you have now become a real Oxford student.' I realized that students and bicycles were inseparable at Oxford. All student cycles were so old that it seemed as if the wheels might fall off while they were being ridden. Only a few students had cars. When you lived in college it was much more convenient to use a bicycle. For those living outside the same did not apply. I was occasionally given lifts by a graduate student whose car, too, was old and you never knew when it might break down. When it came to both clothes and vehicles, it seemed to be the fashion for Oxford students to go on using them in spite of their being old and somewhat dirty.

Readers may conclude from all the above that all Oxford students were outstanding students, but there were a number of odd people at Oxford. I have already mentioned the girl with a star mark on her forehead; there were also some students who dressed in punk style. Some were too clever and their statements sometimes outrageous. Talking of bright people, in the year when I went to Merton a girl at the tender age of thirteen was admitted to read mathematics. She did better than any other maths student and although no one can graduate unless they have completed three years at the university she took the final exam at the end of her second year.

There were also some odd people among the dons who might best be described as eccentrics. One went out in midwinter wearing nothing over his shirt, another never had his hair cut, yet another did all his research in a room with the curtains drawn. Generally speaking, however, dons were so knowledgeable that they were virtually walking dictionaries. I have already mentioned that some undergraduates when invited to a meal at high table found it difficult keeping up with the conversation as the dons were too sharp and knew too much. I heard of one don at Merton who at a quiz was the only person who answered all the questions correctly.

Lewis Carroll, the well known author of *Alice in Wonderland*, whose real name was Dodgson, was a don at Oxford. His college was Christ Church where he taught mathematics. Liddell, the master of Christ Church, had three daughters. Going up the river by boat one day with them and a colleague and being asked to tell a story he recounted a story which had Alice, the second daughter, as its main character. This became *Alice in Wonderland*. T. E. Lawrence, the main character in the film *Lawrence of Arabia*, was a fellow of All Souls.

I have written in these chapters about students and dons at Oxford, but I would like to record here how fortunate I was while I was at Oxford to have the help of Sir Rex Richards, the warden, Professor Mathias and Dr Highfield. I shall write about Professor Mathias and Dr Highfield in a later chapter, but I cannot find adequate words to express here my deep appreciation of the kindness of Sir Rex Richards. I had one year with him as warden. He invited me to tea and to meals in his house with other students and always kept an eye on my life as a student in his college. Shortly before I left Merton the new warden Dr Roberts assumed his post, but Sir Rex had been warden during the most important part of my stay and looked after me so well.

I have recently had the chance to read Adam Smith's *The Wealth of Nations*. He won a scholarship to study at Oxford and spent seven years at Balliol from 1740. In a dire critique of the situation then prevailing at Oxford he wrote: 'In the university of Oxford, the greater part of the public professors have, for these many years, given up altogether even the pretence of teaching.'[2] Now, two-hundred-and-fifty years later, so far as I could see, there was not the slightest sign that Oxford was anything like what Adam Smith had described. It seemed to me to be an educational establishment which was outstanding both in terms of scholarship and teaching.

---

[2] Book Five, Chapter 1, Part 3 of *The Wealth of Nations*

CHAPTER 6

CULTURAL LIFE AT OXFORD

―――――□―――――

Films, theatre and music

All sorts of events took place in Oxford. In addition to films and concerts there were performances of plays, musicals etc. There were Phoenix cinemas as well as ABC theatres in the town. I quite often went to the cinema, partly to improve my English, when good films or ones which had had good reviews or were interesting were shown in Oxford. I have already mentioned the film about Gandhi. I enjoyed the 007 series of *Octopussy* films and was interested to see David Lean's *Passage to India*. I thought the latter very well directed and I shall never forget the fine performance of Peggy Ashcroft as the leading lady in the film. Once, a friend of mine from a certain country, who was a student at Merton, invited some of us to see a film produced in his country which he, himself, had not yet seen. But it turned out to be pretty incomprehensible and he kept on apologizing for inflicting the film on us, although you can never really tell whether a film is good or bad unless you see it for yourself.

I went a number of times to the Oxford Playhouse which was run by the Oxford University Dramatic Society (OUDS). The OUDS, incidentally, elected me as Honorary President. On one occasion after the performance I went to the reception attended by former members of the OUDS. There were many famous people there, but unfortunately I did not know who was who and could not put names to faces. I learnt at this time that Peggy Ashcroft, John Gielgud, Richard Burton, Peter Brook and other famous stage people had close connections with Oxford, even if they were not necessarily members of the OUDS. After I had returned home in 1988 OUDS came to Japan to give some performances: on that occasion I was able to enjoy a performance of Shakespeare's *As you like it* at the Globe theatre in Shibuya. It was a very good performance and made me feel nostalgic about my time at Oxford.

I have already mentioned that when I was staying at Colonel and Mrs Hall's I had been to Stratford-on-Avon and seen *Henry VIII*. After joining Merton I was invited to join a group of members of the MCR to visit the Royal Shakespeare Theatre at Stratford to see *Twelfth Night*, *The Comedy of Errors* and other plays. The texts are all difficult to understand; so I used to read the story before going to see the play and so managed to follow the plot. I was surprised to see *The Comedy of Errors* produced in such a modern fashion. One of the characters was a policeman, in a contemporary uniform and riding on a bicycle. One of my companions muttered to me after the performance: 'Do you think Shakespeare would approve?'

Performing plays was a very popular pastime at Oxford. In the summer amateurs from the colleges would put on outdoor performances. At Merton these were done on a temporary stage in the back garden. Of course there was a charge for tickets, but alcohol was served in the interval and it made a good evening. In my first year I missed the performance as, for some reason or other, I had gone out that evening, but in my second year a *Commedia Dell'Arte* play was performed and I was urged by a Canadian friend, who was playing the part of a gate-keeper, to come along to the performance. So I went with a number of other fellow-students. Our friend suddenly appeared on the stage, said his two or three lines and hurriedly left the stage. It is quite a different experience when someone you know is performing. I thought that he had performed his part well, but one of those sitting near me thought it quite ordinary. I could have had a good view of the play from beginning to end without paying if I had used binoculars and looked out from the window of my room, but I would have missed the atmosphere. One evening, while performances were taking place in the garden and I was working in my room, I heard a roaring sound. I discovered it was pouring with rain. When I looked out into the garden to see what had happened to the

Films, Theatre and Music

play I saw that brilliant lights had been turned on and the play was continuing while the audience got drenched. Soon, as is common with English weather, the rain stopped, but I thought it must have been tough for the performers and the audience. I heard that Dr Highfield had been one of the victims of the shower.

I learnt that on another day there was to be an amateur production of *A Midsummer Night's Dream* in the garden at Magdalen. So I decided to go along. I was particularly struck by the fairies, who had put black paint all over themselves. This may be normal in Britain; I thought it an excellent idea for the fairies who wanted to remain invisible in the darkness.

I also went to concerts from time to time. The performers varied; in some concerts the performers were mainly Oxford students but in others British and foreign professionals performed. Concerts put on at Merton included performances by the Kodály Choir in the college chapel. I also went to an excellent performance of Haydn's *The Creation* in the Sheldonian Theatre by the choir of New College. This hall is the place where Haydn performed his 92nd Symphony, the one he selected from his many symphonies as an expression of his gratitude to the University for conferring on him in 1791 an honorary degree of doctor of music. As some of you may know, the 92nd is now called the *Oxford Symphony*. I was much moved by being able to hear a work by Haydn in this hall with its historical connections with him. I was also invited from time to time by a student of Queens with whom I played tennis to attend chamber music concerts at his college. The conductor was one of my music friends who taught music at Brasenose.

I also enjoyed opera. I was invited to Covent Garden Opera House in London by Prince Charles and Princess Diana to see Mussorgsky's *Boris Godunov*. I was also invited by the Royal Opera to see Rossini's *The Barber of Seville*. I remember vividly going twice to the opera at Glyndebourne. In my first year I saw Richard Strauss's *Arabella* and in the following year Rossini's *La Cenerentola*. Glyndebourne is an aristocratic country house some ninety kilometres south of London where operas and concerts are performed every year. Men wear dinner-jackets and women evening dress. In the interval members of the audience enjoy special Glyndebourne-style picnics in the garden.

I still remember clearly how much I enjoyed the opera as well as the excellent picnic and the conversation which accompanied it.

There was one other opera occasion while I was at Oxford which I will never forget. That was a performance in English by an English opera company at the Apollo Theatre of Wagner's *The Mastersingers of Nuremburg*. I was very interested to hear a Wagner opera performed in English. I wondered whether the beauty of the original would be lost in translation, but I need not have worried. In the interval I met by chance a member of the MCR and asked his opinion. His view was much the same as mine. I wanted to ask a German member of the MCR what he thought, but he was not there and so I was unable to seek his opinion. As it was such a long opera there were a number of intervals. During the long interval we remained in our seats and ate the sandwiches which we had brought with us. Many other members of the audience did the same. The performance began at 5.0 p.m. and ended at 10.50 p.m. Bruce, my police escort who had been sitting next to me, had looked downcast and had not been looking forward to the evening, but after it was over he muttered: 'Not too bad.'

Finally, in the context of concerts I should like to refer to the Holywell Music Room in Hollywell Street. This dates from 1740 and was the first purpose-built hall in Europe designed for musical performances. I went there on many occasions. It was here that I heard the Allegri Quartet and on one cold winter's evening at the beginning of November I heard an English singer give a rendering of Schubert's *Winterreise* which I found very moving. I was also invited to a *shakuhachi* recital by my friend P who, as I explained earlier, had taken up the instrument. The hall was intended for Western music but I thought that the *shakuhachi* sounded well there. The hall was near the *Turf Tavern*, a pub which I have mentioned previously. One of the precious memories of my time as a student at Oxford is of discussing music, while drinking beer, with my friends after concerts at Holywell Music Room.

I shall also never forget attending an international get-together of viola players in the Isle of Man. The Isle of Man is an island in the Irish Sea about half way between England and Ireland. It is known for Manx cats (cats without tails) and for the motor-bike races which

Films, Theatre and Music

are held there. I attended the International Viola Players Association on the island in August 1984. At the meetings I heard famous viola players give lessons and recitals and from talking with others at the meeting I learnt a good deal about playing the viola and composing music. The purpose of the congress was to enable famous viola players and those with connections with viola-playing from many countries to meet and to promote friendship among the participants as well as an understanding of the viola through recitals and lessons. Although the Isle of Man is part of the United Kingdom it has its own parliament and bank notes. As a result, while it is termed a crown dependency and has the Queen as its sovereign, it is largely an independent state. Motor-bike racing can be held in the Island because the English law forbidding such racing on English roads does not apply in the Isle of Man. The island's banknotes cannot be torn as they are printed on material containing plastic. You also find locally-issued banknotes in Scotland and in the Channel Islands.

Enjoying chamber music

I was particularly glad to be able to take part in musical activities while I was at Merton. I had wanted to find opportunities to play from the time I entered college, but my hopes were fulfilled much earlier than I had expected. I cannot remember exactly when but one morning at breakfast a student sitting next to me chanced to remark that he was studying music. I told him a little nervously that I played the viola and said that I was hoping to be able to play in a chamber-music group. He was a post-graduate student named W; he undertook to find others to join the two of us. On 26 November 1983 we had our first meeting as a quartet in Merton's summer house. On this occasion the first violin part was played by a woman undergraduate from Merton, the second violin was played by W, the 'cello by a woman student from Somerville while I played the viola. I do not remember what piece we played and unfortunately I did not keep a note of it.

As I recall the occasion the other three players were very good. They all asked me what I wanted to play and kindly agreed to perform the piece I selected. We did various repeats of bits which we had not played very well but we worked hard at it and completed all the movements. We began mainly with Haydn, but went on to play pieces by Mozart, Beethoven, Schubert and other composers. We started with quartets such as *The Lark, Fifths* and *The Birds*. We tried various quartets in the *Haydn Set*, composed by Mozart in his middle period. During the year I became pretty busy in my work and could not give much time to playing chamber music.

Early in the New Year I was asked if I would play the viola in a concert sponsored by the MCR. The request came from a woman student at Merton who played the clarinet and who wanted to perform a trio together with another student who played the piano. They needed a viola player to make up the trio and had heard that I played the instrument. I learnt that the piece they wanted to play was a Mozart trio, the *Kegelstatt*.[1] I had heard a recording of this piece, but I had not seen the score and asked for time to consider their request. I really wanted to take part: so I went to a music shop and bought the score. When I read it I came to the conclusion that I could manage it and said that I would take part. We had many practices in Merton's summer house. The piano player took the lead and we worked hard repeating difficult bits over and over or bits where we failed to play in time. I remember even now the way the pianist expressed her approval when we got it right. The concert took place in the Merton's Mure Room on 1 March. Many of my friends came to hear us and almost all the seats were filled. In the second movement the viola has a prominent role but there are some difficult passages. I managed these alright and the third movement went without any problems. I felt relieved that my first concert at Oxford had ended without mishap.

Apart from practising for this concert I continued to practise with the members of the group I have already mentioned. As the girl who played first violin in our group was in her final year and very busy, a don from Brasenose agreed to take over from her. Dr B was doing research on the German composer Spohr.[2] Following the concert in March, especially after the middle of April in the Trinity Term, we

---

[1] Trio for viola, clarinet and piano in E flat, K498
[2] Louis Spohr 1784–1859

Films, Theatre and Music

met as a quartet almost once a week on a Saturday or Sunday morning. If one of the three others was unable to take part in these regular meetings the absentee would generally be responsible for finding a substitute. On the first occasion on which Dr B took part we played Haydn's quartet '*Fifths*' which we had practiced with the others before. I was surprised to hear how well he played. Of course the others also played well. It was very helpful to get his advice on the use of the bow and on playing in time together, but we also got him to suggest pieces which we might play. It was due to him that we played Schubert string quartets and the Brahms' clarinet quintet as well as Spohr string quartets and other works.

I had always been very interested in the string quartets of Mozart and Beethoven and had hoped to be able to play them while I was at Oxford. The others were happy to go along with my wish and almost every week we concentrated on practising a work by one or other composer. We began by playing Beethoven's first quartet, the first of the six in Opus 18. In the last movement of the second quartet in the series there was one point where we all burst out laughing. Interested readers may like to guess where this happened. I recall that we were all quite pleased by our performance of the fourth quartet of the series. From the seventh onwards the quartets became more difficult, but I felt that the depth of sound in these later quartets was special to Beethoven and although they were technically difficult to play they gave me great satisfaction. Of course, we progressed in stops and starts. The eighth is known as the Razumovsky quartet number two; the last movement has to be played by each part at a dizzyingly fast tempo, is full of complicated manoeuvres, and there are places where the parts must not converge. Often in such places I would find to my dismay that I was playing together with someone else's part. I almost felt that I could hear Beethoven laughing. In the ninth, the next quartet, I made another mistake. In this, the third Razumovsky quartet, there is no interval between the third and fourth movements and the fourth movement begins with a solo melody on the viola. The movement is in the form of a fugue and the other instruments take up the theme one by one. This means that the viola part is particularly important at this point. I had not realized this as I had never played the piece before. Towards the end of the third movement I had unfortunately lost my place, and was counting on the interval to find it again, but just when I thought the third movement must have come to an end the other members of the quartet gave me an odd look and B said: 'Hiro, it's your turn to play!'

I would like to mention one more episode in our playing. This happened on one cold day in winter while we were trying to play Haydn's quartet entitled *Seven Last Words on the Cross*. I had brought the score with me. The summer house felt particularly cold that day. This piece, which consists of seven movements, contains many very slow sections, and we were all so cold that after we had played several of the movements, we decided to call it a day. By the way, I have never played this quartet through to the end.

We managed to play all the Beethoven quartets from number one to number eleven, the *Serioso*. Thus, we played all the seventeen quartets up to the four composed in Beethoven's middle period including the quartet entitled *Die Grosse Fugue* (*The Great Fugue*). We played all the quartets by Mozart from his Haydn set onwards with one exception. Haydn composed a huge number of quartets and we had a go at most of those which had been given names. While we were playing one of these B commented: 'In Haydn's music there are elements of modern jazz.' We all nodded in agreement. Among his quartets without names we tried playing Haydn's quartet in F minor, Opus 20, No. 5 and were much impressed by the piece. Apart from works by Beethoven, Mozart and Haydn we greatly enjoyed pieces by Schubert. We began with his *Rosamunde* quartet and on B's recommendation we tried his *Death and the Maiden* quartet. This sounded quite different from Beethoven. We enjoyed the depth of feeling of the music in Schubert's quartet and were tempted to try other pieces by Schubert. B wanted us to try Schubert's quintet with two cellos which Mrs Hall had liked so much, but when I looked at the score I was put off by the length and we never played it while I was at Oxford. When I returned home and did manage to play this wonderful piece I much regretted that I had not played it while at Oxford.

The four of us in the quartet gave some concerts. As on the occasion when I had played in the clarinet trio, the first concert was held in the Mure Room at Merton and we played Dvorak's *America* quartet. We also played Haydn's *Fifths* quartet at Worcester College. I shall

Films, Theatre and Music

never forget the words which W addressed to the audience at the beginning of our performance of the Dvorak quartet: 'This quartet consists of one Japanese and three English members. We are performing the quartet called *America,* a country to which none of us belongs.' The concert at Worcester College took place at lunch-time. A number of students from Merton as well as of Japanese studying at Oxford came along to hear us perform. I was impressed by the fact that white wine was served to all who attended the concert.

Among musical events, other than those to do with chamber music, which I shall not forget is a performance of Handel's *Messiah* held in a church in London as part of the celebrations marking the three-hundredth anniversary of the births of Bach and Handel. This was given by the Oratorio Association of Japan whose concert in Japan had been attended by my mother. Strangely enough, my birthday, which is 23 February, happens to be the same as Handel's. So it was a happy occasion for me that the *Messiah,* which is one of my favourite works and is typical of his compositions, was being performed, in commemoration of the three-hundredth anniversary of his birth, in the country, which he regarded as his second home. The sounds of the music reverberating in the Church were most impressive. I was surprised to see that when the famous *Hallelujah* chorus was reached nearly every member of the audience immediately stood up. This dates back to the time of King George II when the King deeply impressed by the music had stood up at this point. The same Oratorio Association gave another concert in London in September 1985 and visited Oxford where I took part in their performance. In addition to pieces by Handel they played the *Greensleeves Fantasia* (by Vaughan Williams) as well as *Spring Sea*[3] for flute and harp duet. As I was leaving Oxford in the next month I invited Professor Mathias and other dons who had been so helpful to me while I was at Oxford as well as some Oxford friends to the concert. The memory will always remain with me of a moment at the end of the concert when I was asked to stand up for the final piece, *Auld Lang Syne,* which had been selected without my knowledge as a farewell message of good

---

[3] *Spring Sea* is the English for *Haru no umi* composed for *koto* and *shakuhachi* by Miyagi Michio, the blind *koto* player who died in 1956.

wishes. The conductor who made this kind gesture towards me passed away some years ago.

Visit to places associated with musicians: England and music

While I was at Oxford I was able to visit not only many parts of Britain but also a wide variety of countries in Europe including places with musical associations. At Salzburg in Austria I visited the Mozart House where he was born and was kindly allowed to play on the viola which he had used. In Bonn in Germany I visited the house where Beethoven was born. Talking of Beethoven, I shall always remember joining in a performance by the Vienna Philharmonic Orchestra in the Beethoven House on the outskirts of Vienna where Beethoven is said to have written his famous Heiligenstadt Testament. At Prague I visited Dvorak's house where I was allowed to play on his viola and I saw many of his possessions.

Readers may wonder whom I might mention among British composers. In earlier times there were Henry Purcell and John Dowland. Handel lived for a long time in England and readers may recall that there is a memorial to him in Westminster Abbey. As for modern times readers may think of Elgar's *Pomp and Circumstance* and *Love's Greeting*.[4] He was a thorough Englishman, who was born in 1857 and died in 1934. I visited his house in Worcestershire. It was a cosy compact residence where a number of compositions in manuscript together with his violin and various other personal possessions were exhibited. Among these I was very interested to see the huge collection of press cuttings about Elgar which had been collected by his wife who clearly had a mania for collecting. I remember that these were stuck all over the wall. Among English composers dating from after the nineteenth century I should mention among others Britten, Delius and Vaughan Williams. Undoubtedly the Beatles must be added to the pages of musical history while Andrew Lloyd Webber, who wrote the music for *Cats* and *Phantom of the Opera*, may be regarded as representative of modern English composers. His

---

[4] '*Love's Greeting*', the English name for Elgar's *Salute d'Amour*, was composed in 1911 for piano and violin, but later arranged as a string quartet. It also appears as a piece for classical guitar. '

Films, Theatre and Music

Requiem was composed while I was at Oxford. The author of the Cats poems, the English poet, T. S. Eliot (1888–1965), spent a year at Merton.

So you see, Britain has produced a number of famous composers. Moreover Britain has attracted many foreign composers. Handel spent a long time in England and died there at the end of his long stay. I have already written about Haydn's connections with Oxford. He wrote many of his final symphonies in London. Mozart also came to London and gave a concert there. Mendelssohn was popular in London and earned the trust of Queen Victoria and Prince Albert. Dvorak was awarded an honorary doctorate by Cambridge University and his eighth symphony is known as *England*. Brahms, unfortunately, failed to receive his honorary degree from Cambridge. He had been born in a harbour town but disliked travelling by sea and is said to have refused to travel to England to accept the honour. I do not know whether this is true or not.

However, it seems to me that English people have something of a complex about music in England. They think of Britain as a country which musicians visit and seem to think that their country has not produced many musical figures. My friend W complained that works by English composers were rarely performed, but once when I visited the flat of a friend who was fond of music, I praised a piece of music which he was playing on his tape recorder. This was *Variations on a Theme of Thomas Tallis* by the contemporary composer Vaughan Williams. When I left he lent me the tape, saying: 'I am delighted to be able to introduce works by an English composer to even one more individual who wants to get to know them.' I do not know how far this work is known among music lovers in Japan. It is a marvellous work with a beautiful melody. Probably the work by Vaughan Williams which is best known in Japan is his *Fantasia on the Theme of Greensleeves*. I also like very much his *Lark Ascending*.

Delius came from a German wool merchant's family. He was born in Bradford in Yorkshire but spent more than half of his life outside Britain. As a result some English people do not regard him as an English composer. His music is not always easy to understand, but I think that his *On Hearing the First Cuckoo in Spring*, as well as many of his pieces for wind instruments and strings and his 'cello concerto are superb. Many of Elgar's short pieces for wind and strings are rather plain, but I came to like his first symphony, his 'cello and violin concertos, his piano quintet and his string quartets. I bought a tape of the first symphony in an Oxford record shop and was deeply impressed by it when I listened to it in my rooms in college. I was surprised to discover that a film which I saw at Oxford took this work as its main theme. Apart from these composers I enjoyed Holst's *The Planets,* Britten's *Young People's Guide to the Orchestra,* Walton's viola concerto and music by Howell. [5]

While I was at Oxford I felt that I should get to know and appreciate the music of English composers. So I went to concerts and bought tapes and records. I keep them in my study as treasured souvenirs of my time in England.

I was very fortunate while I was studying at Oxford to be able to see and experience many films, plays and concerts. There are of course also opportunities for me to see performances in Japan, but although Oxford is a comparatively small community there were so many artistic activities close at hand and I was surprised at how easy it was to keep in touch with them. I was fortunate in being able to live for two years in a society where the arts played an easy and natural part in conversation and were an everyday topic.

---

[5] Herbert Howells, born 1892, who succeeded Holst at St Paul's Girls School.

CHAPTER 7

SPORT

———□———

Rowing

Beginning with rugby, many sports originated in Britain, and there are lots of British people who enjoy sports on a daily basis. It is amazing how many sports clubs there are at Oxford University. In the town, too, there are many sports facilities. Anyone wanting to take part in sports would find Oxford a well-endowed environment.

Probably the best known sports club in Oxford is the rowing club. The annual boat race between the Oxford and Cambridge clubs has been held ever year since 1829. I was fortunate in being able to watch the race in two consecutive years. The first was in March 1984. On the 17th, the scheduled date of the race, the Cambridge boat, while practising for the race that day, crashed into a barge which was anchored nearby and was badly damaged. As a result, the race was put off until the following day. So I went to the Thames again on the 18th and saw the race from on board another boat. The river banks were crammed with spectators and the shouts of encouragement to the crews never ended. As the Oxford boat went downstream and the river became wider there was a slight curve where there was the usual competition between the two crews to determine which side to take on the curve. Oxford won both the races I saw.

There were rowing clubs in each college. At Merton the crew would be up at six in the morning running and training, I gathered that one of the crew members was inclined to over-sleep; so the other members of the crew would go to his room and wake him up.

The Thames and I

When I was invited to the rowing club party in my first term I was asked whether I would like to be their cox, but I declined as I had only rowed a number of times in a four in Japan and had no experience of an eight. However, in my second year I felt that I really would like to row a boat on the Thames. So I asked the captain of the rowing club if I could join in the practice and he willingly agreed. Some days later, I found a rough note in my pigeon hole listing the days, times and place for practice.

The practice began with the crew, which was a mixed one of men and women, carrying the boat out of the boat house. The girl behind me kindly explained how the boat should be carried. The girls in the crew were a really sturdy lot. Even those of slender build had plenty of physical strength. I learnt that there were rules about how you got on board as well as various methods of practising rowing after you were on board. One way was not to move the sliding seats but only use your arms to row; another was to row a number of times with all your strength, followed by several strokes using a little less force. On this occasion the boat captain and the girl I have just mentioned kindly helped me by explaining how it was done. I enjoyed going on the Thames in the boat, but I think that the other members of the crew supported me as a beginner and I realized that it would be difficult for me to become a team member and practise regularly. Moreover, when I was at High School I had found that the oar hit me in the stomach and I had trouble pushing it back. This is popularly called in Japanese *hara-kiri* or cutting the stomach. I wondered what it was called at Oxford; if my memory is correct it is termed 'catching a crab'. The 'Torpid' competition between colleges took place in Hilary Term while 'Eights Week' was held in Trinity Term. In both competitions, which date back to the beginning of the nineteenth century, the aim is to bump into the boat of the other college, hence the term 'bumping races'.

Tennis and Squash

Apart from rowing I particularly enjoyed tennis. I was chosen to play for Merton and thus had the opportunity to take part in competitive matches with other colleges. At the beginning of the Trinity Term in

Sport

1984 I received a note from the captain of tennis urging me to take part in 'college practice'. I had met him at MCR parties and on other occasions and as a result we had played many sets together, but I did not know what he meant by the term 'college practice'; out of curiosity I accepted the invitation. 'College practice' took place on the college's lawn tennis courts. I had expected that the practice would involve a lot of hard work and I was surprised by the fact that it simply meant taking part in doubles with other members of the college. But the tennis captain seemed to have watched my play closely and some days later I received a note from him giving the name of my pair as well as instructions on when and where to attend a match and with which college. I remember that I was number three seed in Merton's team of six. The inter-college matches, which generally took place once a week during the Trinity Term in my first year, were played on the lawn tennis (grass) courts which every Oxford college possesses. Merton's courts were near the student quarters belonging to St Catherine's college. There were two hard courts and three grass courts in a corner of the sports ground which faced St Catherine's. I enjoyed playing on grass. There is much less strain on the knees than on a hard court, but at first one had to get used to the way the ball bounces on grass. On a grass court the ball coming towards you seems to slide as it rises. If you are at all careless you are liable to miss the ball or be late with your swing. Even so, once you get used to a grass court it is like nothing on earth, it is so wonderful. The captain of tennis or one of his colleagues told me when and where matches were to take place either through a note in my pigeon-hole or by word of mouth when we met in hall. Singles and doubles matches were decided by the best of three sets. The colleges against which we played were St John's, Worcester, Oriel, Queen's, St Catherine's and Wolfson. I got to know those against whom I played in singles matches and as I mentioned before I even went to concerts together with the player from Queen's. I remember clearly a singles finals match with him which took place on a very hot day when he disappeared to have a drink of water. In the intervals between matches we continued to practise in order to improve coordination with our partner and to get used to playing in lengthy matches. In the end, Merton's performance that year was only fair.

The Thames and I

We played hard in our matches, and in true English fashion tea was served in the interval between matches. At tea we did not treat our opponents as enemies, but chatted amicably eating biscuits. However, I was careful not to eat too much when the tea interval occurred between my singles and doubles matches.

Returning to my main theme, I might add that I was particularly struck by the physical strength of my opponents. Therefore, when my opponent combined good technique with physical strength, I often found myself totally defeated. However, even when I was clearly weaker than my opponent, there were times when I returned all the balls using every ounce of strength in my arm and my opponent became tired (or irritated) and lost his poise; I was then eventually able to win the game. Still, I felt a certain handicap in playing against such tall fellows with their powerful serves and strokes.

I have fond memories of the matches against other colleges in which I played for Merton and I shall never forget the many friends I made as a result of playing tennis on grass courts. I recall the face of the captain of tennis who, irrespective of the results, would always say to me after the game: 'Well done Hiro!'

I also had plenty of opportunities of playing tennis other than in college matches. J, the chairman of the MCR, greatly enjoyed tennis and he would invite me and his friends to play on courts not far away from the college on the University sports ground facing Iffley Road. After tennis one day I went with them to a nearby pub where they looked at me wondering who this odd fellow was, but I was glad to lubricate my throat even if I had to admit that the beer was not cold.

I often played with other members of the MCR. There were many tennis enthusiasts in the MCR who would meet in the common room after lunch and decide on the order of play. The level of play varied, but playing tennis, sometimes switching between doubles and singles with different members, is a pleasant way to spend an afternoon. We normally played on Merton courts. As the Merton grass courts were used for official matches I generally only played on them when I was playing for the college and instead used hard courts. On the subject of grass courts I remember an occasion when members of the MCR wanting to use the grass courts were unable to do so. One day when the members met M who, as I have mentioned,

Sport

became chairman of the MCR in my second year, had a brain wave and proposed that we should use grass courts belonging to other colleges. When we went to a certain college, we found the gate to the court open and it looked as if we could make free use of their court, but only a few minutes after play had commenced a fierce-looking official appeared and I recall that we had to leave the court after we had only been playing for a few minutes.

My tennis friends in the MCR were of various nationalities. In addition to English there were Americans, New Zealanders, Germans, Philippinos and Australians. On Merton courts I usually played with a slightly larger racket. I mentioned, when I wrote about doing my washing, that I had met H, a German. He asked if he could borrow my racket as he thought that there was a greater chance of hitting a ball with a large-sized racket. As I was lucky enough to have two rackets I was able to lend him one. Unfortunately, while he was playing with my racket he hit himself in the face with the racket, perhaps because the ball he was playing had too much top spin. He lost some blood and had to go to the hospital where he needed a number of stitches. Laughing, he said to me: 'It's your fault, Hiro.' Feeling that I did indeed have some responsibility for his mishap I decided to give him the racket as a souvenir. I do not know whether he is still using the racket, but I am sure that he still associates the racket with me and jokes that I brought him bad luck.

On one occasion after tennis we held a barbecue party in the gym nearby. I recall that in my last term at Oxford, when we were all assembled for tennis, someone proposed a party. The sky was cloudy and it looked as if it would rain, but after the game I was able to have my fill of delicious barbecued food. I greatly enjoyed the conversation at the party which was also attended by members of the MCR who did not play tennis.

I would like to relate one other story about tennis. One day, when I was playing singles with one of my Merton doubles partners and managed to win, we got soaked at the end of the set by a sudden rain storm, but we played on and our shirts and hair became sopping wet. We hastened back to Merton; unfortunately, our return coincided with meal time and my college friends, waiting in the queue outside hall and seeing me dripping wet and carrying a racket, teased me by calling out in unison: 'water tennis!' Is this I wonder another English expression?

When I think of tennis in England my thoughts immediately turn to Wimbledon in the summer. I was fortunate in being able to go to Wimbledon on three occasions. The matches I remember best are the singles matches between Connors and McEnroe and Becker and Curren.[1] I had the good fortune to be able to watch the matches sitting next to the Duke of Kent, the President of the club. In the Connors/McEnroe match it seemed to be a one-sided affair with McEnroe in the lead and I remember the Duke muttering: 'Come on Jimmy!' The match between Becker and Curren was also an interesting one. Becker won but I thought his behaviour peculiar. Those concerned with the championship seemed to want Curren to win. The special atmosphere of Wimbledon with its long history lies in the attitudes of the crowd of spectators and reflects, I think, one aspect of Britain. Another English feature of Wimbledon is the serving of tea in the interval. I shall also never forget being able to play tennis twice on grass courts at Wimbledon thanks to the connection I made during my stay with Colonel Hall.

At Merton there is a 'real tennis' court. (This is called '*Le jeu de paume*' in France, 'Court tennis' in America, and 'Royal tennis' in Australia.) 'Real tennis' is the original game as it developed at the court of the King of France under the name '*le jeu de paume*' and spread to England. In Shakespeare's play *Henry V* there is a story of how the Dauphin of France sends King Henry a set of tennis balls.

M happened to know something about 'real tennis' and I was able to play on a number of occasions. The 'real tennis' court was on the other side of Merton Street. The rules of 'real tennis' are frankly complicated and weird. The court is indoors and the shape of a crown is carved on the side wall. Various lines, whose meaning is unclear, are painted on the surface of the court. The net across the centre of the court is the same as in normal tennis. The rackets are narrower and longer than modern tennis rackets and seem to be strung with sheep gut. The ball is roughly the same size as in ordinary

---

[1] In the men's singles at Wimbledon in 1984 John McEnroe (US) beat Jimmy Connors (US) and in 1985 Boris Becker (Germany) beat Kevin Curren (US).

tennis, but is heavy and hard like a baseball. The game begins by the server hitting the ball to a protruding section that looks like a roof, and when the ball hits the ground, the player hits the ball again to continue the game. Points are apparently scored as the ball crosses the centre line. It is also said that points can be gained by hitting the ball into a number of holes [literally depressions] in the side wall. Although I played the game two or three times I never really grasped the rules.

I wonder how many readers understand why in tennis the scoring is 15–0, 30–0 and 40–0. I wondered about the origin of these terms but learnt the answer by chance from one of the Merton dons. According to him the method of scoring in tennis is connected with the counting of time. Fifteen and thirty can be easily understood by looking at a clock, but why forty? He said that forty-five was difficult to pronounce and so forty was chosen. I found this *a* convincing theory. In tennis zero is pronounced 'love'. According to one theory the French used the term '*l'oeuf* to count zero in '*le jeu de paume*,' since an 0 being a long elliptical shape looks like an egg which in French is '*l'oeuf*'. When the game was brought to England, the English people thought it sounded like 'love' and this word accordingly came to be used in scoring in England. But there are also various other theories including ones which suggest that tennis scoring is related to gambling.

Another game with similarities to tennis is squash. It is also played in an inside court and makes full use of the walls. The rules are not as complicated as in 'real tennis'. The two players face the back wall and play the ball in turns against the four walls making sure that it does not bounce more than once. The ball which is struck hard against the wall may rebound against the back wall and the other player returns it without letting it bounce twice. It is a really tough game. The captain of tennis at Merton was also a very good squash player. When I played with him I soon realized his superior power. When we played together he always stood in the centre of the court and I found myself running all around him and spent my time picking up the ball. Towards the end of the game I felt exhausted but he did not seem a bit tired. I also played with a Canadian member of the MCR but I was beaten. An interesting thing about squash, irrespective of the game itself, is the fact that a red or a yellow mark painted on top of the ball shows the way the ball will bounce. A ball with a red mark will bounce high, one with a yellow mark will have a low bounce. Clearly, the less the ball bounces the more the players have to run. Another interesting fact is that after you have been playing for a bit with a ball with a yellow spot it begins to bounce as if it were alive. I did not play squash as often as I played tennis, but I found that a short time playing squash involved a considerable amount of exercise. I enjoyed playing squash if it was raining and the tennis courts could not be used. Whereas in tennis you use the whole arm, in squash you mainly use the wrist. I do not know whether this was good for my tennis or not, but I thought that strengthening my wrist had benefited my tennis.

Jogging, climbing, skiing and other sporting activities

Jogging was another sport which I enjoyed in my time as a student. Going out from Merton's gate you soon come to Christ Church Meadow. From the entrance it is about two kilometres round the meadow. At one point you come to the banks of the Thames. Jogging there when the weather was fine made one feel good. I often jogged there of an evening and would see the same faces each time. We would exchange greetings but I never discovered their names. Apart from Christ Church Meadow another route on which I also enjoyed jogging was running along the Thames from where Folly Bridge crosses the river on St Aldate's Street as far as Iffley Lock. I shall also refer to this route when speaking of going on a walk with Dr Highfield. From Iffley Lock this route took you near the Church up Iffley Road via the High Street to Merton Street. It was probably about six kilometres in all. It seemed to be good exercise for my police escort who followed me on his bicycle.

Another sport I enjoyed was mountain-climbing. I had done some climbing in Japan and had always dreamt of climbing in Britain. Readers will know that Great Britain consists of England, Scotland, Wales and Northern Ireland, but I expect many would have difficulty in describing the geographical location of mountains in Britain and may even wonder if there are any real mountains in the British Isles.

Sport

If you open your map you will see that there is a range of mountains from the centre to the northern part of Scotland and that there are mountains also in the north of England and in North Wales. These mountains are mostly around one thousand metres high, which is roughly the same height as the hills in the Oku-Tama range. As readers will know the highest mountain in Britain is Ben Nevis in Scotland which is 1344 metres high.

From the very day I arrived in Britain I had it in mind to climb the highest mountains in England, Scotland and Wales, but I did not have accurate information about them and much as I wanted to achieve my ambition I was not sure that I would have time to accomplish it. I soon realized that the highest mountain in Britain was in Scotland, but I did not know how high it was or how suitable it was for ordinary climbers. It was in the following summer of 1984 that I managed to climb Ben Nevis. I planned a leisurely trip to Scotland mainly round the north and central part of the country. I found that Ben Nevis attracted many climbers; my police escort told me that if one kept to the normal route it was quite a safe climb and thus my wish to climb Ben Nevis was realized.

The weather was fine on 16 July, the day fixed for the climb. I went by car from Lord Campbell's house near Fort William where I was staying. I was accompanied by a friend of Lord Campbell's son and his wife. From the car Ben Nevis did not look particularly impressive as a mountain but I noticed from the map that there were some steep cliffs at the back of the mountain on the opposite side from the climbers' path. When we got to the beginning of the path I realized that Ben Nevis was indeed a big mountain. Perhaps because it lies in such a northerly latitude there were no wooded areas on its slopes and grass stretched right up to the summit. It became rather cloudy and we could not see the summit which was sheathed in mist. The path had been well maintained and the slope was not too steep, but it was uphill all the way. So it was fortunate that the sun was obscured. We passed various people coming down the mountain and I was interested to hear in addition people talking in German, French and, as I later realized, Danish. After we had passed the lake, which lay half way up, the outlook round about made me realize we had gained considerable height, and I had the same sort of alpine feeling that I get when climbing in Japan's high mountains. After passing a snowy ravine we came to the summit but found ourselves in dense fog and could not see anything. It had taken us just over three hours.

The second mountain, which I climbed on 27 July 1985, was Snowdon, which at 1085 metres is the highest mountain in Wales. There is a small mountain railway that runs up to the summit, but I had made up my mind that I would climb on foot the highest mountains in Scotland, Wales and England. So I climbed up the path which is located on the opposite side of the mountain from the railway track. In contrast to the climb up Ben Nevis, which was a climb straight up the mountain, I felt on this occasion that it was like walking on a ridge. I was spurred on by the sight of the summit with its bare rocks, which I saw from the small lake on the way up, but the climb was easier than that of Ben Nevis and I reached the top easily. The view was obscured by mist and I felt rather depressed when I heard the sound of the train, but I was happy that I had made the climb on my own two feet and appreciated the mountain's comparatively large number of different views. On the way down I followed the path by the railway for part of the way; fortunately, the weather improved and I enjoyed some unexpected views. People waving to me from the train; people looking curious and puzzled; I wonder if I shall see such a sight again.

I went on from Wales to the Lake District where I had been once before. My objective this time was to climb Scafell Pike, which at 978 metres is the highest mountain in England. On 29 July having met up with three fellow students we left our lodgings at Borrowdale to climb to the top of the mountain. The path up the mountain was similar to that up Snowdon, but as we climbed we never seemed to see the summit and I realized that this really was quite a mountain. After we had been climbing for about two hours we came to a beautiful lake where some tents were pitched. Presumably, these belonged to people who were hiking in the mountains. At about this time clouds began to form and hide the mountain tops. When climbing we had occasionally needed to use our hands but it had not been a difficult climb. Threading through the mists we reached the summit in about three-and-a-half hours. The mountain tops

Sport

appeared and disappeared in the mist and formed a range of rocky mountains. It reminded me of a Japanese mountain range but the biggest difference was probably that, however high you climbed, you kept on encountering sheep.

In this way I managed to climb to the top of the three highest mountains in Britain. I had not been lucky with the weather, but the paths with their ups and downs and the surrounding scenery were different from anything I had experienced in Japan and provided an interesting contrast. British mountains are not particularly high but you get the feeling that you are among high mountains perhaps because Britain lies in such a northerly latitude. There may not be many high mountains in Britain but the country has produced many outstanding mountaineers such as Mallory and Bonnington. Moreover, in the Meiji period it was Walter Weston, the English Missionary, who called Japan's central mountain range 'The Japan Alps' and spread knowledge of Japanese mountains around the world.

I also tried golf on several occasions. I was introduced by one of the dons at Merton to a golf course some fifteen minutes away by car where I had some lessons from a golf pro. It felt good when the impact was right, but I felt pretty wretched when I missed the ball or my club tore up a piece of turf. I am sure that the pro was a good teacher, but I found more attraction in sports where I had to move around more. Nevertheless, I was glad to be able to wield a golf club in Britain, the home of golf.

I suppose that racing should also come under sports! Ascot is famous for racing and I was fortunate in being able to go to 'Royal Ascot' in both 1984 and 1985. It was a colourful occasion. The Queen and members of the Royal Family, who came in horse-driven carriages, were greeted with much applause on their arrival. It was a magnificent sight as those attending doffed their top hats. The Queen is very fond of racing as I could see standing by her side. I was fortunately able to watch the races from the royal box and although I did not understand much about racing I saw the races from start to finish and was overwhelmed by the atmosphere. I noticed that when the Queen entered the enclosure without anyone saying a word a passage was opened to allow her through the throng. I was much impressed by how relaxed the Queen seemed. For the first time in my life I had a bet on a horse race, but it was a spectacular failure. As it was only a one pound bet it did not have any serious effect on my purse.

Winter sports essentially mean skiing. I had the good fortune to be invited two years in succession by Hans Adam, the Crown Prince of Liechtenstein, to stay a few days in his house. From there we could go out skiing not only in Liechtenstein but also in both the Austrian and Swiss Alps. The Crown Prince and his wife Princess Mary had three sons and one daughter. The Crown Prince and his eldest son accompanied me skiing and we all had a relaxing time chatting after our expeditions. On the first occasion a former ski champion who was a member of the police guards for the household of the Prince of Liechtenstein set a course for us to follow and guided me over the course. In the second year temperatures in the Austrian mountains recorded minus 25 degrees centigrade. I was impressed by the extent of European skiing resorts.

I was also invited by the Grand Duke of Luxembourg and his family to stay in their chalet in Switzerland at Cran Montana ski resort and I enjoyed skiing in fresh snow. I thought that the Crown Prince was a very fine skier. I also spent a few days skiing with Colonel Hall and his family at the French ski resort of Meribel. Meribel, which is near Albertville where the winter Olympics were held, is a famous and extensive skiing area. The Halls and I skied around the resort. The area of snow is so vast that one cannot go around it all in one day. I was also able to do some skating on a rink nearby with Colonel Hall's daughter. Afterwards, Colonel Hall said to me more than once: 'I thought that the Prince would stop skiing but I was wrong he was a non-stop skier and I was exhausted.'

I have happy memories of all the sports with which I came in contact during my time studying abroad. Sports often come up in conversation and the fact that I had taken part in sports was often a helpful starting point for a conversation.

With apologies to the English, who regard cricket as their national sport I have to confess that I could not understand the rules of the game. Still, the sight of the players in their white shirts and trousers standing out on the greensward which forms the pitch makes a lovely picture which seems to fit the English landscape. There is

Sport

something about the cricket bat that makes me think of a rower's oar, and I wonder if it did not have some historical connection with the Vikings. I also wonder what the connections are between cricket and baseball and at this stage I find it more interesting to think about this than to try to understand the rules of cricket.

CHAPTER 8

LIFE AS A RESEARCH STUDENT AT OXFORD

Why I decided to do research on the Thames as a highway

I have described various aspects of my life at Oxford, but my research was, of course, the most important part of my life there. My two years at Oxford were so precious to me that I did wonder if it would be a waste of time to spend them on the sort of research which I could do in Japan. However, looking back I realize that my research contributed significantly to my experience at Oxford. It certainly enabled me to have many valuable experiences, meet many people and to get the feel of what was involved in research. The theme of my research at Oxford was transport on the river Thames in the eighteenth century. I should first like to explain how I came to study this subject.

From the time when I was a child I had been interested in roads as a means of transportation. In my position I could not go outside the gates whenever I wanted to, but when I wandered along the paths in the grounds of the Akasaka palace, I felt that I was making a journey into a part of the world I did not know at all. For me these paths played an important role as a means of connecting me with the unknown world. It was, I think, when I had only just started school that I found, when wandering around the Akasaka palace grounds, a sign which read '*Ōshū Kaidō*'.[1] The sign was a modern one, but I was excited when

---

[1] The Ōshū Kaidō was an old highway connecting the northern provinces with Edo (now Tokyo).

Life as a Research Student at Oxford

I learnt that according to old maps and experts on the subject an old highway had indeed passed through the palace grounds during the Kamakura period (1192–1333). Then in my first year at high school when I was reading with my mother Bashō's[2] *Oku no Hosomichi* I became even more interested than I had been before in travels and in transport. Perhaps for this reason my main interest during my first two years at elementary school was learning about the road system and the posting stations along the highways in Edo Japan.

At university I had studied in the history department in the faculty of letters. The focus of my interest gradually moved to the transportation system in the medieval period (from the eleventh century to the end of the sixteenth century) on which little academic research had been carried out. The transportation system in this period developed from the post station[3] system which came into being under the political regime based on the early legal system[4] adapted from Chinese models. It led to the transportation system in the Edo period (1603–1868) of the post-station town[5] system which was developed under the joint shogunate and domain structure.[6] However, as I began my studies I found that there were only a limited number of documents relating to land transport in this period. So I decided to concentrate on the history of sea transport in the Muromachi period (fourteenth to sixteenth centuries) where comparatively more research materials were available. My graduation thesis was a study and analysis of the transport of commodities such as salt, rice, timber and other raw materials in the Inland Sea.

I took up the theme of transport in the Inland Sea in medieval Japan as I had come across some relevant documents. These had been discovered by chance by Mr Hayashiya Tatsusaburo, a Kyoto historian, in a second-hand bookshop in Kyoto about thirty years ago. As I was working on my thesis, I heard from Mr Hayashiya that the papers he had found were going to appear in print. I realized

---

[2] Matsuo Bashō (1644–94) was Japan's foremost haiku poet. *Oku no Hosomichi* describes his journey to the northern provinces.
[3] *Eki-sei* 駅制.
[4] *Ritsuryōsei* 律令制
[5] *shukuekisei* 宿駅制
[6] *bakuhantaisei* 幕藩体制

from my studies at university that research into sea transport in the medieval period had not got very far: fortunately, these documents had come to light just as I was about to take up the theme of sea transport in the Inland Sea. Their publication was most valuable for my research. These documents which were produced in 1445 consisted of the detailed records over one year of duties paid by all shipping entering Hyogo Kitazeki (the northern customs post of Hyogo) which is the modern port of Kobe and which was then part of the domain of the Tōdaiji (temple in Nara). These documents and the customs house records of the port of Lübeck in northern Germany, dating from about the middle of the fourteenth century, are historically important materials. I continued my studies on this theme for about a year as a post-graduate and then I moved to England. There can be no doubt that the methods, which I had learnt in Japan, of how to deal with, read and research historical documents, despite the differences between Japanese and English historical material, stood me in good stead at Oxford.

I decided that, as this was relevant to my previous studies in Japan, I would do research into transport by water in Britain, while I was at Oxford. But when I started at Oxford I had not reached any firm conclusion about the form this should take. English history was outside my special field of study and I realized that it would be far from easy to learn about the background to transport and distribution problems in the period which I wanted to study. I also recognized that research into transport by water in the Middle Ages in Britain, which was related to my studies in Japan, presented particular difficulties as the relevant historical documents in England up to about the seventeenth century were written in Latin and I had never studied Latin. I had, therefore, an immediate problem, as I started my studies at Oxford; how was I was going to read such material in Latin? I only had two years to complete my research and I faced an immediate challenge to the pursuit of my studies.

Professor Mathias

A solution to my problem emerged in discussions with Professor Mathias. As I have already explained Professor Mathias of All Souls had been chosen as my supervisor and Dr Highfield as my college tutor and adviser. Professor Mathias's speciality was the economic history of modern Britain. His work *The First Industrial Nation* has been translated into Japanese and has been widely read as an introduction to modern British economic history. Dr Highfield's speciality was the history of medieval Spain but he was also an expert on the history of Oxford and in 1988, together with Professor Christopher Brooke and Wim Swaan, he published an illustrated book about the buildings and architecture of Oxford and Cambridge. I had been invited to meet both Professor Mathias and Dr Highfield before I had started at Oxford. During my first term I had tutorials with Professor Mathias about historical materials. I went for walks with Dr Highfield and learnt a great deal from him about Oxford by seeing things for myself. All this led me to the study of transport on the river Thames.

In my first term I did not reach any decision on what the exact theme of my research should be. Professor Mathias began by concentrating on a summary of the history of transport in Japan. At his request I wrote an essay outlining the history of transport from ancient times up to the Edo period (1603–1868). Professor Mathias urged me to express more of my own opinions and think about issues such as why horse-driven vehicles were not developed in Japan. This made me apprehensive about how my studies would progress. Apart from my tutorials, I attended Professor Mathias' lectures to learn the general lines of British economic history. Lectures lasted one hour and were given in a not very large classroom in the Examination School and were attended by twenty to thirty finals students. The Professor wore a gown and gave his lecture from a desk on a dais on which he spread his papers. He had an excellent delivery, occasionally writing on the board to explain particular points. With my limited knowledge of English I found it difficult to take in everything he said; so with his permission I brought along a tape-recorder and thus was able to listen again to his lectures back in my rooms. It took time but gradually I began to understand better and this was of benefit to my researches. I also went to similar lectures given by Dr Patrick O'Brien, also of St Anthony's, and attended seminars at the Bodleian Library for students beginning to study history. At these seminars the lecturers, apart from the coordinator, were different each week. The main theme was how to use historical research materials. I found the advice on how to use the Bodleian library particularly useful. Courses of lectures lasted for one term. This did not take place in my first term but I was particularly interested in the course of lectures on the history of Oxford buildings which both Professor Mathias and Dr Highfield urged me to attend. In line with the general thrust of my studies I read books about canals in England, a subject which Professor Mathias knew well and concentrated on expanding my basic knowledge of the subject.

My first term came to an end without my having made a real start with my research. One day after the beginning of my second term I told Professor Mathias that I wanted to study transport on the river Thames. One of the impressions which I had gained from the previous term was that the Thames had played an important role in the transportation of goods within England and I had come to have a real affection for this river which flows through Oxford. I guessed that it should be relatively easy to find in Oxford the necessary historical materials about a river flowing through the city. Professor Mathias, after giving this matter some thought, said that the first problem was to discover how much material there was. As a first step, I should take a look at the historical records, which no one had yet studied, about the toll road which went through Oxfordshire (the Oxford turnpike) in the Oxfordshire County Record Office and then decide how to proceed. When I responded that I particularly wanted to look at transport by water as that was in line with my studies in Japan, Professor Mathias suggested that in that case I should have a look in the Record Office to see what materials there were relating to transport by water.

The County Record Office was in the basement of County Hall a little outside to the west of the centre of the city. Having promised to meet Professor Mathias at the Record Office on a certain day I made my way there. I had no difficulty in finding the hall but I could not discover the entrance to the basement. So I went into the main entrance with my police escort. There I encountered a number of smartly dressed and solemn-looking people and I thought that I must have gone to the wrong entrance by mistake. But one person

Life as a Research Student at Oxford

said: 'I know who you are' and when I asked the way to the basement he kindly told me where to go. Despite the fact that I was wearing jeans I had been recognized. Of course, my visit to the Record Office was entirely a private matter and Professor Mathias had no need to let County Hall know in advance about my visit. I still have a vivid memory of the visit that day. The Record Office was quite light although it was in the basement. I was impressed to see there a variety of individuals including old people, women and obvious students studying the records carefully. I learnt afterwards that ordinary English people are very keen to find out more about the history of their families and that roughly two thirds of those using the Record Office are people looking into their genealogy. Every time I made use of the records in the office I had to enter my name in the visitors' book and explain the purpose of my visit. It was clear from the book that many of the visitors were engaged in genealogical research. In the reading room there were all kinds of information about the various types of records and files held there and where they were to be found. These were piled up in shelves reaching up to the ceiling. Professor Mathias immediately introduced me to the archivist, Mr Burns, who was of great assistance to me in my researches while I was at Oxford and explained to him the nature of my proposed research, asking how much material there was in the record office about the river Thames. Mr Burns disappeared into the back for a moment and shortly after emerged carrying a box nearly a metre long and covered in dust. The box contained a large number of papers relating to the river Thames. The appearance of this dusty commonplace-looking box determined the theme of my two years research at Oxford.

Let me now explain briefly about the Thames. The river has its source in the east-facing slopes of Gloucestershire in the South-West of England. It is 340 kilometres long and after the Severn it is the second longest river in England. The length of the river Thames, by the way, is 30 kilometres shorter than the Shinano River which is the longest river in Japan. Towns on the river going from the estuary towards the source include London, Windsor, famous for Windsor Castle, Henley-on-Thames, where the Henley regatta is held, Reading, Abingdon, Oxford and Lechlade. Many readers will know that London was a Roman city. When the Romans were going up the river Thames the topography of the area and the size of their ships forced them to land where London now lies. As a result, the port of Londinium was developed. According to *A Thames Companion*, written jointly by Mary Pritchard and Humphrey Carpenter, the name of the river derives from the Latin *teme* meaning dark. The Celts, with their religious belief in rivers, found the river Thames, surrounded as it was by marshlands which were difficult to develop, dark and mystical. It must be assumed that this feeling spread among the peoples who arrived there later and led to the Thames being given this name. This is a very interesting theory.

Before I started to read the documents in the Record Office I discussed with Professor Mathias and Mr Burns what particular aspect I should study. It was agreed that I should investigate the facts about the quantities of malt, a raw material for making beer and whisky, transported by boat on the Thames and about the skippers of these boats. I began by reading the records of the Oxfordshire Quarter Sessions. The reason why I studied the transport of malt was that malt was subject to duty. This meant that if any accident occurred which affected the malt in transit on which duty had already been paid the merchants concerned could claim a refund on the portion lost. From the court records I could learn the addresses of the merchants, the amount of malt transported, the places where boats had sunk and other facts about the transport of malt. The records had been preserved because malt was a taxable commodity. As I had decided to research the period from 1750 to 1800, I inevitably concentrated on these records for this period. The records which I looked at were not the originals but copies which had been made in the early twentieth century. As a result, the writing was fortunately easy for me to read. I was not used to eighteenth-century handwriting. So this was a great help to me, but as I progressed I came across places where I thought mistakes had been made in copying and I had to go back to the originals.

Next, I began to do some research in *Jackson's Oxford Journal* in the Bodleian Library. In this weekly local paper I found many interesting articles about topics related to my research. These included the names and numbers of the boatmen and details of the discussions at meetings of the Thames Navigation Commissioners about improvements designed to facilitate navigation and shipping on the Thames as well as information about merchants trading in malt and coal on the river. Fortunately, there was an index in the library covering issues up to 1790. So I was not faced with the laborious task of leafing through quantities of papers to find what I was looking for. Unfortunately, there was no index for the years between 1790 and 1800. So sitting in a separate room in the library I had to go through the papers, which were bound together in a binder and from which clouds of dust rose as I turned the pages, and note down important points on cards. This was a particular chore when I was suffering somewhat from hay fever. I covered the papers up to 1790 in my first year and went through the papers for the remaining ten years in parallel with my other researches. I only finished the last ones shortly before I left Oxford.

I must explain briefly here about the Bodleian Library which was a great boon to Oxford students and researchers. It stemmed from Duke Humfrey's Library which had been built in the latter part of the fifteenth century and which was rebuilt by Sir Thomas Bodley in the seventeenth century. It contains today over fifteen million books and forty thousand manuscripts. I should add that the Bodleian is one of the very few libraries in Britain which automatically receives a copy of every book published in the United Kingdom. Sir Thomas Bodley, the founder of the library, believed that the rule that books should not be taken out of the library should apply to everyone, even the king. As the library contains many old books, photocopies cannot always be obtained and requests are often refused. It took time for a photocopy to be produced even if permission were given. Consequently, you saw many students and researchers in the reading room making notes from books in the library.

To obtain permission to use the Bodleian Library you had to have the approval and recommendation of your supervisor. I recall that in my case the procedures were not at all complicated and permission was given quite readily as I was kindly accompanied by Professor Mathias. I cannot unfortunately now remember the full procedure, but having completed the necessary details on the form I had my photo taken for my permit. My expression in the photo was one of surprise as I looked up towards the bright light shining in my face. But a bigger surprise was that on receiving my permit I was handed a piece of paper covering the rules which must be observed when using the library (such as treating library books with care). Permit-holders were obliged to read these aloud there and then in their own language. In my case I was given a copy of the rules in Japanese which I duly read out. I recall that the Japanese text was not in very good Japanese. This had been, I gathered, the tradition at the Bodleian since the seventeenth century.

Whenever you entered the Bodleian Library you had to show your pass. To search for a book you looked in the huge catalogue in the reading room. The bound volumes of the published index up to 1920 were in one room. The index for later publications was in an adjacent room. So in order to find a book quickly it was necessary to know whether it was published before or after 1920. You could look up books either by the title or by the author's name. There was no problem in consulting a book you were looking for if they were on the open shelves, but if they were in the store you had to complete a form giving details of the book you wanted and hand this in at the desk and wait for it to be brought out. When I was at Oxford the procedure was that the librarian had to fetch each book separately from the store and as this took a comparatively long time I used to order on the previous afternoon the books I wanted to see the following day.

As I have already indicated, the Bodleian Library included subsidiary libraries such as the Radcliffe Camera, the New Bodleian Library (referred to below as New Bodleian) and the Science Library. The Radcliffe Camera which was a round building with a large cupola on top in Radcliffe Square could be reached from the Bodleian Library by an underground passage. The New Bodleian was in a building on the other side of Broad Street. Copies of *Jackson's Oxford Journal* which I wanted to consult were held in the New Bodleian.

The first time I went to the New Bodleian I did not realize that you were supposed to check in your belongings and only allowed to take a necessary minimum of items into the library. The doorman was looking down and did not stop me; so I took all my belongings in with me. But, unfortunately, when I came out I was stopped and sternly told that, in future, I must check in my belongings before entering the library. I gathered that pages from old books and documents were sometimes torn out and taken away by readers. Once, when I was collecting my belongings, a student whom I had never seen before said to me: 'I remember how good the food was at Merton.' He must have noticed the magenta Merton scarf I was wearing that day. Each college has a different coloured scarf.

I recall another incident involving the New Bodleian. That was when my umbrella was stolen. It was raining pretty heavily that day, if I remember correctly, and I had gone to the New Bodleian with the umbrella that I had recently bought in London. On the ground floor there was an umbrella rack and I carelessly left my new umbrella there before going upstairs to the reading room to continue my research into *Jackson's Oxford Journal*. When I had finished and went out my umbrella was no longer there. Someone had either taken it by mistake or gone home with it deliberately because it was raining. The rain was coming down harder than ever. When I told the porter that my umbrella was missing he responded: 'What again! I don't know how many times this has happened today!' If it was found he promised to get in touch with me, but there was no hope of my umbrella turning up. Accordingly, I returned to college some ten minutes away through the wet streets and got soaked through. I liked that umbrella and regretted the loss. Whoever had taken it had managed to get home without getting wet, so I reckoned that I had contributed to his welfare. Needless to say, once I was back in my rooms I immediately took a bath.

Apart from items relating to the Thames, there were many other interesting articles in *Jackson's Oxford Journal*. One theme to which I felt like devoting a little time was reading reports of concerts in Oxford. Thus, in my first year, in addition to attending lectures, I spent time in the library and the record office reading the accounts of court proceedings and researching newspaper reports, but by the end of the year I could see the direction in which my studies of the history of transport by water on the river Thames should take.

I had tutorials with Professor Mathias either every week or every other week. His room was on the second floor of the Hawksmoor Tower which had been built to a design by Nicholas Hawksmoor who had been a disciple of Sir Christopher Wren who had designed the Sheldonian. Professor Needham, whom I had met when I had been invited to lunch at All Souls by Professor Mathias before I had started at Merton and while I was staying with the Halls, had rooms on the floor below. There was a sofa near the door of Professor Mathias's room and his desk was at the back. There was a door on the right at the back of the room which seemed to lead to a telephone and typing room. Tutorials took place on the sofa. When I was asked to prepare an essay I would send it to him in advance and the tutorial concentrated on an appraisal of what I had written. As my research progressed and I prepared questions for discussion the tutorial would begin by my making a presentation on which Professor Mathias would comment. He would explain problems in easily understandable language and advise me that on such and such a point I should read a particular book. Occasionally, he would return to his desk to look for a document or book. There were always piles of documents and papers on his desk, but as far as I can remember, with one or two exceptions, he always found what he was looking for. 'I must tidy up' was a phrase I heard Professor Mathias say from time to time during tutorials. The main subjects of my essays were the transport of coal and malt on the river Thames during the eighteenth century. As he wanted me to produce various relevant charts and documents I spent some time searching for the necessary material in the Bodleian Library, the specialist history library immediately on the other side of Broad Street and Merton College library. I could not find a book about the transport of coal that I was looking for even in the specialist history library, but I came across it by chance in the most convenient place of all, namely the college library. I was pleased and relieved when I found the book.

    I had collected a good deal of material about the transport of coal and malt on the Thames, but I realized that writing an essay confined to the transport of a single commodity only in relation to the river Thames was not enough. I needed to think about transport of malt in other areas and also about the significance of the transport of such a commodity in the eighteenth century. The knowledge which I could acquire from books was important in this context. At first, I felt that the burden of reading so many books for my tutorials was a heavy

Life as a Research Student at Oxford

one and I needed speed-reading techniques to get through such a huge quantity of books in the limited time available. Of course, it would not do just to cut and paste bits from books. I needed to add my own explanations and opinions. In addition, as I had to write in English the preparation of my essays was a very onerous task.

In the weeks when I had to present an essay I often did not get to sleep until late at night. All my essays were prepared in long hand and it must have been a hard job for Professor Mathias to read them. When I thought that I was getting used to reading quickly and that my essays were getting a little better I was pleased when he said to me: 'This is a much, much better essay than the last one', but then I was disappointed as I realized that the last one must really have been bad and I was rather apprehensive about what he might say about my next effort. After my essay had been looked at critically Professor Mathias invariably gave me directions about the next topic and issues that I should cover. I have to say that although he had described my essay as good he had noted many mistakes in my English. In this way my tutorials and my personal researches were inextricably connected. Although I normally wore jeans, I usually wore a tie when I went for my tutorials. At the end of the tutorial as I said goodbye Professor Mathias would appoint a day and time for my next tutorial. If I had not written an essay that day he would urge me rather sternly to write more quickly, but normally he would say 'good' or 'very good' when he sent me on my way. Often he would treat me to a glass of sherry which he kept in his rooms.

It can be seen from this that my tutorials with Professor Mathias were very substantial but I should point out the differences between my experience at Oxford and the relationship between teacher and student in seminars on medieval Japan in the history department of the faculty of letters in the graduate division of the Gakushūin University. (This was under the direction of Professor Yasuda Motohisa and I shall refer to these as Yasuda seminars.) The Yasuda seminars were attended by second- to fourth-year students specializing in medieval history and the students in each year would form a group and would, for instance, read and discuss a text consisting of a record of the *bakufu* in the Kamakura period. As a result, junior students could always look for help and guidance from senior students in the group. As there were a large variety of aspects to be studied by students specializing in medieval history, Professor Yasuda, who had spent nearly twenty years as a leading teacher in Gakushūin University, had the assistance of sub-teachers who had studied under him. Their task was to help students working on particular themes with which they were familiar. In this way, when the time came for students to write their graduating theses, sub-teachers would come round to the houses where students were staying together to discuss problems and students could be put in touch with seniors who had done research in a similar field. When I came to write my graduating thesis I learnt a good deal about reading and analysing historical texts related to my themes from Professor Yasuda and seniors who had a detailed knowledge about the history of the distribution of commodities as well as from senior students who were not experts in this field. Thus, as a result of attending Yasuda seminars I had a good deal of help and guidance not only from the professor himself but also from seniors in classes above mine and from others who were up to twenty years senior to me.

At Oxford, while I had the benefit of one-to-one tutorials with Professor Mathias in his rooms and from attending his seminars, I did not have contact with senior students of Professor Mathias in the same way as I had had in the Yasuda seminars. Thus, although I gained from thorough man-to-man contacts with my professor I had few opportunities of developing contacts with other scholars and in particular with researchers in related fields. My experience of the Yasuda seminars showed that guidance from the sub-teachers had been very useful. They shared our interest in research and were able to discuss problems which arose in our studies. They also provided good opportunities to meet other researchers in similar fields.

In mid-December, towards the end of my first year at Oxford, Professor Mathias kindly took me to see the Iron Bridge on the river Severn and its museum in North-West Shropshire. The Iron Bridge, which was completed in 1779, was the first bridge in the world made of iron, which as a student of the time of the Industrial Revolution I should not miss. Professor Mathias having given me an account of the bridge then accompanied me to the adjacent museum where he and the museum curator explained the exhibits. We went round the

Life as a Research Student at Oxford

museum, which was in what had been a warehouse, built in 1838, and outside on the site of an iron works, which had continued to operate until the end of the nineteenth century. I was impressed to discover that the first blast furnace, which had been one of the driving forces of the Industrial Revolution, had been preserved. Professor Mathias knew the specialists in economic history throughout the world and, when I visited continental countries, scholars and researchers introduced to me by Professor Mathias guided me to historical sites in their countries. In France, for instance, I was taken to see various canals and in Norway I was shown round the city of Bergen.

In my second year Professor Mathias thought it would be useful if I was able to have the advice of another specialist as well as of himself and suggested Dr Morgan who had studied under him while at New College. Dr Morgan, whose speciality was the history of trade, was then teaching at Bristol University, which lay some 100 kilometres to the west of Oxford. At Professor Mathias's request Dr Morgan agreed to come over from Bristol to give me his advice.

Visiting record offices

Dr Morgan had ginger hair and a somewhat stern face. At first, I did not find him very easy but as we progressed in our talks I realized that he was a good sort. Although he was not an expert in the history of transport by water this was, he said, a good opportunity for him to study the subject. He played the bassoon and was very knowledgeable about music.

The reason why I had chosen to do research into transport on the upper reaches of the Thames was that it was geographically convenient for me while I was studying at Oxford. The Thames passes through the counties of Gloucester, Oxford, Buckingham and Berks before reaching London. So if I wanted to study the upper reaches of the river it would be necessary for me to collect information not only from the record offices and libraries in Oxfordshire but also from offices and libraries in other counties. Whenever he was able to do so Dr Morgan accompanied me on such visits.

The first record office I visited four or five times in the course of my enquiries was at Reading. This was in the corner of a modern building and quite different from the equivalent in Oxford. It was much more spacious and comfortable, but at Oxford the relationship between the users and the archivists was much closer and the atmosphere for research students much better. At this office I looked at the Thames Navigation Commission's report on their investigation into the state of the river and the records of the Berkshire Quarter Sessions in order to find out the state of navigation and the transport of malt on the river Thames at that time. Unfortunately, the record was largely a handwritten one and this made my investigations hard work.

There were also various historical documents in the Gloucestershire record office and library about the upper reaches of the river towards its source. In the latter half of the eighteenth century there was an increase in the transport of goods along canals constructed between rivers. In 1791 the Thames and Severn Canal was completed; this connected the Thames and Severn rivers at Lechlade in Gloucestershire, the highest navigable point on the Thames. The office held many papers, emanating from the Thames and Severn Canal Company, which were very useful for my study of the arrangements for the distribution of commodities in the second half of the eighteenth century. In addition, I found many other papers relating to transport by water.

I also visited the Buckinghamshire record office in Aylesbury, about an hour by car from Oxford, the Public Record Office in London and the Guildhall Library in the City of London. I did not find much of use for my research in the Aylesbury office. In the Guildhall Library I found various insurance company records relating to insurances taken out in respect of the assets and personal property of boatmen and coal merchants and malt traders on the Thames. These were useful in studying the social position of those involved. The records of the Sun Fire Insurance Company had been computerized and were easy to use, but it was a time-consuming task to go through the huge amount of material which had been retained in order to find the facts relating to the people I was studying.

I was always accompanied by one of my two police escorts when I went to these various places. He usually spent his time reading a book which interested him, but he would help me as necessary by

Life as a Research Student at Oxford

noting on cards information about historical documents and assisting me in deciphering difficult passages. As the record office in Reading was in one corner of the county hall there was a cafeteria in the same building. But this was not so at the Guildhall. In this case the chauffeur who had driven me there looked for the nearest pub. Fortunately, he found a good one nearby and every time I visited the Guildhall I went there; it became a favourite of mine. By the way, pub-users in the City of London look quite different from those who go to pubs in Oxford. In the City people in suits and ties, if they cannot find a table to sit at, try to find a space to put down their food and with their beer in their hand talk and laugh – a sight you rarely saw at Oxford.

Dr Morgan told me later on that once when we went to the Guildhall library it seemed that another Japanese researcher was also there at the same time. I had put the name 'Naruhito' on the application form for the document which I wanted to see. The attendant must have thought that this referred to the other oriental person there and saying 'Mr Naruhito' put the papers for which I had applied in front of this man who was greatly disconcerted. However, all the papers which I had requested were delivered to me without a hitch and I was unaware of what had happened. Shortly afterwards, Dr Morgan and Professor Mathias, who were at a conference together, by chance met the Japanese involved. He had seen Dr Morgan by my side and apparently mistaken him for my police escort. What a series of coincidences and rather amusing!

The Public Record Office was in two locations, at Kew and in Chancery Lane in London. The records, which I wanted, were at Kew, but the older ones were in the Chancery Lane office. I also went to the Greater London Record Office for some items. I did not find many relevant documents in the Public Record Office at Kew, but I was interested in the way documents were requested there. You first entered into the computer all the details of the records you were seeking. You then received a pocket-sized receiver. When the documents you required were ready a red light flashed on the receiver and you heard a sound. The receiver thus let you know automatically that your papers could be collected from the desk. The receiver worked wherever you were in the building. In the Greater London Record

Office I was fortunately able to find a paper listing the amount subscribed and the names and occupations of the subscribers to the Thames Navigation Commission; I made a copy of these lists.

In parallel with these investigations I spent some time looking for various documents and records in Oxford. *The Victoria History of the Counties of England,* which contained details of the history of each English county, was very useful in my study of the counties through which the Thames flowed. I also found a number of valuable articles about transport by water. In addition, I discovered that the *Parliamentary Papers* in the basement of the Radcliffe Camera contained some valuable information. Parliamentary approval was required before rivers could be repaired and for the construction of canals. This meant that parliamentary papers were important sources for my study of water transport. I was really surprised how much relevant material there was in these parliamentary records. All the details about the progress of repairs to rivers, about the number of trips made by boats and about the various problems of the river had been recorded. The parliamentary records had been printed and this saved me a great deal of trouble in reading them. I still remember nostalgically the time I spent following the very small print, making notes on cards and inserting onto tables details from these documents; they had a peculiar smell from the store where they had been preserved. *The Universal British Directory* held in the Bodleian Library, which contained the names of merchants active in each place at the time, was also useful to my investigation of those engaged in transport, as well as of merchants involved in the coal and malt trade. When the name Daniel Defoe is mentioned, everyone thinks immediately of *Robinson Crusoe*, but Defoe was a great traveller and in the eighteenth century he went round Britain observing the state of each area of the country. In his account of his travels he recorded among other things the price, means of transport and route taken by coal, as well as details of the trade in malt between Reading and London. I found this most useful. In addition, I discovered the Oxford City Apprentice Records in Oxford City Library; these gave details of the apprentices in eighteenth-century Oxford and were useful for my study of the transport enterprises and malt merchants and their apprentices in Oxford at that time.

Life as a Research Student at Oxford

I recorded one by one on cards the points which were relevant to my research. At first reading and analysing the records took time, but in this way I made contact with the raw materials of history and I felt happy that I had come in direct touch with the age I was studying through my struggle to read the papers and by breathing in the dust arising from these old papers. I found the officials in the record offices most kind and had the impression that they understood very well how to search out the documents I needed. In particular, I recall how helpful Mr Burns as well as others in the Oxfordshire County Record Office were. He taught me not only how to read difficult words, but was always trying to find where records relating to water transport on the Thames could be found. It would not be an exaggeration to say that every time I went to his office I was able to glean some new information.

Dr Highfield

I cannot record here all the happy memories of my time at Oxford, but my first intellectual excitement after I started at Oxford came from the Oxford historical walks which I did with Dr Highfield who was my college supervisor in college.

Dr Highfield, whose speciality was the medieval history of Spain, was a graduate of Magdalen, but he was also very well informed about English history and recently contributed a forty-page article about early Oxford colleges to the first volume of *The History of Oxford* and, as I have already mentioned, in 1988 he had produced with Professor Brooke and Wim Swaan an illustrated and comparative account of the building of Oxford and Cambridge Universities. This book was in preparation when I was at Oxford. When I was about to leave in the summer of 1985 I often used to see him walking round Oxford accompanied by a photographer.

Dr Highfield, who looked somewhere between fifty and sixty, was a bachelor and lived in college. With his white hair and thick spectacles, and the sly grin he used to give you as you passed him in the street or when he told a joke, there was something special about him which made you think of a wizard riding on a broomstick. As soon as I had joined Merton he used to visit me in my rooms once a week

The Thames and I

when we would discuss the progress of my studies. Afterwards, we would go out on a walk to look at historical buildings in Oxford. To be honest, when we went on our first walk, I did not realize that this would be the first of some ten historical walks which I would want to record. I thought that he had invited me to go out with him to stretch our legs as a bit of relaxation. However that may be, I must say that through these walks I was able to learn the outlines of the history of Oxford. In addition to the enjoyment gained from seeing the buildings in their historical context I was able to deepen my understanding of the connections between Oxford and my own field study of water transport on the Thames.

My first walk with Dr Highfield was on 15 October 1983. It was pouring with rain and we spent about an hour going round Christ Church meadow. During our walk he explained that the present course of the Thames was different from what it had been in medieval times and that the boundary between Merton and Christ Church Meadow had at that time been part of the city wall. He also told me that the boatmen and boat owners in seventeenth- and eighteenth-century Oxford had lived in an area near Folly Bridge which was not far from the meadow by the Thames. (He had already realized that I had begun to be interested in transport on the river.) As we went along the explanations, which he gave me, aroused my interest in the history of the city of Oxford and of the connections between its inhabitants and the river. I remember clearly to this day the intellectual excitement which I felt at the time. I also recall, after he had warned me to be careful about slipping in the rain, the sight of Dr Highfield making a spectacular fall.

My walks with Dr Highfield took place mainly on Saturdays or Sundays; in my first term alone we took seven walks together. Looking again at my diary to see where we went, I find that on 15 October we went to Christ Church Meadow, on 22 October to the Botanical Gardens and to Magdalen, on 29 October to Queen's, on 5 November to the University Park and to the northern part of Oxford, on 12 November to Worcester [college], on 4 December to Iffley Lock and church, and on 11 December to the neighbourhood of Oxford Castle.

In our walks Dr Highfield did not just comment at random on any old buildings which we passed. He selected two or three and concentrated on the important points about each. I was therefore able to understand without difficulty what he wanted to show me and able to absorb and remember what he said. The following are some examples: the seventeenth-century classical gateway to the Botanical Gardens, the water wheel which is recorded in the eleventh-century Doomsday Book and which lies just above the creek by Magdalen, the plaster work in the ceiling of the library at Queen's, which was completed in the eighteenth century, and in the college chapel, as well as the Baroque gate to the college, the modern buildings of Wolfson by the University Park and the Victorian gothic-style brick buildings of Keble. I remember him saying, as he drew my attention to the pointed entrances and windows in the upper part of these buildings with their peculiarly gothic-style features: 'The gothic-style of the thirteenth to the fifteenth centuries was revived in the Victorian era.'

Before we went to Iffley on 4 December Dr Highfield took me to Merton College library and showed me part of a thick green book and explained: 'Here is the parliamentary resolution of 1624 about the construction of Iffley Lock. The purpose of the lock was to facilitate the transport of stone for building purposes from Headington near Oxford to London and of coal for heating from London to Oxford. On our walk today let us have a look at the lock and the twelfth-century church there.' The documents which he showed me demonstrated that there was no way at that time of getting by barge as far as Oxford and that a great deal of effort had been put into solving this problem.

It was a bright and warm autumn day when we went to Iffley. Dr Highfield carried under his arm a number of volumes about Oxfordshire buildings by Pevsner, the British architectural historian, and walked vigorously along the path by the river Thames as if he was drawn on by invisible forces. I had to make a considerable effort to keep up with his fast pace. I saw then what he had meant by the words when he said on our Christ Church Meadow walk: 'We shall take our exercise walking round the meadow.' At the same time I realized that the speed with which he walked reflected his passion for scholarship which I began to share.

Iffley Lock lay below a small hill in beautiful country. At today's newly renovated lock there were a number of leisure boats and people chatting amiably waiting before the lock gates for the lock to open. There was no sign now of the difficulties which had faced earlier navigators on the river or of the efforts which had been expended in building the lock. But it was very useful for my later studies to see with my own eyes how the lock operated. We crossed over the lock and went towards the church. There were few vehicles on the quiet paved road up to the church. The church blended in with the old buildings around and the general atmosphere made me think of the Middle Ages. The church was on top of the hill. It was a symmetrical and elegant small building. I liked this building as soon as I saw it. The doorway at the front of the building with its Norman decoration was so well preserved that one could hardly believe that it had been built in the twelfth century. Dr Highfield explained in detail about round Norman arches and the decorations surrounding doors. It was an unforgettable walk which had taken us to this ancient and fine twelfth-century church.

On our final walk that first term Dr Highfield took me to Oxford Castle. Oxford Castle had been built in 1071 five years after the Norman Conquest by Robert d'Oilly who had been appointed governor of Oxford by William the Conqueror. As the castle is now within the precincts of Oxford prison it is not open to the general public, but we were able to get a general view of it from the path which follows the stream beside the castle. Dr Highfield pointed out that there used to be a water wheel standing just below the tower and mound which were all that remain of the old castle today, and as we moved south along the creek he said that this area was called Fisher Row and was the second of two areas where those engaged in the carriage of goods had lived (the other area being by Folly Bridge). Finally, he noted that Oxford prison was in the precincts of the castle and commented with a laugh: 'You see the castle's role has not changed in over a thousand years!'

The first time I was invited by Dr Highfield for tea in his room was shortly after I had begun my stay with Colonel and Mrs Hall to improve my knowledge of English. I shall never forget my first impression of him as he greeted me. He was standing erect in a dark blue suit with piercing but kindly-looking eyes peering through thick spectacles and raised his hand to welcome me. Sitting me on the sofa

Life as a Research Student at Oxford

by the window he showed me a book and said that he thought I might find it useful to glance through the book before I began my studies at Oxford. This was an outline history by J.H. Clapham of the economic history of England in the Middle Ages. It dealt with a period before the eighteenth century, which I was proposing to study, but the section about transport in the Middle Ages was very useful for my later studies. Dr Highfield, putting an electric lead into an ancient and battered electric kettle, began to make tea. While Colonel Hall was discussing with Dr Highfield how I was getting on with my language studies and what the next steps should be, the kettle in which the water had boiled began to spew out steam as if it was about to explode. Somewhat scared, I moved away from the kettle, but Dr Highfield was obviously used to the ways of his kettle and, removing the cord, put in the tea. It was very delicious tea. As I was finishing my tea he asked me if I would like to hear a record and while waiting for me to reply put on a record of Haydn's *Military Symphony*. His record-player looked as old as his electric kettle, but the sound reproduction was good.

After I entered college I used to visit Dr Highfield's room in connection with the essays which I had to prepare for presentation to Professor Mathias. He readily replied to all my trifling questions and produced relevant papers for me to look at. When he could not give an immediate response he would make a memo of the details I wanted and would put his reply in my college pigeon hole. Sometimes, if he came across things which might be relevant to my studies, he would follow the same procedure. Unfortunately, however, I found his handwriting very difficult to read and occasionally I had to seek the assistance of my police escort, but trying to read his handwriting was good practice for my reading of hand-written historical documents, which I had to look at in the course of my researches.

Among the happy memories of my association with Dr Highfield were the visits we made to operas together. The first of the operas we saw was Beethoven's *Fidelio* on 26 October. There was a scene at the beginning of the opera when a woman was ironing; it looked just like the ironing we did at college, and struck me as funny. It was a good performance but it seemed rather a gloomy opera. This was the first time I had been to an opera in England. The last opera, which

The Thames and I

I saw with Dr Highfield, was *The Marriage of Figaro* in a fine production at Glyndebourne; it left a deep impression on me. People with whom I went to operas while I was at Oxford were Mrs Storry (wife and later widow of Richard Storry, the outstanding and irreplaceable scholar of Japanese at Oxford), Mr and Mrs Fuji and my police escort. I greatly enjoyed opera; this was a great boon from my stay in Oxford.

After the opera I usually had a meal with Dr Highfield. We had supper in a cosy and very quiet room, down some stairs, a little below the rooms occupied by Merton dons. Drinking wine (the Spanish wine we drank after *The Marriage of Figaro* was especially good) we talked until late about the opera we had seen.

I cannot record here all my happy memories of Dr Highfield, but I made one major blunder in my relations with him. It happened when we were taking one of our walks in Oxford. Generally at the end of our walk we discussed when and where our next walk should take place. On one walk both I and my police escort failed to note this down in our notebooks. The day in question happened to be that on which the Oxford Colleges boat races took place and I had gone to the Thames to watch them. It was some time after three in the afternoon when I returned to the porter's lodge and looking in my pigeon hole saw a memo in Dr Highfield's handwriting saying that he had been waiting at the lodge from two o'clock. I was greatly embarrassed and immediately went round to his rooms. He did not seem in the least put out and when I apologized for forgetting our appointment, saying that I had gone to watch the boat races, he responded gently: 'I thought that you might have gone to see the races. They are an important tradition at Oxford and it was a good idea to watch them.' As I could not think of anything to say in reply I quickly left his rooms after promising that I would not make such a mistake again in the future. I still feel guilty that I had wasted his precious time; I knew that in his capacity as a tutor he had many students to supervise and that this left him little time for his own researches, but I was somewhat relieved by the thought that it had been the boat races which I had been to see on that occasion.

Among my memories of Dr Highfield I recall the time when in my last summer we visited the upper reaches of the Thames and the

Life as a Research Student at Oxford

Thames and Severn canal. We first looked at three bridges across the upper reaches of the river. The first one was called 'New Bridge', but the adjective new was far from appropriate in this case, as it was an old bridge built in the fourteenth to the fifteenth century. I wonder if it was called 'new' much in the same way as New College was so termed. Dr Highfield explained that the stone used to build this bridge had come from the Cotswold Hills which extend from the western part of Oxfordshire as far as the eastern part of Gloucestershire. The next was 'Tadpole Bridge' but no one apparently knows why it was so called. The last was 'Radcot Bridge' which was also said to have been built in the fourteenth century and, according to Dr Highfield, Cotswold stones had also been used in its construction. Our next objective was Grafton Lock some kilometres upstream, but he suggested that instead of using the car we walk along the path by the river. However, it was further than it appeared from the map and the grass was growing high beside the path. Eventually, we managed to push through the grass thickets and reached the lock, although in the process we suffered from the sharp pricks of the grass.

The lock-keeper kindly agreed to show us round and let us see some photographs of the floods which had swamped the area some years earlier. Dr Highfield, feeling perhaps that he had been responsible for forcing us to go through the 'jungle' on our way to the lock, decided to go back the same way with the driver to collect the car from Radcot Bridge and he left me and my police escort at the lock. Having seen them off I heard more about the floods from the lock-keeper. While we were talking, a boat came down the river and at the suggestion of the lock-keeper I and my police escort joined the boat as far as Radcot Bridge and set off in pursuit of Dr Highfield and the driver. The boat contained a couple who were going down the Thames as far as London. We spotted Dr Highfield and the driver some distance away and shouted after them, but we were too far away for them to hear us. As I have mentioned earlier, Dr Highfield keeps up a fast pace and our hopes of reaching Radcot Bridge by the time they did so were dashed. When we reached the bridge we found that he and the driver had already left by car to pick us up at the lock. I remember that we had to wait a few minutes before they appeared again at the bridge. I remember it did not take more than a few minutes before the smiling face of Dr Highfield appeared again at the bridge.

After we had had lunch at Cirencester we went to look at the Thames and Severn canal which had been shut at the beginning of the twentieth century and has turned into stagnant pools of water. I could not help feeling sad at the contrast between the vitality of the surrounding green fields and the canal which no longer had any life. I must mention the Sapperton Tunnel which was over three kilometres in length and was opened in 1789. The entrance to the tunnel with its fine stone construction reflected the combined technical skills of the time. I was impressed by the self-confidence of those involved in the construction. Dr Highfield made some very interesting comments here. He pointed out that the tunnel, which had been constructed, was too narrow for the horses, which had pulled the barges, to enter; so the boatmen lying down on boards placed across their boats would propel the boat forward by pushing their feet against the ceiling and side walls of the tunnel. In other words, the boats were propelled by human feet. He pointed out a pub which stood near the entrance to the tunnel and explained that, while the boatmen were struggling to push their boats through the tunnel, the horses and their drivers would take the road above the tunnel to the other end and then spend the time in the pub until the boats appeared. No doubt this was why there was a pub at both ends of the tunnel. But it does seem to me that they showed rather a lack of fellow feeling by passing the time having a drink while their companions were struggling away inside the tunnel.

After we had had a look at the tunnel we went to see the source of the Thames but unfortunately the water had dried up and we were unable to see where the river started. Our last stop that day was at Lechlade where we looked at St John's Lock which is the highest lock on the Thames. There was a stone monument by the side of the lock, which had originally been at the Crystal Palace in London and had been moved to the source of the Thames. According to the plate on the lower part of the monument it had been moved there in 1974. A number of leisure boats arrived at the lock while we were there and the lock-keeper had a busy time opening and shutting the lock. The people on the boats looked relaxed. In the background I could

Life as a Research Student at Oxford

see the small tower of a pretty-looking church on the other side of a meadow. This was undoubtedly the highlight of our seven-hour tour that day.

I learnt a great deal over my two years in Oxford from Dr Highfield. He taught me so much during our walks about the history of Oxford, helped me in so many ways while preparing my essays, accompanied me to the opera and took me to the upper reaches of the Thames. His influence on me has been incalculable. Dr Highfield was in every meaning of the word my 'moral tutor' in guiding me through the difficulties, hardships and joys of the pursuit of learning.

Preparing my thesis[7]

Based on the historical materials which I had collected during my two years at Oxford I analysed the state of water transport on the Thames, concentrating on the people who had been involved in improvements to the river and navigation on it, and on the transport of agricultural commodities including coal and malt. The following is a brief outline of my dissertation.

Generally speaking, English people in the Middle Ages were more interested in using rivers to help them to live rather than as transport routes. As a result, rivers were dammed to provide traps for fishermen and waterwheels for millers of corn. This led to endless disputes between those whose primary interest was in the dams and fish traps and those who wanted to use their boats on the rivers; the Thames was no exception.

In the thirteenth century a compromise was reached between those engaged in the carrying trade and the millers leading to what were called 'flash locks'. These were movable water gates which allowed boats to pass through the dams, which I have just mentioned, but the boatmen had to struggle hard to prevent their vessels from capsizing in the fast flowing and turbulent waters when the gates were opened. There were a number of incidents of boats

---

[7] This was produced as *The Thames as Highway, A Study of Navigation and Traffic on the Upper Thames in the Eighteenth Century* by H.I.H. Prince Naruhito and printed at the Oxford University Press Printing House in 1989.

capsizing. The millers also needed time for water levels to rise sufficiently so that their water wheels would work properly again.

In the seventeenth and eighteenth centuries the expansion of London and the development of agriculture in the surrounding area led to increasing importance being attached to rivers as highways. The technical innovation of 'pound locks', contributed to a solution of the disputes between the millers and those engaged in transport. You will still find many examples of this type of lock on rivers and canals. 'The pound lock consists of a chamber, made of bricks and stones, enclosed within two sets of gates fitted with two sluices. A boat enters the chamber to go downstream. The gates are shut and the water is drained from the chamber through sluices in the lower gates, till the water inside is equal to that outside. Then the lower gates are shut and the lock chamber is filled with water entering through sluices in the upper gate.'[8] As a result of the invention of the 'pound lock' boats were able to move up and down from fast-flowing sections of the river without displacing large amounts of water. The Thames Navigation Commission which was established in the middle of the eighteenth century carried out a series of improvements to the river, including the construction of 'pound locks', designed to speed up transport on the river. During the 1790s – the so-called era of canal mania – various canals were built with junctions to the Thames. This led to significant changes in the nature of transport of commodities on the river. I added as an example of these changes some observations on the Thames and Severn canal.

I realized that as a result of various improvements made to the river there had been a striking increase in the quantities of commodities transported on the river, a decrease in accidents to boats following the construction of 'pound locks' and a reduction in tariffs for the transport of commodities. The average tonnage of boats on the Thames at that time was seventy to eighty tons. Although 'pound locks' had come into widespread use, the boatmen still faced problems in passing through the remaining 'flash locks'. When there was a drought there would not be enough water and when there were

---

[8] Quotation from C. Hadfield *British Canals,* Newton Abbott, 1984, page 22.

floods there would be too much; these conditions hindered navigation. The Thames and Severn Canal Company owned boats of their own which participated in navigation on the rivers.

The transport of coal on the river Thames was very important. The Thames Navigation Commission set the tolls for transporting coal and the contribution to be made towards improvements to the river. At the beginning of the eighteenth century the river was used to transport coal to Oxford from London, to which it had been brought from Newcastle. But towards the end of the eighteenth century coal from Wales and the Midlands could be transported more cheaply to Oxford via the Thames and Severn Canal and via the Oxford Canal which connected the neighbourhood of Birmingham with the Thames. This led to fierce price competition and gradually coal from Newcastle was displaced. Generally, merchants who dealt in coal were not simply coal merchants but combined the business with dealing in various other commodities such as timber. I found many interesting records about these merchants as well as about those engaged in transport business. The fact that they mostly lived in the vicinity of the river was due to its being convenient for their trades.

The transport of agricultural commodities was as important as that of coal. The most important commodities were grains including malt for use in brewing beer. Prior to the construction of canals these commodities had followed the opposite course to that of coal, going down stream to London. But the development of canals facilitated the exchange of commodities between London and the midwestern part of England via the Thames. According to the records, unlike the coal merchants who lived near the Thames, the malt merchants lived in a wider area. As a result, they used horse- or hand-driven carts to carry malt to the nearest river. The transport of malt was seasonal and influenced by the appropriate time for brewing, the winter being the most important season.

Let us take a quick look at the transport of commodities other than coal and malt up the Thames from London. I was surprised to find how many different commodities had been carried by boats belonging to the Thames and Severn Canal Company in the period between September 1794 and the end of 1797. Apart from a number

The Thames and I

of agricultural products I found thirty-five different items including a variety of manufactured goods such as metal products, dye-stuffs presumably for use in making textiles, alum, cider, wine, ale and other alcoholic beverages except rum, items from the colonies including sugar, tobacco, rice and tea, as well as stone, and timber. This made me realize what a huge trading centre London was. But it was interesting that there was no reference in the statistics to coffee, which was beginning to be appreciated in England, but was presumably not yet a popular drink. Among manufactured goods there were items which seemed to have come from Scandinavia and countries on the Baltic Sea. Together with the many items originating in the colonies they painted a picture of London as an international city.

The above is a rough sketch of my thesis. I was very pleased that recently it has been produced under the title of *The Thames as Highway* under the imprint of Oxford University Press. I shall never forget the help I received from so many people, especially Professor Mathias and Dr Highfield. When I returned to Japan and was organizing the results of my research, I recognized once again the assistance, which I had received in my researches, from the well-stocked British libraries and record offices and from their respective archivists. They have, without doubt, made a significant contribution to the high level attained by English historical research. When I re-read *The Thames as Highway* I relive my days by the Thames. Apart from all my efforts to collect records about the river I recall so many happy moments – my walks beside the river with Dr Highfield, the sights of the softly flowing Thames and the beautiful landscape around the river, which helped to cure the weariness resulting from my studies, the days on which I jogged beside the river and the times when from the top of the boat house I watched enthusiastically the college boat races. It is seven years since I left Oxford and even though the river is on the other side of the globe the name of the Thames conjures up in me feelings of affection and nostalgia transcending distance and time. While I was at Oxford the Thames was the prop of my life and of my studies. I dearly wish that I could see the river again with my own eyes and re-live the happy days of my youth beside the Thames.

Life as a Research Student at Oxford

Canals past and future

From the standpoint of the history of transport since the eighteenth century, I should like to add a few words, about how the Thames has changed. The coming of the railway age in the nineteenth-century had a huge impact on river and canal transport including transport on the Thames. The first railway in England was completed between Stockton and Darlington in 1825 and coal could be transported from the inland Durham coal fields to the coast. The railway between Liverpool and Manchester opened in 1830 and marked the real beginning of the railway age, but the construction of railways did not lead to the immediate demise of canals. According to parliamentary papers pottery and china were being transported via the Oxford canal in the middle of the nineteenth century; breakable items were carried on canal boats rather than by rail. By the 1860s commodities, particularly coal, were generally transported by rail. After the First World War commodities began to be moved by lorry and the role of canals in the transport of commodities came to an end. As a result, many canals, which had hitherto been prosperous, were closed and the water ceased to flow in them. The sight in these days of fishermen with rod and line fishing in the 'pound lock' pools shows how far canals have declined from their past prosperity. But in recent years canals have developed into leisure facilities for pleasure boats and many canals, which had been shut, have been revived for leisure purposes. Moreover, as water supplies become increasingly strained, proposals have emerged for canals to be used to carry water from areas of plenty such as North Wales to those where water is in short supply. The cost of making an existing canal usable is about one tenth of that of laying a pipe line while the operational cost is about one seventh. The construction is said to be fairly simple involving the placing of pumps at key points to change the direction of water flow. Canals, which were one of the important products of the Industrial Revolution, are finding new uses these days and being revived for leisure purposes or for water supply.

In Europe the Rhine, Main, Danube Canal was completed in September 1992, thus linking the three rivers and providing a means of moving commodities from the North Sea to the Black Sea.

The countries through which the route passes are from the North, Holland, Germany, Austria, Czechoslovakia[9] and Hungary, Yugoslavia, Rumania, Bulgaria, and Moldavia (which was part of the former Soviet Union), thus linking Western and Eastern Europe. Today when relations between Eastern European countries and those in Western Europe are becoming closer it has an important role to play in bringing the economically advanced and the less developed areas closer together. This year [1992] marks the completion of the European single market. I shall be very interested to see how canals are used in the future.

---

[9] At the time the Prince was writing the Czech Republic and Slovakia had not become independent states.

CHAPTER 9

TRAVELS IN BRITAIN AND ABROAD

———□———

Weekend drives in the countryside around Oxford

During my two years at Oxford I managed to travel a good deal in Britain and Europe. I propose to begin by describing some weekend drives I made in the neighbourhood of Oxford. As, of course, I did not have a driving licence, I arranged for my police escort to be my driver. Sometimes he and I went out on our own; on other occasions I took Oxford friends with me.

On many weekends I went into the Cotswolds which stretch from the north-west of Oxford to the neighbouring county of Gloucestershire. When I looked from a high point with a wide view of the countryside I could see the beautiful Cotswold villages – groups of the local honey-coloured stone houses clustered around church towers.

Burford on the western fringe of Oxfordshire, with its gently sloping High Street and attractive buildings on each side was beautiful, and I was attracted by the town of Bibury in Gloucestershire on the way from Burford to Cirencester. I was interested in the differing shades of the honey-coloured stone with which the houses in the various villages on the way were built, and Bourton-on-the-Water with its houses reflected in the river had a charm of its own.

Cirencester was a Roman town. Most towns whose names end in 'cester' or 'chester' trace their origin to Roman times. Chester in the north of England, Winchester and Dorchester in the south were said to have been Roman garrison towns. The roads which meet at

Cirencester were mainly straight roads. It is well known that the Romans built straight roads in order to facilitate the transmission of information and the speedy movement of their troops. The sayings 'all roads lead to Rome' and 'Rome is eternal' are well known. When I looked at these straight roads and saw that these Roman roads were still being used today, was it a hasty conclusion to think that they had indeed preserved an eternal life? I had once visited Cirencester on a cold winter's day. After having a look at the town and while I was looking for the remains of the Roman theatre I came across a mound. There was a depression in the middle of the mound and children were tobogganing on the slopes where there was still some snow. This was where the Roman theatre had been. There was no hint here of 'eternal Rome'; I could only feel the loneliness and emptiness of the place.

On the borders of south-west Oxfordshire and Wiltshire there is a huge image of a white horse carved into the chalk slopes of a hill. According to one theory, it originated in the time of King Alfred around the ninth century. It must have been a huge job to create it. You can walk over parts of the horse on the upper part of the hill; as you find your way the horse seems so big that it is even difficult to estimate what part you are standing on. I visited this spot twice. On the first occasion there was a heavy rain storm; on the second it was a fine day and I was able to see clearly from quite far away the whole shape of the white horse. But, as I gazed at it this time I thought that although it did look like a horse, it could also be some other kind of unknown animal. There are various other white horses elsewhere but I was told that this was the oldest of them all.

The visits which I made to towns and villages on the Thames were interesting. I particularly enjoyed drives and walks on the banks of the river from Wallingford, south of Oxford, to Goring and Henley. There were many attractive places near Oxford to visit at weekends but I cannot describe them all. If I had passed my time at Oxford without seeing these places I should have been like a man who remained in 'the dark spot under the lighthouse',[1] so I made every effort to explore the area round Oxford.

---

[1] The Prince was quoting a famous Japanese proverb *Tōdai moto kurashi*.

Travels in Britain and abroad

Trips in Britain involving overnight stays

The first time I stayed away anywhere in Britain was in December of my first year when I visited Broughton Castle. I spent some days staying with Lord and Lady Saye and Sele and again experienced the warmth of English family life. Broughton is a beautiful castle surrounded by a moat. It is magnificent both inside and out. Lady Saye was a viola player and we played duets. Neighbours came round and we sang carols. As a result of this visit, when my parents visited England in the following year, they stayed at Broughton.

That same month I visited Cambridge which is also a university town, but in Cambridge the colleges are closer together and I had the impression that it is more of a university town than Oxford. I thought that the gently sloping lawns down to the river Cam with the colleges in the background were especially attractive. I had particularly wanted to visit Kings College Chapel but, unfortunately, as this coincided with the middle of a recording session, this was not possible.

In the latter part of December I visited Chester and York in the north of England. They are both fine walled cities. In Chester there are remains from Roman times all over the place. York was so named after the Viking conqueror Jorvic and a Viking museum was under construction there. York Minister is a huge white cathedral, whose dignified grandeur cannot be easily described and which I found overwhelming. I climbed up the staircase to the top of the cathedral; it was a long climb and I was quite out of breath. There was a superb view of the Minster from on top of the walls. The atmosphere of the narrow streets of the city and the surrounding buildings created a feeling that one was back in medieval times. I found strolling round the city most enjoyable.

There were many other places in Britain where history seemed still alive. For someone who had studied medieval history in Japan, as I had done, it was exciting to walk round these historical towns with their savour of olden times and shadows of the past; it seemed like travelling in a time machine. I felt much the same excitement when I visited Prague in Czechoslovakia and old towns in Italy, such as Siena and Orvieto. There are also historical towns in Japan but

I do not think that they convey as a whole quite the same feeling of being back in a past age.

In 1984, I spent nine days in Cornwall in the south-west of England. Although it was only April, I felt immediately that the sun was stronger there. Someone from an aristocratic family, whom I had met soon after I started at Oxford, introduced me to some families who were living there and while staying with them I made various trips. At the house of the Galsworthys near Truro I was shown a magnificent garden. The camellias were particularly fine. There were also many precious books in this house. When after a meal I asked a question the host would suddenly disappear, and then reappear with a large volume and proceed to answer my question. They were a very pleasant couple and I had a relaxing two days with them.

In June I went to Liverpool in the north-west of England in order to be present at the opening ceremony for a Japanese Garden. Liverpool was the home base from which the Beatles overwhelmed the world. I visited the museum devoted to their memory and listening to the deeply familiar beat I took a trip down memory lane.

In July I made a long tour of eleven days to Scotland. I spent most of the time in the Highlands, but I also went over to the Shetlands, the most northerly islands in Britain. There were no trees there that could really be called trees, but I saw some Viking dwellings called brochs[2] which looked as though they were the result of haphazardly piling up stones. This place made me feel that I had come to the most deserted and lonely spot at the northern tip of the country. As in Helsinki, the capital of Finland, which is on the same latitude, it was still so light at midnight that one could read a newspaper. By the way, when I asked in the Shetlands what was the nearest place the reply was 'Norway'.

Returning to the mainland of Scotland I went to Glencoe and Loch Ness. Here I was looked after by Lord Campbell whom I have already mentioned. Talking with Lord Campbell's family and representatives of other clans in various parts of Scotland I could not help noting their resentment and the grudge they bore towards

---

[2] A broch according to the OED is 'in Scotland a prehistoric stone tower'.

England, because, half-defeated by the English, they had not been able to adopt a direct descendant of the Stuarts as their king in succession to the English king. How many times did I not hear on this journey the remark 'The English destroyed everything!' The Campbells liked to sing 'The Skye Boat Song'. This was a song in which there was a touch of sadness and told the story of how Bonny Prince Charlie, the descendant of the Stuart King James I (formerly King James VI of Scotland), had been forced to flee to the Island of Skye although he had been born a royal prince. I could not avoid noting in their expressions, as they sang, their feelings, which cannot be easily put into words, of affection for their homeland of Scotland and for Prince Charlie. Scotland is part of the United Kingdom but retains its own currency[3] and Scottish banks print their own notes and mint their own coins.

I was again in Scotland that September when I had the good fortune to be invited to spend a few days with the Queen and Prince Philip at Balmoral near Aberdeen. I was much impressed by the way they enjoyed their holidays in the wide open spaces around Balmoral.

In March 1985 I visited South Wales. I was surprised to see that, when the train reached Newport, which was the first station in Wales, the names of the stations were in Welsh as well as in English. On this occasion I only visited the southern part of the Principality, but I found the Welsh kindly people and felt a different sort of warmth there than I had felt in England and Scotland. The Welsh are famous for their love of singing and they naturally break into song on every sort of occasion. I joined in several times. I went on by train to Durham in northern England to attend a world kendo championship meeting. Looking out of the train window on arrival the sight of the cathedral towering up above the city was stunning.

In April I went to Lincoln in the east of England. The daffodils were blooming in the gardens of Doddington Hall outside Lincoln. I shall also never forget the beauty of Lincoln cathedral. After I had met the Mayor of Lincoln at the Guildhall I went on towards Peterborough stopping for lunch at the George Inn at Stamford as

---

[3] While Scottish banks still issue their own notes and there are a few Scottish coins there is no separate Scottish currency.

recommended by Professor Mathias. On the following day I travelled on from Peterborough to Norwich. Norwich is an example of an English medieval city; the stone cobbled road up to Elm Hill in the middle of the city had a medieval feel about it. I had a guide who showed me round; it was interesting the way in which he kept on talking about places that were haunted by ghosts as if this was the most natural thing in the world.

In June at the beginning of the long university summer holiday I visited the University of Essex.[4] In the neighbourhood I also visited the River Stour, which is famous for the paintings of the Hay Wain and the watermill[5] by Constable, the outstanding nineteenth-century artist. It was raining that day but this made the greenery more vivid and beautiful.

In July Lord Cranborne whom I had got to know invited me to stay. I spent a pleasant day with the Cranbornes playing various sports and enjoying other activities. That month I also went to the south-east of England visiting Dover among other places. I saw the famous white cliffs of Dover and was impressed by the construction of Dover castle and the beautiful medieval town of Rye. I shall also not forget the three days I spent that month staying with Sir Peter Miller, the Chairman of Lloyds Insurance, at his house on the Channel Island of Sark. There are no cars on the island. The only means of transport are tractors, horse-drawn carriages and bicycles. We naturally went round on bicycles. For the first time, I also had the experience of diving in a wet suit. In August, I visited Portsmouth and the Isle of Wight among other places in the south of England. I really did get round quite a bit!

While I was at Oxford I stayed at a 'Bed and Breakfast' in the neighbourhood. Many people will have seen notice-boards advertising B and Bs as they are called. In B and Bs ordinary people offer a bedroom in which guests can stay and provide breakfast the following morning. These are the English equivalent of Japanese *minshuku*. When I arrived there in the evening the lady of the house showed

---

[4] The University of Essex was established in 1965. When the Prince visited the university it had just opened a department for Japanese studies.
[5] Flatford Mill.

Travels in Britain and abroad

me to my room and politely explained to me how to use the shower. After this she told me where I could find a television set if I wanted to watch TV. And having told me to make myself comfortable she disappeared into another part of the house. The landlady did not, of course, know who I was. My police escort made sure of this. For breakfast the following day I had a plate of delicious bacon and eggs, far tastier than what you would get in a hotel. I put 'Hiro' as my name down in the visitors book and returned to Oxford.

I must add one other thing. In my visits to English manor houses I came across many places which had lots of Chinese and Japanese *objets d'art*. In one manor house near Broadway there was a huge collection of Japanese armour. I also saw many pieces of Arita and Imari ware as well as *ukiyo-e*. In some cases, it was not easy to tell at first glance whether the objects were of Chinese or Japanese origin, but I felt nostalgic on seeing so many oriental pieces. There were also many collectors of netsuke in ivory decorated in many ways, and more discussion of netsuke than you will encounter in Japan. I was indeed frequently asked about netsuke. It was interesting that some *objets d'art*, gradually being forgotten in Japan, were so popular in England.

I think that I did pretty well in grasping my opportunities in travelling so much in England during my two years stay there. My deepest impressions were of the English countryside with its carpet of green fields, of the old towns with their historical flavour and of the simple life of ordinary British people. The chance to see the true face of Britain was a most valuable experience for me.

Travelling round Europe and meeting European royal families

As I mentioned briefly in the chapters devoted to the arts and to my studies, I also visited many countries in Europe. I shall now summarize what I did.

When my parents visited Norway I met them in Bergen as a result of the kindness of His Majesty the King. I shall never forget sailing up the fjords together with the Crown Prince and Princess of Norway (now the King and Queen) and spending a night on board ship. I was warmly entertained by their Royal Highnesses and I recall the relaxing time I had with them. Just as with the Belgian Royal family I was impressed by the strength of the friendly ties between the Japanese Imperial and the Norwegian Royal families. In Holland the Queen of the Netherlands with the Prince Consort and their children, despite their busy schedule, kindly entertained me by taking me on a cruise. While travelling in Spain I called on the King who was then staying at his villa in Majorca and lunched with Their Majesties, the King and Queen of Spain. The King, realizing that I had made the visit to the island in order to call on him, asked whether there was any place in Majorca which I particularly wanted to see after lunch. Although it was not on the original schedule I replied that I would like to see the house where Chopin lived with Georges Sand. The King asked Crown Prince Philip to arrange this and he kindly accompanied me there. I have mentioned my contacts with the families of the Grand Duke of Luxembourg and the Prince of Liechtenstein in Chapter 7 about sports.

I recognized that the warm welcome I received from European royalty was due to the friendly relations, which my parents had built up with them over the years. I realized, indeed, how fortunate I had been and the importance of continuing these ties for future generations.

I visited in all thirteen countries in Europe. It is a pity that I cannot mention them all separately. I recognized the importance of getting to know not only Britain but also European countries. I was able to see for myself that although the countries of continental Europe are part of the same land mass their history, people and cultures all differed. Britain and Japan are both separated by sea from their adjacent continents, but I could not avoid noting that the distance between Britain and the continent was short and this had led to British culture and society being greatly influenced by Europe.

CHAPTER 10

LOOKING BACK ON MY TWO YEARS' STAY

―――――□―――――

The English people as I saw them

In concluding this memoir I should like to say a few words about my impressions of England, and record a few of the feelings which made up my experience of Britain.

One point I should make to begin with is that in Britain the old and the new exist harmoniously side by side. Soon after my arrival, I attended the official opening of parliament and saw for myself the way in which Britain is a traditional country. At Oxford, I saw students wearing the traditional cap and gown pass in the streets youngsters in punk rock garb, but I did not feel that it was out of the ordinary. It seemed to me that both reflected the spirit of the place. This was after all a country which produced the Beatles and the miniskirt. I felt that, while the British attach importance to old traditions, they also have the ability to innovate. Take sports, for instance; there are many sports such as golf, rugby and cricket which started in Britain. The Industrial revolution took off in Britain before any other European country.

At Oxford, I could not avoid feeling the weight of tradition. I could see this in the solemn ceremonies which were performed in the same way as they had been for centuries, in the clothes which students had to wear for the entrance ceremony and the fact that the ceremony was conducted in Latin. I was impressed by the importance attached to history as shown for instance in the Latin Grace said at High Table in college and by the antique silver used there.

The Thames and I

The college system is too complicated to explain in a few words. But I thought that the way in which students in different disciplines lived and ate together and were given the opportunity to provoke one another's intellectual curiosity was admirable. At the Gakushūin, where I studied in the humanities faculty, the different subjects were taught on different floors. Even if you were in the humanities faculty it was difficult, unless you made a major effort, to establish contacts with students studying other subjects in the same faculty. It was even more difficult to do so with students in other disciplines.

What did Oxford students think about tradition? What view did they take of the coexistence of tradition and innovation? Some students declared that their respect for tradition was no more than superficial. Some also thought it strange to be asked such a question by a Japanese, as they thought that Japan was a country where tradition was highly valued. Some older people boast that they take traditions seriously and are proud of behaving in accordance with tradition.

It was not only in my life as a student that I felt the weight of tradition. I often felt it strongly when I was invited out to British homes. In old houses I often saw portraits of the family's ancestors hanging on the walls. In some cases the walls seemed to be totally hidden by portraits and I would be told about each of those portrayed. I felt that each family wanted to preserve carefully their tangible and intangible legacies.

I am sure that I was not the only one who felt that, while at first sight there was something incompatible between the old and the new in Britain, British society had been sufficiently flexible and discerning to ensure that there was no confrontation between the two.

My second point is my belief that the British usually take a long-term view of things. I felt that the character of the British people lies in generally not forcing the pace when dealing with immediate problems and in thinking about the future implications of what they do. We can see this in the way in which buildings are put up. Let us take as an example the building of a great cathedral. Most of them took many centuries to complete. The stone mason who cut the first stones would never see the completed building, but as he loaded

Looking back on my two years stay

each stone he would see the future cathedral in his mind's eye. Cathedrals are not the only large buildings made of stone. We Japanese tend to be absorbed by what immediately confronts us. I do not think that we are very good at thinking about things in the long term. I think this can partly be explained by the difference between living in a building made of wood, which can be done relatively quickly, and one made of stone, which requires much longer to complete.

In the context of the difference between stone and wood I should mention the difference between Japan and Britain in relation to privacy. It may be due to the kind of houses they live in, but the British attach a great deal of importance to their private life and to their own space and time. In talking with British people I had the feeling that they were prepared to discuss personal matters up to a certain point, but that there were some aspects of their life on which other people should not trespass. At places such as country houses, people observe notices saying 'private', and although there is no fence or anything to stop one from going beyond people rarely go past the sign. The British like to enjoy their holidays to the full. It seemed to me that they look on their vacations as an important opportunity to store up energy for their future work. In brief, on the basis of their traditional individualist beliefs, they defend firmly what they regard as strictly personal. There is a tacit understanding that certain areas are mutually inviolable. Is not this the difference of identity between people who live in spaces which are separated from the outside by stone and those who live in spaces separated by very thin partitions made of substances like paper and wood, which can easily be penetrated by anyone?

I have already mentioned how adept the British are at social relationships, and the way they show consideration for others by, for instance, holding doors open for people behind them. I was also often aware of their inconspicuous acts of warmth and sympathy towards the disabled. In this context, when in my first term I was attending a lecture by Professor Mathias in the examinations school, I noticed that the group of students who were walking and chatting in front of me moved to the side and a gap opened up. I wondered why and saw a student walking with a straight back and carrying a white stick. The group of students while continuing to walk and chat had stepped aside and allowed him to pass without any fuss. I saw this kind of thing many times. Although it seemed the most natural thing in the world, I was moved. I am sure that similar things happen in Japan, but perhaps I had not personally experienced them. It seemed to me that in Oxford disabled people could walk around the streets and live and behave with dignity. Thus, they were able to merge easily and well into the life of Oxford. It seemed to me that importance was attached everywhere in Britain to wheel-chair access and that consideration for the needs of disabled people had spread widely in Britain.

Finally, I think that I managed in my two years stay abroad to get a glimpse of the attitude of British and continental people towards 'light'. In England the winters are cold and the skies cloudy. In midwinter it was still dark at eight o'clock and it became dark again around three thirty. When I was in my rooms in college I felt the cold and the draughts coming through the cracks and often longed for the warmth of life in Japan with its well-heated rooms. One consolation in winter was the fact that the grass remained green throughout the year. If winter seemed long the spring was lovely. The daffodils, which had sprung up all over the place, formed a yellow carpet and the multicoloured crocuses poked their heads through the turf. One can readily understand why Europeans make spring itself such an important artistic theme. In Japan, perhaps because the four seasons are so distinct, the attitude towards them seems to me a little different; from *Manyōshū*[1] days the blossoms of plum and cherry have been seen as symbols of spring, and the sound of the cuckoo as a harbinger of the arrival of summer.

In Europe, sunshine contributes greatly to making people feel that the spring has arrived. With the arrival of April the hours of sunshine lengthen and there is more chance of the sun coming out. It may still be quite cold, but people enjoy sun-bathing. The many Gothic cathedrals one sees in Europe have large stained-glass windows letting in the maximum amount of light possible. I cannot

---

[1] Produced in about AD 760, the *Manyōshū* is the oldest collection of Japanese poems from the Nara period 710–784.

help but wonder if that is not a reflection of the peoples' deep yearning for light.

Light has a connection with fashion. It seemed to me that the clothes generally worn by British people were sober and lacking in colour. The fact that this did not seem out of harmony was, I thought, because it was appropriate to the British climate. The bright colours adopted by fashions in Paris and Milan seemed to reflect the brighter sunlight of the south. I went to Paris in the spring and felt that the sunlight was brighter there than in Britain. Paris buildings are beautiful not so much because they are white but because their white colour is enhanced by the sunshine.

The European approach to light and the philosophy that goes with it are rather different from that which we Japanese adopt. Light is an abstract concept and doubtless each individual has a different feeling in his heart about it. I was struck by this when back in the bright sunshine of Tokyo I began to feel my thankfulness for sunshine gradually ebbing away.

On Leaving Britain

At one of my tutorials in my last Trinity term I heard Professor Mathias say: 'Your remaining time in Oxford is fast coming to a close and will probably end like a burst of fireworks!' I took this to heart and determined to spend my last days at Oxford to the full. Fortunately, I had very largely completed my investigation of the historical materials relating to my thesis. So I wondered what there was that I still wanted to accomplish outside my research and what things I wanted to do once more. I began to think about how many more times I would be able to do the sort of things which had been part of my daily life there such as talking with my fellow students in the MCR and in hall. I began to realize that even the smallest things in my daily life had been really important to me. At the same time, I went over once again the Oxford streets which I had got to know so well; I revisited my favourite spots and took photographs of each of them. Every little street and square brought back happy memories of my two years at Oxford. If I revisited Oxford I should probably never again be able to wander round freely like a student.

The town would remain the same; what would be different would be my position in life. When I thought about things like that I was overtaken by a strange feeling of uneasiness, and wished that time would stop. Fortunately, all the places which I remember so fondly are recorded in the photographs in the albums in my study and, of course, in my head.

As my last days at Oxford became so few they could be numbered on the fingers of one hand, my friends in the MCR gave a farewell party for me in the room I had got to know so well. This took place in the evening and almost every member I knew in the MCR and those I had got to know in the JCR turned up. C, who was in charge of the MCR accounts, made a speech at the start of the party in which he recounted some 'strange' stories about my life at Oxford. He spoke about my interest in the history of transport and the fact that I had nearly all my meals in hall, which he thought 'strange'. Then he presented me with a commemorative mug in which I had to drink at least five mugs full of some liquid which he had concocted from unknown materials (I think it was a mixture of various types of liquor). I duly performed this task! I think it was pretty strong stuff! All those present asked me when I would next come to Oxford, in what way I would perform my official duties, and would I pursue my research at Oxford? Many members of the MCR took three years to complete their research papers, so there was some talk about meeting again next year if I was coming back to Oxford after the vacation. It was sad for me to have to say farewell to those whom I had got to know so well over the last two years. This had been a happy time for me – perhaps I should say the happiest time of my life – and I owed this greatly to their cooperation and consideration for me.

In this way taking so many memories away with me I left my rooms in Merton at the end of September and spent my remaining days in Britain with the Fujis at their house or in the ambassador's residence in London. I was kindly invited to farewell receptions by the Japan Society and other Anglo-Japanese organizations and I was able to express my thanks to almost all those who had helped me during my two years stay.

Looking back it seemed to me that the two years had passed in a flash but I had learnt a great deal. I had had many interesting

Looking back on my two years stay

experiences not least at Oxford. Among my experiences were, of course, doing my own laundry and ironing! I had been able to see Britain from the inside and meet many people. Through these meetings I had learnt much about British society. I had also, seeing it from the outside, reappraised my own country. All these were irreplaceable experiences for me.

On the afternoon of 10 October I left Heathrow, where I was seen off by Colonel Hall, Japanese residents in Britain and representatives of the Japanese Embassy. As the London scene gradually disappeared from view I realized that an important chapter in my life was over. A new page in my life was opening, but I felt a large void in my heart and as I stared out of the windows of the plane I felt a lump in my throat.

POSTSCRIPT

―――□―――

As I wrote this account of my time studying abroad and reviewed the various memories which passed through my mind, I realized that I had come to grips with all sorts of issues while I had been at Oxford. Fond memories of each scene flashed through my mind like a revolving lantern. I faced one problem in writing this book; it was seven years since I had left Oxford. Although I could remember a good deal, there were limits to the extent to which I could recall individual events. However, fortunately while I was at Oxford, I had jotted down each day what I had done and had kept these notes. I was able to put these together with the memos made by my police escort and through these I was able to recall my experiences. My diary in English, which I had written while I was staying with the Halls and which had been checked by my English teachers, was also useful and the pamphlets and leaflets about places which I had visited on my travels together with the tickets and other items, which I had kept, were a real treasure-trove. I had taken over two thousand photographs while I was at Oxford and these were very useful for reference. In addition, the official telegrams which had been sent at the time naturally provided background material. After I came home the occasional essays which I had written about my studies were also valuable memory aides and these have been incorporated into this book.

In September 1991, I revisited England to attend the Japan Festival[1] and was delighted to be able to meet once again many of

Postscript

those who had helped me during my time as a student. I was much gratified to receive the award of an honorary doctorate from Oxford University. I revisited Merton where I met Dr Roberts, the warden, Dr Highfield and other dons of the college and was able to get together again with some of the students whom I had known and who were pursuing their researches. I was invited to a pub by the student I mentioned earlier who had been learning to play the *shakuhachi*. As I trod the familiar streets that evening I felt that Oxford had not changed and nostalgic memories welled up within me. I want to keep these memories sacred and I look forward to the chance of returning there once again.

In conclusion, I want to reiterate my sincere gratitude both publicly and privately to all those who helped me in so many ways, eased my path and made my stay so enjoyable. In particular, I would like to express my thanks to Professor Mathias and Dr Highfield as well as Dr Morgan for their guidance and assistance with my research, to Colonel Hall who received me so kindly in his home and to others with whom I stayed while I was in Britain, to Ambassadors Hirahara and Yamazaki and the staff of the Japanese Embassy in London, and, of course, to my two police escorts.

We make many of our own memories but many are also made by others. Thanks to all the warm friendship I received while I was abroad I have lasting and happy memories of my fruitful stay in Britain.

Finally, I wish to express my thanks to Professor Naitō Yorihiro, President of the Gakushūin School, and to Professor Hayakawa Tōzō, President of the Gakushūin University, for encouraging me to recall the happy days of my youth and write these memoirs.

Prince Naruhito
Winter, 1992

---

[1] The Japan Festival in the United Kingdom in 1991 marked the centenary of the foundation of the Japan Society. The Kyoto Garden in Holland Park in London, which was opened by the Prince of Wales and the Crown Prince, is a permanent memorial of the Festival.

BIBLIOGRAPHY

Andō Nobusuke, Koike Shigeru and others, (Edited): *Igirisu no seikatsu to bunka jiten* (Dictionary of British life and culture) Kenkyusha, 1982.

Ugawa Kaoru: *Igirisu no shakai-keizaishi no tabi* (A journey through British social history), Nihon kiristokyōdan shuppankyoku, 1984.

Koike Shigeru (editor): *Igirisu*, Shinchōsha 1992.

Mikasa no Miya Tomohito: *Tomhito-san no egeresu Ryūgaku*, Bungeishunjū 1991.

John Bergh,(translated by Kamei Akira and Tamaki Yutaka) *Daisakkyokuka no Shōgai*, Kyōdō Tsūshinsha, 1978.

In addition to guide books to Merton College and *The Story of Oxford* published by the Oxford Museum, there are other reference works such as:

Christopher Hibbert (edited): *The Encyclopaedia of Oxford*, London, 1988.

Michael Hall & Ernest Frankl: *Oxford*. Cambridge, 1981.

Anthony F. Kersting & John Ashdown: *The Buildings of Oxford*, London, 1980.

V. H. H. Green: *A History of Oxford University*, London, 1974.

Christopher Brooke & Roger Highfield: *Oxford and Cambridge*, Cambridge, 1988.

Nikolaus Pevsner: *The Buildings of England, Oxfordshire*, Middlesex, 1974.

Howard Colvin: *Unbuilt Oxford*, London, 1983.

Anton Gill: *How to be Oxbridge*, London, 1986.

Mari Pritchard & Humphrey Carpenter: *A Thames Companion,* Oxford, 1981.

John Gagg: *Canals*, London, 1982.

John Arlott: *The Oxford Companion to Sports and Games*, Oxford, 1977.

Daniel Topolski: *Boat Race*, London, 1985.

Malcolm D. Whitman: *Tennis-Origins and Mysteries*, New York, 1932.

INDEX

Personal names[1] and place names outside Oxford and London.

Abingdon, 12, 22,103
Adam, Hans, Crown Prince of Liechtenstein
— see Liechtenstein
Akasaka Palace, 98
Akishino, Prince, 64
Albert, Prince, 83
Alexandra, Princess, 3
Alfred, King, 37, 130
Allegri Quartet, 76
Andrew, Prince, 3
Anne, Princess, 3
Ascot, 95, 96
Ashcroft, Peggy, 73
Ayer, Bruce, police escort[2], 61, 62, 76, 145
Aylesbury, 112

Bach, J.S. 81
Bacon, Roger, police escort, (see also endnote 2) 61, 62, 145
Balliol, John de, 37
Balmoral, 133
Barclay, Mr (friend of Colonel Hall), 14
Bashō, Matsuo, 99
Beatles, The, 82, 132
Beatrice, Queen, 13

Becker, Boris, 90
Beethoven, Ludwig van, 78–80, 82, 119
Belgians, King of the, 62, 135
Ben Nevis, 93, 94
Bergen, 135
Besselsleigh, 22
Bibury, 129
Blacker, Dr Carmen, viii
Bodley, Sir Thomas, 105
Bonn, 82
Bonnington, Chris, 95
Borrowdale, 94
Bouchier, Dorothy, Lady (Britton), x
Brahms, Johannes, 18, 79, 83
Brighton, 6
Britten, Benjamin, 82
Broadway, 64
Brook, Peter, 73
Brook Shields, 68
Brooke, Professor Christopher, 101, 115
Broughton Castle, 63
Burford, 129
Burns, Mr, Oxfordshire County Records official, 103, 104, 115
Burton, Richard, 73

---

[1] The Prince's fellow students are generally referred to by an initial and as such are not listed in this index.
[2] There are references to 'my police escorts' on a number of other occasions, but as the Prince does not say which these have not been indexed.

Index

Cambridge, 18, 131
Campbell, Lord, 93, 132, 133
Canterbury, 6
Carpenter, Humphrey, 104
Carroll, Lewis, 72
Charlie, Bonny Prince, 133
Charles, Prince of Wales, v, vii, 17, 75, 145
Charles I, King, 41
Chedworth, 17, 54
Cheltenham, 15
Chester, 131
Chichibu, Princess, 18
Chiselhampton, 21
Chopin, Frédéric, 136
Cirencester, 122, 129, 130
Clapham, J.H., 119
Clifton Hampden, 12
Connors, Jimmy, 90
Constable, John, 134
Corcos, Mr (Philip) and Mrs (Diana), 9, 11, 12, 20–2
Cran Montana, 96
Cranbourne, Lord, 134
Culham, 12
Curren, Kevin, 90

Defoe, Daniel, 114
Delius, Frederick, 82, 83
Diana, Princess of Wales, 17, 75
Doddington Hall, 133
Dover, 134
Dowland, John, 82
Durham, 133
Dvořák, Antonin, 80–3

Edinburgh, 17–19
Edinburgh, Duke of, see Philip, Prince
Edward, Prince, 3
Elgar, Edward, 82
Eliot, T.S., 83
Elliott, Mark

Fort William, 93
Fuji Akira, Counsellor (and Mrs), 8, 14, 19, 22–4, 53, 120, 142

Gagg, John, 11
Gakushūin, viii, ix, 109, 110, 145

Galsworthys, 132
Gandhi, 29, 73
George II, King, 81
Gielgud, John, 73
Glencoe, 132
Glyndebourne, 75, 120
Goring, 130
Grafton Lock, 121
Greenwich, 10
Guildhall Library, 113

Haddington, Earl and Countess of, 18–20
Hadfield, C., 124
Hall, Colonel Tom (also Halls), x, 3, 7, 10–17, 20–2, 54, 62, 64, 96, 108, 118, 119, 143–5
Hall, Edward, 7, 10, 15, 16
Hall, John, 7, 15
Hall, Lucy, 7
Hall, Mariette, Mrs, 7, 12, 13, 80
Handel, George Frideric, 43, 81–3
Harvey, Dr Barbara, 58
Harvey, Dr William, 41
Hastings, 6
Hawksmoor, Nicholas, 107
Hayakawa Tōzō, Professor, 145
Hayashi Tatsusaburo, 99
Haydn, Joseph, 75, 77–80, 83, 119
Headington, 117
Helsinki, 132
Henley-on-Thames, 5, 103, 130
Henrietta Maria, Queen, 41
Henry II, King, 33
Henry V, King, 90
Highfield, Dr Roger, vi, x, 4, 28, 29, 39, 47, 57, 63, 64, 72, 75, 92, 101, 102, 115–23, 126, 145
Hirahara Tsuyoshi, Ambassador, 1, 2, 5, 8, 55, 145
Hitchcock, Alfred, 67
Holland, 13
Holst, Gustav, 84
Howard, Professor Michael, 29
Howell, Herbert, 84
Humfry, Duke, 105

Iffley, 117, 118
Iron Bridge (Shropshire), 110

Index

Irvine, A.C., 45
Isle of Wight, 134

James I, King, 133
Japan, Emperor and Empress, (during the Prince's stay at Oxford Crown Prince and Princess of Japan, later Heisei era Emperor (given name Akihito) x, 62, 63, 136
Japan, Showa era Emperor (given name Hirohito), 17,22

Kent, Duke of, 90
Kew, 113,
Kodály, Zoltán, 43, 75
Kyoto, 99

Lake District, 20, 94
Lawrence, T.E., 72
Lean, David, 73
Lechlade, 103, 112, 123
Liddell, Dr, 72
Liechtenstein, Crown Prince of, 96,136
Lincoln, 133
Liverpool, 132
Lloyd Webber, Andrew, 82
Loch Ness, 132
Luxembourg, Grand Duke of, 96,136

McEnroe, John, 90
Machimura Akiko, x
Macmillan, Harold, Earl of Stockton, 35,
Mahler, Gustav, 19
Majorca, 136
Mallory, George Leigh, 45, 95
Man, Isle of, 76, 77
Mansfield, Earl and Countess of, 3, 19, 20
Margaret, Princess, 3
Marlow, 6
Mary, Princess of Liechtenstein, 96
Mathias, Peter, Professor, vi, x, 3, 5, 16, 17, 39, 47, 54, 63, 72, 87, 100–11, 119, 126, 134, 141, 145
Maunsfield, Henry de, 44
Mendelssohn, Felix, 83
Meribel, 96,
Merton, Walter de, 41
Methuen, John, British Envoy to Portugal 1691, later Lord Chancellor of Ireland, 60

Mibu Motohiro, 1
Milan, 141
Miller, Sir Peter, 134
Mizoguchi Kenji, 68
Morgan, Dr, 111, 113, 145
Morris, William (Oxford motor manufacturer) 51
Mozart, Wolfgang Amadeus, 19, 78, 80, 82, 120
Mussorgsky, Modeste Petrovich, 75

Naitō Yoshiro, Professor, 145
Nakagawa Tosu, Ambassador, 8
Needham, Professor Rodney, 16,108
Netherlands, Queen Beatrice of the, 13, 136
Newport, 153
Northampton
Norway, King of, 135
Norway, Crown Prince and Princess of, 135
Norwich, 134

O'Brien, Dr Patrick, 101
Oilly, Robert d', 118
Oman, 68
Orvieto, 131
Oswald, Sir Michael, 13
Ozu Yasujiro, 68

Paris, 141
Peterborough, 134
Pevsner, Nicholas, 117
Philip, Duke of Edinburgh, 1, 17, 18, 133
Portsmouth, 134
Prague, 82, 131
Princeton, 68
Pritchard, Mary, 104
Purcell, Henry, 82

Queen Elizabeth II, 2, 3, 17, 63, 77, 95, 133

Radcot Bridge, 12
Reading, 103, 111–14
Richards, Sir Rex, 3–5, 24, 25, 28, 31, 41, 63, 72
Roberts, Dr John, 72, 145
Rossini, Giachomo, 75
Rye, 134

149

Index

St John's Lock, 122
Salzburg, 82
Sand, George, 136
Sapperton Tunnel, 122
Sark, Island of, 134
Saye and Sele, Lord and Lady, 63,131
Sayako, Princess (Nori no miya), 64
Savile, Henry, 42
Scafell Pike, 94
Schubert, Franz, 13, 76, 77, 79, 80
Scone Palace, 19
Shakespeare, William, 21, 74, 90
Shetland Islands, 122
Salisbury, 9, 10
Siena, 131
Simmonds, Dr John, 16, 17
Smith, Adam, 72
Snowdon, Mt, 94, 95
Spain, King and Queen of, 136
Spain, Crown Prince Philip of, 136
Spoht, Louis, 78, 79
Stamford, 133
Stonehenge, 9
Storry, Mrs Dorothie, 120
Storry, Dr Richard, 120
Stour, River, 134
Stratford-upon-Avon, 21, 74
Strauss, Richard, 75
Swaan, Wim, 101, 115

Tallis, Thomas, 83
Thatcher, Mrs, 3, 49, 58

Thomas à Becket, 33
Truro, 132
Tyninghame Castle, 18, 19

Ugawa Kaoru, 39, 58

Vaughan Williams, Ralph, 81–3
Victoria, Queen, 83
Vienna, 82
Visconti, 67

Wagner, Richard, 76
Wales, 133
Wallingford, 130
Walton, William, 84
Weston, Rev.Walter, 95
White Horse, The, 130
William of Durham, 37
William of Wykeham, 37
William the Conqueror, 118
Wimbledon, 15, 49, 90
Windsor, 1, 103
Wordsworth, William, 20
Wren, Sir Christopher, 31, 108

Yamazaki Toshio, Ambassador, 145
Yasuda Motohiro, Professor, 109, 110
York, 131

Zuckerman, Pinchas, 18